start p. 94 Maya

Praise for *Decoding Doomsday*:

*"Doug Woodward's new book, **Decoding Doomsday**, should come with its own sound track. Perhaps it was my imagination, but I kept hearing that threatening music from the movie, Jaws, ringing in my ears as I turned each page... Woodward leaves no stone unturned in his search for answers. From the Mayan calendar to the Jewish Feast Days; to the mysterious Bible codes; to the Hopi Calendar that predicted oil spills and nuclear war... Woodward pursues every possible angle and conspiracy, true or false, searching for truth. Isaac Newton; Plato; Nostradamus; Martin Luther; Francis Bacon; Adolf Hitler; Madame Blavatsky... even a Hebrew professor at New York City University in 1844 by the name of George Bush! They're all part of this remarkable story."*

- Bob Ulrich, Contributing Editor and Director, *Prophecy in the News Magazine.*

*"Douglas Woodward and I have been friends for several years. Although he is a Christian and I, an orthodox Jewish Rabbi, we both share the conviction that the Bible is God's message to humanity. As such, it is much more than just a history of a particular people. It is a roadmap to the future. While I can't endorse all of his conclusions, I can confirm the encyclopedic value Douglas has brought to **Decoding Doomsday**, as well as the educational and entertainment value of his writing. The reader will be thoughtfully stimulated and engagingly delighted all at the same time!"*

- Rabbi Daniel Lapin, President of the American Alliance of Jews and Christians, author of *Buried Treasure* and *Thou Shall Prosper.*

"From earliest times, ancient shamans, high priests and prophets of doom have predicted the end of the world. Apocalyptic literature from numerous cultures forecast a moment beyond which civilization will no longer exist, at least not as we have known it. In recent years the Mayan calendar with its December 21, 2012 catastrophic day of apocalypse has led to dozens of books, websites, and films speculating whether the ancient Mesoamerican astronomers and their advanced calendar cycles accurately predicted a dazzling and soon-coming end of humanity, or the dawn of a golden age. What should Christians make of this and other end-of-the-world speculations? S. Douglas Woodward surveys not only the history of Mayan scholars, but pseudo-archeologists, channelers, mediums, shamans, megalithic monuments and alternative historians to uncover a startling truth about the Apocalypse. What he unveils should be of vital concern to every Bible believer."

- Thomas R. Horn, publisher and author, *Apollyon Rising: 2012* and *Forbidden Gates.*

D0206909

"Douglas Woodward has authoritatively addressed the red-hot topic of the 2012 prophecies from a unique perspective that non-believers and believers alike will find fascinating, informative, and entertaining. This book is one of the most well-researched and credible manuscripts I've encountered on the subject – and believe me, in the last couple of decades, I've read just about everything concerning 2012 and its relation to Bible prophecy. Doug combines solid biblical facts with deep analytical insights from secular history, resulting in a number of astounding contemporary connections. **Decoding Doomsday** is a masterpiece of well-founded research. If all the 2012 talk has you shaking your head and turning away, think again. This book will give you conclusive answers from a biblical perspective … answers that you can trust. Doug's ever-present sense of humor also shines through the work, bringing a light touch to a very heavy subject."

- Gary Stearman, Pastor, Author, and Editor of *Prophecy in the News Magazine*.

"S. Douglas Woodward states simply the heart of his research for his book, **Decoding Doomsday**: 'The reality and proximity of Doomsday is the ultimate question.' And, that's where the simplicity ends, so far as the depth of this volume is concerned. The author has tackled perhaps the most titillating topic of these times for Planet Earth. Many other writers have of late made the assault. The difference is Woodward – rather than simply tackling head-on – surrounds the matters involving the Mayan 2012 enigma and prophesied/ predicted doomsday from a multi-faceted empiricism that is breath-taking in its scope. No other work on the subject, to my knowledge, provides so many levels of insight".

- Terry James, Author, *The Rapture Dialogues, The American Apocalypse, and The Nephilim Imperatives: Dark Sentences*.

"Doug and I have known each other for a couple of years and have a number of things in common. We are both active in the entrepreneurial world, live in the Seattle area, and are authors on prophetic topics. What I especially appreciate about Doug's book, **Decoding Doomsday**, is that it's not just intelligent, but entertaining. It takes prophetic discourse to another level. It doesn't require the reader to know much about biblical prophecy, yet it's an intriguing learning experience even for those who have already studied numerous books on the subject. I commend him to you for a good read."

- Bryan Mistele, CEO, INRIX Inc., and author, *The Truth About Prophecy in the Bible* and *The Truth about Eternity and the Spirit World*.

Table of Contents

Table of Figures

Acknowledgements

I wish to thank a number of family and friends for their efforts in reviewing early versions of the manuscript and providing helpful feedback.

First, my thanks to Rabbi Daniel Lapin, a good and gracious friend, who has provided a wonderful foreword testifying not only to his generosity of spirit, but also to his exceptionally lyrical writing style and his keen insight into the inestimable asset we Jews and Christians share in the sacred Scriptures. His willingness to share his wisdom here may seem surprising to some. But it's typical of his spirit and the many insights into the Hebrew Scriptures he shares each time we sit down together.

I am also greatly appreciative of Bob Ulrich, Operations Manager at Prophecy in the News, who provided encouragement and a number of helpful suggestions in the formation of this book, its title, and overall marketing plan. Thanks also to Bryan Mistele, a celebrated fellow author on these same subjects and CEO of a brilliant young company, both accomplishments of which he should be very proud. Bryan offered a critical eye to the content of the first half of this book and made several perceptive suggestions.

My brother Phil continues to be a source of encouragement which I greatly appreciate. Likewise, my father also deserves my thanks for being my number one fan and my mother-in-law for her continued love.

My biggest thank you is however saved for my wife, Donna. She has continued to put up with many nights apart as I work dutifully in my office upstairs. She'd much rather have me downstairs sharing time together, enjoying television, and the company of our little dogs. Donna, you share in the impact and success of this tome, for you carried much of the burden of keeping things in order while I worked. I love you more than I can possibly say in this little allotted space.

S. Douglas (Doug) Woodward
Woodinville, Washington
July, 2010

ix

S. Douglas Woodward

I dedicate this book to my wife
Donna Wilson Woodward
and to my children,
Corinne Noel Wilson Woodward
and Nicholas Stephen Wilson Woodward.

May God continue to bless all of you
who I so greatly cherish.

Foreword

This encyclopedic work is really a monumental achievement on the part of my friend, the gentleman and scholar, S. Douglas Woodward. Though he is a Christian and I am an Orthodox Jewish rabbi, we have enjoyed the occasions on which we have been able to discuss the ideas that gave birth to this volume.

Some would wonder how this is possible. The answer lies in what we have in common.

We now live in the first generation in over two thousand years, in which there are many people who consider themselves literate and educated yet remain utterly ignorant of the most published and printed book in the history of humanity — the Bible. Among those who know something of the Bible, there are many who see it as a vaguely interesting ancient artifact; no more than an archeological curiosity. But many others such as the distinguished author of this book as well as I, recognize the Bible as God's message to humanity. That is what we have in common.

My own view is that if indeed, this majestic and mysterious tome is nothing more than the mental meanderings of successive tribes of Bedouin scribes; I have a far too busy life to waste even a nano-second on it. I find Shakespeare to contain far more skillfully rounded characters and Churchill to contain far more inspiring speeches. I'd turn to Wodehouse for more entertaining writing and to Peter Drucker for more useful information.

But if, however, I am right and Scripture is nothing more and nothing less than God's comprehensive matrix of all reality, why, there is nothing in all of human literary achievement more important for me to master. It is this shared conviction that lay behind Douglas Woodward's extensive odyssey of spiritual exploration that resulted in this work.

After all, the story of western civilization shows that though the Bible starts by describing how God created the universe, it is the Bible that was the catalyst for mankind's creation of the most durable and desirable form of civilization the world has known. It can hardly be an accident that the overwhelming majority of scientific and medical discoveries of the past millennium occurred in Christendom, an old fashioned word but a useful one describing societies in which the Bible played a formative role.

It can hardly be coincidental, a word by the way, that doesn't appear in Scripture, that indigenous capital markets only arose in societies that sprang from the pages of the Bible. Yes, argue as one might, it requires academic athleticism to squirm one's way out of the inevitable deduction that somehow the Bible influenced the development of airplanes, Novocain, and the business corporation, not to mention indoor plumbing and waterborne sewerage systems. And the world continues to demonstrate its preference for Bible-based civilization by voting with its feet, moving en masse to countries enjoying the legacy of their Judeo-Christian origins.

It is no accident that today, both bathrooms and banks in Beijing, Bombay, and Bangkok finally resemble their counterparts first found in Brussels, Boston, and Bristol. All of this is not to trumpet the superiority of western societies but to articulate clearly my conviction that regardless of who adopts it as a blueprint for civilization, the Bible somehow develops the systems best suited to the peculiar needs of the human race.

The Bible was not only the first book ever printed on the newly developed printing press in about 1450, but it was also the first book ever published in the newly independent United States of America.

In its early pre-Revolutionary-War years, Harvard, a college founded by Puritans who were denied higher education in England, placed a far greater emphasis on the study of the Bible in its original Hebrew than any other university in the world. By 1776, ten universities stood on American soil and they all required study of the Bible in Hebrew. Puritan minister Increase Mather, a future president of Harvard, was named thus because his parents translated the Hebrew name *Yoseif* (Joseph) correctly.

America's Founders saw America as trying to step under the protective umbrella of God's covenant with ancient Israel. For instance, Jefferson, Adams, Madison and almost all of America's Founders were indirectly initiated into much of the Oral Torah, the commentaries that British author George Eliot termed "the great transmitters." Their direct sources, especially John Locke, developed their theories of individual rights, property rights, religious toleration, and a federal republic form government based on the biblically derived theories of great 17th century scholars such as British Jurist John Selden and Hugo Grotius and his Dutch contemporaries who in turn were taught by the Dutch rabbi, Menashe ben Israel, close confidante of the artist, Rembrandt, and friend of Oliver Cromwell. Grotius, Selden, and their contemporaries developed their "laws of nations" and theories of "natural law" based on the teaching of the Jewish sage, Maimonides, and the oral Torah, including extensive study of the *Noachide* laws. Their theories focused on the first chapters of Genesis, which they understood as having universal application to (all) mankind, and they became the philosophical foundation for the creation of America.

I write of all this and more because I want to convey a basic validation of Douglas Woodward's quest if not of all his conclusions. The Bible is far more than the accumulated legends of long forgotten nations in now irrelevant wars and struggles. It is even far more than a telephone directory of do's and don'ts. It is not a history book of the past – *it is a roadmap to the future.* To seek guideposts to that future within its pages makes all the sense in the world.

For this reason John Wycliffe labored mightily in the 14th century to create an English language version of the Bible. He was followed by William Tyndale who devoted his life, indeed he later sacrificed it, in order to make the Bible accessible to the masses of English speaking people. The great British historian John Richard Green, writing in 1874 described 16th century England thus: "England became the people of a book, and that book was the Bible."

Later, the spirit of those Biblically-sculpted Englishmen crossed the Atlantic. One of my most treasured possessions is a reproduction of William Bradford's seventeenth century book, *History of the Plymouth Plantation.* Bradford, who had come over on the Mayflower, was the second governor of the colony and filled the first twenty or so pages of his manuscript with words and sentences in Biblical Hebrew which he painstakingly translated. He describes Hebrew as the language in which God spoke to the patriarchs and the language in which Adam named all creatures and explains this as the reason he wanted to study the Lord's language. Thomas Jefferson would later describe Hebrew as "the very language of the divine communication."

As Samuel P. Huntington writes, "Americans have always been extremely religious and overwhelmingly Christian. The 17th-century settlers founded their communities in America in large part for religious reasons. Eighteenth-century Americans saw their Revolution in religious and largely biblical terms."

The journey that led me to friendship with Douglas Woodward probably began with the first time I crossed the Atlantic and came to America.

Hoping to see as much as possible of this vast new land during the short visit I had planned, I picked up a full set of United States maps from the now defunct Texaco store in mid-town Manhattan. Returning to my Brooklyn boarding house, I set the maps out on a large table and began poring over them in eager anticipation of my forthcoming road trip.

Suddenly my eye locked on to the town of Salem in Kentucky. Wow! Salem is the Biblical name for Jerusalem. How weird, I thought, as the ancient words of Genesis echoed in my mind: "And Malchizedek, King of Salem, brought out bread and wine" as he prepared to bless Avraham Avinu. How could the king that ancient Jewish wisdom identifies as Shem, the son of Noah, of the city that is similarly identified as Jerusalem, come to life in a small southern town. I was jolted from this reverie as Salem, Massachusetts leaped at me off the page. Then Salem, Oregon, and then, my goodness, Salem, Illinois, followed by Salem, Indiana, Salem, Arkansas, and then nineteen other Salems! I was aware of no other Salems in any of the many other countries I had visited in Africa and Europe. What was going on here?

As if hypnotized, my gaze was drawn to Hebron, Texas, then Hebron, Ohio, followed by nine more Hebrons. With maps flailing around the table, I quickly homed in on Zion, New Jersey, Zion, South Carolina, and another six Zions. How about Jericho, I wondered. Well, there just for starters was Jericho, Vermont and Jericho, New York.

The mountain of Moses, *Har Nevo*, memorialized in Nebo, Louisiana, and Nebo, Missouri along with two or three others. (Remember that the second letter of the Hebrew alphabet reads as either a 'b' or a 'v' depending on punctuation.)

How about twenty or so Lebanons or New Lebanons, eight Bethlehems, about a dozen Bethels (mouth of God) and a Piel, Washington, (mouth of God). Rehoboth, Goshen, Canaan, and New Cannan. There was no end to this! But you get the idea. To a recent arrival in New York with the dust of Kennedy airport still on his hat, this was all quite an astounding discovery. And it was a discovery that ultimately led to my many Christian friends and brothers, among whom is the hard-working author to whom you are indebted for the delights awaiting you in the pages ahead.

Rabbi Daniel Lapin
Mercer Island, Washington. 2010
President, The American Alliance of Jews and Christians.
www.aajc.org

Preface

When I decided to write on apocalyptic themes one year ago, I hardly realized the breadth of additional study required to do the topic justice. During my 35 years of adulthood, I had already read no less than 100 books on the subject of *the last days*. However, since the writing began, I've found it necessary to devour several dozen more. The sheer weight of relevant new material was overwhelming. I soon recognized that to accomplish my goal I must research the subject of biblical prophecy and the Apocalypse afresh, as if my prior study had been devoted to topic quite unrelated to the end of the world.

During the past decade, many new insights have found their way into books about *the last days*. Nevertheless, I still found two major deficiencies or gaps in the available published works:

- The first shortfall was the absence of a book in popular style that provided an explanation for how the notion of Apocalypse developed historically in Christendom and how that reflects on the prophecy teachers of today.

- The second was the lack of a published account on the many attempts to *decode Doomsday* (historic and contemporary) in order to develop an intellectually honest, culturally enlightened, and historically sound approach to the effort.

Consequently, I've written two books during the past fourteen months. The first book addresses gap number one, while the second naturally directs itself to gap number two.

In my first book, *Are We Living in the Last Days?* I delineate the three essential Christian positions on the Apocalypse developed over nearly 2,000 years of Christian history. I distinguish the Jewish and Christian concept of Messiah showing specifically why Christian theology breaks with its parent religion. I also defend the idea of *vision* as a means to comprehend the revelation of God for the last days. This issue is crucial for couched in the *visions* of the two foremost apocalyptic authors of the Bible – the prophet Daniel and the Apostle John – the Bible's most important and detailed prophecies are expressed. The bulk of the first book presents the major Protestant views on the prophetic topics of greatest interest such as the meaning of Armageddon, the Antichrist, the Rapture of the Church, the Seven Seals, the Seven Bowls of Wrath, etc. The book's primary thesis: *How we interpret the Bible (what theologians call our **hermeneutic**), determines what we believe about the Apocalypse.*

In some respects this book, *Decoding Doomsday*, belongs first. It's intended for the reader who wonders if the massive attention paid to 2012 is justified.

What's my angle? I attempt to examine the various 2012 sources in a comprehensive review to judge *whether the end of the world as we know it* is truly imminent. Style wise, I assume the reader prefers reviewing the data directly without a preemptive dogmatic conclusion on my part. Therefore, my approach is *to present the facts, analyze the data, and draw reasoned conclusions.* While I admit to being (or attempting to be) an ardent and orthodox Christian, my *modus operandi* is to present the facts with a critical eye and avoid reference to biblical passages as any sort of *proof text*. My reference to Scripture won't be to cinch an argument, but to analyze it just like any other source. Therefore, I rarely quote the Bible until we look directly at its message in the second half of this book.

Because I am, by nature critically minded and not easily persuaded to take things on faith, I ask investigative questions seeking an honest understanding of any particular witness' account, be it biblical or some other ancient source. I consider the prevailing reputation of any purveyor of wisdom vitally important. Likewise, I dismiss predictive assertions which fail for want of clarity or ability to present the original source accurately. Without this type of interpretive method, unwarranted speculation reigns.

It's my hope that you, the reader, will find this book helpful to arrive at a satisfying perspective on the challenge (and even necessity) of *decoding Doomsday*, as well as deciding what that personally means *to you*. With that stated intent, I commit my work and present this book.

Overview of this Book

The suspicion most everyone has when encountering the subject of Doomsday is that those attempting this investigation are clearly unbalanced or obviously escaping unhappy circumstances. As Lawrence Joseph joked to two Mayan shamans (the Barrios brothers, in his book *Apocalypse 2012*), when asked why he was so interested in what the Mayans had to say about the coming apocalypse (paraphrasing), "With my divorce this year my life came to an end, and so I've decided that everyone else's should as well."

Nevertheless, as Joseph asserts in all seriousness, we'd be foolish if we didn't seek out every piece of information that might avert or reduce the destructiveness of Doomsday. In addition, if Doomsday turns out to culminate in the *Second Coming of Christ* (as Christian's understandably label it), there are eternal reasons to come to grips with what's happening in the days ahead. To put it simply: *The reality and proximity of Doomsday is the ultimate question.* Joseph's unsettling quip also infers something else that we are likely to avoid discussing: *Doomsday is an existential matter.* There's no disputing that Doomsday is a matter of life and death — and that's as *ultimate* as it gets.

I have no desire to create a lengthy introduction, but allow me to outline how I will systematically address such a complex topic. After all, tackling an issue of this magnitude requires an organized approach at the very least.

Let me say at the outset that a key to understanding my emphasis on history is very simple. Hidden in our past are clear indications of our future. We can know what the future holds if we understand our history. *The past is the key to our future.* Only a historical approach can decode Doomsday.

So for starters, in **Part I**, we will provide an overview of *the history of Doomsday.* Our first chapter begins with elements of today's popular culture that infuses much of our entertainment with doomsday discussion. Next, I will briefly analyze *the nature of our culture today,* how its change over the past five decades influences the whole conversation of Doomsday.

In the second chapter, I engage with some of the most acclaimed voices speaking to the issue of Doomsday. These voices have new accents, but come from ancient sources. Here we will look at the 2012 commotion caused by (1) the *Mayan scholars* and New Age authors, (2) *Novelty theory* and the relevance of a sacred Chinese book, the *I Ching*, and finally (3) the value of using *the Bible Code* to predict the end of days.

After summarizing this contemporary phenomenon for context, we embark upon a detailed historical inquiry. First, I identify *the origin of the concept of Apocalypse.* It's important we understand from *whence* the idea of Doomsday arises; as we shall see, this origin serves as the dominant motivation for most apocalyptic scenarios over the past 2,000 years as well as the most widely-held apocalyptic scenario today. These many specific date-setting attempts predicting the end of the world become our next topic in Chapter 4. Logically, before we attempt decoding Doomsday, one of our foundational issues is the history of the many methods *employed* (and all of which so far notoriously *failed*), to determine the world's last day. It's no stretch to suppose the most obvious objection to my thesis can be succinctly summarized, "Hundreds of others have predicted a date and been wrong – why do you think you will be any different?" Naiveté may play a part, intellectual curiosity another, but my conviction is at the core of it and remains undaunted: We can obtain this knowledge if *we earnestly seek it.* We can be enlightened by building upon the mountains of research compiled through the centuries by studying the smartest insights our species has recorded – with some of those recordings handed down to us in surprising ways. In the worst case, what others presaged and how they derived wrong conclusions offer us many lessons illustrating *how not to approach this challenge.*

In **Part II**, we dig deeper into the natural history of the planet as well as the biographical and sociological history of the most popular "prophets" whose predictions stimulate Doomsday thinking today. In Chapter 5, we begin with modern Science's recent discoveries that there have been many more *mini-doomsdays* than previously understood; proving that *cataclysms are actually the normal course of life on planet earth.* For while we might think ourselves safe from catastrophic demise, Science demonstrates that major destructive events should be expected at least once in each millennium with minor catastrophes transpiring several times each century. Indeed, it's now exceedingly evident that no generation is exempt from cataclysm.

A case in point: We often lament how in the 20th century and beyond, human beings can trigger their own Doomsday with advanced weapons or genetic manipulation gone wrong. The power to end the world already rests in our hands. However, it's a fact worthy of reflection that ours isn't a unique situation in this regard. At the beginning of the 13th century, Genghis Khan led a well-trained cavalry armed with a compact and exceedingly brutal bow (his *weapon of mass destruction*), which laid waste to Asia – from Iraq to China. The death toll from his empire building totaled three million or more – all in less than three decades.

After our lesson on natural history, we will study the history of the Meso-american people in Chapter 6. We will focus mostly on the *Maya* in an extend-ed manner delving into their implied predictions and the correlation of their calendars to their prophecies. Next, we will look at the supporting data from other North American Indian sources such as the Aztecs, the Hopi, and the Cherokee. After looking at these Indian prophecies and how they interpreted them, in Chapter 7 we will do a walkthrough of the much more recent and highly peculiar circular activity characteristic of our Mother Country. Not only will we discover fascinating things about the wisdom of pre-historic Britain, we will uncover how this history is connected to the perplexing activity present today in the phenomenon known as Crop Circles and how this phenomenon also connects to Doomsday.

In the next three chapters of this section, we will consider the input pro-vided from three distinct but equally fascinating subjects. First, we will consid-er the principal *esoteric sources* that have had far more impact upon our world than most realize. This history is enormously fascinating and relevant as we shall see. After we discuss the topics of the occult, UFOs, and secret conspiracies (and what they have in common), we will move on to highlight the prophecies and relevance of history's greatest prophet outside the Bible: Nostradamus. Here I will offer some surprising new findings refuting most of the so-called experts who approach the prophecies of "Dr. No" from an esoteric or naturalist perspective. Then we will launch a discussion on Sir Isaac Newton, regarded by many as one of history's premiere Doomsday decoders.

Next, in Chapter 11, we will drill-down (as we say today) on the colorful history of what amounts to a true age-old world religion and how it has influ-enced America – *Freemasonry.* If the meaning of the Knights Templar is of in-terest you, you will want to consider how these Knights of 800 years ago are distinctly connected to today's America. One of the most often asked questions is, "Where is America in Bible Prophecy?" Here I provide the surprising an-swer.

Linked to these surprising findings will be an even more astonishing analy-sis: The true identity of the Antichrist (Chapter 12). History and the Bible tell us not only *what* he is but *who* – once we have decoded these ancient sources properly. The Antichrist has many names as we shall see, but his ancient name will catch most readers by surprise – and tell us how to recognize him once he reveals himself sometime in the years ahead. *Soon!*

No discussion of Doomsday would be complete without speaking to the manner of World War III (Chapter 13). Did you know that the Bible actually tells us that there will be three regional wars with the final culminating in a war world-wide in scope? It not only informs us regarding who the participants are in each war, but tells us who wins and who loses. It's so detailed that the ancient book of the Jews and Christians can be read side-by-side with today's newspapers to complete the story and let us know what's really going on behind the scenes.

In Chapter 15, I endeavor to sum up what we learned and offer reasoned and specific conclusions regarding what lies ahead. I will set forth a simple methodology for decoding Doomsday – how we should analyze the facts we've documented in order to draw sensible conclusions. It will become apparent that the topic of decoding Doomsday proves not only a rational task yielding clear-cut results; it's a noble effort to which we should aspire.

The world *as we know it* may soon end. Given the immense challenges of our times, we can't afford not to face these facts. Thus, Chapter 16 finishes with a meditation on the dangers of denying Doomsday, leaning on concepts from psychoanalysis and philosophy to explain why a preoccupation with Doomsday can be healthy. Lastly, I will offer several key reasons we must focus on the outcome of our age, lest we be caught unprepared.

Given that I take the tact I do, it's rather clear that this book is not just a history of Decoding Doomsday, but an apologetic for *why we should concern ourselves with it.* Millenarians have always been criticized as intellectually bankrupt and emotionally unbalanced. It would be a shock to the intellectual community if there could be a reasonable justification for why we should be mindful of the potential outcome of the human race. In the final section, we will examine the Bible and its most widely held scenario for what the future holds.

We know the skepticism of today's academics has been based upon a rigid *naturalism* – a denial of the possibility of spiritual reality playing any role in what happens to life on earth. This closed-mindedness is changing; for as we will see, spiritualism has and continues to be a driving force behind apocalypticism of all sorts, especially today's enthusiasm (if not euphoria) for anticipating the events associated with what we now call, "2012."

Therefore, I conclude with a counter-argument that humankind face Doomsday earnestly the same way individuals must face their personal death with the blinders off, fully understanding our predicament, and preparing ourselves for the inevitable.

PART I:
THE HISTORY OF
DOOMSDAY

Chapter 1:
A Culture Obsessed With the End of Time

If the button is pushed, there's no running away,
There'll be no one to save with the world in a grave,
Yeah, my blood's so mad, feels like coagulatin',
I'm sittin' here, just contemplatin',
I can't twist the truth, it knows no regulation,
handful of Senators don't pass legislation,
and marches alone can't bring integration,
When human respect is disintegratin',
This whole crazy world is just too frustratin',
and you tell me over and over and over again my friend,
ah, you don't believe we're on the eve of destruction.

P.F. Sloan

The Eve of Destruction

It was a time of war and protest. A newcomer named Barry McGuire scribbled a song he'd recently heard on a napkin and then recorded it on July 14, 1965. The next day, a radio DJ leaked the P.F. Sloan song, playing McGuire's recording on the air. It became an instant hit.

Within a few weeks, it was number one on the charts. The tune was catchy but Sloan's lyrics sparked a mountain of controversy. The song warned of *apocalypse*. The words protested the in-

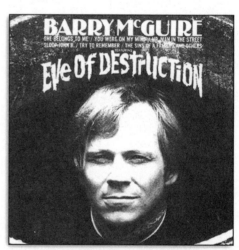

FIGURE 1 - ALBUM COVER FOR THE EVE OF DESTRUCTION

volvement of the United States in Vietnam. The *Cold War* was at its height, the civil rights movement was just getting off the ground, and the terrors of nuclear war were "clear and present dangers" of the day.

The song was banned on some radio stations in the US, most of England, and all of Scotland. Conservatives said it symbolized everything negative about the young people of the sixties. It was an audio icon.

If ESPN's Chris Berman would stop referring to retired baseball star Mark McGwire as "Mark – Eve of Destruction – McGwire," this song would be entirely absent from our 21st century culture. Barry McGuire, who later converted to Christianity, continues singing religious songs. However, it's the one hit wonder for which he's best remembered. After all, it's not just anyone the "Establishment" singles out as an emblem for what's wrong with *all young people*.

2012 – The Movie Is Released Today

As I begin my writing, Roland Emmerich releases his movie *2012* (November 13, 2009). It's no doubt going to be a special effects extravaganza. It seems only fitting to start this manuscript on the day this movie blockbuster declares the Apocalypse lies only 37 months away.

The Studio has hyped the movie *2012* for almost a year. The first trailer previewed a massive tsunami lapping over the peaks of the Himalayas. "**Who.will.survive.2012,**" the web site for the movie, provides a stirring synopsis: "Never before has a date in history been so significant to so many cultures, so many religions, scientists, and governments. *2012* is an epic adventure about a global cataclysm that brings an end to the world and tells of the heroic struggle of the survivors."

Whether the movie is a success at the box-office or a flop, it has already popularized the seminal ideas that gave rise to the movie: Mayan prophecies of destruction, scientific scenarios of doom, and cross-cultural histories of the end of the world. They all point to the same doomsday date.

Recent Movies of the Apocalypse – a Fan Favorite

2012 is hardly the first movie focused on the Apocalypse. This very same year (2009), the movie *Knowing* hit the theaters, exposing audiences to an apocalypse featuring supernatural foreknowledge of the end. A series of hand written arcane codes, plucked from a time capsule buried at an elementary school 50 years prior, hid this prognostication. The fantastic plot line was built upon a similar prediction of the apocalypse as *2012* – massive solar flares from our sun disrupting and then overcoming earth's protective covering, its powerful magnetic field and atmospheric shield. The characters are shocked to learn that excessive radiation from the sun will cook the whole population of the earth, its animal life forms, as well as humanity itself. Can anyone save humanity?

Spoiler alert (skip to the next paragraph): Salvation of biblical proportions assures the continuance of humanity through an "ark" from outer space apparently manned by angelic beings. It's not your normal Hollywood ending. As a modern retelling of Noah's Ark, critics thought the ending rather predictable and a bit cheesy.

The 2007 movie *I Am Legend* portrays a much grimmer picture of the end of humanity. Will Smith stars in a classic story by the same name, a remake of the 1971 movie, *The Omega Man* (which starred one of my old time favorites, Charlton Heston). In this story, a genetically re-engineered measles virus infects all humanity. Everyone is wiped out except for the bad guys, 12 million "*Darkseekers*" who can't stand the suns' radiation even in normal doses (UV sun block anyone?). When does the main part of the movie take place? When has the Apocalypse come? In 2012, of course!

The movie, *12 Monkeys,* (1995) by Terry Gilliam, is another film where humanity is driven underground due to a virus gone bad (of course, when is there ever a good virus?) Then there's that number 12 again. Like a bad penny...

We could mention other movies with similar story lines: *Resident Evil 2 – Apocalypse* (2004) and *Resident Evil 3 – Extinction* (2007). Again, the villain is a deadly virus. However, instead of creating creatures that hide from the light, traditional horror movie fans were thrilled to see the film's monsters made to resemble old-fashioned zombies. Innovation isn't always the smartest way to please the movie-going crowds.

Let's recap a recent history of these terrifying world-ending events made manifest by the movies:

- *Death from nuclear annihilation:* The ***Planet of the Apes Series,*** first movie by the same name in 1965 starring Charlton Heston; The ***Mad Max Series*** (first installment with Mel Gibson in 1971), and the 1960's classic (featuring much more plot and acting with only one special effect – a deserted San Francisco), with Gregory Peck, ***On the Beach.***

- *Death from the machines:* ***The Matrix Series,*** first installment in 1999 starring Keanu Reeves; ***The Terminator Series,*** first of many, with the "governator" Arnold Schwarzenegger in the auspicious year 1984.

- *Death from asteroids:* (1) ***Armageddon*** (1998) – it's certainly good we have Bruce Willis to save the world; (2) ***Deep Impact*** (1998), the better of the two movies plot-wise with a more believable solution to the problem of "when worlds collide." However, the box office liked *Armageddon* much better.

- *Death from aliens:* (1) **Independence Day,** (1996) also made by 2012 director, Roland Emmerich); (2) **War of the Worlds** (2005) in which director Stephen Spielberg gets in the game; (3) **The Day the Earth Stood Still** (2008), a not-so-popular remake of the 1951 classic.

- *Death from climate change:* (1) **Waterworld,** (1995) produced, directed and starring Kevin Costner – a really bad movie that proves you never want to have your name listed more than twice in the credits; (2) **The Day After Tomorrow** (2004), produced, directed and written by, wait for it… Roland Emmerich once again.

Clearly, humanity's survival is the provocative plot of more popular movies than at any previous time since movies became an essential part of our culture. Where would the Apocalypse be in the mind of many without the special effects now commonplace in our films?

Additionally, it doesn't take much analysis to recognize the biggest bogeyman we fear at any given moment becomes the threat we see in celluloid:

- In the 1960's and 70's, we were freaked out by *the unnerving cold war and the ghastly prospects of nuclear annihilation* that we barely averted during the *Cuban Missile Crisis* of October, 1962.

- In the 1980's and 90's, we began to speculate *how computers would someday control many facets of our lives.* It didn't take much precognition to foresee computers taking away all notion of humankind's mastery of the world. It was only a matter of time until one day we would wake up to the reality that machines were competing with us for the label *highest intelligence* and they could apparently win the contest – not only in chess matches, but in waging war too.

- Later in the 1990's *our fears turned more and more toward outer space.* We obsessed over evil aliens and the possible catastrophe caused by a comet or asteroid striking the earth. With many near misses disclosed to us by scientists in the last ten years, we know it isn't so far-fetched that space could bean us with a fastball coming at us so quickly and with so little notice – there will be no time to duck. We know it did in the dinosaurs' time; it seems inevitable our species is next in line.

- Today we focus our fear *on the changing global climate.* It's getting too hot to handle and this heat could mean a polar meltdown. Since 40% of the world's population is located within about 40 miles of the coastline, it's no small thing to raise sea level a foot or two worldwide.

- Closely linked to the issue of climate change is *our sun; changes in its behavior may spell our doom.* We understand that the sun goes through cycles too; the next solar maximum (when sunspots and solar activity are at their highest) could be a real lollapalooza. It just so happens, Science has already promised this will occur at the end of 2012.

The Impact on Television

Over the past few months, the *History Channel* and the *Discovery Channel* have had a field day developing sensational documentaries and airing them repeatedly. In fact, the *History Channel*, created a completely new series, **The Nostradamus Effect,** based upon the possible convergence of history's doomsday prophecies with current events.

ABC has just launched a new series, **V,** which is really an old series updated (the original was aired in 1984). It appears outer space yields yet another race of creatures proclaiming its eagerness to save humanity (so they say). Moreover, they aren't even Democrats. So, guess who's coming to dinner? (Warning: While we may find ourselves at table with "the Visitors," we may not be honored guests).

Haven't we seen this theme before? We certainly have. For nine seasons the **X Files** provided us with a great story 'arc' featuring the "black oil" that would infiltrate our bodies and turn us into one of them. We saw graphically in the first **X Files** movie how this oil ultimately turns us into creatures resembling the **Alien** monster from that series of horror films. It certainly appears that we can learn some lessons here.

Do you remember the line from Homer's *Iliad* (the story of the Trojan War*)?* "Beware Greeks bearing gifts!" What gift you ask? That Trojan horse of course! It looks like our visitors from distant worlds, (aka *reptilian aliens*), may employ the same strategy as ancient Greeks. We must conclude a good stratagem never gets out of date nor is it limited to just our little corner of the galaxy. "Those that do not learn from history are destined to repeat it." Just remember you heard it here first: *"Beware aliens bearing gifts."*

Indeed, we lament our lost heroes – no more macho Marines; gone are the days of *Westerns.* Adventure now has nothing to do with "Cowboys and Indians." It's obvious that if John Wayne were an actor in his prime today, he wouldn't be riding a horse; he'd be flying a space ship.

The Inevitable Doomsday – Going Viral

However, even more plausible (since historical precedent matters), is a cataclysm brought on by *microscopic organisms*. Rational scientists with both feet on the ground speculate that virus mutations could cause worldwide plagues. The recent experiences of SARS and H1N1 are present day points in fact. Nevertheless, history gives us even stronger examples that we shouldn't overlook. Viruses and bacteria in times past have caused true cataclysms killing millions at a time. The "Black Plague" in Europe (from the fifth century forward) struck repeatedly. Our kids still sing about it:

Ring around the rosy, (the rose-colored blemishes)
Pocket full of posies, (flowers to cut down on the smell)
Ashes, ashes – all fall down! (The burning pyre of bodies collapsing into an ash heap)

Likewise, when Columbus discovered America it wasn't all good news. The natives encountered European grown diseases for which they had no immunity.

So we see that apocalypse has already occurred in America – we just weren't present in the 16th century to witness it firsthand. Some experts estimate that 80% or more of the native population died as a result. 50 million indigenous peoples contracted to only 8 million by 1650. That is a death toll.

In the past 100 years, the *Great Flu Pandemic of 1918* stands out as an empirical, all-too-scary benchmark. Compared to war, it's no contest. 50 million people died between 1918 and 1920, almost seven times the deaths of World War I. Three percent of the world's population died from this "Spanish Flu" and an estimated 30% of the population was infected. With today's population approaching six billion, such a widespread breakout could kill 200,000,000 people and infect 2 billion. We have no idea how overwhelmed our health care systems would be.

Today, we fear *Ebola*, a virus that broke out in Africa and has appeared again there at least seven times in the past 33 years. So far, an air borne version hasn't escaped laboratories where it's studied (an airborne version did exist in Reston, VA, but was destroyed there after dramatic steps were taken to eradicate the outbreak in the test animals). Nevertheless, the experts say, "It's only a matter of time before it goes global." Unlike the flu of 1918, it won't be the case that 1 out of 10 infected with the virus dies. It is more likely the inverse: 9 out of 10 persons won't survive.

Of all the fears we have of how the apocalypse can befall us, it may be obvious that only "death by virus" is predictable, rational, and worthy of all the effort we can muster to keep it from becoming reality. *Science poses no skepticism whatsoever on this possible cause of the calamity to end all calamities.*

How the World Has Changed

If one fact seems certain in describing the cultural transformation over the last 40 years, it's this:

- **1969:** Fantastic phenomena (out-of-this-world) can't be taken seriously.
- **2009:** Mundane explanations (of this world) are out of the question!

In the 60's we were adopting the brave new world of Huxley and Orwell, assuming that *reason* should direct all our decisions, miracles can't happen to anyone, and Science is the new religion our world should embrace.

Today, any meaningful solution to the age-old questions of "Why Are We Here?" and "What Does Life Mean?" better contain a big dose of *spirituality* or the *paranormal;* otherwise we aren't impressed.

Just how big a change has been going on? Let's take evangelicals for example. Evangelical Christianity dominates the church scene in America today. Mega churches (8,000 or more attending Sunday services) are growing by leaps and bounds. One national periodical in 2005 (*Newsweek*) suggested that the equivalent of a two new mega-churches opened every week in America. Such places of worship proclaim a historic version of the Christian faith and believe in the literal truth of the Bible.

Not that it's the *old time religion* winning the day in every quarter. Some seek spiritual solutions from cabbalists and gurus, from parapsychologists and mediums, from new age thinkers and purveyors of alternate medicine, from shamans as well as wizards. Many others seek more respected spiritual insights from traditional eastern mysticism and especially the likes of Jungian psychology.

However, not everyone buys into spiritual solutions to our problems. There are cultural holdouts. I would be remiss if I failed to point out the "new atheism" of raging agnostics like Richard Dawkins (*The God Delusion*), Christopher Hitchens (*God is Not Great*), and Daniel Dennett (*Breaking the Spell: Religion as a Natural Phenomenon*). From the perspective of these particularly outspoken atheists, everyone outside their club is too illiterate, irrational, superstitious, or uninformed to *see the light* quite the way they do. This group has proclaimed themselves in a robust lack of modesty, "the *Brights*" (since they confidently intend to *illuminate* the rest of us).

Their worldview is actually quite simple: There is no God, there is no realm of the spirit, and there is no afterlife. Miracles don't happen. In addition, to these atheists the real evil is *the rest of us that believe in such things.* To be more specific: The world's largest problems are *a direct result of religious fanaticism.* This elite group heralds a rallying cry for atheists and agnostics everywhere to stand up and fight the good fight against the supernatural, the old religious way of thinking, and those that advocate it.

Will this view win the day? It's not too likely. This is the 1960's worldview gasping for one last gulp of air. When you think about it, it's apparent that the group is pretty well doomed right from the start. After all, if too many people join the club, the exclusiveness loses its luster. By definition, the "elite" are only special if they are no more than a select few. And it only takes one indisputable miracle on prime-time TV to finally bring this point of view to an end.

In stark contrast, today more than ever before, the common person resolves the fundamental question of *meaning* with *religion and spiritual explanations.* Just look at the rise in the interest in the paranormal or the rapid growth in Islam and Mormonism worldwide. Spiritual worldviews still predominate. Moreover, if you want to affect a change throughout the general culture, a few antagonistic atheists can't outdo a spiritually based movement in dedication or accomplishment. Maybe the *new atheists* know this and it's why they talk with such vitriol, quick to attack any manner of religious thought.

One thing's for sure: When it's crystal-clear that Doomsday looms, the atheist will second guess their doubt quicker than you can say, "The fool says in his heart, there is no God." As many a veteran of combat would attest, "There are no atheists in fox holes." There won't be any atheists when Doomsday comes either – just those who stand firm in *the belief their God will deliver them* or those who can't outrun the destruction that approaches in plain sight.

Jesus said, "As in the days of Noah, so shall it be in the day when the Son of Man comes." He went on to say, paraphrasing, "It will be business as usual. People will be celebrating, getting married and assuming that the future goes on forever. But in Noah's day, (despite their optimism about the future and their skepticism about a catastrophic event), they elected to ignore the warnings. Finally, the floods came and washed everyone away."

Noah loaded the Ark and raised the loading ramp. For seven more days the sun shined and Noah and his family waited. Outside the crowds gathered and jeered. But then the floods came. In another day or two, the water rose to frightening heights. The *Brights* of that day stood outside the Ark with water up to their waists, beating on the doors. They thought surely Noah would open the doors. But the decision was no longer in Noah's hands. The Bible says "and God *shut the door.*" Once the day and the hour finally arrived, time had run out. There was no chance to alter the decisions that had been made.

Will it really be like this when Doomsday comes? Is 2012 the only Doomsday scenario we need to worry about? Do other sources of ancient wisdom beside the Bible warn us about the future? What do we need to know to gauge exactly where we are on the Doomsday timeline? Are some voices more reliable than others? Are there really more reasons to worry about the future today than 50 years ago? Isn't preoccupation with Doomsday evidence of neurosis? Shouldn't we accentuate the positive and downplay the negative?

My job will be to answer these questions and many others just as interesting and important. But you'd better hold onto your hats. Despite the fact that I don't make many predictions, I do predict this is going to be a wild ride.

Chapter 2:
Old Voices – New Messages

Do not awaken slumbering beasts;
They are guarding secrets
Deeper than you know.
Do not provoke their interest
or you will flee
before the reddened eye and bared teeth.
Sleeping Dogs guard the gates of hell
and feast upon the arrogant or unwary soul -
Who fears not the past, is a fool.

Geraldine Moorkens Byrne

Dead Civilizations Speak from the Grave

O ld adages are hard to beat. The "advice of sages through the ages" is a wisdom we do well to heed. Moreover, it's easy calling some of these aphorisms to mind:

"Opposites attract."

"Let sleeping dogs lie."

"Quiet! You might wake the dead."

So, you ask, what do you do if the dogs wake up? Clearly, you have to deal with the dogs. As to not waking the dead, I suppose the advice intends to stave off zombie attacks. They both sound like good ideas to me.

But if I had to choose, I'd rather deal with the dogs.

Nevertheless, when it comes to *pop prophecy,* over the past 30 years or so, *we've had to deal with the dead* – dead civilizations and primeval voices to be specific. Indeed, there have been a number of ancient sources lying as quiet as sleeping dogs for several millennia. In the last three decades, these sources have been *awakened* so to speak. They have been unearthed, decoded, or updated in such a way to coalesce in what appears to be a common timeframe predicting the world's end. They all arrive at the same conclusion: *2012.* Specifically, on December 21, 2012, the world as we know it will no longer be the same. What's most intriguing is, as I just stated, these sources aren't imaginative books or movies – *they are ancient sources of wisdom that have been with us for thousands of years.*

Let's listen to these "old voices with new messages" briefly to get a sense of what they forecast. On the one hand, we will be surprised to learn that our ancient ancestors were actually a lot smarter than we thought. On the other hand, unlike the plethora of publications that find synchronicities and coincidences heralding the end of the world in 2012, when we carefully study the authentic testimony, we may learn some of the messages have been twisted by modern day, *2012 enthusiasts* – many of these sources never intended to pinpoint the date when everything falls apart.

The Mayan Calendars and Their Knowledge of the Heavens

There are many great and notable empires in the history of the ancient world: The Egyptians, the Persians, the Greeks, and of course, the Romans. However, except for Egypt, none of these empires speak to the world today. Quite unexpectedly, it's one empire in particular, the Mesoamerican Empire of the Maya, which has captured our attention at the beginning of the 21st century.

We now know that the empire of the Mayans (if we include the *Olmec's* – their prior relations as well as their successors, the (Aztecs) may have lasted over 4,000 years (roughly from 2600 BC to 1500 AD), which would make it the most enduring empire of all time. Certainly most experts agree it lasted at least 1,000 years reaching its zenith around the 7th or 8th century AD. Then, as a "force to be reckoned with," suddenly, the Maya civilization all but vanished. We have educated guesses, but we don't exactly know why or how, after such a glorious past, its extinction ensued. Mel Gibson's movie, *Apocalypto,* assumes that Mayan civilization collapsed because of its decadence and lust for blood, which reached its height just before the arrival of Cortez and the Spanish Conquistadors in the 16th century.[1] History challenges this view however. It appears the demise of the Maya commenced long before that event – perhaps 800 years prior.

Great architecture and amazingly accurate knowledge of the workings of the heavens characterized the Mayan civilization. The Mayans understood the cycles of the sun, the moon, the length of earth year (accurate to at least four decimal places), the cycle of Venus (its procession as seen from earth, a *five-point appearance*)[2] and even the cycle of the spiraling galaxy. (It's one of the great-unsolved mysteries of our day: How could a culture without many of the most basic sciences (such as metallurgy, the use of gunpowder, and many other practical inventions – most noteworthy being *the wheel*), know something so advanced as how heavenly bodies move through the skies?

This knowledge gave rise to a series of calendars. The most famous, the *grand cycle* of the "long-count calendar" actually tracks the time it takes for the earth to wobble its way around through the zodiac (our earth tilts 23.5 degrees and spins like a top – one circle of this wobbling spin cycle takes about 26,000 years – 25,630 to be precise). The Mayans understood this phenomenon and created a calendar predicting a complete cycle concluding on December 21, 2012.

This cycle also coincides with the sun standing perfectly between the earth and the exact center of the Milky Way Galaxy (our home galaxy in a universe of billions of galaxies). When this invisible eclipse happens, the sun rises at a point on the horizon where it touches the center of the Milky Way's so-called *dark rift*. This *place* (which is really no more than our vantage point) is the long and jagged, dare I say, *fudgy middle* of the Milky Way – scientifically known as the layer of cosmic dust and perhaps dark matter that hides most of the stars between the galactic center and us. While this galactic eclipse is unusual, does it mean anything significant to life on earth?

FIGURE 2 - A PANORAMA OF THE MILKY WAY GALAXY

Many experts in Mayan folklore believe it does. They divide this 25,630 solar-year period into five segments each about 5,126 solar years in length. According to these researchers and writers, we are supposedly now living in the fifth of these five periods.[3] Each period concludes an "age" or epoch – and a cataclysm of biblical proportions accompanies the completion of every one.

Reinforcing the Bible's story of Noah's Ark (and perhaps its approximate timing too), the last epoch concluded in 3,114 BC when the earth experienced a calamitous flood killing virtually all life on the planet. The next epoch will end on 12-21-2012. Some say this period will end with enormous worldwide earthquakes. Others say that this epoch will end in fire. Then there are those that believe the cataclysm will once again be a flood (an interpretation of the very last page of the *Dresden Codex* – one of the few Mayan manuscripts still preserved today – resident in Dresden, Germany). All believe there will be a time of dramatic events that will purify the world and cleanse humanity of its fallen ways and mistaken perspectives.

Many of today's writers on these subjects see only a time of transition or transformation. The drama may not be cataclysmic but cosmic. Human beings will suddenly understand that there is much more to the universe than what we know today. We will come to appreciate that the realms of nature and of spirit are a single reality, a union of the *seen and the unseen*. Our *fall from grace* (metaphorically in this context), has been our failure to appreciate this underlying unity and our tendency to dwell only on material things. As a result, we have lost our souls. On December 21, 2012, the alignment of the earth, sun, and galactic center will provide the impetus to remake our world and to change all of us for the better!

Exactly how this happens isn't explainable in terms of human physiology or psychology. Most scientists can only wag their heads in ridicule. But advocates talk of a force or power that emanates from the middle of the galaxy and once it ceases its contact with us (apparently as the sun blocks our connection with it) it will have an enormous impact upon the earth. Humankind (depending upon whom you listen to) may be destroyed or suddenly rehabilitated from its cold-hearted ways and be ushered into a time of peace and harmony. The song, *The Age of Aquarius* from the Broadway musical *Hair*, celebrates this *human change of mind*. Indeed, I can still hear the *Fifth Dimension* sing its chorus four decades after making it their number one hit in 1969: "No more falsehoods or derisions, mystic crystal revelations, and the mind's true liberation." Aquarius dawns!

We will probe further into this Mesoamerican cosmology and its prophecies in a later chapter. For the moment, we will leave the Maya here, only with a summary of the two principal alternative interpretations of their *2012 prophecies*:

- View one: We will experience the end of the world.

- View two: *No worries.* We will change in a dramatic way and all will be better and brighter.

But for now let's look at other ancient voices that seem to agree with the Maya, suggesting the very same crossroad lies just ahead.

The I Ching

Another ancient empire whose wisdom is creating a commotion today is China. The ancient book, the *I Ching*, (or *Yi Jing*), commonly translated as "the book of changes" was supposedly created in the legendary era of Fu Xi, one of

China's first emperors, living between 2900 and 2800 BC. Like the prophecies of the Maya, it's noteworthy that the history of this wisdom appears to begin almost 5,000 years ago. Confucius, who lived 2,300 years later (around 550 BC), considered the *I Ching* a fount of insight. He declared it a book worthy of dedicated study. Some scholars even believe that Confucius wrote the extensive commentaries accompanying the copies we have today. The book itself focuses on processes, balancing opposites and the inevitability of change. At its core are sixty-four "stick figures" composed of six horizontal lines. Lines are either solid or are broken with a space in the middle. These lines are stacked up six high.

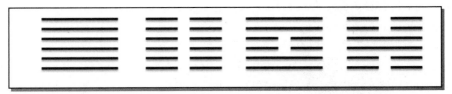

FIGURE 3 – EXAMPLES OF THE SIX LINE HEXAGRAMS IN THE I CHING

This sequence can therefore create sixty-four (64) unique variations or characters of six lines each.

Each of the sixty-four hexagrams potentially provides us with personal truths in a process known as "divination" (where one seeks guidance from a supernatural source). Like casting lots, crystal ball gazing, scrying, and water witching, *divination* attempts to contact spiritual sources to help in decision-making. *Theistic religions typically spurn divination as evil, since it leads to calling upon other deities, causing a failure to exercise faith in God as the only source to guide our destiny.* Religions that are *polytheistic* (that believe there are *many* gods) couldn't care less about this concern. From their perspective, if we can get an opinion from a supernatural source of wisdom, "we're all ears!" Listening to such gods and seeking their counsel seems like a smart idea, particularly if they have proven in the past to know something about the future.

The *I Ching* is relevant to our story because of two brothers – Terrence and Dennis McKenna – that unite its use to their theory of the Universe's *essence*. They connect the *I Ching's* principles to what they label *Novelty Theory* or *Time Wave Theory*. This exotic hypothesis of how time and eternity interact is our next topic.

Time Wave Theory

In the 1970's, the McKenna's went on a trip to the Amazon and studied the effects of various psychedelic drugs on perception. They searched (but never found) the plant known as the "oo-koo-he" which contains a chemical substance, *Dimethyltryptamine*, alias, DMT. The common name for the fun juice derived from it is *Ayahuasca*. On their way to the oo-koo-he, they encountered mushrooms and got stuck with them instead. *But they still experienced a great trip* (in more ways than one). With such promising good times ahead, Dennis urged Terrence to sample the goods (which they both ingested). You might call it *doing primary research* (a firsthand investigation – purely for the sake of science of course), in which they actively took part in ingesting the drugs and experiencing their direct affects.

One of their conclusions was that by ingesting this class of drugs, primitive humans began to "speak in tongues" (otherwise known scientifically as *glossolalia*). The *chemical brothers* theorized that language actually developed in these creatures (our forebears) from these experiences of exuberant expressions in which they verbalized sounds without meaning. All oohing and cooing aside, while being a truly provocative position on the origination of language in humans, at the very least it wouldn't be the first time that native folk were accused of taking drugs to get in the spirit of things. However, for McKenna, this was no laughing matter: He echoed Dr. Timothy Leary (UC Berkeley, Harvard), the intellectual leader of the "hippie movement," in the 1960's, regarding another similar drug known popularly as LSD. Like Leary before him, who had also taken a trip south of the border to check out some special mushrooms, he concluded that *drugs were the gateway to God.*[4]

Terrence experienced visions of speaking insects and all manner of weird and wacky things. This is quite a story unto itself. But what we are interested in here is the imaginative leap he made connecting his experiences in the Amazon to the *I Ching*. Why did he make this leap? Terrence encountered a being he called *Logos*,[5] who he believed was the spiritual source (a god?) behind all religions. During his many experiences in a trance state, this spirit being told McKenna that what he needed, more than a good high, was spending some quality time studying the *I Ching*.

Terrence evaluated the 64 hexagrams of the *I Ching* and noted that if you multiplied 64 by 6 (the number of lines in each character figure), you would arrive at 384, which just so happens is almost an exact lunar year (13 months of 29.5 days). He thought, "Eureka! The *I Ching* must be a calendar system too." This obviously meant there was a relationship between the calendar systems of the Chinese and the Maya. Well, maybe it wasn't completely obvious. Nevertheless, to both of the McKenna brothers, it was a real epiphany.

The next leap was just as imaginative. McKenna decided that the *I Ching* could actually provide insight into the way that "time works." He purposed that time is itself an animated reality that is intentional – which is an intriguing way of saying that time *thinks* and time *creates*.[6] (Perhaps this insight isn't too hard to conjecture if you have been eating 'shrooms' to excess.) In fact, McKenna suggests that time *innovates* and actually, increases the rate of innovation as it moves along.[7] A corollary to this idea is that time *accelerates* (and who hasn't experienced the phenomenon of time going faster as we get older?) In an interesting *about face,* McKenna's thinking transforms the creative force of God – normally equated with eternity – into "*TIME* as the god-force." In the McKenna's view, *TIME* draws us all forward to a moment of special significance. *TIME* is intentional, goal-directed – *TIME* has a plan.

Therefore, McKenna began to map world events and the rate of innovation and he noticed an interesting pattern. It seems that *mega-events* (extra big, world changing occurrences – in my childhood days we called them "red-letter dates" because they appeared that way in our Encyclopedias), happened in a cycle that shows progression into an ever-increasing rate of change. TIME is moving toward an exponential rate of innovation – new things will come on the scene more and more frequently.[8] When TIME reaches the conclusion where change is in fact constant, (differentiation and evolution are occurring without as much as a hiccup), we will have achieved a *singularity* (an infinite state), where the world is transformed, and the capacity of human consciousness is likewise catapulted into the stratosphere. However intelligent we are now is not worth celebrating. After we hit this *singularity,* also known as *time wave zero,* we become a whole lot smarter and aware of many spiritual realities whose existence or meaning we doubt today. We might even recognize our place in the universe's grand scheme of things. We will achieve "cosmic consciousness."

Well, there's no harm in admitting McKenna was an optimist.

McKenna also determined a full human life-cycle according to the *I Ching* was a smidge more than 67 years. Using this time span as well as its multiples or its "fractals" (a convenient way of giving yourself lots of latitude when finding patterns in something as asynchronous and puzzling as history), these *time waves* could be proven to be empirical realities. After all, if you can map it on graph paper it must be scientific. Use a computer and you have *uber*-science.

Finally, McKenna decided that the penultimate (second-to-last) mega-event was the unleashing of the atomic bomb on Hiroshima in 1945. Next, all he needed to do was to add 67 years (plus that smidge) to this date and arrive at the calculable answer to the world's climatic ending – 2012. Seems simple doesn't it?[9]

The book that made these brainstorms public appeared in 1975: *The Invisible Landscape – Mind Hallucinogens and the I Ching.*[10] According to McKenna, the coincidence of his date for the end, December 22, 2012 and the Mayan date of December 21, 2012 was something that he couldn't have contrived, at least the way he tells the story. After all, he published his book years ahead of the Mayan "discoveries."

Also, it should be pointed out that since his end date just so happens to be within 24 hours of the Mayan calendar conclusion, from his perspective (and many others) this amounts to be truly independent if not scientific confirmation[11] that the world will end on December 21 or 22, 2012. Therefore, McKenna and many of his supporters believe – drum roll please – *Doomsday has been decoded!*

So what do I think? From my point of view, the McKenna's actually have an innovative hypothesis worth considering, but they just haven't made the case. Additionally, they are hardly the first to argue there's a pattern to history spurred on by a force behind it all. In philosophy, one of its greatest minds, G.W.F. Hegel saw the force as the *geist* (spirit) while Karl Marx "turned Hegel on his head" and saw it as "lively matter" (materialism) working through class struggle within history. This *force* (whether mind or matter) did its work through a process they both called the *dialectic.*[12] Their argument was far more complete than the "Time Wave Theory" although philosophers of history today might question whether Hegel or Marx were offering overly aggressive (forced) interpretations of how "history" (aka, TIME) works. Additionally, given how the McKenna's derived their insights (from drugs, trances, and spiritual voices in their heads), not many scientists would find their conclusions particularly credible either.

The Hindu Calendar and Civilization's Genesis

While it's not the basis for the same amount of conjecture, most writers discussing the Mayan Calendar as a means to decode Doomsday are quick to point out that the *Kali Yoga* calendar of the Hindus begins with a start date of January 23, 3102 BC. Additionally, one interpretation in Hinduism asserts that the ultimate great cataclysm would occur 5,000 years later (around 1898 AD). Is this loose prediction in fact noteworthy?

If you read many authors of books on 2012, you would think it is. They frequently cite it as "yet another near-ironclad corroboration" of the theory. However, most people sensitive to science and empirical evidence suppose that any discrepancy of this length *isn't a small inaccuracy*. "Missing the mark and calling it good," is just as bad as fabrication. Unlike "horse shoes and hand grenades," *close doesn't count in prophecy* – especially if you seek to prove something in the world of *facts* capable of withstanding critical scrutiny.

Nevertheless, I would be remiss if I didn't admit that many books touting *2012* as the end date point out consistent testimony from many other cultures that civilization has a documented beginning[13] around 3100 BC. This is so not only in the Mayan, Hindu, and Egyptian cultures, but also in the culture of perhaps the world's oldest city, Uruk, in *Mesopotamia* (which is ancient Sumer in present day Iraq). A quick look at Wikipedia, however, warns against making too much of this theory, at least in the case of Uruk, for the archeologists tell us that there were in fact many cities built upon this site – all of which date back 2,000 years further, to 5000 BC. What is so special about 3100 BC in the history of Uruk? Only that this is when its inhabitants built their first temples and created Uruk's encircling walls.

Given these facts, what are we to make of *this possible start date* for civilization? While it may be true that this is when people began to make records permanent, it might not mean the beginning of civilization itself. It more likely means that some cataclysm in their recent memory made keeping a lasting *impression* of this history necessary. If you happen to subscribe to the view that the biblical flood of Noah was an historical event (but occurred prior to 2400 BC, a date many evangelicals suppose), it would seem more than plausible that permanent record keeping became preferred to oral tradition, in order to document the truly important events worth sharing with future generations. Otherwise, when another flash flood comes rushing down the valley, it might wash away the artifacts of your culture and all evidence of your existence.

We should also point out that Hinduism shares many religious elements with the Mayans. Indeed, perhaps they both came from an even more primitive pagan religion, which asserted what these perspectives had in common:

- These religious systems believed in many gods, yet both regarded one god primary and more powerful than all others.

- Both share a belief in the connection of heaven and earth, the obvious connection of the sun and the seasons, as well as the not-so-obvious linkage between the stars and our human consciousness.

- Additionally, both of these cultures utilized *lunar* and a *solar* calendars (while the Mayans actually have 20 calendars, Hinduism has nine).

Finally, there is the most important theme they appeared to share – human consciousness connected to the heavens. Both cultures repeat this theme many times in their respective religions. Certainly it's this connection that catalyzes the view of many who see a human consciousness transformation in the "heavenly" cycles which play themselves out in 2012. However, there is at least one major noteworthy difference. Hinduism proposes a second sun around which our visible sun rotates. According to Hinduism, when we are closest to this second sun, our consciousness heightens; when we are far away, our awareness of the sacred drops. As the group *The Police*, (and their lead singer, Sting) advise:

> *There has to be an invisible sun*
> *It gives its heat to everyone*
> *There has to be an invisible sun*
> *It gives us hope when the whole day's done.*

Is this idea crazy? Surprisingly, there is a strong scientific argument for a "second sun" as an invisible dwarf star around which our sun *dances in rotation*. We'll take a quick look.

It's a fact that most stars in the cosmos appear in pairs; stars are "doubles and not singles" according to traditional astronomy. This second sun theory also leverages the so-called "precession of the equinoxes" as empirical proof for its validity. Walter Cruttendon of the Binary Research Institute says our sun is no different:

> The precession of the equinox is observed as the stars moving across the sky at the rate of about 50 arc seconds per year, relative to the equinox. Conventional theory holds that this phenomenon is due to the gravity of the sun and moon acting upon the oblate spheroid of the earth causing the axis to wobble (the *lunisolar* theory). The alternative explanation advanced by the Binary Research Institute is that most of the observable is due to solar system motion, causing a reorientation of the earth relative to the fixed stars as the solar system gradually curves through space (the binary theory or model). We find the binary model better explains acceleration of the precession rate, better predicts changes in the rate, answers a number of solar system problems and has none of the paradoxes or inconsistencies associated with *lunisolar* precession theory.[14]

Whether or not there is an invisible sun causing this phenomenon, it's a fact that more than one group of ancient people discovered the "precession of the equinoxes." It's pretty obvious that when you don't have electricity to light up the night, you study the stars. Thus we arrive at a theme we will return to frequently: Stargazers were *everywhere* in the ancient world.

I can also safely say given that Hinduism is the world's third largest religion (with adherents near one billion worldwide) there are many points of view on many different topics within Hinduism, just like any other religion. We do the Hindu religion a disservice by asserting that Hinduism concurs with the Mayan "end of time" on 2012. This is the same as saying: "Catholics and Protestants are on the same page when it comes to the sacraments." The informed know better.

But there is more. While it is true that Hindus generally believe in four epochs through which time *cycles*, the current world age supposedly won't be complete until after 4000 AD, (some say 400,000 AD!), and apparently the present time is only age two. Believing in Karma and reincarnation – human beings and all living creatures get recycled endlessly – the concept of the world ending (the way we westerners conjecture), is an illogical concept to the Hindu. If we conclude, after we connect the dots, that the Maya and the Hindus shared a similar concept of where time is going, much less a western notion of an "omega point,"[15] we are not very being good anthropologists. My point being: There are many instances where 2012 evangelists aren't being good anthropologists either.

The Bible Code

While these ancient sources of wisdom are intriguing, from our western point of view, the ancient source of wisdom we are most familiar with and pay the most attention to is, of course, *the Bible*. Like the other sources of ancient wisdom given new voices, fresh insights derived from the Bible during the two most recent decades may put a completely new light on the relevance of its prophecy.

In 1996, Michael Drosnin, a writer for the *Washington Post* and the *Wall Street Journal*, published a book called *The Bible Code*. His view popularized several contemporary Jewish and Christian scholars as well as other biblical authorities from times past (including Sir Isaac Newton). What view? Hidden deep within the Bible are *implicit codes that validate the explicit story the Bible tells*.

The book gave numerous striking examples, many now called into question, but others that provide solid evidence that Drosnin was onto something genuine. These examples supplied by Drosnin show how their originator *encodes* the *Torah* (the first five books of the Bible, also known as the *Pentateuch*).

What precipitated Drosnin's book was an academic paper prepared by a team of mathematicians from Israel, headed by Eliyahu Rips. Rips, et al, developed the paper reviewed and blessed through a peer review in a mathematics journal published by *Carnegie Mellon University* (Pittsburgh, PA) in 1994. In the paper, Rips demonstrated how he discovered a coding technique implicit in the original Hebrew of the Bible that was a major revelation – literally. Using an equidistant letter sequence (ELS), an encoding technique known to cryptologists, Rips shows how the Bible contains many surprising and meaningful hidden messages. Rips used one particular example to set out his thesis and submit it to "Peer Review." He identified the full names of numerous famous Jewish Rabbis living throughout the ages and the date of their birth. Through the technique, one finds *these personalities in the book of Genesis.* The paper also worked out the mathematical or statistical significance, i.e., "what are the chances this was a coincidence?"[16]

After it created a furor, the periodical *Statistical Science* published the paper as well. The editor of the journal indicated that as mysterious and inexplicable as this is, it stands up to scrutiny – the phenomenon persists. The team that examined the paper wasn't prepared for an ancient text encoded with information about modern day personalities – which was their way of saying (paraphrasing), "We didn't start out assuming that Rips was right in the claims he made. But the evidence proves his claims can't be easily disputed."

The "father" of the ELS concept was a Slovakian Rabbi, Michael Ber Weissmandl,[17] living at the time of World War II. The Rabbi noted that if you begin the book of Genesis and Exodus, pick the first letter, skip 50 letters, and continue throughout each book, you spell TORAH (which in Hebrew is four letters, a *tav, vav, resh,* and *heh*). If you start at the end of the final two books (Numbers and Deuteronomy), and move backwards 50 letters at a time in the same manner, you spell TORAH again, this time in reverse.

In the book, Drosnin highlighted a number of startling examples, many of which extended beyond the Torah into the books of the prophets (such as Isaiah and Daniel). Being from Oklahoma City, the example that seemed to match the historical details of the Timothy McVeigh bombing of the Alfred P. Murrah Building on April 19, 1995, fascinated me. I found it compelling, although at first blush, I thought it dubious.

But Drosnin didn't just cite historical examples – he ventured further. He actually used the technique in an attempt *to predict the future.* For instance, he believed the codes suggest that someone will assassinate Benjamin Netanyahu (and so far, half-way through 2010, Netanyahu is very much alive, well, and guiding the State of Israel , apparently to President Barak Obama's annoyance). Drosnin also indicated that there are Bible codes that indicate the end of the world either in 2000 or in 2006. Likewise, as you might have noticed, this failed to happen.

Since his predictions appeared to be phony, those who believe fervently in the Bible codes took aim at his techniques. They saw how Drosnin was consistently finding encoded messages – but his examples had skips of thousands of letters to create "the encoded message." Additionally, since he was an admitted atheist, ascribing this phenomenon to a far superior intelligence (clearly obsessed with the Torah, but ironically not the Hebrew God), made Drosnin's claims more unbelievable. Certainly, many believed Drosnin's strange perspective sucked him down a rabbit hole. To Bible Code enthusiasts, Drosnin was, at best, a learned crackpot who had an interesting *way with words*, biblical words in particular. At worst, he was a fraud.

Not long after Simon and Schuster published the book, *The Bible Code*, Eliyahu Rips posted on his web site that he did not support Drosnin's contentions and felt his many examples were not in fact accurate or representative of how one should use the technique. Additionally, one of the team working with Rips was Doron Witztum, who on June 4, 1997, released a statement on the Internet worrying that Drosnin's lack of scientific methodology would upset the legitimacy of the Bible Code phenomenon. Witztum was proven right; soon academics at other institutions sought to discredit the notion of finding hidden codes in the biblical text through the ELS technique. Scanning through a Hebrew version of *Moby Dick*, one debunker composed sensible phrases telling of assassinations and other horrible events using the ELS technique.[18]

Despite the fact that there are now academics that believe you can find codes using ELS in just about any novel you choose, the ELS coding/decoding schema as it pertains to the Bible hasn't been discredited. In addition, it's important that the original supporters of the ELS notion discredited Drosnin themselves, indicating the fault is not in whether ELS exists in the Bible, but how one goes about looking for such patterns. Since the time the most torrid debate concluded, scholars who believe there are hidden messages encoded in the Bible have begun to establish guidelines for what likely merits attention and what doesn't.[19]

So what should we conclude about the Bible Code and its ability to predict the end of the world? Most experts suggest that using the *Bible Code to pinpoint Doomsday is certain to fail.* This is so because its primary use is not prophetic. It exists to underscore that the Bible has a supernatural author. It *authenticates* (validates) the Scripture as God's Word or special revelation to us. Because these codes couldn't happen by accident, the author must have abilities far surpassing human intellect. Therefore, since the Bible claims to be authored by God through His prophets (in the *Torah's* case, through Moses), *it would seem illogical to suppose that it's mistaken about its own authorship.* Indeed, how could the Bible contain so much evidence of supernatural foreknowledge, perhaps detailing scores of future events, but be dead wrong at the outset regarding who wrote it?

Given that both sides of the argument make strong points, what should we conclude about the Bible Code? As fascinating as it is and although potentially useful if not revelatory, *the Bible Code is not intended to decode Doomsday.* Likewise, most Bible scholars would say that the Bible Code doesn't predict the future at all. Even though the Bible proffers vast numbers of prophetic passages throughout its pages, the Bible isn't a tool of divination. The Bible's doesn't hide its prophecies – the Bible exposes them openly and makes them *available to the public.*[20]

In short, decoding Doomsday through using Bible codes doesn't seem to be what the original encoder, the Hebrew God, had in mind.

Chapter Summary

Ancient voices do provide insight into many things. However, have the voices really predicted the day the world ends? We will study Mayan prophecy and its religion further in this book because it appears to merit additional scrutiny. However, *this is the only source studied here that deserves such careful analysis.* As we shall see, other North American Indians living in the current day, along with other sources of wisdom, appear to provide further corroboration of the Mayan prophecies. We should consider them carefully.

We've also noted here that not every source of wisdom that scholars cite as relevant to 2012, actually speaks to the 2012 end date, even though for any particular source there seems to be at least one or two erudite supporters who insist it does. The reality is that, upon impartial study, we can summarily disqualify such authorities. They become irrelevant to decoding Doomsday.

The primary case in point: The connection between the *I Ching* and *Time Wave Theory*. This linkage fails to warrant additional consideration. Even though many within the New Age movement find Terrence McKenna a true genius (apparently he was a spell-binding speaker), very few religious advocates believe enlightenment comes from walking down the path he followed. Talking to insects and taking drugs are not exactly compatible with mainstream spirituality. Most responsible psychologists or scientists would be wary too. The McKenna's findings have more to do with the "paranormal" than with either philosophy or science. This is despite the many complicated pharmaceutical formulas cited in their book and the computer software utilized to promote the concept of "Time Wave Zero." However close some of their methods comes to science, their conclusions clearly aren't. What they propose hasn't stood the test of time. They fail to amass much in the way of hard evidence to vindicate their argument.

In seeking to establish when civilization began making permanent records, the Hindu calendar attracts attention. However, it's a stretch to see a match with the Mayan's "calendar conclusion" and what the Maya apparently *concluded* it meant. Hinduism itself doesn't corroborate the ancient Americas' prophecy for how the end will come. To the contrary, Hinduism contends the world isn't due for a day like December 21, 2012, for at least another 2,000 years. Therefore, we shouldn't connect what we label *"2012"* to Hinduism.

Finally, the Bible Code is another controversial phenomenon emerging in the last dozen years or so. Its discoverers, as well as other scholars employing it today, consider the Bible Code limited to *authenticating* the Bible's primary messages. *They don't assert it has the ability to decode the moment of the Apocalypse.* For that insight from the Bible, if it does exist, we will have to look elsewhere.

In conclusion, there are "ancient voices" that testify to the future of our world. But it's not a large chorus or a choir. It's more like a trio or a quartet. And since the number of singers is really quite small, we need to audition each of them before allowing any to join the group of singers we put on tour. Another way to make this point (but staying with the music analogy), is that *there are lots of folks jumping on the 2012 bandwagon.* But that doesn't prove the musicians are playing the right tune. It's just the reverse. *We need to offload the players muddling the melody to hear the tune we paid to listen to in the first place.*

Notes

¹ The timing of the Spanish is tied to the Aztecs, not the Maya. If we speak of the Aztecs, Mr. Gibson's thesis is historically valid.

² Which is supposedly where the *pentagram* originates as an occult symbol.

³ The Maya and Cherokees say we are in World Age Five while the Hopi indicate that we are only in epoch number four. However, we will see later that they nonetheless are predicting the same sort of destruction.

⁴ As we go through the book, take note of the number of people that have used drugs to encounter the spiritual realm.

⁵ This is clearly a convenient borrowing of a particular appellation for Christ in the Christian tradition. "In the beginning was the Logos, and the Logos was with God, and the Logos was God" (John 1:1). The Logos was the "spoken word of God" (God speaks and it comes into being).

⁶ Alfred North Whitehead heavily influenced the McKenna brothers. Published in 1929, *Process and Reality* was Whitehead's famous work. God, to Whitehead, was not a static, outside-the-realm-of-time observer, but actually "grew" through time. This would influence theology in the 1970's creating a school known as "Process Theology." The New Age adopted the Priest/Theologian Teihard de Chardin (another "process theologian") as one of their own.

⁷ Apparently, we humans are in fact only unwitting actors directed by this animated force of time. So much for free will.

⁸ Apparently, it never crossed his mind that the rate of change might be increasing because of population growth (more people to change things) and information growth (more and better ways to record events). It would seem a plausible explanation for the same phenomenon.

⁹ According to Daniel Pinchbeck, McKenna actually posited 2012 as the end date because the theory worked better (the events lined up better). He didn't derive 2012 from the theory but picked it. Why did he pick it? He knew that the eclipse of the sun across the Milky Way's middle was in 2012. He just didn't know about the Mayan Calendar's end date. Consequently, one can dismiss a bit of the "synchronicity" often championed regarding his theory. 2012 was contrived.

¹⁰ It's hardly an easy read. To make much sense of it, you need a degree in Pharmacology, Process Theology (Whitehead), Shamanism, and grounding in Chinese Philosophy. Obfuscation certainly makes the smart seem smarter.

¹¹ It is true that archeologists discovered most of what we know about the Mayans, their calendars, and their beliefs only in the last 30 years. José Argüelles and his promotion of the so-called harmonic convergence of 1987 (when the earth first began to cross the galactic equator), was the moment of the Mayan "coming out" with the theory they knew the outcome of world history.

12 Philosophers define "the dialectic" as one reality begetting its opposite and then the two opposites combine into a *synthesis*; the process repeats, *ad infinitum.*

13 The ancients' typically recorded their history on stone or clay tablets.

14 See *http://www.binaryresearchinstitute.org/index.shtml.*

15 An "omega point" is a more generic way of talking about a day of "doom" or a conclusion to history and TIME (as we know it). Omega equals "the end." Pierre Teihard de Chardin coined the term for the culmination of all things.

16 Those odds, of course, would be many millions to one.

17 Historians credit this same rabbi with saving the lives of over one million Jews from the holocaust.

18 When one compares the extensive codes uncovered in the Bible with these "contra-coding searches" which try to discredit the ELS technique, a fair review concludes the Bible much more likely to yield meaningful codes that correspond to the explicit meaning of the text where they are found. *The dissenters' "findings" should make us cautious, but not dubious.*

19 One book cited in my bibliography, *Bible Code Bombshell,* by R. Edwin Sherman, does a nice job of providing a history of the code and the rules that should govern its use.

20 This is not to say that interpretation is unnecessary because clearly it is. Prophecy scholars would quote Jesus who said, "Search and you shall find, knock and the door shall be opened." The implication is that the meaning of prophecy is discernable to those who truly seek it.

Chapter 3:
Tracing the Origins
of Apocalypse

To the East, Africa was a neighbour, across a short strait of sea miles.
The great Egyptian age is but a remnant of The Atlantian culture.
The antediluvian kings colonised the world
All the Gods who play in the mythological dramas
In all legends from all lands were from fair Atlantis.

Donovan

Atlantis and Alternate History

In the first two chapters, we've seen evidence that our favorite apprehension is Doomsday. Why is this? Scientists state the world is millions of years old (actually 4.5 billion) and that as a species we've been around for much longer than we can remember. However, no matter how old the world is, the questions are still the same, "Why do we think that *our time has come*? Why don't we assume things will just continue in the same path?"

In asking why humankind is so obsessed with the end of the world for the better part of the last 2,500 years, we also must ask another question – "exactly *when* did this worry begin?"

While not all of humankind consciously shares this anxiety in equal parts, as Carl Jung would say, it does appear to be in our *collective unconscious*. (You may recall that Jung was a disciple of Sigmund Freud, but unlike Freud who seemed fixated on sexual motivations, Jung was much more inclined toward investigating the realm of the spirit to diagnose psychological disorders). Jung believed there are *archetypes* in the *universal memory* that humans subconsciously share. These archetypes are symbols of meaning – and they seem to have a life of their own. We unwittingly encounter them in our dreams and visions. Experts often reckon them the origin of our myths. The fact that we have them in common validates that we tap into is a "collective unconscious mind." This *mind* transcends our individual minds.

Since the notion of Atlantis, a supposed advanced civilization destroyed in 9600 BC (mentioned by Plato around 380 BC in his *Timaeus* and *Critias* dialogues), one archetype of humanity's pending destruction is very old indeed. While it's true that Atlantis for traditional historians is at best *a tall tale*, there are many authors who contend Atlantis *really existed*. Furthermore, the convinced assert there is much more to Atlantis than merely a myth of destruction. After all, we named the second biggest ocean, the Atlantic, after this missing continent. Even Georgians found it worthy to name their capital after too.

Nonetheless, to find these modern day advocates for the theory of Atlantis, you must resort to *alternate history* – which is a polite way of labeling a historical rendering "more likely fable than fact."

According to those that take *alternate history* seriously, the world experienced the great cataclysm that sunk Atlantis around 12,000 years ago just as Plato indicates. There were precious few survivors of this apocalypse. According to this theory, those that did manage to survive wound up in Egypt.

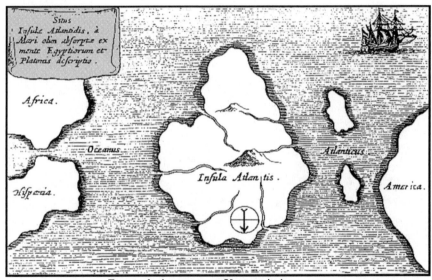

FIGURE 4 - ATHANASIUS KIRCHER'S ATLANTIS

Traditional history (and Egypt's national scholars) records that Pharaoh Khufu built the first of the Pyramids (ca: 2850 BC). However, alternative history contends the descendants of those that fled Atlantis built the Pyramids, and certainly the Sphinx, perhaps as much as 6,000 years earlier.[1] Furthermore, these most sophisticated pyramids were not tombs to safeguard mummies. To the contrary, their builders created them to safeguard *ancient knowledge for the ages.* Exactly what do we mean by ancient knowledge?

Also known as, *"prisca sapientia,"* this ancient knowledge is something that many enlightened scientists and philosophers of the 16th and 17th centuries believed once existed, but was subsequently lost to humankind through the ages. Keep in mind – these enlightened ones were hardly members of *the fringe element*. Scholars like Francis Bacon and Sir Isaac Newton (who we will study thoroughly later), were convinced ancient humans possessed this knowledge – and *the study of their archaic monuments and historical records would decode it*. Make a note of this. It's key to our study.

FIGURE 5 - THE PYRAMIDS OF GIZA

How did pre-historic man derive this arcane wisdom? That's a fascinating question because in essence, many believe "only the gods" knew this information and therefore, such insight *was beyond humanity's ability to uncover without supernatural (or at least extraterrestrial) means*. The Egyptians learned this transcendent knowledge directly from extraterrestrials or, indirectly, from an advanced and even more ancient civilization, namely, *Atlantis*. Presumably, the Atlanteans were our direct connections to the extraterrestrials. By surviving (supposedly) the catastrophe of 10,000 BC, Atlanteans passed down this knowledge to subsequent generations.[2]

Case in point: The very architecture of the Pyramids information appears *encoded* and may address issues like: "Where did we come from?" "How big is the world?" and "When we will experience another world-wide catastrophe?"[3]

Attributes of the construction are fascinating. These structures point true north, are completely symmetrical, and possess over a two and a half million stones weighing 2.5 to 50 tons apiece. Given that we have little to no equipment that can accomplish similar construction today, this is no "mean" feat. Furthermore, despite this enormous weight, the Pyramids haven't sunk into the earth one inch. Moreover, the builders placed the stones so tightly that the space between the stones is less than 1/50th of an inch. That's so close it's impossible to slide a piece of paper in the crease between the stones.

FIGURE 6 – ORION'S BELT

Then there are the astronomical features. Many scholars (traditional and alternate) now agree that the layout of the Pyramids models the three stars in Orion's constellation (his "belt" – an idea proposed by Robert Bauval in his book, *The Orion Mystery*). Additionally, the long and narrow "air shafts" inside the Great Pyramid of Giza target specific locations in the sky – pointing to very specific stars preeminent in particular constellations (e.g., Draco, Sirius), causing some believers to suppose these pointers locate the origin of our alien visitors – the extraterrestrials who designed the Pyramids and supplied the requisite technology. Maybe it's where ET phoned home.

However, is there really information encoded into the architecture of the Pyramids that only "out-of-this-world" beings could know?

When we dig deep into the little known facts, we learn that it's apparent these ancient builders did indeed encode ancient knowledge into the Pyramids *that wouldn't have been available without advanced instrumentation.*

- Students of the pyramids contend that the location of the Pyramids lies exactly at the center of the landmasses of the world. It also stands at an elevation equal to the "mean" elevation for all the earth's continents considered together.

- If we take the ancient Egyptian cubit to be 25.025 inches, a reasonable assumption as we will see later, the length of each side of the Giza Pyramid is 365.2422 cubits – almost exactly the length of the solar year within a few minutes.

- Likewise, the height isn't random. The slope of the four sides yields a height of 232.52 cubits. If twice we divide the length of a side (365.2422) by the height (232.52), the result is an especially interesting number: 3.1416. Pie (π) anyone? However, there's more.

- Take the altitude, raised to the power of nine. You wind up with 91,840,000. Transformed to miles, that number is the mean distance to the sun – give or take a mile or two. But how would anyone know to calculate this number? Perhaps it's because for every 10 feet you ascend the Pyramid at its perilous 52° slope, you rise in altitude by 9 feet.[4] And before you object that our "mile" can't be the same as an ancient metric, hold your peace. We will cover that later too.

Apparently, astronomical knowledge wasn't just ancient wisdom peculiar to the Maya. Clearly, the Egyptians were equally well versed in this knowledge too. However, does possessing this arcane wisdom suggest that those living on both sides of the Atlantic acquired this knowledge from survivors of Atlantis? Alternatively, did both peoples encounter ET and learn these facts from aliens such as Erich Van Däniken, author of *Chariots of the Gods,* supposes?

Both peoples built pyramids with great sophistication in their methods. Both had astronomical information that modern man has only possessed for about the last 80 years or so. Each society recorded its history in hieroglyphs. Some of these glyphs can be interpreted to refer to *ancient astronauts* and to gods with similar abilities. Thus, it appears the idea of *ancient wisdom* has merit.

Nevertheless, should we jump to the conclusion that the know-how came from Atlantis?[5]

Perhaps we should consider another structure that causes the plot to thicken further – an edifice that historians call the *Labyrinth*.

No less than the father of history himself, *Herodotus*, traveled to Egypt from Greece and saw this structure around 450 BC (of course, he saw the Pyramids too – it was hard to miss them). As impressed as he was with the Pyramids and the intelligence it took to build them, he indicates in his account that the Labyrinth is far more amazing. He says in his *Histories*, "From what I have seen it is hard to believe that they (the rooms) are the work of men." This structure was massive in size (over 3,000 rooms) with half of the buildings above the surface and half below. Traditional historians admit such a structure existed, but for the most part, the ravages of time destroyed it. Only the foundation stones (recently found by modern day archeologists) are all that remain.

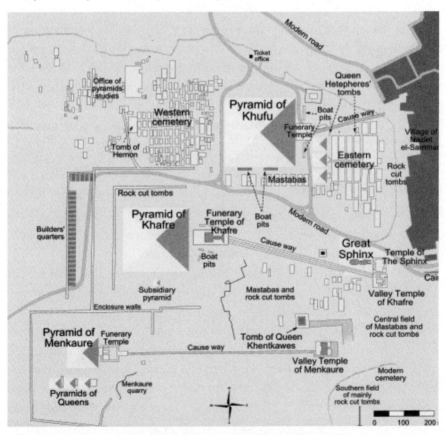

FIGURE 7 - THE GIZA PYRAMID COMPLEX

Some allege that the Labyrinth contained far more ancient history and wisdom than the Pyramids. One such person is alternate history writer, Patrick Geryl, who has been trying to fund an expedition to explore this structure for years (he believes there is much more remaining of the structure than what archeologists admit). Furthermore, he contends that no matter what the cost to excavate it is, it will be worth it. Geryl believes that the Labyrinth, once "decoded," discloses the *next cataclysm*, along with what we must do to survive it.

However, Geryl's writings are scattered and difficult to follow. It isn't obvious why he expresses such certainty about our gloomy fate. Additionally, Geryl makes most of his assertions without citing reliable authorities. Due to this lapse, it's hard to take him seriously. Additionally, Geryl faces an even bigger problem than the lack of funds necessary to go gallivanting around the Egyptian desert. In his opinion, the next cataclysm takes place in 2012. His time (and ours apparently) *is running out*.

But why is 2012 relevant to Geryl? He points to a most unusual astronomical phenomenon that happened once before in 9782 BC. This was the year of the so-called *transit of Venus* – this is when Venus crosses the Pleiades from our perspective.[6] The planet rarely loops through this spot in the sky.[7] In fact, the next time that it repeats this movement is, of course, *in 2012*. Geryl believes the wisdom of Egypt discloses *this is the seminal sign that cataclysm approaches*, since it was the essential sign to the Atlanteans that their culture was coming to a catastrophic end.

The Worldwide Flood

However, the tale of Atlantis might not be the only primordial source of our obsession with Doomsday. Another story of catastrophe, equally fantastic, may be the primeval cause: *The worldwide flood of Noah.*

Like the tale of Atlantis, the flood of Noah is an account that most secular historians seriously doubt – ascribing it to the realm of *myth*. While they sometimes acquiesce, agreeing that there may have been a spectacular localized flood in the old Mesopotamian world, this is as far as most will go.[8] Confidently, they assert that such a flood wasn't worldwide and it certainly didn't wipe out all of humanity or the animal kingdom. Secular history dismisses this watery cataclysm, seeing no scientific basis for how it could happen.

Despite this skepticism, the *Book of Genesis* maintains that Noah's flood was an historical event. Furthermore, those who study the chronology of the Bible ascertain that this flood transpired in the year 2348 BC. (With the names of ancient personages, along with their age when they begat their progeny, Bible scholars can create a very detailed chronology of the world.[9])

Furthermore, other cultures also contribute to a legend of a great flood. The Mayans suggest that the last age (epoch four of five) was destroyed by flood. Could it be that the Great Flood of Noah was the concluding event of the last Mayan age (3114 BC) and is the starting point for the next 5126-year period in their "long-count" calendar?[10]

Assuming that such a flood did occur the issue is whether it was closer to when the Hebrew Bible specifies (2348 BC) or when the fifth age of the Mayan calendar began five millennia ago (764 years earlier than the biblical chronology). What's in common in both accounts is the conviction that a great deluge occurred about five thousand years ago and it dramatically changed human civilization.

Although outside the scope of our study, we could demonstrate that a worldwide flood is a shared memory of *virtually every ancient culture*. If we accept this thesis, it becomes evident that such an event would produce a similar account of devastation and a universal apprehension that what happened before could happen again.

So do our doomsday fears spring from the flood of Noah? For the past two hundred years, popular *scientific enlightenment* has inundated us with wave after wave of skepticism (no pun intended) as regards the historical validity of the Bible. Critics skewer no Bible story as much as the tale of the *Great Flood* (with the possible exception being, "Jonah and the Whale"). Therefore, despite considerable evidence from ancient cultures as an explanation for the *origin* of our apprehension, Noah's Flood isn't the strongest contender.

In the final analysis, both stories (the destruction of Atlantis and the worldwide flood of Noah), whether true or not, are too distant being beyond recorded history. Therefore, it's hard to believe they're the basis for so much worry over the world's end. True, a subliminal fear resulting from these accounts may hide in our collective subconscious. Nevertheless, history provides a much more vital and *empirical source* for our concern.

To get at the real origin of our *doomsday dread* in the Western World (and the Middle East), we must study a much more recent element of the Bible. In particular, one primary biblical prediction drives the greatest amount of consternation on the topic of Doomsday – the belief that *God will send an anointed one, a messiah, to set things right in the world*. This powerful (and perhaps divine) figure will end sin, oppression, and injustice.

Would that this predicted deliverance only came on the heels of good news! Unfortunately, by all accounts the Messiah comes at *the climax of THE Apocalypse*, a time of unsurpassed destruction, dismay, and death.

Today, there seems to be little that Jews, Christians, and Muslims can agree on; however, they all hold in common the notion of Messiah. For all three monotheistic religions (Judaism, Christianity, and Islam), the idea of an *anointed one* is central to their faith. Moreover, all three envision this as a cataclysmic moment. Thus, we see the prophecies of Messiah and Apocalypse wound together. The Coming of Messiah for the Jews, the Second Coming of Jesus Christ for the Christians, and the coming of the 12th Imam in Islam (as well as Jesus Christ who is a secondary figure in Islam), all go hand-in-hand with the Apocalypse.

As they say, there is no free lunch.

That's why I contend that for the western world and the Middle East, the *coming of Messiah and the circumstances surrounding his appearance are the fundamental cause of our doomsday fears.* In the following chapter, we will amass considerable proof for this assertion, detailing the many examples of predicting Doomsday tied to messianic fervor. However, in the remaining portion of this chapter, our goal is to first understand the specific origin of *apocalyptic thinking* and then, secondly, see how the world's most famous Messiah contributed to this vision of the end of the world.

Daniel's Prophecy - 70 Weeks in Jewish History

There seems to be little debate: *The prophecies in the Book of Daniel first spawned messianic and apocalyptic fervor.*[11] Tradition holds that the author of the Book of Daniel was the very prophet himself.[12] His tomb in northern Iran is revered even to this day.

The Babylonians carted off Daniel to their fair city when they destroyed Jerusalem and its first amazing temple, the *Temple of Solomon* (completed around but no earlier than 960 BC). King Nebuchadnezzar smashed Israel between 606 and 586 BC. Writing in Babylon toward the end of his life and after an amazing career in public service as a loyal subject to the Babylonian kings, Daniel predicted the Messiah Prince of the Jews, previously spoken of by Moses and by King David in the Psalms, would soon arrive on the scene.[13]

Daniel predicted a series of specific events would transpire over a 490-year period, commencing with the commandment for the Hebrews to go forth from Babylon and rebuild the walls and the city of Jerusalem (see *Daniel*, Chapter 9).

From the date of this proclamation by a future king, 483 years would pass. History records this to be *Artaxerxes'* proclamation on or about March 14, 445 BC. At the conclusion of this period, the Messiah comes.[14] First, Daniel asserts in his prophecy that Messiah ends sin and brings in righteousness; immediately thereafter, he is "cut off" (which is a Jewish idiom meaning *put to death*). After the death of Messiah, the Prophet Daniel indicates that there would be another follow-on period of seven years to the previous 483, completing a 490-year epoch.

However, halfway through this final seven years (which equals 1,260 days or three and one-half years), a great imposter – a "man of sin" will appear. He will enter into the temple of the Jews (necessarily rebuilt at that time) and proclaim himself to be God. This announcement leads to no end of trouble. Jesus called this event (while referencing Daniel the prophet), "the *abomination of desolation*." Here is our first *clear-cut* biblical encounter with the notorious character we have come to know as the *Antichrist*.

How and when the final seven years are fulfilled is quite another matter altogether. *Nonetheless, in decoding Doomsday, it's pivotal.*[15]

FIGURE 8 - COIN OF ANTIOCHUS IV EPIPHANIES (PROFILE) WITH APOLLO ON THE REVERSE SIDE

The rabbinical scholars at this time looked intently for Messiah to appear. One in particular, Rabbi Nehumiah, predicted that the Anointed One would come to the nation no later than in the Jewish year 3760 (or 1 BC in our Gregorian calendar). Christians, who know about this Rabbi's prediction, believe he was a worthy teacher in his own right. For by some accounts, *this very year is when Jesus Christ was born in Bethlehem of Judea.*[16]

However, before we talk about Jesus of Nazareth, we should understand a bit more about Jewish history – specifically, the history transpiring *after* Daniel and *before* the Roman destruction of Jerusalem in 70 AD. This allows us to put the ministry of Jesus in proper context amidst the apocalyptic times in which he lived.

Messianic and Apocalyptic Times

Throughout the period from about 170 BC to the great earthquake of 31 BC, there was tremendous turmoil in Palestine. Around the beginning of this period, a Syrian King, *Antiochus Epiphanes*, desecrated the Temple in Jerusalem in a failed attempt to "Hellenize" the Jews (i.e., force them to worship the Greek gods and transform their culture along the lines of the Greek world). After about three and one-half years of fighting the tyranny of Antiochus (note the connection to the 1260 days of Daniel's prophecy), the Jews led by Judas Maccabeus overcame the Syrians and freed themselves.[17] For the next 100 years, the Hebrews would remain independent until the Roman emperor, Pompey, conquered Jerusalem in 63 BC.

With the ending of the Hasmonean Dynasty in 37 BC (the dynasty established by the Maccabees), considerable internal conflict arose between the political rulers who ran the country (the next dynasty, that being the *Herodians*), and the religious leaders composed of several splitter groups we know from the New Testament gospels as the *Sadducees* and the *Pharisees*.[18]

The Sadducees were secular in orientation, actually one of the first groups of lawyers that, like today, the common people loved to hate. We know the Pharisees as the super self-righteous law abiding citizens that became the arch-enemies of Jesus. They were a classic example of hypocrites prac-

FIGURE 9 - CAVES AT QUMRAN

ticing a religion "by the letter rather than by the spirit of the law" – the Levitical Law in this case.

Another intriguing group existing at the time was the *Essenes*. This group withdrew from the Jewish society in the first century BC because they believed the government was corrupt and the Jewish priesthood wasn't authentic. It was their view God hadn't properly ordained it. The Essenes settled in a place called *Qumran*, about 12 miles east, southeast from Jerusalem, on the banks of the *Dead Sea*.

Through the help of a Bedouin sheepherder (throwing rocks into the many caves in the area), archeologists discovered the handiwork of the Essenes in 1947. The story goes, after something went crash, the shepherd climbed into the cave and found dozens of clay jars. As worthless as these old pots must have seemed at the time, what they contained was perhaps the most remarkable archeological find since we started caring about such things. It was the ultimate example of potluck!

FIGURE 10 - THE ISAIAH SCROLL FROM THE DEAD SEA SCROLLS

The Essenes had meticulously gathered, scrupulously copied, and carefully stored the many historic books of the Hebrew Bible (practically the entire collection of writings) as well as many other works contemporary to their time – usually regarded as *apocalyptic literature*. One particular writing is noteworthy because it appears to be original with the Essenes and has Doomsday *written all over it* (or more precisely, *throughout*). Today, we know it as the "War Scroll." We will have more to say about it in a few moments.

The Essenes were convinced the Apocalypse was just around the corner. This fear drove the Essenes to safeguard discretely the religious writings of the Hebrews, hiding them in the many caves in the Dead Sea region. Hence, archeologists labeled them the "Dead Sea Scrolls." They placed these scrolls in over 900 clay jars (hand printed on animal skin – no printing presses or paper then!) Amazingly, due to the arid climate of this area, these scrolls fared well, preserved through the past two millennia.

This discovery was astounding because it allowed scholars to compare biblical manuscripts today with those from 2,000 years ago – writings created literally at the same time that Jesus walked the earth. To their astonishment, scholars soon learned that no more than a handful of changes had crept into the Bible during the last 2,000 years. It was quite a shot in the arm for Bible fans.

What is equally relevant to us as far as the Essenes are concerned is that they were history's *first religious fanatics who believed the world would soon end*. They were the "survivalists" of their day – opposed to the secular government and the religious leaders who they deemed heretics. Sequestered in this desert region, they avoided moral and religious corruption and awaited the final battle between cosmic good and evil. They were also history's first recluses who lived *ascetic* lives (a *Spartan* existence you might say). As such, they set the example for *monasticism* in the centuries that followed.

One special leader, known as the *Teacher of Righteousness*, led the Essenes. Based upon the writings in the *War Scroll*, we learn the Essenes may have considered themselves the *Sons of Light*. If so, they regarded their enemies as the *Sons of Evil*. They were convinced that a great war would occur in their lifetime. As it turned out, a catastrophic war did occur – *and they were some of the most unfortunate participants.*

In 66 AD, angered by the continued rebellion of the Jews, the Roman armies decided to take action. Titus, soon to become Caesar, moved against the Jewish homeland. Josephus, the Jewish historian known for his *Antiquities of the Jews* and *The Jewish War*, told of the exploits of this war as a keen firsthand observer. He relates that in 70 AD the Romans conquered Jerusalem, destroyed the Jewish Temple,[19] and killed or captured everyone in the city. Although the Essenes entered the battle as the good guys fighting the Roman infidels, the Romans didn't get the memo. They mercilessly massacred the Essenes.

Ironically, the *War Scroll* indicates that the expected great battle wouldn't be against the Romans, but against an evil figure known as Belial[20] and his hordes originating from *Mesopotamia*. Therefore, it's probable that the Essenes realized that the fracas against Rome wasn't the final conflict of which they wrote. Clearly, the Romans weren't from Mesopotamia. Furthermore, the War Scroll predicts that the Sons of Light will fight not one but seven battles, the last one apparently the "mother of all battles." Given that the circumstances differ, we now see the War Scroll as the Essenes' uniquely worded prophecy envisioning a future conflict, enlisting a distinct group called the *Sons of Light* against a future evil king, Belial, and his *Sons of Darkness*.

Nevertheless, in regards to the fight against Rome, they committed 100%. And that, as they say, was the end of the Essenes.

The Most Celebrated Messiah of this Troubled Time

Amidst all this tumult, one *Jesus of Nazareth* arose. Living in this tense time after the Herodians took over from the Hasmonean clan (37 BC) and before Rome retook and destroyed the city and its temple (70 AD), Jesus preached a similar message to that of the Essenes: "The Kingdom of God is at hand." He launched his teaching upon this core assertion. Virtually everything he said and did was an attempt to reinforce it. Even the model prayer he taught his disciples to say begins with praise to God, but quickly follows with the supplication "Thy Kingdom come." Closely tied to this Kingdom's coming, was the prediction that destruction was near. Just as the Hebrew prophets Isaiah, Zechariah, and Joel all proclaimed, the coming of the Kingdom was synonymous with "The Day of the Lord." A great war must precede the peace that comes with the Kingdom. As Isaiah taught, "Plowshares must be beat into swords before they can be remade back into plowshares." Jesus warned the leaders of his time, "How is it that you can predict weather from the clouds in the sky, but you can't interpret the signs of the times?"

Jesus was very much a man of his times – an *apocalyptic Rabbi* inclined to use frightening images of hell to reinforce the seriousness of his point (he mentions hell or *Gehenna* 11 times in the four gospels). Without repentance, disaster loomed. Like the Essenes, he chided the religious leaders for contaminating the religion of Moses. He aligned himself with the historic Hebrew prophets who had continually challenged the kings and priests of Israel for failure to stay true to the Law of Moses. He saw the government and the priesthood utterly corrupted. As a result, he proclaimed that God was soon to judge them for their actions. "You brood of vipers! How can you escape the wrath to come?" His colorful analogies fueled the controversy with his opponents. "After you make a convert, you make him twice as fit for hell as you are yourselves." "You are white-washed tombs, a pleasing spectacle on the outside, but inside you are full of dead men's bones." To the religious Jew concerned about purity, this insult was about as derogatory as you can get.

FIGURE 11 - A REPLICA OF HEROD'S TEMPLE IN JERUSALEM'S MUSEUM

Jesus was not a reformer and certainly had no stomach for diplomacy. Jesus refused to reconcile himself to the religious and political institutions as long as they continued down their path to destruction. "You must put new wine into new wineskins. If you put new wine into old wineskins, the skins will crack destroying the wineskins and wasting both." Despite this, he did not identify with the Essenes or the other insurrectionists of his day, the *Zealots*. Like the prophets, he had no intention to take up arms and revolt against the existing powers. "Those who live by the sword will die by the sword." "If my kingdom were of this world my followers would fight; but because my kingdom is not of this world, they do not."

However, neither did Jesus side with the prevailing views of what constituted proper behavior and proven righteousness. Jesus dined with tax collectors. They were the most hated of men; the Jews saw them as collaborators with the enemy. Likewise, he spoke with prostitutes and allowed the "unclean" to touch him. He reached out to the lepers and restored their dignity. Jesus challenged conventional wisdom. It wasn't just about following the dictates of the law. It involved much more. "Unless your righteousness exceeds that of the Pharisees, you shall in no wise see the Kingdom of God."

His concept of true religion was particularly revolutionary. "Blessed are the poor in spirit; blessed are the meek; blessed are they that hunger and thirst for righteousness." Possessing power didn't prove your religious commitment. He turned to the poor and taught the common folk his message of an "inward transformation," instructing his followers to seek God in secret, and "God who sees in secret will reward you." Neither did he believe that true religion was sentimentalism or ecstatic experience. *True religion is evident in the everyday actions of how we treat one another.* "If you are at the altar and wish to give a gift but remember you have something against your brother, first go and restore your relationship with your brother and then return to the altar and give your gift."

His concept of success shocked the masses. "How hard it is for a rich man to enter into the Kingdom of God. It is easier for a camel to pass through the eye of a needle than for a rich man to enter in." Being rich did not signify God's endorsement. Neither did giving alms in public prove one's worthiness. Jesus educated his followers to avoid letting your "left hand know what your right hand is doing." "Don't seek the praise of men – seek the praise of God instead." "Don't be like the Pharisees who give alms when the trumpet sounds to call attention to their act. I tell you they have their reward. Instead, give in secret. And God who sees in secret will reward you."

Like many Rabbis in his day, Jesus took on disciples and trained them in his method for understanding the Scriptures. He explained only to them the hidden meanings of his teachings communicated to the masses through parables.

After only a year or two of public ministry, it seemed clear that Jesus was headed for a confrontation with the Pharisees who objected to his interpretation of the Law and particularly his regular practice of healing the sick on the Sabbath. It only angered them more when he proclaimed, "The Sabbath was made for man and not man for the Sabbath."[21] Jesus was turning the cherished idea of Jewish religious observance upside down. Many common people loved it since they felt shunned by the religious leadership. The institutions of the day cared little for the wants and needs of the *average Joseph*.

Intended as proof of God's endorsement, the gospels contain many examples in which Jesus performs miracles of healing and demonic deliverance. Jesus himself refers to these works as proof of his authority and his claim to divinity and equality with God – a point of view that ultimately solidified his opposition and mobilized them to take action. "For which of my good works do you pick up stones to throw at me? Believe me because of what I say or believe based upon the works themselves."

Jesus began informing his disciples that he would ultimately not survive the coming confrontation. He spoke in indirect language but later plainly, how his enemies would crucify him in Jerusalem – like the other prophets before him. After all, "It is not fitting that a prophet should perish outside of Jerusalem."

Jesus first appeared during his final Passover holiday, by riding into Jerusalem on the back of a donkey. This symbolized his intention to maintain a peaceful demeanor (compare the image of Jesus and the donkey to that of Alexander the Great and his legendary horse *Bucephalus*). Nevertheless, the priestly leadership feared that the "rabble" would try to make him King, by force, if necessary. Consequently, when he was apart from the crowds they arrested him for sedition. His betrayal by Judas, his disciple, was late at night "on Preparation Day" (the day before Passover, after the "last supper"), in his favorite but secret place to pray – the *Garden of Gethsemane* on the *Mount of Olives*. A large military cohort took him into custody. His disciples scattered to save themselves.

After the rush to judgment by the Jewish court, the Sanhedrin, and then the Roman governor, Pontius Pilate, he was crucified in Jerusalem under the aegis of Rome in the spring of AD 30. The gospel records the high priest Caiaphas saying, "It is fitting that one man die on behalf of the nation, rather than the whole nation is destroyed." Buried in a borrowed tomb near the place of his crucifixion, after only three days, his body disappeared.

His disciples testified that God had resurrected him *physically*. They had seen him, talked with him, eaten with him, and after several weeks, they testified they saw him ascend into heaven.

At that very same moment, they indicated that angelic beings appeared to them and told them that just as they had seen Jesus leave and disappear into a cloud in the sky, he would soon return in the same way. Consequently, the disciples believed they had been commissioned to go and preach the things that Jesus had taught them throughout the whole world, including the teaching of *his soon return to judge the world and commence the Kingdom of God.* As we now know, they were *much more than merely effective* in accomplishing this mission.

As we read in the writings attributed to them, his disciples seem convinced that they were living in the last days. Hence, they evangelized everywhere because Jesus, now called Christ, *would come back at any moment.* This sense of drama, of expectation, of impeding intervention by God himself was hardly anything less than *the impetus for proselytizing the entire world.*

Remarkably, amidst persecution, torture, and thousands of martyrdoms, the teaching of this Judean sect even overturned the Roman Empire itself.[22] Three centuries after the crucifixion, the teachings of Jesus had replaced emperor worship as the state religion.

Originally, the Romans executed Jesus to keep the peace. The Hebrew leaders demanded his death to maintain the status quo. How difficult it would have been then to predict that a supposed criminal tortured to death on a cross, by sharing an apocalyptic vision for the future, could shake the institutions of the ancient world to the point of capitulation!

As his disciple, John said at the opening of his gospel, "He came into the world he created, and unto his own people, but his own people did not welcome him." Perhaps it's the greatest enigma of all time – how the teaching of Jesus radically changed the history of the world when even his own race had rejected it, he himself was murdered for his teaching, and that after only three years preaching.

What should we make of these things? If we set aside whether or not what the disciples testified was true and consider only what they taught, it becomes very clear that this new sect of the Jews, called Christianity, is a religion based upon an apocalyptic expectation. Certainly, the amazing events surrounding the life, death, and proclaimed resurrection of Jesus – this "Christ" – set this movement in perpetual motion. Nevertheless, it was the fervent belief in the *Second Advent* (or Second Coming of Christ), which drove the movement forward so ferociously that as even the secular leaders living at the time said, "This teaching has turned the world upside down."

As we have seen, the times before, during, and after were filled with calamitous wars, earthquakes, and political intrigue. There was widespread anxiety that the nation of Israel was on a precipice. Many believed it was only a matter of time before cataclysm ensued.

Before being crucified, in three of the four accounts of his "passion" (the final week of his life), Jesus taught his disciples that his return would be surrounded by frightening signs in the sky, by wars and rumors of wars, by earthquakes, famines, pestilence, and false messiahs. One of his most enduring teachings was that his disciples should always be on the lookout for his soon return. "Watch – for you know not when the Son of Man comes."

His most precise prediction focused on the Jewish Temple. He predicted that enemies would destroy the Temple and leave no stone unturned. "When you see Jerusalem surrounded by armies, escape to the mountains." In 70 AD, when the Romans burned the Temple, the gold from the Temple melted into the cracks between the stones. To salvage this gold, the soldiers separated the stones, claimed the gold, and tore the Temple down to the ground, stone-by-stone. They threw many stones over Jerusalem's walls, into the valley below in a stunning fulfillment of Jesus' improbable prophecy.

Jesus' three most notable disciples, in writings attributed to them, forecasted many other prophetic events tied to the end of days: Peter, Paul, and especially John whose vision of *the end* we know as the Revelation of John. In particular, John's writing does much to "decode Doomsday." It's in his *Apocalypse* (the alternative name for Revelation), where biblical prophecy reaches its zenith.

Apocalyptic Thinking, a Trademark of Authentic Christianity

For now, I wish mostly to underscore how essential the whole theme of apocalypse is to understand the essential nature of Christianity. *The imminence or any-minute aspect of the second coming of Christ* **explains the evangelistic fervor of its followers.** The *mission of the church links inextricably to the climax of Jesus' return at the end of days.* It's no wonder that most Doomsday predictions during the past 2,000 years resulted from Christians seeking the day when Jesus would make good on his promised return.

This does not mean to infer such speculation is unwarranted. To the contrary, my point is we should expect such *rampant speculation from true believers.* Christians "who predict the end of the world" illustrate the most predictable behavior of all. After all, how could they avoid complete captivation by the possibility of Jesus' return, bringing the Kingdom of God to this earth? It's the very premise of Jesus' worldview *and his ultimate mission statement.* It's at the heart of motivating Christians to be zealous in their daily affairs. "For we know not when he shall return."

As the dominant religion of the western world for almost 90% of the last two millennia, we can easily establish that our preoccupation with Doomsday is a direct result of the Christian perspective of what history portends. Christianity, and to a lesser extent Jewish Apocalypticism, is the origin of our captivation with Doomsday. As we will see in the next chapter, almost all the groups and movements (and there have been hundreds), which assert a specific date when Doomsday would finally happen, do so based on the promise of Christ's return. The return (or first coming from the Jewish perspective) of the Messiah is the motivation for date-setters to proclaim the time of the end. To put things into perspective, as intriguing as the recent eruption of interest in 2012 is, the Mayan phenomenon is only about four decades old. The first mention in modern times was from the book by Michael D. Coe, *The Mayas*, in 1966. In stark contrast, we can't fully appreciate two thousand years of history in the western world without factoring in the Jewish expectation for Messiah and the Christian insistence on the Second Advent of Christ. Both contend this event involving Messiah is the concluding historical event to which all of history is drawn. That is why some scholars have said, perhaps tongue in cheek, that history is "His story."

Therefore, the logical next step in our study is to turn our attention to chronicling this history of "failed dates and false hopes" to prove this point. Furthermore, by doing this analysis, since our intent is to discern how we might decode Doomsday, it's best to learn as many lessons from the past as possible – lessons regarding methods tried and failed to pinpoint the final day of business as usual.

Notes

[1] This group of alternate historians is sometimes lumped together in a not so flattering bunch called the "Pyramidiots." Graham Hancock and Robert Bauval would be the two most famous of the bunch. James (J.J.) Hurtak and Richard Hoagland would be two others who connect the Pyramids to "The Council of the Nine" – supposedly extraterrestrials mirroring the "nine gods of Heliopolis," aka the Ennead, who various mediums purportedly have channeled since the 1950's. We will discuss much more about this paranormal perspective in a later chapter.

[2] The movie, *10,000 BC*, briefly alludes to "ancient ones," who guided the construction of the Pyramids. The movie provides a very quick glimpse of the one remaining being, known as the "Almighty," who appears to be a giant and an alien.

Roland Emmerich made this movie too. (There is a pattern here!) Was Emmerich inferring these beings to be *Atlanteans*, Nephilim (i.e., "demigods" spoken of in the Bible, see Genesis 6:4), or extraterrestrials? Although he did not acknowledge this fact, Emmerich was clearly familiar with "alternative history speculations" concerning the origin of the Pyramids as well as when they were built. The constellation Orion and the notion of a coming Messiah from there is also big part of his story.

3 Plato's father, Plato, and one of his biographers two hundred years after Plato's death, supposedly went to Egypt and wrote down the story of Atlantis from a particular temple where the story was engraved. Each made the trip separately over several hundred years. Unfortunately in the 2nd century BC, the temple was destroyed.

4 This information is from Patrick Heron's book listed in the bibliography, pages 2 and 3. Skeptics might contend, "Figures don't lie, but liars figure."

5 Later in the book, we will delve into the "henges" in England and the remarkable work done by Christopher Knight and Alan Butler, which argues that ancient wisdom existed there 1,000 years before the Egyptian Pyramids. Knight and Butler provide an explanation for at least a portion of this knowledge, which doesn't require an "out of this world" explanation.

6 The Pleiades is the fuzzy pack of stars (usually regarded as seven) we see with the naked eye but with field glasses explodes into hundreds of stars.

7 Known as "the transit of Venus," the looping effect comes from the fact that we are orbiting the Sun just as Venus is. Being much closer to the sun, the appearance of the orbit of Venus from Earth appears like a loop over a series of nights, although according to some sources this eclipse on December 21, 2012, will actually be in the noonday Sun, right where the Sun will also be. It can't be observed when it occurs.

8 Mesopotamia literally means "between the two rivers" and refers to the rivers Tigris and Euphrates. Thus, we know today's Syria, Iraq, and Iran collectively by this ancient name.

9 This date may be quite precise if you are willing to grant that we can count on the accuracy of the Hebrew genealogies and that, as they are given, they are *contiguous* – without any gaps. However, not even all Evangelicals agree that we should regard the genealogies in this way.

10 According to most Mayan scholars, we are living in *age five*, which completes in 2012 – the next age, if there is one, begins on December 22, 2012.

11 Other Hebrew prophets, especially Isaiah, contain many messianic prophecies, but they did not have a proximate historical affect to the extent that Daniel did.

12 Modern liberal scholarship believes the author wrote almost 400 years later than tradition teaches. In their view, the book derives its name from *its principal*

character who is Daniel (born, circa 610 BC – died circa 530 BC), and not because Daniel actually wrote it.

13 Actually, Jacob (renamed Israel) prophesied that his son Judah would be the tribe from which "Shiloh" would come. Christians believe Shiloh is a messianic name referring to Jesus. Muslims believe it refers to Mohammed.

14 We know these years as "prophetic years" of 360 days instead of 365.25 days. The end of the 483 prophetic years appears to point to April, 30 AD, and to "holy week" otherwise known as Jesus' passion. Scholars still debate this date, some suggesting as early as 28 AD with some proposing 32 AD. At issue is, "Which Messiah candidate died during this window of time?" The answer is rather obvious.

15We will delve into this when we look at the Prophet Daniel later.

16 Scholars debate the exact date of Jesus' "birthday" – it may have been as early as 7 BC, (pinpointed by a triple conjunction of Jupiter and Saturn) or it may have been four years later when there was a triple conjunction of Jupiter and Venus in 3 BC. Because Herod died in 1 BC, not 4 BC as most scholars report, using some astronomical sleuthing, a date of 3 BC is the most logical date to select for Jesus' "birthday". A manuscript corruption of Josephus commencing in 1544 (the gospels tell us Joseph took Mary and Jesus went to Egypt until Herod's death), is the source for the inaccurate dating of Herod's death. Jesus' date of conception is the most likely "date of birth" because this was consistent with how Hebrews understood when life begins. If true, Mary conceived Jesus in September and his birth was in June. See *Bethlehemstar.net* for a lively discussion of this dating. Later I will purpose that his birthday may have been on Pentecost which might have occurred at this time.

17 This revolt is known as the Maccabean Revolt and is told in the Apocryphal books, *I and II Maccabees*. *Chanukah* commemorates this same period; specifically the battle over the Jerusalem Temple and the associated miraculous event, in which one-day's ration of lamp oil burned for eight consecutive days.

18 King Herod's dynasty came to power because of deals it struck with Rome. The Herodians were hated not only because they were complicit in Roman rule, but also because they were of mixed blood and insincere in their commitment to the Jewish religion.

19 This temple was the temple of Herod, "the second Temple," Solomon's Temple being the first.

20 This personage is an early name for the "man of sin" aka *Antichrist*.

21 According to the Law of Moses, failure to honor the Sabbath was punishable by death. The fact that Jesus challenged this and later declared himself "lord of the Sabbath" was yet another expression of his claim to divinity as Christians assert.

22 Some diminish the triumph of Christianity over Roman "state religion" believing that it was just a political move on the part of Constantine attempting to save the empire. His conversion was staged. Given the history of Rome and the hatred it had for Christians, this conclusion doesn't easily follow from the facts.

Chapter 4:
A History of Failed Dates and False Hopes

I always avoid prophesying beforehand,
because it is a much better policy to prophesy
after the event has already taken place.

Winston Churchill

Classifying Methods for Decoding Doomsday

To substantiate our thesis from the prior chapter, we will recap the most dramatic doomsday dates of the past 2,000 years.[1] First, we will highlight that there are no less than *ten particular methods* used in times past to decode Doomsday. The dates selected relate to a particular prophet proclaiming the *end of days* – a proclamation with at least one specific rationale. Each claim for "why we know when it will happen" falls into these ten categories:[2]

- The (1) *symmetry of the date* itself (500 AD, 1000 AD, 1500 AD, 2000 AD); (2) its tie to an *anniversary of a major event* like Pentecost or (3) a *numerically significant or symmetrical space of time* between events (e.g., 1000 years since the crucifixion of Christ).

- (4) *Noteworthy signs in the heavens*, especially in modern times, with sightings of flying saucers, which many interpret as a means to save a remnant of humanity from the coming cataclysm. Throughout history, comets are the most common portent signaling "bad times ahead." Eclipses of the sun and moon may also have a part to play in this speculation.

- (5) *A prediction from a self-proclaimed messiah* that the world ends at such-and-such a time; typically only this group of believers will be saved (e.g., David Koresh, Jim Jones, and Charles Manson).

- (6) *Encoded timelines in ancient structures* (the Pyramids of the Maya or Egyptians); or (7) *repeated astronomical events* in the constellations or motions of the planets. Planetary conjunctions are the most frequent sign of a pending momentous event.

- Finally, we will see examples in which Christian "expositors" calculate the end-date based upon: (8) *biblical numerology;* or (9) some *particular marker* they believe crucial to pinpoint the date the world ends (e.g., the time span of a "biblical generation"); or (10) the *specific numbering of verses* in the Bible tied to dates and times.

In documenting these missed dates, we underscore that "the expectation of the soon return of Christ" is the *primary cause for apocalyptic expectation in the western world,* at least *until* the last three decades. In the last 30 years, the momentum has shifted partially to natural causes (motivated by recent scientific discoveries), new age speculations, the meaning of the Mayan calendars, or decoded Egyptian pyramids which (*to some authors*) provide reliable predictions for Doomsday.

Another purpose here is to underscore how when someone predicts Doomsday, he or she resorts to *decoding* something. Usually, they decode the Bible, but often they decode ancient architecture or another sacred book.

Rarely are claims predicting Doomsday based on a simple but clearly worded revelation supposedly from God to an "anointed individual." It's an unfortunate universal truth that as soon as someone says, "God told me that the world will end on _____" (*Fill in the blank*), it's time to run as far and as fast as you can. In cases like this, the messiah-like person always displays a destructive personality; he or she usually commits suicide and leads the rest of his or her group to do the same. An announcement from such a megalomaniac is a dead giveaway that the only Doomsday they will witness is their own.

Again, the fact that Christians (more than any other group), have been responsible for apocalyptic date setting *doesn't* mean that this obsession is due to *a misinterpretation of the Christian message.* As I've said before, it reinforces the essential apocalyptic nature of the message originally given by Jesus Christ to his apostles and thereafter, from the apostles to their churches – soundly calling into question any Christian perspective that denies *apocalyptic fervor as fundamental to the Christian viewpoint.*

That being true, the issue isn't whether Christians will speculate on the time of Christ's return. They have and will continue to do so. The question for Christians is therefore, "How can a more accurate understanding of the Holy Scriptures cause believers to establish a more balanced and biblically informed set of expectations as to the *when* and the *how* the apocalypse will transpire?" In other words, "Jesus is coming;" but *how should we then live* in the meantime?

The issue for *non-Christians* who believe in prophecy is quite different. It amounts to determining which pagan or secular source for foretelling Doomsday offers the most evidence to support such a claim. As we proceed through the remainder of this chapter, we will also consider this *second opinion* (doomsday predictions from non-Christians sources).

The Predictions for the Messianic Event before 1000 AD

Emerging from the first century AD, Jewish expectations for Messiah were unabated. The most important event for Jewish messianic anticipation was the *Bar Kochba* rebellion of **135** AD. This revolt was the final straw for Rome. After destroying this rebellion, Jerusalem was renamed *Aelia Capitolina* by the Emperor Hadrian and the remaining Jewish population was sold into slavery, and dispersed throughout the world. Hadrian forbade the Jews to enter the city – a decree that stood for 300 years. Nevertheless, Jewish expectation of messiah still wasn't sated.

Therefore, many of the doomsday dates identified in the 2nd and 3rd centuries AD remained driven by Jewish speculation on when the messiah would come. *Rabbi Dosa* said the messiah would come around **400** AD. *Rabbi Judah ha-Nasi* said the messiah would come 365 years after the Romans destroyed the Temple (**435** AD).

However, Christians get credit for the most advanced calculations to determine the end of days. Christian church fathers *Hyppolytus* and *Lactantius* writing in the third century predicted that Jesus would return in **500** AD based upon the belief that God created the world in 5500 BC and this would be the conclusion of 6,000 years of creation history. They may have relied upon a Roman theologian *Sextus Julius Africanus* (living earlier in the second century) that believed there had been 5531 years from creation to the resurrection. Therefore, the *Parousia* (the Greek word the New Testament used to label the events surrounding the Second Advent[3]) would be in **500** AD. *Irenaeous*, another early theologian of the church, appears influenced by this calculation too.

In essence, the "messianic millennium" (1,000 years spoken of in the *Revelation of John*) would be the final millennium, creating a "week" of millenniums (7,000 years). The notion continues to be a strong rationale even to this day. The core issue to determine the timing of the end is to figure out the moment of beginning – "precisely when did God create Adam?"[4]

One final example from this period (a colorful one): One Christian priest in Rome predicted that Christ would return in **500** AD based upon the dimensions of Noah's Ark. As fantastic as this rationale might seem today, no doubt the idea seemed *seaworthy at the time*. Other noteworthy examples:

- A group known as the *Montanists* founded in **156** AD held that God through Christ would found a New Jerusalem in Phrygia (modern day Turkey). Montanus was a believer in ecstatic mysticism and believed in the "immediacy" of the experience of God. This viewpoint saw God's three persons (Father, Son, and Holy Spirit) as different modes of His expression. This view lost out to the *Trinitarian* view canonized at Nicaea. According to one source, this appears to be the first bona fide Christian cult formed specifically around the belief of Jesus' soon return and the formation of a New Jerusalem. *Tertullian* was a follower of Montanism and was the most famous defender. This sect continued for over 600 years mostly in the area where it began.

- Another group of North African Christians, the *Donatists*, believed that Christ would return **in 380 AD.** The Donatists were unwilling to forgive those that fell away from the faith during the vicious persecutions at the beginning of the fourth century; thus, they separated from the rest of the church. Eventually, the emperor Constantine called a church council becoming directly involved to settle the matter. However, the matter was not so easily resolved. The accompanying figure (*See* below, **Figure 12**), points out that St. Augustine, living almost 100 years later, clashed with this sect.

FIGURE 12 - ST. AUGUSTINE ARGUING WITH THE DONATISTS

The End of the First Millennium to 1500 AD

There were many predictions for the end of the age during the 10th century leading up to 1000 AD. Here are just a few:

- In 950 AD, Adso of Montier-en-Der wrote a "Treatise on the Anti-christ" predicting he would be unveiled in **1000** AD.

- The last of the Carolingian dynasty fell with the death of King Louis V in **987**. This led many to believe that Antichrist would come to fill the vacuum.

- King Otto II of Germany had *Charlemagne's* body exhumed on Pentecost in the year **1000** supposedly to forestall the apocalypse. (*Charles the Great* had been dead for about 175 years – but you never know when a resurrection of the Antichrist might finally come to pass! The resurrection of the first and greatest Roman emperor, Charlemagne, to become Antichrist might have seemed a good bet at the time. The fact that Emperors ruled for 1006 years until Napoleon's demise is a point to consider).

- Signs in the sky were also noteworthy at this time. Halley's Comet appeared in 989 AD and many observed a supernova in 1006 AD. Making matters worse, the Moslem caliph, Al Hakim, chose this time to destroy the Holy Sepulcher in Jerusalem. Perhaps Al Hakim thought this action would bring about the apocalypse. (If so, Iran's President Ahmadinejad, in 2010, seems eager to follow in Hakim's footsteps.)

- One of the most interesting dates near this time was March 25, **970** AD. The *Lotharingians* thought the date significant because the date of the Annunciation fell on the same date as Good Friday (this was when the Angel Gabriel told Mary she would become pregnant by the Holy Spirit and birth Jesus). This group also believed that this day was when God created Adam, the Red Sea parted, Mary conceived Jesus, and Pilate crucified him. With so many anniversaries (all happening on the same day), the Second Advent must have appeared to be an "odds-on" cinch.

Mel Sanger makes these comments about **1000** AD:

> This year goes down as one of the most pronounced states of hysteria over the return of Christ. All members of society seemed affected by the prediction that Jesus was coming back on Jan 1, 1000 AD… the magical number 1000 was primarily the sole reason for the expectation. During **December, 999** AD, everyone was on their best behavior; worldly goods were sold and given to the

poor, swarms of pilgrims headed east to meet the Lord at Jerusalem, buildings went unrepaired, crops were left unplanted, and criminals were set free from jails.

As the year 1000 AD progressed, nothing happened. Nevertheless, the theologians of the day connected dozens of other events in the 11th century to Christ's soon return, leading to the conviction that the Apocalypse *was already underway* – it just wasn't clear to anyone the exact moment it had begun. Despite not knowing this important piece of information, most predicted the *Parousia (His coming)* would break forth nevertheless.

In **1284**, *Pope Innocent III* believed the Second Coming would transpire because it was 666 years after the birth of Islam. Here we combine multiple factors: heresy, numerology, and a space in time between events.

In 1147, *Gerald of Poehlde* proclaimed the return of Christ in **1306** when the Millennium *ends*. He believed it began with the coming to power of Constantine in 306 AD (a symmetrical time span of 1,000 years, or a millennium, based upon an anniversary).

Many mystics and seers believed that the Millennium would finally conclude in **1500** AD. Again, a symmetrical date motivated the conviction.

The Messianic Predictions from 1500 to 1700 AD

Three particular outbreaks of concern pointing to the coming of doomsday took place during the 16th Century. The first, around **1525**, was a peasant revolt led by Anabaptist Thomas Müntzer (this occurred around the time of Luther's reformation, an apocalypse for the Roman Catholic Church – *metaphorically speaking*). The authorities quickly and brutally extinguished the revolt.

Another Anabaptist, Melchior Hoffman predicted Christ's return to Strasburg in **1533** in which God would save only 144,000 *select*. The rest of the world would perish.

In **1534**, more blood would be shed but to a lesser extent. Again, the *Anabaptists* fueled this uprising. Jan Matthys took over the city of Münster, throwing the entire population out. Dispossessed of their city, the populace regrouped and lay siege. After a year of fighting, everyone was dead. Truly, this was a self-fulfilling apocalyptic prophecy.

Martin Luther of course conducted his reforming business during this period. When did he believe that Christ would return? According to Luther, it would be no later than **1600** AD.

However, the events in the 16th century were minor compared to what was to happen in the 17th century. The strongest anticipation of the end would be an English affair. Imagine if you will, a story in a then contemporary newspaper:

> **London: September 6th, 1666.** *It has been 1000 years since the birth of Christ plus 666 years (the number of the Beast). The city is ablaze. 70,000 homes are on fire. The blaze has destroyed 87 parish churches. St. Paul's Cathedral caught fire and is destroyed. This very same year over 100,000 succumbed to the Bubonic plague. Then, there are the comets. Not one, but two comets appeared only last year. What more warning do we need that the end is near?*

Such an imaginary account recaps the main happenings. It's no wonder that Sir Isaac Newton spent his free moments searching the scriptures to learn if Christ would return in this ominous year of **1666**. Newton eventually decided that this wasn't the date. Nonetheless, as he was inclined to do, he would systematically assemble his thoughts on the subject. Newton would exit this experience with his own prediction – the end of the world was still 400 years away – he wrote that we should witness it, but not before **2060** AD. In a subsequent chapter, we will explore how he derived this date.

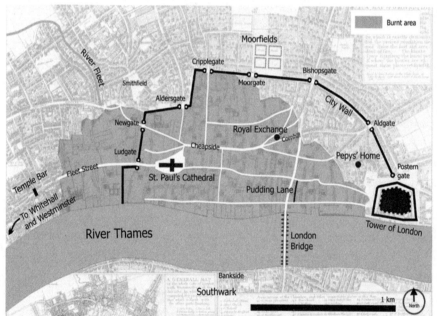

FIGURE 13 - THE PORTION OF LONDON DESTROYED BY THE GREAT FIRE OF 1666

However, Newton wasn't the only one looking for the end. A radical group called the (*Fifth Monarchy Men,*) spurred on by the conflict between Charles I and Parliament, was certain the return of Christ would occur in **1666**.[5]

Oliver Cromwell, a figure that recent history has chosen to villianize, calmed down such radicals. He also allowed Jewish immigration to England during this time. While Jewish discrimination continued, Cromwell allowed the Jews to worship openly. This was one of the first examples in hundreds of years of Christians coming to the aid of Jewish believers. Cromwell began a trend that other Bible-oriented Christians would follow in the centuries ahead.

In America, the Puritans believed the end was likely in **1697** (so said Cotton Mather); and in **1700,** John Napier revised an earlier prediction to this new date. Americans believed this period wasn't the climax of the Millennium, but the beginning. No doubt, an unspoiled new world helped Americans see the goodness yet to be.

Napoleon sought to conquer the Middle East during 1798 and **1799**. Although not widely known, in 1799 he published a letter to the Jews of the world to return to their homeland in Palestine.

Many saw Napoleon playing the role of the Antichrist as he "pitched his tent" in Israel in a manner reminiscent of the prophecies of Daniel. Napoleon even helped to gather up a would-be council of the *Sanhedrin* in Paris to reinstitute the Jewish Levitical government. However, after Napoleon's uncle (a Bishop living in Paris at that time), warned his nephew that he may be unwittingly falling into the role of Daniel's Antichrist; Napoleon immediately ceased supporting the effort.[6]

Millerites and Millenarians of the 19th Century

Joining in the predicting business, *John Wesley,* the founder of Methodism asserted that the Millennium would begin in **1836**. The Great Beast of Revelation 13 would arise 3.5 years earlier in **1832**.

William Miller, the founder of the *"Millerites,"* led one of the most famous separatist groups (following in the manner of the Essenes and the Montanists). Miller studied the Bible carefully, determining that **1843** to **1844** would be the grand finale. An unusual meteor display (a sign in the heavens) assisted Miller's proclamation. However, after the failure for this to come to pass (known as *"The Great Disappointment"*), the movement had to rethink their viewpoint. Sanger quotes one upset follower after the failure of this yearlong wait for the end: "The world made merry over the old Prophet's predicament. The taunts and jeers of the 'scoffers' were well-nigh unbearable." Despite this, the Millerites didn't give up. They shifted their proselytizing into high gear[7] and continued to come up with more dates: **1845, 1849,** and **1851**.

In **1856**, the *Crimean War* gave rise to the view that Armageddon was just around the corner. In this war, Russia sought to pull Palestine away from the Ottoman Turks. Resulting from this conflict, some 19th century Bible scholars saw the much-anticipated invasion of Russia into Israel, aka the "War of Gog and Magog" (a key upcoming event often mentioned in today's evangelical prophetic scenarios and one we will discuss later).

FIGURE 14 - WILLIAM MILLER

Miller was the forebear to many *Seventh Day Adventists* groups today sporting what could be called a *strict constructionist* view of the Bible and its manner of interpretation. As their name suggests, the Adventists maintain believers should honor the Sabbath on Saturday and not Sunday – the 7th day of the week rather than the first day of the week (Christ was resurrected on a Sunday and Christians came to see this day as the Sabbath accordingly). Although orthodox in most articles of faith, they contend that Christians should maintain certain other Jewish traditions too.

In **1862**, John Cumming of the Scottish National Church estimates *the end of 6,000 years of creation has concluded*. Once again proving to be a popular rationale for the return of Christ, he asserted the Millennium of the Messiah was beginning at that time. Of course, it didn't happen as he predicted.

In **1835**, Joseph Smith, the founder of *Mormonism* predicts the Second Coming of Christ will occur in 56 years, or **1891**. Smith follows in the long line of founders of Christian sects that emphasize *eschatology* (the study of last things), to rally his troops.

In **1900**, Father Pierre Lachèze foresaw Doomsday occurring eight years after the Temple in Jerusalem is rebuilt (the rebuilding of the Temple is a recurring theme in evangelical prophecy today). Of course, the Jews didn't rebuild their temple then and we are still waiting today for the groundbreaking ceremony.

In addition, in **1900**, 100 members of a Russian cult, the *Brothers and Sisters of the Red Death*, commit suicide to prepare themselves for the end of the world. This is *one of the first apocalyptic groups* not expressly formed around a biblically motivated rationale.

The Jehovah's Witnesses – Record Holders for Failed Dates

William Miller just didn't found the Millerites that morphed into the Seventh Day Adventists; he also influenced one *Charles Russell* who founded the *Jehovah's Witnesses* in 1914. One of the first and strongest dates the Witnesses (and others) suggested in the 20th century was 1914. The Witnesses employed a number of mathematical calculations that (as we shall see) other Evangelicals utilized throughout the 20th century and into the 21st.

The Witnesses selected **1914** because it was 2,520 years from a starting date of 606 BC, connected to the time of judgment when Nebuchadnezzar first captured the Kingdom of Judea and began to relocate Jews from Palestine to Babylon. *We will learn later that the number 2,520 is central to how Newton decoded Doomsday and key to Biblical numerology.* In this instance, it refers to a time of judgment and its fulfillment.

To explain the rationale: The Mosaic Law dictated that every seven years the land of Israel was to lie fallow (uncultivated) – thus creating a Sabbath rest for the Land. However, the Jewish nation ignored this law. Hence, in Ezekiel's history, the prophet tells us that a failure to learn the lesson would multiply the *judgment sevenfold*. The failure of the land to enjoy its Sabbaths was a period of 360 years (apparently from around 966 BC to 606 BC). Nevertheless, the Jews (according to the Jehovah's Witnesses) didn't learn their lesson; therefore, God multiplied the *360 years by seven* for a total judgment of 2,520 years. That span of time leads us to 1914 – and the end of the world, *as we know it*. Of course, we know that 1914 was an auspicious year indeed, marking the beginning of World War I. Despite *The Great War* (also known as the "war to end all wars"), the Messiah didn't return. As a result, the Witnesses scrambled for an explanation and other possible dates.

The year **1994** was the next date selected after it was determined that 1914 was only the beginning of the *end time*. The length of a generation was determined to be *eighty years* (actually it's seventy, see Psalm 90:10) and a *full genera-tion must pass before Jesus returns* (a specific marker—rationale *number nine*.) Je-sus had said, "I tell you that a generation shall not pass until all these signs I foretell shall come to pass." However, did he mean a generation in the future? Alternatively, did he mean the generation alive at the time of his ministry?[8] No doubt, the gospel writers record Jesus saying this. Assuming it relates to a fu-ture series of events, there are two issues: First, is the *length of a generation* in the Bible 70 years, 80 years, 40 years, or perhaps as little as 33 years? This question is difficult enough. However, it doesn't stand-alone. The second question is, *"when does the countdown begin?"* Both matters remain problematic for "date setters" today. We will discuss this too later.

Of course, 1994 came and went – yet another disappointment.

As it turns out, Jehovah's Witnesses selected many more dates than just these two. In addition to 1914 and 1994, they selected **1918, 1920, 1925, 1941, 1957, 1975,** and **1994.** As Sanger notes, *they hold the record for the most failed dates* – hardly the best way to establish one's credibility in the interpretation of Bible prophecy.

Other doomsday dates in the 20th Century break new ground:

- **1954:** The *Brotherhood of the Seven Rays* a UFO cult, led by Dorothy Martin, believes a great worldwide flood will destroy the world. This cult is the group studied by Leon Festinger in his book, *When Prophecy Fails.* Festinger invents the term "cognitive dissonance" to disclose what happens when a person holds two conflicting beliefs that must be reconciled. Beginning with this group, *we begin to see occult movements predicting Doomsday.* Christians no longer have the only apocalyptic game in town.

- **1960:** Charles Piazzi Smyth, a *Pyramidologist,* predicts the Millennium would begin. Enter yet another source for pinpointing Doomsday – groups that believe *other ancient religions and their monuments can* clue us in on the day when the world ends.

- **1962:** Jeanne Dixon predicts Antichrist's birth in February of this year. If true, he is 48 (in 2010) and living in the world today. (In case you were wondering, Barak Obama was born in August 1961).

- **1973:** David Berg (aka Moses David), leader of the "Family of Love" predicts the Comet Kohoutek will destroy the United States. I remem-ber reading one of his tracts before my freshmen English class (in col-lege) at that time. Berg missed this prognostication (and I'm glad – I loved college and met my wife there). He will later revise his prediction to **1993**.

Doomsday Predictions – 1980 to 2000

The pace of Doomsday predictions begins to pick up dramatically in the decade of the 80's.

- **1981** – Many evangelicals predict this to be the date for the *Rapture*. Hal Lindsey's book, *The Late Great Planet Earth,* heavily influences this belief. The book asserts that the rapture must occur no less than seven years before the actual, visible, *Second Coming of Christ*. Lindsey's interpretation (based on *Dispensational* Theology, a type of evangelical interpretation existing since about 1840), builds upon his view that *a biblical generation is 40 years* and the starting point for the countdown was 1948. Therefore, the Second Coming is in 1988 and the Rapture seven years before.

- Lindsey was quite explicit. In his book, *The 1980's: Countdown to Armageddon*, Lindsey answers one skeptics' question, "Why do you think that all the various prophecies will come to pass during *this* generation?" His response: "The answer is simple. The prophets told us that the rebirth of Israel – no other event – would be the sign that the countdown has begun. Since that rebirth, the rest of the prophecies have begun to be fulfilled quite rapidly. For this reason I am convinced that we are now in the unique time so clearly and precisely forecast by the Hebrew prophets."

- **1982** – A rare planetary alignment in which all planets line up on one side of the Sun (the so-called, "Jupiter Effect"). Many predict massive earthquakes. Others see this as a remarkable "sign in the heavens."[9] Yes, there was an earthquake or two that year like any other. However, none was so noteworthy that the doomsayers felt vindicated.

- Also in **1982**, the *New Age Movement*, specifically the followers of *Madam Blavatsky* (the famous theosophist), *Alice Bailey*, and *Benjamin Crème*, working through the *Tara Centers* take out a full page ad in the New York Times (and many other newspapers worldwide), declaring that "The Christ is Here" by which they meant, *Lord Maitreya*. This so-called *Christ* is actually the Buddhist concept of an ancient master who has been waiting in the wings until the world was ready. Unfortunately, for this group at least, Maitreya is a no-show. But no worries, he's just delayed until **2012**.

- **1987** – José Argüelles predicts this is the beginning of a transformation of human consciousness, known as "the harmonic convergence." The world will experience dramatic change. Thus begins the *galactic eclipse* that isn't complete until 2019. Furthermore, many scientists point out that the exact year of the eclipse was 1999. Moreover, enthusiasts are dismayed since little if anything happens in 1987. Within a few years, they regroup and begin to talk up the "real" date we should take note of – **2012**. (Today, Argüelles remains a "cross-over" star in both the New Age and Mayan "camps"). The reason why 2012 is the key date for the galactic eclipse seems somewhat random. Nevertheless, true believers point out that the Maya set this day as the end of their *long-count calendar* to coincide with the sun's movement into the dark rift.

- **1988** – A book is published, *88 Reasons Why the Rapture is in 1988*. Many people get excited. Hal Lindsey had emphasized this date.[10] However, there is no apocalypse and no rapture.

- **1993** – September 13th, Rabin and Arafat sign a peace treaty. Many see this as the covenant spoken of in the *Book of Daniel*, Chapter 9. If so, it's to last for precisely seven years. Apocalyptic authors do the math and decide the end date will be seven years later, in the year 2000. This is a good date to pick because it's symmetrical and may be the conclusion of 6,000 years of "creation history."

- **1994** – Reginald Dunlop claims the last coded date in the Pyramid of Giza is 1994. Therefore, this is the end of the line! Here we have another prediction of Doomsday tied to ancient monuments.

- **1997** – The group *Heaven's Gate* commits suicide. Another comet does us in – this one is *Hale-Bopp*. Supposedly, the Council of Nine (through James Hurtak and Richard Hoagland)[11] confirms there's another heavenly object hidden behind the comet, the future home of those selected to be saved. Heaven's Gate, parodying *the Brothers and Sisters of the Red Death*, believe their ticket to ride is to kill themselves (please don't ask me to explain their logic).

- **1998** – Edgar Cayce, the Sleeping Prophet predicted decades before that there were be a *pole reversal* and it would create a massive disruption of the oceans and the earth's crust. This would also lead to the rediscovery of Atlantis. Of course, many 2012 sages today repeat this not-so-probable prediction. Nevertheless, 1998 didn't yield this event. Thank goodness for our sakes. Cayce still sleeps well since he doesn't have to account for missing this one.

- **2000** – Another millennium comes and goes. This year has even more speculation and excitement than 1000 AD.

- **2000** – The Y2K bug bites business. However, the bite isn't too deep. The alarming warnings about the coming computer crash were due to the *two-digit year* coded into most of the world's software. Although this bug did catch programmers off guard (we programmers might diminish the error by relabeling it *a design flaw*), in the end new accounting software installed in the '90's swatted it silly. Nevertheless, the commotion catches many notable evangelical prophecy scholars crying wolf. This leads the prudent to ask, *"Will 2012 be another Y2K?"* Will evangelical prophecy authors use the popular hysteria to ramp up the evangelism? The glut of books dedicated to the 2012 topic makes it appear so. Then again, *maybe 2012 is the year we've all been waiting for after all.*

- **2000** – A conjunction occurs between Jupiter and Saturn (in the constellation Taurus). Is this the Star of Bethlehem? This conjunction appears in 2000 just as it did in 7 BC. Does this signal the birth or revealing of the Antichrist? Does this star mean Christ is coming back?

Dates in the 20th Century Often Used for Doomsday Markers

Key dates that figure into doomsday predictions in the 20th century can be summarized as follows:

- **1917** – The British put forth the *Balfour Declaration and retake Jerusalem* from the Turks (British General Allenby does the honors). Afterwards, Winston Churchill, Woodrow Wilson, and other European leaders meeting in Cairo, restructure the Middle East forming the nation states of Iraq, Saudi Arabia, Palestine, and Transjordan (aka the British Mandate of 1921). Churchill's reckoning as to how the whole area should be carved up *sows the seeds for the current crises of the Middle East.* His motivation then: Britain was running out of money and *couldn't afford to police the world.* Many Americans today would appreciate Churchill's dilemma – it sounds so very familiar.

- **1948** – The United Nations *recognizes* Israel in spite of protests from its Arab and Egyptian neighbors. Through this action, the UN ignites a hot spot that flares still today. Most evangelicals see this as the fulfillment of *Ezekiel's prediction of the Valley of Dry Bones* (Ezekiel 37), i.e., the return of the Jews to their native land. This is a key marker for Biblical believers that the *end of days* is fast approaching.

- **1967** – Israel wins *the Six-Day War and the retakes Jerusalem from Jordan*. Many proclaim this to be the "end of the time of the Gentiles" – a period identified by Jesus in the Gospel of Luke. From this date forward, many Bible-believing Christians assert that only one generation will pass until Jesus returns. The question is, *is this really the end of the time of the Gentiles?*[12] Indeed, there's a keen argument against the view that "the time of the Gentiles" concludes with this event: Moshe Dayan immediately chooses to return the Temple Mount to Jordanian control, handing it over to the agency known as the WAQF. Not being particularly religious, Dayan believes this is the politically correct thing to do. His decision stuns Orthodox Jews (as well as Freemasons and evangelical Christians looking for a rebuilt Jewish Temple) and thereby appeases no one but the Arabs in East Jerusalem – at least for a short period of time.

Of course, the date setting goes on and on into the 21st century.

However, this is a good point to "leave it there" as they say on the cable news. We will take up the predictions of this last decade (2001 to 2010) as we continue in the chapters ahead.

Notes

1 In this chapter, I owe a debt to Chris Nelson's web site *(http://www. ab-hota.info/index.htm) and* Mel Sanger's research (see the bibliography), which supplements my own, recapping the hundreds of noteworthy examples of "date setting" that has punctuated Apocalypticism throughout the Christian era. We won't look at every one (see Nelson's site at the link listed above or Sanger's paper for a more complete discussion of the topic). My contribution here is primarily distinguishing the "ten methods for decoding Doomsday" and "putting things in perspective."

2 By categorizing the top ten methods for decoding Doomsday down through history, I don't mean to imply that it logically follows that these rationales are necessarily off base. One or more may be noteworthy and proven right!

3 The word *Parousia* means "coming" but in a personal sense, such as "in two weeks I will be with you in person." That adds some additional depth to his coming.

4 Not all orthodox believers insist that the world is only 6,000 years old – but they do believe that Adam was a special creative act of God. God may have literally

formed Adam from the clay, or Adam may have been the result of God implanting a new type of soul or spirit into "homo sapiens."

5 The Fifth Monarchy refers to the fifth Kingdom mentioned in Daniel, Chapter 2. The Fifth Kingdom is the Kingdom of the Messiah.

6 Likewise, the famous seer *Nostradamus*, whose prophecies predict there will be three Antichrists, saw Napoleon as the first of the three to enjoy the title. (Cited by David Flynn in his book, *The Temple at the Center of Time*, pg. 173, citing John Holland Rose, *The Personality of Napoleon*, pg. 243).

7 "Proselytizing after prophecies fail" is one of the sociological behaviors believers typically exhibit. Getting others to believe what you believe, especially after your beliefs have faltered, is a keen way to reinforce your faith. Festinger documented this behavior in his 1956 book, *When Prophecy Fails*, which we will discuss again briefly in the chapter on Esotericism and UFOs.

8 Jesus' prediction of the destruction of the Temple and "the other signs" he discloses in his "Olivet Discourse," were fulfilled within a 40-year time span from his death (30 AD) to the time of the destruction of the Jewish Temple in 70 AD. Nevertheless, is there yet "another fulfillment" where "in the last days" the events repeat themselves? Evangelical Christians, specifically Dispensationalists, believe this will in fact happen.

9 I viewed the alignment that year on a very clear night. It was spectacular!

10 For the record, despite his reputation as an alarmist, Hal Lindsey was instrumental in shaping my thinking about the relevance of Christianity to my life. I owe him a debt, as do many evangelicals, as he caused me to think carefully about what the prophecies in the Bible mean to my life in the 20th (now 21st) century. For that, I am most grateful.

11 The "Pyramidiots" don't publicize their connection with the "channeled Nine" and Heaven's Gate. However, if you do the research, you'll see that they are strong believers in the Council of Nine, suggest the "secondary object behind the comet," and therefore, ultimately share some responsibility for these suicides (See *The StarGate Conspiracy* in the Bibliography). We will discuss this more in Chapter 8.

12 Not every evangelical scholar believes this is the proper interpretation. Some noted conservative theologians, including John Walvoord (former President of Dallas Theological Seminary) do not believe the time of the Gentiles necessarily ends until Jesus Christ physically returns at His Second Coming. That is my position too.

PART TWO:

DOOMSDAY PROPHETS

Chapter 5:
Science Predicts the End of the World

Some say the world will end in fire, some say in ice.
From what I've tasted of desire
I hold with those who favor fire.
But if it had to perish twice,
I think I know enough of hate
To say that for destruction ice
Is also great and would suffice.

Robert Frost

Recent Doomsdays Just Discovered

Not long ago, after over a century of investigation, we finally discovered why the dinosaurs disappeared. As it turns out, the research was rather startling. Science informed us that a meteor or comet struck the earth in the Yucatan Peninsula near Mexico City wiping out the giant reptiles in the "fifth great extinction event."[1] This event destroyed almost all life, kicking up so much dust into the atmosphere that it caused what we now call, a *nuclear winter*, (or more precisely, a *meteorite winter*).

However, since this event was estimated to be 65 million years ago, it's easy to think, "No worries. That kind of mega-disaster seems way out of the ordinary. Why be alarmed? Dinosaurs had their fun in the sun – it's time for nature to move on."

Even when we consider it more thoroughly, isn't this catastrophe proof positive that these kinds of things happen so infrequently, eons apart, that we have no practical reason to fret?

If the Yucatan meteorite was all we had to consider, then yes, there is no reason to be vexed. The odds are in our favor. One- chance-in-65 million is not a bet I would take. So, shouldn't we just toss aside this fact and forget about it? Regrettably, scientists today would respond, "Not so fast." As it turns out, during the past three decades, science has uncovered many decimating disasters that we previously knew nothing about. Indeed, *science continues to demonstrate that cataclysms are actually commonplace on our planet.*

This perspective is quite a change from what was "the planetary norm" 40 years ago. Back in the 70's, tales of natural disasters happening in our time were about as credible as ghost stories. However, like paranormal stories today, no longer do we find it easy to dismiss them as yarns invented to scare kids sitting around a campfire.

Given the newfound merit in respecting Mother Nature's often nasty temperament, let's discuss one of sciences most recent doomsday discoveries to point out just how frequently and recently the worse things seem to happen to our world.

The Last Ice Age and the Younger Dryas Event

Our first little-known, but recently discovered catastrophe happened only about 12,000 years ago (circa 10,000 BC), known as the *Younger Dryas Event.* Before we talk about it in detail, we need first to place this extraordinary event in the context of how humans settled North America.

The textbooks taught my generation that certain peoples populated the new world from only one origin, heading in one direction. Coming across an ice bridge that follows Alaska's

FIGURE 15 - ALASKA'S ALEUTIAN ISLANDS
AS SEEN FROM EARTH ORBIT

Aleutian Islands, ancestors to Native Americans first began to appear in the western portion of the continent and then spread east. Asians immigrating from Siberia and Japan settled the Americas. In the 1970's, this was no theory; it was simply a matter of fact.

However, in the past 30 years or so, anthropologists and geologists learned that this is only part of the story. In fact, two or three different sources of Homo sapiens seeded the population of the Americas. Based upon the discovery and analysis of humankind's early *artifacts* (bits and pieces of things humans made), we now know that about the time the population in the western Americas was starting up, pre-historic explorers arrived from Europe on the eastern seaboard, in the area from Virginia to New Jersey. Now remember, this wasn't the settlement of Jamestown – that would be 13,000 years later. No, this populace was apparently from the area we now know as Scandinavia or perhaps northern France. Scientists gained this new insight from the study of the most basic of utensils; specifically, how prehistoric humans chipped out small channels from their arrowheads to make stronger arrows. While not totally confirmed to the satisfaction of all anthropologists, most now believe that European ancestors to Native Americans, known as *Clovis Man*, were hunting and gathering their way across this eastern region.

So, what does Clovis Man have to do with cataclysms? The "Clovis Clan" is relevant because of what happened soon after they got their start in the New World. Soon after occupying an area on the eastern seaboard, *wild weather virtually wiped out Clovis Man.*

Looking at a broader timeframe, this period was at the end of the last great ice age, which had been underway for some 60,000 years. Although still overlaying much of the North American land-mass (what are today the states of Michigan, Minnesota, North Dakota, Montana, and Washington), glaciers were steadily receding as the earth began to warm. Suddenly something out of the ordinary happened that stopped the glaciers from retreating to the north. Specifically, this strange event blocked the drainage of the melted ice, which in turn led to a great catastrophe.

Normally, the runoff would find its way down the muddy Mississippi. Instead, a drastic event transpired, creating an ice damn near today's Great Lakes. The fresh water produced from the melting of these massive glaciers began heading a different direction. Instead of going south, it started going east through what is today the St. Lawrence River. The spillage of this fresh water into the northern Atlantic altered the saltiness of the water there. The net affect: By mixing with the salt water at this latitude, the water ceased being *heavier*, thus stopping the sinking process of the *saltier* water, which in turn caused the ocean currents to come to a screeching halt in the North Atlantic. Eliminating this affect

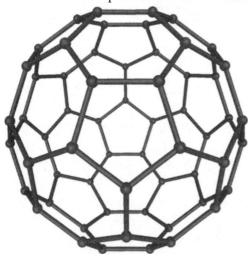

FIGURE 16 - THE CARBON STRUCTURE OF THE 'FULLERENE'

(known as the *thermohaline circulation* driven by differences in salinity of the waters in the Atlantic),[2] reinvigorated the ice age for another thousand years.

The *Younger Dryas Event* was an absolute cataclysm for all *fauna* (that includes humans) in the eastern half of North America. The horrendous weather (note: *massive climate change*, the cause for the major cataclysm) drove Clovis clan members (those few that survived) westward in search of new sources of food. Eventually, Clovis Men met the Asian immigrants living in the middle of the continent. After they became acquainted, we can safely assume they shared more than just bow- and-arrow technology.

Consequently, Native Americans aren't only descendants of Asian stock, but a genetic blend including a northern European gene pool too. It's also possible that peoples from other quarters (Polynesia) who settled in South America joined in the populating party. As it turns out, pre-historic Americans were quite diverse in their genetics, somewhat like we Americans are today. (It appears our American *melting pot* began long ago. Other countries might disparage us with a statement like, "Once a nation of mutts – always a nation of mutts." But then, our hybrid vigor does make us a great people and a much admired nation of humbled masses yearning to be free.)

As you might expect, eventually the ice damn broke and fresh water followed its normal course south – the ocean currents returned to normal in the North Atlantic. However, the story doesn't end there. We must backtrack and ask, "What caused this ice damn in the first place?" Would you believe it was *another major cataclysm?*

Science has been studying the soil that accompanies the artifacts of Clovis Man in certain sections of the country.[3] What they discovered was the most likely event creating the ice damn (and causing the change in how fresh water flowed away from the melting glaciers), was *an asteroid or comet striking the earth in the area we know as southern Canada*, smack dab in the glaciers, leaving a giant crater in the ice that caused the ice blockage.[4] We know this because of the presence of tiny, little pure carbon spherical shapes known as "Fullerenes" (aka "Buckyballs," named after Buckminster Fuller, famous for the *geodesic dome* shape that these little balls resemble).

These tiny bits of carbon sport a molecular formation uncommon on earth. As such, their composition tells us exactly where they come from – well at least that they come from *out of this world.* Additionally, scientists find the fullerenes layered throughout the soil set down at the time of Clovis Man. These little balls are telltale signs of a *close encounter of a third kind* (i.e., *contact* – using Steven Spielberg's lexicon.) Upon impact, they were scattered around the region; thereafter, the draining waters dispersed them across today's Mississippi Valley region.

What this all means is that a *comet cataclysm nearly annihilated Clovis Man.* Keep in mind this wasn't 65 million years ago. This was only about 12,000 BP (years *before present*).[5] As I said at the outset of this chapter, in the past 30 years or so, we've learned that *cataclysms are commonplace in the natural history of our earth.*

It's for these reasons that scientists (whether they like it or not), *have become today's most prominent Doomsday prophets.* Consequently, for the remainder of this chapter, we will summarize the various ways that Science testifies *our entire species could be wiped out at any moment.* Most of these causes of cataclysm *are the stuff of today's popular apocalyptic scenarios.* What should unnerve us most is that each of these catastrophes has happened many times – and in some cases, very recently in our planet's natural history (that is, within the last few thousand years). Catastrophes are "anything but unprecedented."

In short, we simply aren't as safe as we once thought.

Super Volcanoes and Nuclear Winter

In the literature of 2012, one of the most frightening things we uncover is how America is home to the world's largest volcano – and we really didn't know this either *before the last couple of decades.*

One of nation's favorite national parks, Yellowstone, doesn't just *contain* the volcano – it *is* the volcano. The *cone,* if you will, is actually hundreds of square miles, covering the entire valley where Yellowstone lies. Such a sizeable volcano has a special name, a *caldera* (coming from the same root word as *caldron*). That is why we see so much seismic activity in the area. The whole region is churning. Geysers, mud pits, and boiling water all bubble out of the ground. You could say its nature's way of letting off steam.

It just so happens that this caldera we call Yellowstone erupts every 600,000 years. When this occurs, it's a major catastrophic event for the entire planet. In its last eruption, it blasted enough dust into the atmosphere to cover the landscape downwind with several feet of volcanic dust. We learned about it when a paleontologist began digging fossils out of a hillside in Nebraska. He wondered, "Why are they buried so deep in volcanic material?" He hadn't seen evidence before of such a massive volcanic event in the Great Plains.

However, it's because of this *dusty death* (thanks to Shakespeare for this nearly alliterative phrase), scientists started looking for a suitable cause. After studying the continent from photographs taken from outer space, they finally determined that the culprit (or caldera that is), was Yellowstone.

We know now that not only did North America suffer at its eruption, but also as I mentioned before, when this much dust is kicked up into the atmosphere it's bad news for everyone. Such an event would put the planet into a *volcanic winter* and within a few years, instigate another ice age. Indeed, the recent ice age cited above (commencing about 75,000 years ago), was most likely due to yet another caldera blowing its formidable top. We can safely conclude Nature's pattern repeats itself, again and again.

Today's 2012 authors like to point out that Yellowstone is way past due for its next massive eruption. Its last detonation was 675,000 years ago – so it's about 75,000 years past due. We see signs that tell us so – like the base of Yellowstone Lake that bulges and flows water out at one end. The whole valley is rising from the expansion of the heated earth beneath it. It doesn't take an expert in volcanism to speculate that something big is about to happen.

Scientists debate the cause for the Yellowstone caldera. Some say it's the large amount of uranium lying beneath the park. Generating massive amounts of heat, this explanation suggests that Yellowstone is like a nuclear reactor ready to blow. However, that is the minority report.

In contrast, the majority believes that Yellowstone is one of the earth's so-called *hot spots*. This phenomenon is caused when heat from beneath the earth's *crust* comes to the surface – superheating the outer layer in that location.[6] Science suspects our earth has as many as 30 hot spots like Yellowstone. The reason we don't know about them is that mostly they hide deep in the oceans.

However, one oceanic hotspot we do know about is right in the middle of the Pacific Ocean. Over millions of years, the earth has slid across this hot spot and has literally *given rise* to the mountains that peak above the water there, becoming our national paradise, *Hawaii*. Today, the Big Island of Hawaii is sitting right on top of this hot spot, which is why its volcanoes normally spew and sputter so much lava.

As with the other scientific phenomena highlighted, only *recently has science learned the reason the earth acts the way it does.* It turns out the earth consists of a number of major and minor "plates" that move over the surface of the planet. This theory is known as *Plate Tectonics* (a theory so widely accepted that most experts *no longer consider it a theory* – see the figure below, which illustrates the various plates and their respective movements relative to one another).

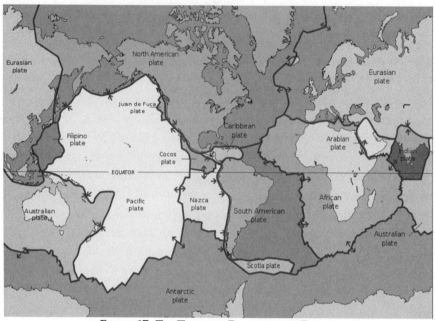

FIGURE 17 - THE TECTONIC PLATES OF THE EARTH

Although Yellowstone may be past due to blow, shouldn't we recognize that there is no way to tell whether it will simply continue to boil for another 10,000 or 20,000 years before "going off?"

Scientists admit that's so. On the other hand, it could also be ignited by any number of other catastrophes unique to this moment in time in which we live.

However, before we go there, let's review recent records of two other astounding eruptions.

The Eruption of Thera and the Destruction of the Minoans

The year is 1628 BC. An advanced civilization, the *Minoan*, is thriving on the Island of Crete. In some respects, its architecture is rather modern including running water and sewage. The Minoans decorate their halls with expressive frescoes showing an unusual and colorful perspective of life atypical of the period. It's an ideal setting. The weather is perfect. The Minoans have no standing army; peace reigns supreme. Leveraging their superior shipping capability, their economy thrives. They become *captains of trade* throughout the Mediterranean. Along with the Phoenicians and Egyptians, they are one of the few elite civilizations of the period. However, this is all about to change.

An island north of Crete, *Santorini*, also known as Thera, literally explodes creating a massive caldera in the aftermath. It sends mountains of dust into the atmosphere. It's so significant that scientists blame it for bringing frost to China in July. It may have been the explanation for the collapse of the Xia Dynasty. In the northern hemisphere, tree rings in California, Ireland, England, and Germany demonstrate the climatic effect (confirming the date of the explosion and its worldwide impact).

Just how powerful was the impact of the Santorini eruption? We can better grasp its immensity by comparing it to the details of the famous explosion of *Sumatra's Krakatoa in 1883*. The Krakatoa eruption was the first major event in history known by persons throughout the world *within a two-week time span* (thanks to advances in technology – specifically, the telegraph was working overtime since the transatlantic cable had been deployed on the ocean floor in the 1870's). Here is the summary of the Krakatoa explosion from Wikipedia:

> On August 27, a series of four huge explosions almost entirely destroyed the island. The explosions were so violent that they were heard 3,500 km (2,200 mi) away in Perth, Western Australia and the island of Rodrigues near Mauritius, 4,800 km (3,000 mi) away. The pressure wave from the final explosion was recorded on barographs around the world, which continued to register it up to 5 days after the explosion. The recordings show that the shockwave from the final explosion reverberated around the globe 7 times in total. Ash was propelled to a height of 80 km (50 mi). The combined effects of pyroclastic flows, volcanic ashes, and tsunamis had disastrous results in the region. The official death toll recorded by the Dutch authorities was 36,417, although some sources put the estimate at more than 120,000. There are numerous documented reports of groups of human skeletons floating across the Indian Ocean on rafts of volcanic pumice and washing up on the east coast of Africa, up to a year after the eruption... Weather patterns continued to be chaotic for years and temperatures did not return to normal until 1888.[7]

Scientists estimate the volcanic impact of *Thera's eruption* to be from *four to ten times more powerful than the explosion of Krakatoa*. The tidal wave created by the eruption of Thera may have topped 400 feet as it hit Crete devastating the Island and destroying the Minoan civilization. Despite their advanced technologies, their economic sophistication, and their artistic value to civilization, nature knows no favorites. Another culture simply bit the dust.

FIGURE 18 - 1888 LITHOGRAPH OF THE 1883 ERUPTION OF KRAKATOA

One team of scholars suggests that the survivors (which boarded a few remaining ships and sailed to the mainland) can be traced to Gaza in Palestine. This group of survivors thrived there, becoming the Philistines, ancient rivals to the Jews.[8] The Bible appears to verify this fact (*see Jeremiah 47:4*). While a fascinating subject in its own right, it's way off track for our study, so we'll have to move on.

For our purposes, the point is that North Americans have no guarantee that *what happened to the Minoans won't happen to us.* We have the world's biggest caldera sitting in our own backyard and it's primed and ready to blow. As we have just seen, recent history foreshadows what the explosion of Yellowstone could mean to us. Failure to prepare for such an event only makes matters worse *if* the inevitable happens in our lifetime.

Solar Cycles, the Solar Maximum and 2012

Even more portentous, the well-documented and frightening natural phenomenon that could affect the entire planet has to do with the natural source of all life – the sun. As most everyone knows, sunspots are magnetic storms. The storms come and go, but follow a pattern. Every eleven years the sun goes through a magnetic pole reversal. By tracking sunspots, we detect where the sun is in this cycle and predict with some level of certainty when storms will be more prominent or will dissipate. The National Science Foundation issued a warning in 2009 that the effect of the next solar maximum on our planet in 2012 may be 50% stronger than the last one – a cycle concluding around 2000, which was a real jackhammer. The 2012 solar maximum could even be stronger than the most famous such occurrence of 1859, the worst on record.[9]

Here is a description of what that one was like:

> From August 28, 1859 until September 2, 1859, numerous sunspots and solar flares were observed on the sun. Just before noon on September 1, the British astronomer Richard Carrington observed the largest flare, which caused a massive coronal mass ejection (CME), to travel directly toward Earth, a journey of 18 hours. This is remarkable because such a journey normally takes three to four days. It moved so quickly because an earlier CME had cleared its way.
> On September 1–2, 1859 the largest recorded geomagnetic storm occurred, causing the failure of telegraph systems all over Europe and North America. Auroras were seen around the world, most notably over the Caribbean; also noteworthy were those over the Rocky Mountains that were so bright, the glow awoke gold miners, who began preparing breakfast because they thought it was morning (emphasis mine).[10]

Another factor that comes into play here is the weakening of the earth's magnetic field, aka the *magnetosphere*. We know from measurements dating back over 200 years that the magnetic field is at the weakest point since we started taking measurements. We recognize that the North Pole is moving too – from Canada toward Siberia. What is most disturbing is that we've identified in recent decades how holes in the magnetic field have opened up, with a particularly horrid one in the South Atlantic. Keep in mind, the value of the magnetic field to life on earth is its shielding of harmful protons and other radiation from the sun. As a result, when we detect holes in our *protective covering,* we should take whatever precautions we can.

Another factor that comes into play here is the weakening of the earth's magnetic field, aka the *magnetosphere*. We know from measurements dating back started taking measurements. We recognize that the North Pole is moving too – from Canada toward Siberia. What is most disturbing is that we've identified in recent decades how holes in the magnetic field have opened up, with a particularly horrid one in the South Atlantic. Keep in mind, the value of the magnetic field to life on earth is its shielding of harmful protons and other radiation from the sun. As a result, when we detect holes in our *protective covering,* we should take whatever precautions we can.

Experts in the field suggest that our world could be in for an enormously disrupting experience. If severe enough, the radiation of the sun can literally *fry our electrical grid.* The possibility looms we could witness potential power outages on the scale never before seen. This concern has been very much on the minds of scientists for some time – they are now careful observers of this activity.

Some years ago (1980), NASA sent a special satellite into space, *SolarMax,* as part of the *Solar Maximum Mission.* Unfortunately, encountering severe problems, NASA couldn't repair the satellite and so it burned up upon re-entry in 1989. Fortunately, there are several other satellites are in orbit today which monitor solar activity and help sci-

25-Feb-2007 13:50

FIGURE 19 - MOON IN FRONT OF THE SUN, TAKEN BY STEREO-B SATELLITE ON 2-25-2007

entists better understand solar processes. One is nicknamed SOHO (Solar Heliospheric Observatory) operated by the High Altitude Observatory (HAO) and is part of the National Center for Atmospheric Research (NCAR), funded by the National Science Foundation. NASA plans for these satellites to provide an *early warning system*; but the question is, "Will the warning come soon enough?"

As mentioned above, we label the specific event we fear the most, a *Coronal Mass Ejection* (CME). CMEs are the giant solar flares we see released from the sun, aka, *prominences*. When CMEs take place, they create energy waves. These waves push particles outward, accelerating them at great speeds.

Occasionally, a CME creates a particle storm approaching earth at nearly the speed-of-light. When this happens, depending upon how large the CME launching the particle storm is, we had better duck.

As Lawrence Joseph points out, some CMEs, if directed right at earth, *could be planet killers in their own right*. What is particularly worrisome, as Joseph comments, is that some of the largest CMEs ever recorded occurred during 2005, which was the most recent "Solar Minimum" – when the sun is supposed to be at it quietest. If such troublesome CMEs happened at Solar Minimum, what will they be like when we reach Solar Maximum in 2012? Furthermore, what will this mean if the earth's magnetic shield continues to weaken?

In a nutshell: We could be in for real trouble.

Joseph connects the wild weather that transpired during September 2005 to solar activity. This is not wild conjecture on his part. While the sun was literally exploding with CMEs, the earth was absorbing this energy and generating some of the strongest hurricanes on record, notably Katrina that devastated New Orleans. Joseph quotes one Sami Solanki, of the Max Planck Institute for Solar System Research, "Except possibly for a few brief peaks, the Sun is more active currently than at any time in the past 11,000 years."[11] What will this mean for potential killer storms in 2012? To say the least, we had better batten down the hatches.

As hinted earlier, the possibility exists that the sun might warm up the earth so much it could lead to all kinds of collateral consequences, particularly the shifting of the tectonic plates (i.e., earthquakes), and the possible detonation of caldrons like Yellowstone. Lawrence refers to these events (one after another, each giving rise to the next), as "the 2012 domino effect."

There seems to be little controversy amongst scientists that the sun is throwing an uncharacteristic tantrum, posing a real threat to our modern wired-world. Science knows it's for real. To quote Tom Hanks from the movie, *Apollo 13,* "Houston, we have a problem."

The fact that not more is being made of the potential destructive effects on our power grid, our coastal cities, and our very way of life (which is so dependent upon centralized electricity), makes me wonder if perhaps there isn't a lot of wishful thinking going on in governments, utility companies, and amongst solar scientists. But if we aren't careful, we just might wind up in the dark – literally – requiring years to bring things back on line.

Then again, maybe there is a lot of prep work underway and the average American just doesn't know about it.

Conspiracy Theory – Underground Building Programs

In mid-January 2010, I watched a first-run episode of Jesse Ventura's television program, *Conspiracy Theory.* The subject was 2012 and the cover-up of a secret plan to build massive underground facilities to protect the government, precisely due to this threat. I saw many different sources interviewed including two authors mentioned in this book, Patrick Geryl and Lawrence Joseph. During their interviews, these authors gave Jesse the *2012 executive summary.* With his consciousness duly raised, he sent his team into action.

One of the staff was the guest of the administrator responsible for the Colorado *Cheyenne Mountain facility,* already in place for many years (created initially to protect the military chain of command in the event of nuclear war). The walk-through of the facility was low-key. My suspicion is that the *administrator* willingly (and literally) opened the doors without concern, since he was thinking, "the threat is over" (after all, we won the Cold War). However, the *interviewer* wasn't thinking "Cold War" but *2012.* Consequently, Jesse's guy asked probing questions and received unsettling answers. Most notably, we heard how the U.S. Government maintains the facility for a select few; should anyone else crash the party, "they will pay a heavy price." Underscoring the threat, the camera swung around as the administrator uttered these words, portraying the facility's heavily armed guards.

Later in the program, Ventura conducted another interview himself with a construction contractor converting missile silos in Kansas into upscale condominiums, in order to "weather the sun storm in 2012" (this project is being privately funded through wealthy individuals). The scale of the activity reported was remarkable. The contractor spoke cautiously during the interview; yet he made it clear there were many more building programs underway (and *underground*) that weren't just for the rich and famous. He felt one project would be of particular interest to Jesse. He recommended that the *Conspiracy Theory* team investigate the strange decor at a nearby airport that he refused to name, but which Jesse quickly determined was Denver International Airport (DIA). What a story this turned out to be.

The Colorado government (no doubt with matching U.S. funds) built the airport in 1995 on 34,000 acres (53 square miles). Budgeted at $1.5B, it was brought in over budget at $5.2B. Many call DIA the country's "Most Inconvenient Airport" (MIA).[12] Smaller than Denver's old Stapleton Airport with fewer gates and runways, one wonders: "Why in the world was it built?" If we buy what the conspiracy theorists are selling, *it's because DIA sits atop a vast underground city and military base.* One Internet site, *Anomalies-Unlimited.com/Denver_airport*, goes into considerable detail. Their commentary relies upon a 1996 interview with Alex Christopher (a woman), apparently in the know about the whole project:

> Well, the gentleman that I was dealing with, Phil Schneider [*SDW - now dead supposedly from a suspicious suicide*] said that during the last year of construction they were connecting the underground airport system to the deep underground base. He told me that there was at least an eight-level deep underground base there, and that there was a 4.5 square mile underground city and an 88.5 square-mile base underneath the airport. It is very unusual that they would allot a 50 square-mile area on the surface at which to locate an airport in the middle of nowhere unless they really planned to use it for something very unusual later.
>
> There is a 10-mile, 4-line highway out to this airport, and there is nothing out there in between the airport and Denver. Not even a service station, at least in September 1995. The people in Denver are really upset with the fact that this airport went in the way it did. There was this fellow who wrote a book in which he made the statement that they had a copy of an audio tape on which a Denver city official was talking with people from the CIA, and that he was paid 1.5 million dollars to allow the "airport" to be built, no matter what it took. It appears that there was a lot more interest in getting the airport built from just officials in the Denver area. They plan on using this facility for something else other than just landing planes.

Cut and pasted across the Internet over the past 15 years, this interview is now an important part of the long-lived and notorious DIA conspiracy folklore. However, not everyone is so easily persuaded. An article in 2007 counters the conspiracy findings since Christopher and Schneider were both conspiracy theorists long before they began poking around at DIA.[13]

Nevertheless, there are some weird twists and turns that we dare not overlook. Most notable are the bizarre murals at the airport that provide ghastly images of children in coffins, dead animals, cities in flame, and soldiers in gas masks. Additionally, the main terminal sports a time capsule topped with a capstone describing the "New World Airport Commission" that contributed to the development of the airport. Then there is that intriguing Masonic symbol on the capstone and the fact officials decided to call the main terminal area, "The Great Hall," reminiscent of the meeting places for Masons in their respective lodges around the world. Oh boy.

Figure 20 - Capstone Commemorating Completion of Denver International Airport in 1994

Government officials really should be smarter. They ought to know how certain actions are interpreted, like showcasing a Masonic symbol on a capstone, authorizing dreadful artwork illustrating Doomsday, and choosing provocative names (referencing the *New World Order* and other Masonic terminology), which can't help but egg on the notion of conspiracy. Whether true in whole, in part, or not at all, the officials at Denver International

Airport shouldn't be surprised the *DIA Underground* is the subject of so many rumors.

At the very least, any team of leaders should realize that *a conspiracy works best when it's kept a **secret***. Parading it in public isn't advisable. Moreover, if you aren't conspiring to take over the world, you should also recognize how easy it is for the court of public opinion to convict you, especially if the allegation is nothing more than guilt by association, or in this case, guilt by *appearance*.

So is there really a conspiracy at DIA? I very much doubt there is. But I must admit that officials there did their very best to spawn the conspiracy hubbub. Indeed, they generated their own form of *"implausible* deniability," agitating the conspiratorial tumult. And for that, they have only themselves to blame.

Shooting Stars and "When Worlds Collide"

We pointed out at the outset of this chapter that collisions of asteroids on Planet Earth aren't imaginary. They happen every day. In addition, when big ones come into play, it means bad news for life on earth.

Perhaps the most powerful recent *close encounter* (with an asteroid) was the *Tunguska* event on June 30, 1908. Tunguska lies four hours east of St. Petersburg in central Siberia. Something sinister devastated Tunguska, which generated heat amounting to 25,000° Kelvin. The blast leveled trees for 1,000 square miles. It also caused a phenomenon known as *bright nights* – which is literally that. Even very far away from the event, perhaps thousands of miles, nights can be so bright photographers can take pictures out of doors, at midnight, without supplemental lighting. Experts believe the cause is either dust or water vapor injected into the atmosphere from a calamitous event somewhere on the globe. In the case of Tunguska, Londoners experienced this *bright night phenomenon*.

Nevertheless, just how big of an event was it? Calculations by scientists suggest that an object, no more than 200 feet wide, was to blame. While size is always a factor, even more important is the speed of the object. The object, whatever it was, entered the earth's atmosphere traveling at 34,000 MPH. About five miles above the earth's surface, it exploded, creating a massive shock and heat wave in all directions. The explosion scorched trees directly beneath it, but left the trees standing straight; whereas emanating outward from the fireball's center, it pushed trees to the ground in all directions with their leaves or pine needles stripped away. Scientists estimate the power of the blast was equivalent to 15 megatons – which equals 1,000 Hiroshima A-bombs.

Research on the nature of the object causing this event continues 100 years later. Concerning the object, there have been many incredible explanations to account for all the amazing empirical data resulting from the event.

One theory: It was a rare giant lightning ball. Another, it was nuclear explosion *caused by an alien spacecraft*.

However, the hypothesis cited by most scientists contends "Tunguska" was a metallic asteroid or an old comet which had lost its ice. Research completed by Italian scholars in the 1990's, found traces of carbon in tree rings from 1908 – a type of carbon that doesn't occur naturally on our planet. (Could it have been *Fullerenes*?) Consequently, science is growing increasingly satisfied that typical solar system phenomena explain the event without recourse to the fantastic. Of course, not everyone is so easily convinced. That's why the debate rages to this day.

How often does this kind of thing occur? One scientist interviewed about the event suggested that (1) basketball size objects hit our planet daily; (2) Volkswagen size objects hit the planet once every six months; (3) Tunguska size objects hit the planet once a millennium.

My review of the data would suggest that a Tunguska-event happens more often than that – only *once in a thousand years* is a very low estimate. Given that water and ice cover three-fourths of the world's surface, it seems logical that in the last 5,000 years, we wouldn't always notice an impact of this magnitude because it didn't hit land. After all, it's only in the last fifty years that we would detect such an impact, even if it occurred in a remote ocean location.

The verdict is this: While Tunguska-like events don't happen often, depending on precisely where the object smacks us, the effects could be so devastating that millions of people might be annihilated in one momentous bang. Doubtless to say, the documentation of the Tunguska event draws attention to the possibility of a repeat performance – and the concern that the next time we get hit, it won't be in a remote wilderness where no one gets hurt.

To sharpen the point, we know that Scientists today are charting about 5,000 objects (mostly asteroids) that orbit the sun. This computerized charting program ensures that we aren't currently on a path to collide with one of these objects any time soon. Then again, the objects we track are less than 20% of the ones we know are out there.

Verifying how mindful we are today of this possibility, check out this article printed on Yahoo's news service (from the Associated Press) on December 31, 2009. We read the following:

Russia may send spacecraft to knock away asteroid
By VLADIMIR ISACHENKOV, Associated Press Writer

MOSCOW – Russia's space agency chief said Wednesday a spacecraft may be dispatched to knock a large asteroid off course and reduce the chances of earth impact, even though U.S. scientists say such a scenario is unlikely. Anatoly Perminov told Golos Rossii radio the space agency would hold a meeting soon to assess a mission to Apophis. He said his agency might eventually invite NASA, the European Space Agency, the Chinese space agency, and others to join the project. When the 270-meter (885-foot) asteroid was first discovered in 2004, astronomers estimated its chances of smashing into Earth in its first flyby, in 2029, at 1-in-37.

Further studies have ruled out the possibility of an impact in 2029, when the asteroid is expected to come no closer than 18,300 miles (29,450 kilometers) from Earth's surface, but they indicated a small possibility of a hit on subsequent encounters. NASA had put the chances that Apophis could hit Earth in 2036 as 1-in-45,000. In October, after researchers recalculated the asteroid's path, the agency changed its estimate to 1-in-250,000. NASA said another close encounter in 2068 will involve a 1-in-330,000 chance of impact. "It wasn't anything to worry about before. Now it's even less so," said Steve Chesley, an astronomer with the Near Earth Object Program at NASA's Jet Propulsion Laboratory. Without mentioning NASA's conclusions, Perminov said that he heard from a scientist that Apophis is getting closer and may hit the planet. "I don't remember exactly, but it seems to me it could hit the Earth by 2032... People's lives are at stake. We should pay several hundred million dollars and build a system that would allow us to prevent a collision, rather than sit and wait for it to happen and kill hundreds of thousands of people," Perminov said.

Along these lines, there is one very frightening prediction made by those doing Bible Code research (and willing to speculate on what could be in store for us in 2012). It just happens to be the prediction of a *massive comet or asteroid impact*. According to these sources, there are two scenarios in the Bible Code. One code structure specifies that the "earth will be struck by a comet" and "the earth will be annihilated." Happily, a second scenario suggests a divine intervention – "the comet will be torn to pieces" before it strikes the earth. Both of these statements are adjacent to 2012 in the encoded text. Does this mean we should take this warning seriously?

Consider this: The Bible isn't the only religious text generating comet collision speculation.

Planet X and the Kolbrin Bible

In addition to the somewhat vanilla impact theory in the Bible Code, is another that goes *way out there* beyond the orbit of the Pluto. We know this theory as the existence of "Planet X" or Planet *Nibiru*. Supposedly, there is a 12th planet (it used to be the 10th; it depends on how many real planets and dwarf planets one considers). This planet has a highly elongated elliptical orbit and only comes near to earth (and the sun) every 3,600 years (which equals one Nibiru solar year). When it does decide to visit, it wreaks havoc on the sun and the earth due to its proximity and dramatic gravitational effect. The theory is, Planet X is on its return voyage and will make its unwelcomed, surprise appearance in 2012.

A notorious source first predicted this mode of doom in 2003. The prophet was Nancy Lieder, host of *Zetatalk.com,* and a self-professed channeler (of extra-terrestrial or spirit guides). She received this announcement from "an intelligent entity" in the *Zeta Reticulli* star system (apparently, a very chatty location in the heavens). Claiming the earth would stop rotating on its axis for almost six days, Leider predicted this would culminate in a *gravitational pole shift* – the earth's polarity would reverse (as mentioned before, a theory common to 2012 authors). Nevertheless, when this failed to happen in 2003, she indicated it had been her intent to fool the establishment via this hoax (akin to the somewhat recent razzing phrase, "made you look"). Therefore, while the poles didn't shift as predicted, *her story did.* The real date to anticipate is 2010.[14]

The Kolbrin Bible

21st Century Master Edition

FIGURE 21 - THE KOLBRIN BIBLE

The most noted spokesperson for the idea of Planet Nibiru is the author and expert of Sumeria tablets, *Zecharia Sitchin.* His major book is entitled, *The 12th Planet.* He connects the idea of Nibiru with its mention on Sumerian (Babylonian) tablets from ancient times (specifically the *Enuma Elish, the creation* account of ancient Sumer). His view is that Nibiru's last visit was 600 BC and the next cycle around the sun won't happen until *one thousand years from now*. Sitchin distances himself from Lieder and other doomsday alarmists preferring instead to support the theory of *ancient astronauts*. Apparently, he regards those that *argue for the existence of extraterrestrials* (and their helping hand) to be more credible *than apocalyptic prophets*. Well, as they say, "we are known by the company we keep." His story is also associated with another ancient source of *wisdom*, hidden from most of us until the past few decades, known as the *Kolbrin Bible*. We read the following synopsis:

> Millennia ago, Egyptian, and Celtic authors recorded prophetic warnings for the future and their harbinger signs are now converging on 2012. These predications are contained in *The Kolbrin Bible*, a secular wisdom text... Nearly as big as the *King James Bible*, this 3600-year old text warns of an imminent, Armageddon-like conflict with radical Islam, but this is not the greatest threat. The authors of *The Kolbrin Bible* predict an end to life as we know it, by a celestial event. It will be the return of a massive space object, in a long elliptical orbit around our sun. Known to the Egyptians and Hebrews as the "Destroyer," the Celts later called it the "Frightener."
>
> *Manuscripts 3:4-6. When blood drops upon the Earth, the Destroyer will appear, and mountains will open up and belch forth fire and ashes. Trees will be destroyed and all living things engulfed. Waters will be swallowed up by the land and seas will boil. The Heavens will burn brightly and redly; there will be a copper hue over the face of the land, 'followed by a day of darkness. A new moon will appear and break up and fall. The people will scatter in madness. They will hear the trumpet and battle cry of the Destroyer and will seek refuge within dens in the Earth. Terror will eat away their hearts, and their courage will flow from them like water from a broken pitcher. They will be eaten in the flames of wrath and consumed by the breath of the Destroyer.*
>
> *Manuscripts 3:10. In those days, men will have the Great Book before them; wisdom will be revealed; the few will be gathered for the stand; it is the hour of trial. The dauntless ones will survive; the stouthearted will not go down to destruction. The Destroyer is also known today as Wormwood, Nibiru, Planet X and Nemesis. There are also troubling prophetic correlations to the future predictions of Mother Shipton's "Fiery Dragon" and the "Red Comet" warning of the Mayan Calendar 2012. While these future predictions are uncertain at best, is it possible for us to know about the Destroyer's previous fly-bys with a great degree of certainty.[15]*

According to experts on the subject, the *Kolbrin Bible* originated in Egypt. Many disillusioned devotees searched for this ancient Egyptian wisdom despite the decisive defeat Moses and his Hebrew God, Yahweh, dished out to their "parochial gods." Years later, the Celts in Ireland nurtured it (as they did many other ancient books, which survived the destruction of Alexandria, Egypt, and later Rome in the 4th century). Consequently, we must ask the question, "How valuable is the 'word' of such gods, so soundly defeated by Yahweh and Moses?" (A rout we see recounted in Cecil B. DeMille's classic, *The Ten Commandments*)

Despite questions about the reliability of these sources, there appears to be enough reason for worry that several folks wrote a survival guide specifically for 2012, when Planet X does its dirty work on Planet Earth. As noted earlier, some theorize this Nibiru notion actually refers to a brown dwarf star, supposedly our sun's invisible twin. Recall *the Police* song referenced earlier (*Invisible Sun*) and the Hindu concept of this second sun as the source of wisdom for humankind (See *Chapter Two*).

Since Sitchin and other's theorize that beings who inhabit Planet X are destined to become our gods upon their return,[16] it should be clear that we have left the world of science far be-

FIGURE 22 – PLANET X FORECAST AND 2012 SURVIVAL GUIDE

hind and are now in the midst of "*UFOology*." We will encounter much more thinking like this in the chapters ahead.

This particular theory of Doomsday aggressively leverages such *pseudo-science* in an attempt to substantiate what many believe is the *most outlandish 2012 apocalyptic scenario yet devised*. It's no surprise that scientists take exception to this theory, calling it *the most aggravating example of pseudo-science in popular culture today*. David Morrison, a Senior Scientist at NASA's *Astrobiology Institute* says:

> He receives 20–25 emails a week about the impending arrival of Nibiru; some frightened, others angry and naming him as part of the conspiracy to keep the truth of the impending apocalypse from the public. Half of these

emails are from outside the US. "Planetary scientists are being driven to distraction by Nibiru," notes science writer Govert Schilling, "And it is not surprising; you devote so much time, energy and creativity to fascinating scientific research, and find yourself on the tracks of the most amazing and interesting things, and all the public at large is concerned about is some crackpot theory about clay tablets, god-astronauts and a planet that doesn't exist." Morrison states that he hopes that the non-arrival of Nibiru could serve as a teaching moment for the public, instructing them on 'rational thought and baloney detection', but doubts that will happen.[17]

Charlatans seek Science's blessing on many a hypothesis; but we must be especially wary of such sleight of hand when the theory is as way out as this one appears to be. *Planet X stretches my credulity to the breaking point.* I might lay awake stressing over comets and meteors, but I doubt Nibiru will generate many night sweats.

Catastrophism – How the Earth Shapes Up

The continued discovery of so many new catastrophes may call upon the evolutionary scientific community to make a major scientific *reversal* – a reversal that has to do with an old controversy between two schools of geological thought on what accounts for *the physical formation and structure of the earth today.*

Two centuries ago, those "doing" Geology argued that the single most important event that shaped the earth was the *Great Flood of Noah.* Geology labels this school of thought *Catastrophism.* This term refers to the theory that a great catastrophe (*The Flood*) formed the earth in the manner that we find it today. However, with the arrival of the *Enlightenment* and the work of Charles Darwin (who begat evolution as the only accepted model for creation and earth science), the Catastrophism *school* not only lost the debate but also became a laughing stock in the modern scientific community.

Geologists label the virtual school holding their view, *Uniformitarianism.* Those who subscribe to this theory believe "the present is the key to the past." Simply stated, that which we see operating today, *small incremental changes working very slowly through millions of years,* gives rise to the world in which we find ourselves. According to this point of view, *uniformity,* the consistent application of processes we witness today – working alongside evolution – is nature's only *dynamo* explaining both origins and change.

What's ironic, given how recently science has unearthed example after example *where a catastrophe dramatically affects the state of our planet,* is that Uniformitarianism appears unfazed. Nevertheless, the scientific findings seem inescapable: *Catastrophes, not just uniform processes, influence the shape of our world.* In making this point, it isn't my intent to argue Evolution and Uniformitarianism are necessarily 100% wrong – that's a very different question. But there is now strong science that proclaims them *incomplete.* Frequent catastrophes are a fact.[18] They dramatically shape the world we live in.

Chapter Summary

So, does science predict Doomsday? It certainly doesn't specify one and only one particular date. Nevertheless, it frequently raises the "Threat Level to Orange." It provides examples and explanations of what has happened in our world, which can and will happen again. Timeframes may be no more than probabilities, but sometimes those probabilities are high. *Betting that nothing bad will happen is going to be a losing bet.* Evidence of Doomsdays past is impossible to ignore. From this perspective, Science predicts *many Doomsdays.*

So let's summarize what we have covered in this chapter. We have seen:

- Clear historical examples where enormous catastrophes have happened that have reshaped our world.

- Proof that earth has been the target of countless objects falling from the sky. When these collisions happen, major changes influence the earth for hundreds if not thousands of years.

- Mounting evidence that massive earthquakes and volcanic eruptions might occur at any moment. Additionally, other out-of-the-ordinary factors could ignite these latent catastrophes in our lifetime.

- One such extraordinary factor is *solar activity.* The sun is more active now than at any time in recorded history. Climate change is happening (*regardless of whether humans and carbon dioxide emissions do or don't make it worse*) creating massive storms (like Katrina) that will devastate regions of our world more often now than in recent decades past. Depending upon the seriousness of this activity, combined with changes in our "Magnetosphere," Doomsday could happen across all of the planet or to at least major sections of the globe in 2012.

- We are more prone to dramatic disruptions now because of our reliance on the power grid for almost every aspect of what we consider modern life – this has dramatic political implications.

- Science is now aware that asteroids or comets are likely to strike us; thankfully, it is also now capable of taking steps to help avert such events. Scientists don't argue against this possibility and don't keep it secret.

- Religious enthusiasts often abuse and misuse Science in an attempt to prove a closely held view about Doomsday. However, religious views that incorporate empirical data don't "contaminate the data" tainting it unscientific just because such views have religious implications. They may in fact provide an explanation scientists lack that can be investigated *scientifically*.

Curiously, we have seen how *science has discovered much of our knowledge of mini-doomsdays in just the last 30 years or so.* Science continues to enlighten us and rewrite the science books my generation used in the 1960's and 1970's.

That being so, I feel compelled to ask, *"what else will science discover to clue us in to what could actually happen to us in the immediate years ahead?"* No doubt, over the next decade or two experts will reveal many more facts of surprising scientific and historical significance. With the advancement of the Internet and its search capabilities, we obtain, store, and make information available at exponentially increasing speeds. Technology advances more and more rapidly – the result is we must rewrite the textbooks as we go. The lesson learned: We had better not grow too comfortable with any cherished theory. All our learning seems subject to change. Science is teaching us anew *to keep an open mind and take little for granted.*

Finally, Science also demonstrates that when it comes to Doomsday, it doesn't take a backseat to any fear mongering prophet. Its predictions are not only believable; they are as frightening as any fictional apocalypse we could imagine. And it just so happens, even the skeptic will find lots of reasons to believe that they are true.

Notes

[1] These extinction events occurred during the last one billion years of planet earth's natural history. Some portentously suggest that another "great extinction event" is long overdue.

[2] This was the condition responsible for the dramatic ice storm featured in the disaster film, *The Day After Tomorrow*, mentioned in Chapter 1.

[3] "A hypothesized *Younger Dryas*, interpreted to have occurred 12,900 years ago in North America, is purported to have initiated the Younger Dryas cooling and population bottleneck or near extinction of the peoples responsible for the Clovis." See *wikipedia.org/wiki/Younger_Dryas*.

[4] Which also explains why it didn't "leave a lasting mark," so to speak. When the snow melts, the snowman is history.

[5] Note that this is about the same time alternate history buffs indicate that a cataclysm destroyed Atlantis. I don't agree with their thesis, but I think it fair to point out.

[6] The crust is a layer of rock 20 to 30 miles thick, sitting on top of the earth's mantle, more than a thousand miles thick, surrounding the core at the center of the earth.

[7] See http://en.wikipedia.org/wiki/Krakatoa

[8] They also point out several passages in the Old Testament that seem to corroborate this as well. See Butler, Alan and Dafoe, Stephen, *The Knights Templar Revealed*, Barnes & Noble, New York 1999.

[9] Some scientists believe that the worst sunspot storm we know in human history about was 500 years ago, but we simply don't have enough data to corroborate how serious its impact was.

[10] See http://en.wikipedia.org/wiki/1859_solar_superstorm.

[11] It's curious how the timing seems to coincide with the destruction of Atlantis.

[12] Dave Kopel, Research Director at the Independent Institute of Golden Colorado had this to say about the airport: "But the real blame for all the design flaws at America's Most Inconvenient Airport lies with former Mayor Pena, the mastermind of MIA, and currently the US Secretary of Transportation. The air traffic problems at convenient Stapleton Airport in Denver (now closed, to prevent competition with MIA) could have been solved by building an additional runway on vacant land at the Rocky Mountain Arsenal (an abandoned federal chemical weapons facility that adjoins Stapleton)... Transportation Secretary Pena calls Denver International "the crown jewel in the nation's transportation system." From a distance, the airport's roof looks more like a circus tent than a crown. Visually

intriguing as the roof is, it doesn't work; when it rains, the rain runs off the roof and onto people standing on sidewalks outside the airport.

The new airport, like its roof, was never designed for the convenience of the traveling public. Instead, DIA was Federico Pena's monument to himself, an illustration of why future airports should be built by private enterprise, rather than by ambitious politicians spending someone else's money."

See *http://www.i2i.org/main/article.php?article_id=501.*

[13] See www.westword.com/photoGallery/?gallery=548937&position=2.

[14] Any takers on a bet that she will retract this prediction in 2010 and push it back to 2012, in order to fall in line with everyone else predicting our doom then?

[15] Taken from the web site where this book is marketed *(http://kolbrin.com).*

[16] Sitchin calls the inhabitants *the Anunnuki.*

[17] See *http://en.wikipedia.org/wiki/Nibiru_collision.*

[18] Therefore, I would hasten to add that the Bible's Flood might not be a myth, just as Catastrophism contends. The Bible can deal with scientific facts too. We may find evidence of the Flood of Noah in the geologic column. Perhaps we should be mindful that just because an incident (albeit earth shattering) is found in the Bible, it doesn't imply that the tale is only legend. The Bible's account can explain empirical data we detect in the world. Catastrophes do happen. Science has proven it so. If the Bible records such events as *history* (and we discover the science to back it up), this may not fully validate the Bible, but neither should we automatically dismiss an account (in the name of science) just because of where we found it. That would actually be very unscientific.

Chapter 6:
End Time Prophecies
of the Americas

Buried beneath the statue the answer hides
Enduring throughout the ages, the transmitter lies
Once the chambers open the signal will be sent
To another world... Far beyond the stars
We were warned of this coming so long ago
Immortal secrets... man shouldn't know
Entering a realm where we just don't belong
We called them and they're coming
Don't open till Doomsday
Destruction's not far away
Don't open till Doomsday
You may not like what you find inside.

The Misfits

The Mayan Calendar and 2012

The Maya are rock stars. Today we see them as great astronomers and seers into our future, resulting from their amazing knowledge of the stars and their ability to develop a solar calendar that is actually slightly more accurate than our own (recall that ours is the *Gregorian* calendar, characterized by having a February 29 every fourth year, the so-called *leap year*).

The popularity of the Maya has grown, most experts believe, because José Argüelles and Terrence McKenna evangelized the western world during the 1980's and 1990's. Since that time, there have been a slew of authors joining the cause. Nowadays, one needs an abacus (or better) to count the number of titles on the subject of 2012 and the Maya.

Perhaps the greatest debate between the experts centers on *whether 2012 is in fact Doomsday or just a moment of human transformation.* Were the Maya truly wise men – spiritual gurus whose advice we should take to heart? Did their methods warrant so much attention as they've received in the past two decades? Can we trust what they tell us about the future? More to the point, *why did 2012 become the point of debate*? What caused the Maya to pick this date?

From the research of John Major Jenkins, perhaps the most capable scholar of the 2012 authors popular today, it appears that the Maya operated with other calendars set to a different "clock" until they discerned that the Sun would "enter the dark rift" of the Milky Way at a future time. Their astronomical methodology correctly indicated that such an event is very rare. However, the symbolism of this event drove their decision to reset the long-count calendar and synchronize the other calendars accordingly.

To them, the *dark rift* was an opening to the underworld. When the Sun aligns with this spot and blocks the earth from its supposed influence, something dark and foreboding will happen. Is it possible that the Maya thought the Sun would slip into the dark rift and cease supplying its life-giving energy?

Today's interpreters suppose there is an energy emanating from the *galactic center* and our disconnect with this power source is the trigger that sets 2012 planetary behaviors into motion – whatever those actions finally prove to be.

FIGURE 23 - KUKULKAN PYRAMID

Whether or not this is the case, it does appear that the moment is unique. The Maya recognized this eclipse happened only once every 26,000 years (precisely, 25,630). Adjusting their calendars accordingly, the Ha'ab (solar), the Tzolk'in (sacred), the *Calendar Round* (synchronizing lunar and solar calendars every 52 years), with this long-count calendar of 5,126 years (and its *great cycle* of about 26,000 years), they determined this auspicious event would occur (on our Gregorian calendar date) of December 21, 2012.

Jenkins believes that Maya created the long count calendar based specifically upon the knowledge of *precession* (the spinning of the earth's axis one time around, which is the cause for this 26,000 year cycle). This learning grew in part from knowledge already cultivated through the *Olmecs* (predecessors to the Maya) plus additional Mayan observation thereafter for at least another 200 years. Jenkins estimates that the Maya completed resetting the long count calendar around 250 BC. Created in 37 BC, the oldest, extant *stele which used the long count dates* is about 2,000 years old.[1] As one would guess, most of these stone pillars are weathered to the point that finding any older legible stele is highly unlikely.

Many critics of the Maya obsession typically challenge the idea that the Maya prophesied anything special regarding the meaning of this moment. "It's just a calendar." Even though I might be inclined to dismiss the Mayan prophecies (since they could threaten "my" Christian cosmology), this *conclusion seems rather ignorant*.

Even a modest amount of study shows that there is an inseparable linkage of the calendar and the meaning assigned to it. Like so many other cultures in ancient times, the Maya were convinced that *to understand what happens on earth, we must appreciate what goes on in the heavens*. In the succinct words of the legendary Egyptian magician and mystic, *Hermes Trismegistus*: "As above, so below." Just a few examples to make the point:

- Each time period *cycles* – past events, happening on certain dates (set by the movement of heavenly bodies), become predictions of similar events on the future "anniversary" (be the length of the period "months," "years," or hundreds of years) – for the Maya, time is a *cyclic* phenomenon. Furthermore, *the cycle is inherently prophetic.*

- Every day of the 20-day "week" of the Tzolk'in had an associated name along with a number of 1 to 13, representing each 20-day period of the 360-day year. This enabled specific implications for divining events, 360 different markers, corresponding to the Tzolk'in days.

- Parents named their children after the day on which they were born – and they believed the spiritual (astrological) value of this day would influence the nature or temperament and future of the child.

- The *Kukulkan* Pyramid at *Chichen Itza* is an obvious "calendar monument" consisting of four sides each with 91 steps and the final step on top (common to all sides) completes the 365 total steps. The terraces divide into 18 segments equaling the number of months in the Ha'ab calendar. The axes running through the northwest and southwest corners are oriented toward the rising sun at the summer solstice and setting sun at the winter solstice. Today, 50,000 people annually witness the slithering serpent come down from heaven as the shadows on these days create this image (the *balustrades* – decorative railings – at the bottom resemble heads of a serpent).

- Mayan destiny connects to the return of *Kukulkan* – the feathered serpent (aka *Quetzalcoatl* of the Olmecs). The return of this *great white brother* will come at the conclusion of the Long Count (December 21, 2012). The ceremony of the slithering serpent on the solstices is to reaffirm the reappearance of Kukulkan in 2012.

So is there any debating this dating? Actually there is.

Carl Johan Calleman, another Mayan scholar, believes the end date should be October 28, 2011, instead of December 21, 2012, claiming that Mayan priests made an adjustment of 420 days in the calendar around 600 AD (adjusting for an apparent error). He based his alternative date upon the study of this same Kukulkan Pyramid.

Others point out (and Jenkins stipulates to this), that the correct timing of the galactic eclipse was in fact 1999. Jenkins strongly contends that the Maya did set their calendar to expire on December 21, 2012 precisely because of the galactic eclipse. However, Jenkins dismisses linking the expected transformation *only to this one day*; it occurs throughout the entire period of galactic alignment from 1983 to 2019.[2] As we've seen, given the history of other Doomsday prophets, this is a smart move on his part.

Mayan Religion and the New Age

Before we delve too deeply into Mayan prophecies, we should ask a question not often asked in today's 2012 literature: *Do 2012 enthusiasts actually share the same religion as the Maya, or are they projecting their beliefs upon them? Are the Maya merely unwitting historical 'silent partners' substantiating the current 'new age' religion?"* Are 2012 authors simply putting words into the Mayans' mouths? I ask this because virtually *all 2012 authors are also card-carrying New Age Movement members.*

The Maya were polytheistic if not "animistic," believing in many gods and deities who dwelt within earthly (and celestial) objects. Today's New Age Movement would deny it holds to *many gods* the same way that ancient cultures did. Its adherents are much too sophisticated to buy into old *animistic assertions.*

The "New Agers" speak about nature with words like "vibrations" and "resonance." No doubt, the Maya thought that nature was alive, particularly since in their trance states, they often *spoke with animals and plants*.[3] Are the modern New Age terms that hearken to quantum physics, string theory and the like, really saying the same thing as the Maya? It seems more likely the New Age movement might not be on speaking terms with the Maya, *literally*. How the Maya would express their worldview might be quite different from what New Age proponents would describe.

In fact, it's true the New Age Movement shares with the Maya a view that *humans are god*, being part of a universal divine consciousness. It's probable that current-day talk about "transformation" may be similar to what the Maya believed. However, did this extend *only to their priests and Kings*? Did the Maya believe that all persons were divine? It seems highly unlikely, given the priests of the Maya performed regular ritual sacrifices. Death to placate or motivate their gods was standard operating procedure. Marx once said, "Religion is the *opiate* of the people." When he made this statement, he probably wasn't thinking about the Mayan version of religion. Watching a fiery human sacrifice in the evening doesn't lend itself to a good night's sleep – particularly, if you know the person fed to the fire. The New Age gang praise how extraordinary and spiritual the Maya were – while they minimize what most spiritually sophisticated persons would deplore. Since offering human sacrifices to the gods isn't compatible with the Judeo-Christian view – a perspective that asserts all humans are made in the image of God – how could it be compatible with a *stronger view* that says we don't just resemble god, but we are in fact divine beings in which "god becomes conscious of himself?"

Mayan Prophecies

Having established that calendars connected events in the heavens with events on earth, what specifically do the Maya predict? This is a fascinating study, particularly when we compare their predictions to other predictions of other pagan cultures.[4] The remainder of this chapter will address the issue.

Looking at Maya prophecies from 30,000 feet, what do we see? Actually, it's not really much of a mystery and doesn't take a lot of decoding. The two most important 2012 predictions are certain:

- *The first key prediction: Many will become gods.* There will be a dramatic change in our consciousness, specifically our self-consciousness. According to advocates, *we will realize our divine nature.* Because the transformation is so dramatic, it helps explain why *some* scholars suggest the Maya (and other Mesoamerican natives) meant the date 12-21-2012 to be the end of all calendars and the end of time itself (experts disagree whether the calendar stops or continues past this date – no consensus exists today on this topic).

- *The second key prediction: 2012 is when Kukulkan (Quetzalcoatl) returns to earth.* When he comes, the Maya believe this will be good news – they will become a great people once again and Kukulkan will set the world right. Other gods will accompany him to restore divine memories. It's as if we will win a *consciousness makeover!* However, as is often said, "No pain, no gain." The Maya firmly believe that like childbirth, we won't experience this rebirth without excruciating birth pangs. This is a time of *purification.* We should expect an agonizing transition on a personal and global basis.

According to John Major Jenkins, *forecasting the end* starts with *understanding the beginning,* i.e., the creation. In his noteworthy book, *Maya Cosmogenesis 2012,* Jenkins points out this duality. The meaning of the Sun entering the dark rift is part of an extensive creation mythology for which he coins the term *cosmogenesis.* The Mayan tale of the "Hero Twins" relates the Maya's creation myth (the "Twins" represent Venus and the Sun). Plus, there is a prediction implied in this myth: The dark rift represents *death* but also symbolizes *rebirth.* The rift not only is a *doorway to the underworld,* but also the *birth canal of the galactic mother.* Venus disappears as the morning star but eventually returns as the evening star. The Maya believed this return symbolizes the victory of the Twins over the Master of the dark underworld.

As a myth, so far so good.

However, here the story gets creepy.

Jenkins points out that the translation for this "spot" in the Mayan language is literally the *black hole,* which is rather stunning because of the usage of this term from today's science. We understand that our galaxy, perhaps like most, has a massive *black hole* at its core. This black hole not only traps all light and catches any object in the web of its enormous gravitational pull, the black hole appears to be the *origin* of stars in the galaxy. If true, the galaxy's center is indeed a cosmic mother. The black hole is the source of the Maya *cosmogenesis.* This is so extraordinary that Jenkins wonders how the Maya could possibly know this.

Indeed, as one studies the astronomical knowledge of the Maya, it's easy to wonder how they got so smart about many things. More than one scholar has speculated that despite the obvious acute observational skill they possess, the Maya seem to discern more than any earthbound intelligence could possibly know, no matter how keen their observational skills.

So how could they be so insightful?

Hallucinogens and the Maya

It's an accepted fact amongst the Mayan calendar experts that the Maya had to have special help to be so tuned in. It's not hard to discover the sources of this assistance. Their hieroglyphs clearly picture them. The first helper was *the magical mushroom*. The *Psilocybe Mexicana* (see figure below) was the primary drug of choice. The second facilitator was *venom* (dried and detoxified) from a *particular toad* (the *Bufo marines* of North America). In both cases, we encounter essentially the same substances that the McKenna's experimented with: *Psilocybin* and DMT. And for the same purpose – they were a Shamanic power tool to induce a trance state. South American Indians, the *Desana, Warao,* and *Kogi,* use these trance aids today. Jenkins deduces that the Maya, many years ago, exploited these substances for similar purposes.

Andrews and Andrews allow that the Maya certainly gained much of their knowledge through careful observation over hundreds of years. However, despite the many years of observation:

FIGURE 24 - PSILOCYBE MEXICANA - JALISCO, MEXICO ©CACTU

This was not enough to explain all that the Maya knew about the sky. For example, the Maya knew a considerable amount about the galaxy and the earth's position in the galaxy. Where would they gain the perspective to know this? No line of sight from the earth can reveal this information! The Maya have their own explanation.

Ceremony for the Maya was an opportunity to open portals and commune with the gods. The Maya considered the sky and the movements of the celestial bodies as the message board of the gods. During ceremony, the Maya achieved trance states that allowed them to open the portals and explore the message board... In trance states, the Mayan shamans were able to perform many extraordinary feats. They were able to perform healing rites, seeming to remove the cause of illness in a type of psychic surgery. They were able to travel among the stars... It was during trance states that some of the advanced knowledge is claimed to have been discovered.[5]

Likewise, Jenkins chides Western scholars for their failure to consider these purported examples of *consciousness projection* (aka "soul travel" or "remote viewing") as a possible explanation for what the Maya knew. He comments:

Something very basic to the Western mindset prevents it from understanding the full profundity of Mesoamerican cosmovision. Scholars can label Maya beliefs and practices, yet they completely *evade* seeing what those beliefs actually mean. For example, scholars do not accept that Maya shamans could actually *journey* to distant times and places. Scholars phrase this as "Maya kings *believed* they could journey to distant locations." In fact, the mental/spiritual capacity for consciousness projection is well known in the Hindu and Buddhist religions, as well as in most animistic worldviews [SDW: *What I call pagan religions*].

Why should the Maya be exempt from such achievements? One begins to suspect that scientific mindset is really far behind the ancient multidimensional paradigms of mysticism and shamanism, where the full potential of the human mind is allowed to manifest. To fully understand Maya culture and cosmology, we must admit the Maya king journeyed to distant places, communed with transcendental wisdom, and periodically conjured his kingdom into being, sustaining it by renewing it at specific nexus-points in the Long Count calendar (emphasis his).[6]

Speaking in defense of Western scholarship, methinks the reason the occidental mind doesn't believe the Mayan shaman-kings could travel to "the Galactic Center" (or back and forward through time), is because our current scholars doubt *anyone* can do it – enlightened scholarship isn't picking on the Maya in particular. As a fellow believer in the spiritual realm, I share Jenkins frustration with the unassailable naturalist assumptions of such modern learning.

Looking at it from another perspective, spiritual experience of the type depicted in these views concerning Mayan cosmology is indeed *a shared, cross-cultural human experience.* Jenkins is quite right: There are connections to other world religions – expressly those that *do not share the Judeo-Christian worldview.* The ability to see entities or objects from another realm (what McKenna called in his book title, *The Invisible Landscape*), to tell fortunes (divination), to travel through time, and to project one's consciousness into a distant place (on the earth or elsewhere in the universe), are all phenomena typically associated with the *occult.*

Did you just hear the door creak?

Such speculation used to be off base many years ago. The occult was no more than fanciful parlor tricks or a pseudo-religion for the well-to-do. But as we noted early on, our worldview today is different. We actually *take the assumptions of the occult seriously.* For instance, during the past 50 years, both the American and Russian military have been conducting experiments on all sorts of mental telepathy and consciousness travel. The latest version of the Indiana Jones movie series, *Indiana Jones and the Crystal Skull* (2008) included this fact in its plot line. The movie, *Men Who Stare at Goats* (2009), may have a silly name but it's a true-life example. (If you doubt this, check out the web sites for the *Discovery* and the *History Channels.* They've produced documentaries that go into considerable detail concerning the subject).[7]

Jenkins describes various neo-Shamans who follow this path today. One is Barbara Hand Clow, who takes her readers onto a cosmic journey to the Galactic Center in her book, *The Pleiadian Agenda.* By taking this space trip (an out-of-body round-trip journey she apparently experienced), her "book trippers" can meet the entities that she calls *the Keepers of Time.* Funny how it just so happens they are set to make an appearance (a return visit) on earth in *2012.*

No doubt traveling with her would be quite an expedition. Nevertheless, I think I'll wait to see if the *Keepers of Time* keep their schedule and come here as planned.

I hasten to point out how noteworthy it is that once again we find information about Doomsday coming to us from sources affected by the *use of hallucinogenic drugs.* Unlike western scholarship as Jenkins labels it, I too believe in spiritual states and in the mind's ability to do far more than we westerners usually grant. As I discussed before, C.G. Jung, a student of Freud, proved the existence of such a spiritual realm from a scientific point of view; though, to this day many scientists doubt his viewpoint is correct. But just as "the worm has turned" in popular culture, it's about to change in academically accepted science too.

Daniel Pinchbeck, author of *2012: The Return of Quetzalcoatl,* cites Jung's influence when taking a shot at the shallowness often visible at the core of many in the New Age: "Our culture has conveniently amputated the concept of spirituality from the processes of life, using it to denote a vast range of commodifiable experiences, self-help movements, and decorative ornaments."[8] Pinchbeck goes on to explain the relevance of Jung's position on the "collective mind" and the archetypes that inhabit it:

> Jung's theory of the archetypes depended upon his understanding of the reality of the psyche, the interconnection of mind and world. He defended this position against any materialist conception. "Not only does the psyche exist, but it is existence itself," Jung wrote, finding this quite obvious when one considered it: "It is an almost absurd prejudice to suppose that existence can only be physical... We might well say, on the contrary, that physical existence is a mere inference, since we know of matter in so far as we perceive psychic images mediated by the senses... Individuals do not invent or generate the archetypes – often they are overtaken or possessed by them, against their conscious desires.[9]

Despite my concurrence with the idea of a spiritual realm populated by entities (or *archetypes* as Jung called them), I am cautious about the trustworthiness of information from such a source that's out-of-this-world. These realities truly have minds of their own just as Jung, from a clinical viewpoint, inferred. When we go on such other-dimensional road trips, the professionals in the mental profession (educated by clinical experience), warn us that we open ourselves to manipulation by non-corporeal beings who have their own goals.

Scott Peck, noted author of *The Road Less Traveled,* perhaps the best book ever written on the integration of religion and psychology, not only concurred with Jung's perspective, he went so far as to analyze evil from a clinical perspective in his book, *People of the Lie.* His book reminds us that at the base of evilness is untruth. Evil people hide from the light. Since in psychoanalysis one is placing oneself in the hands of the therapist to uncover the hidden truths affecting personality disorders and psychosis, undergoing therapy is seeking to come to the truth. *People of the Lie* avoid any encounter with those who could expose them to the truth. They won't allow themselves to be unmasked. That's why evil is so difficult to diagnose as a personality disorder. Peck's analysis even goes so far to discuss the concept of demonic possession, a phenomena he confesses he has personally witnessed in a clinical setting. To Peck, demonic possession is not a myth but a psychological reality that does affect some types of persons, especially those who place themselves in situations where they can encounter such entities as we've discussed.

The Aztec Myth of the Tzitzimime

Given that he isn't so suffused in New Age metaphysics as are most of his 2012 colleagues, it's not surprising that Jenkins makes the same point.[10]

The Aztecs had a slightly different take on the beings that come to earth in 2012. They call them the "*Tzitzimime*" (zit-z-my-me). For the Aztecs, the galactic alignment is not such a good time to roll out the red carpet for gods from outer space or other dimensions.

Jenkins discusses the Aztec myth concerning these visitors who come to earth when the "door opens to the galactic center" in 2012. Apparently, the Aztecs believed these "celestial demons will pour down out of the sky to devour mankind." Jenkins cautions that these beings may not be our unconscious shadows but *"autonomous transdimensional entities, ready to pursue their own agendas."*

Jenkins adds, "Within the New Age Movement, channeling strikes me as a warning of this possibility, and we must be careful not to be duped. We should thus challenge and question, in an intelligent, open, and conscious way, people who claim to be conduits for beings from other realms." Jenkins then recounts a story (and a warning) from a friend whose father had been channeling entities for decades.

> He said to be aware that beings contacted through inner doorways are attracted to human energy and desire to extract a unique kind of energy that living, conscious beings have. In the interest of remaining connected for as long as possible, some of these entities will say many things, much of which does not make sense. My friend's words reinforced my feeling that within some of the recent New Age rhetoric it does not even matter if what is said makes no sense – the very idea that it is the spoken gospel of some transdimensional being or dead Maya king is enough to warrant reverence and loyalty. The danger is that any lapse in our discrimination or good judgment could lull us into an unconscious spell, rather than stimulate our awakening.[11]

If we take this advice at face value, we could (and prudence demands we should) challenge the worthiness of any non-standard source who promises transformation in 2012. We simply can't take "their" word for it. We had better ask, "To what are we opening ourselves up?" Our independence as a conscious entity is not something we should willingly relinquish. Perhaps we better pull back the welcome mat and close the shutters. As I said early on, *"Beware aliens bearing gifts."* When we study the history of such psychic connections in Chapter 8, we will supplement the reasons for such a cautious position with substantial additional historical data.

The Testimony of Daniel Pinchbeck

2012: The Return of Quetzalcoatl, by Daniel Pinchbeck, is perhaps the most fascinating and well-written book in the entire 2012 genre. It's Pinchbeck's personal story, his personal "magical mystery tour" of experimenting with psychedelic drugs (*ayahuasca, DMT*), shamanism, and initiation into drug-centered cults of ancient tribes (like the *Bwiti* of Africa with their drug of choice *iboga*),[12] as well as the first-hand experience of walking amidst freshly created Crop Circles in England. Additionally, Pinchbeck provides a framework for understanding his experience connected to Jung's psychological interpretation of the "soul of man" (or the collective human mind, aka the *Self* or *God*).

To a point, one has to admire the openness of Pinchbeck. He tells us firsthand what it's like to experience the various drugs touted by McKenna and the corresponding visions that result from them. He is an emphatic believer in the spiritual realm, a critic of the materialist, and clear-minded in his expression of what he has witnessed. However, the analysis of his encounters is colored by his religious frame of reference which regards traditional Judeo-Christian thought as a "patriarchal religion," rendered near useless (from his perspective) to modern humankind due to its dogmatic trappings and fallacious world-view of a personal, judgmental God standing distinct and apart from the consciousness of human beings. Pinchbeck believes, like so many others in the 2012 camp, that a raised consciousness is "where it's at." His personal experiences of entities and phantasms, made so vibrant by his extensive drug use, undergird his convictions about what 2012 really means.

For Pinchbeck, the Second Coming is actually the re-emergence of enlightened human beings who regain their ability to contact and influence the "hidden realm." Pinchbeck believes that humans gave up the immediacy of spiritual experience in order to grow their rational and technological skills. This insight is not unique. Trevor Ravenscroft points out in his book, *The Spear of Destiny* (which we will study more thoroughly later), that this quest is part and parcel of the *search for the Holy Grail*. Without this shift in our mindset, we would never have progressed and begat the modern world. However, Pinchbeck believes the time has come for us to shift back the other way. If we don't reaffirm the mythical aspects of truth and don't reactivate our ability to roam amidst the "hidden landscapes" of the spiritual realm (accessed through dreams, drugs, and visionary states), our prognosis is bleak. While Pinchbeck believes that the Apocalypse is actually only an *archetype of the subconscious* (an infrequently quoted view held by Jung), if we don't realign our values and our manner of living, we will destroy the ecosystem of our planet in a matter of a few decades – and then the apocalypse will be experienced *in real-time*.

Pinchbeck's book has something of a surprise ending. Throughout his story, a *spirit entity* has been pursuing him; or so it seems. This spirit finally identifies itself to Pinchbeck and demands that Pinchbeck channel his message. Who is the entity? *It's Quetzalcoatl himself*. Although reluctant to convey his message, and willing to admit that perhaps he is letting his own ego get the best of him, Pinchbeck accedes and scribes the message. What is the earth shattering revelation? *The return of Quetzalcoatl in 2012 is the return of human beings to their true selves*. It's the recognition that our move toward self-consciousness is making us more God-conscious. But isn't this special communication just more of the same? Hasn't Pinchbeck been teaching this lesson to us even before Quetzalcoatl put words in his mouth? Is this epiphany bringing us anything new? Don't other 2012 and new age authors voice the same?

Pogo said, "We have met the enemy and it is us." Quetzalcoatl says, "You meet God when you *come to know yourself*." The Christ in the *Gospel of Thomas*, a Gnostic reinterpretation of the words of Jesus, couldn't have said it better. Once again, as sophisticated and intriguing as the writing is and although the vocabulary is new-age chic peppered with words like, *matrix, metamorphous,* and *vortex*, we come to the same conclusion: It's mystical drivel encased in exceptional pagan prose masquerading as shining new words of enlightenment. How can we not be disappointed? The author acts as if he has discovered fire. Instead, he has just come to the same conclusion as the pagan masters and navel-gazing sages of time immemorial. As a fellow seeker of spiritual truth, I must ask, "How much peace this will really afford Pinchbeck in the long run?" Being possessed by such entities usually has disastrous outcomes.

No doubt, Pinchbeck has received exactly what he had been seeking. He "opened the *doors of perception*" that Aldous Huxley extolled. In the words of *The Doors'* lead singer, Jim Morrison, he "broke on through to the other side." But in gaining these insights, hasn't he *actually forfeited rather than found his soul?*

Other North American Indians Weigh In

These varied connections to the Mayan religious worldview are hardly unique. Other North American natives have similar insights into the future of our world. Not only do the Hopi and the Cherokee share the primary facets of the Maya calendars (including the end date of 2012), they certainly share the same basic worldview. Consequently, it's quite informative to note their predictions. Often documented elsewhere, I will just hit the highlights here.

The Hopi Indians

The "peaceful people" – the Hopi – have sophisticated knowledge of the end times. They possess a *prophecy stone* in their Arizona habitat. Inscribed on the stone are numerous fascinating predictions. There are nine total signs. Let's recount them quickly.

- Sign #1: People will arrive from the east that are white-skinned and steal the land of the Native lands because of their "thunder sticks." Interpretation: Europeans come to America welding guns and conquer the Indian lands of North America.

- Sign #2: People come to populate the lands. Inside "spinning wheels filled with voices," they come. Interpretation: People settle the lands utilizing covered wagons.

- Sign #3: Strange beasts like the buffalo but with long horns take over the plains, overrunning the land. Interpretation: The white man raises long horn cattle and drives them across the land.

- Sign #4: "Snakes of iron" come to cross the lands. Interpretation: The railroad becomes a means for mass travel across the plains.

- Sign #5: A "giant spider web" covers the land. Interpretation: White men erect telegraph, telephone, and power lines.

- Sign #6: Rivers of stone cross the land – they make pictures in the sun. Interpretation: Highways producing mirage-like effects on hot days.

- Sign #7: The Sea will turn black and kill many living things. Interpretation: Oil spills in the oceans.

- Sign #8: "Many youths wearing their hair long like our people, come and join the tribal nations to learn our ways and wisdom." Interpretation: The hippies hang out with the Indian tribes in the 1960's and 1970's. They discover peyote and ancient wisdom.

- Sign #9: A "dwelling place in the heavens" will fall from the sky. It appears as a blue star. Soon thereafter, the ceremonies of the Hopi people will cease. Interpretation: Some say Skylab falls from the sky in 1979. Others the Russian Mir space station in 2001. In both cases, the "shooting star" appeared to be blue.

The prophet, White Feather, provided these predictions to Frank Waters who published them in his 1963 book, *The Book of the Hopi.*

White Feather goes on to indicate that these signs point to great destruction coming. "The world shall rock to and fro. The white man will battle against other people in other lands – with those who possessed the first light of wisdom.[13] There will be many columns of smoke and fire such as White Feather has seen the white man make in the deserts not far from here (*The atomic proving grounds in New Mexico*). Soon – very soon afterward – Pahana will return" (*Pahana is Kukulkan of the Maya and Quetzalcoatl of the Olmecs*).

The Cherokees

Like the Mesoamerican Indians, the Cherokees too believe that 2012 will bring back the great white brother. They call him the *Feathered Rattlesnake* (virtually the same descriptive name given him by the Maya – the "feathered serpent").

The Cherokee prophecies are known as the Rattlesnake Prophecies, aka Cherokee Star Constellation Prophecy, or the Chickamaugan Prophecy (another tribe originally from the southeastern part of North America). The Cherokee set down these prophecies 200 years ago in 1811-1812. A falling of a comet and a great earthquake accompanied the giving of these prophecies.

The Cherokees share many elements of the Mayan calendars. We see this as the prophecy itself includes a snake with 52 scales on its mouth – each point relating to one of the 52 years on their calendar. They call this calendar the "wheel of time" while the Maya called it *the Calendar Round.*

The prophecies mention that when a comet strikes Jupiter (the *Shoemaker-Levy* comet striking Jupiter in 1994), it's time for the Cherokee people to wake up. It also mentions the transit of Venus (2004 and 2012). "And in the year 2004 the Morning Star shall be first and in the year 2012 the Evening Star shall be first. And upon those years the crown of the Feathered Serpent shall bear its colors and honor... And in the year 2012 the Cherokee calendar ends. And all is reborn." However, before the pale one comes (Pahana, Kukulkan), there will be a time of great tribulation, suffering, and hardship.

Another major element of the prophecy is the "three great shakings of the earth." Most interpreters believe these refer to three world wars. "Two great shakings are past, one is yet to come." This portion of the prophecy also speaks of a gourd filled with ashes falling to earth. Some interpret this as an *atomic bomb*; others believe it refers to *a comet that strikes the earth*. Either way, it's bad news for Mother Earth.

Commonalities in the Prophecies of the Americas

If we synthesize the various predictions and emphasize those held in common, we build the following picture of what the prophecies foretell:

- *The time leading up to this climax is a time of purification.* A great time of distress is coming characterized by strong earthquakes, objects falling from heaven, and massive deadly wars.

- *Signs in the heavens will indicate when this occurs.* The transit of Venus and the galactic eclipse all mark the date. "2012" is the specific point in time for the culmination of these events that all native sources identify outright or strongly infer. The consistency is striking.

- *There will be a great man of wisdom coming.* He will be the "white brother," "the pale one," the return of "the feathered serpent." The identity of this white brother is clearly important. For Christians, they would have a very simple explanation. This white brother is either Jesus Christ or he is the Antichrist masquerading as a beneficent leader.

- *Other gods accompany this personality.* Some accounts see this occurrence positively. The gods help earth's peoples relearn the wisdom of old and reestablish their identity as gods. On the other hand, if the Aztecs are right, these gods are *fiends* and not friends – deceptive demons who seek to consume and destroy humanity.

- *The gods will either transform humanity or annihilate it.* The outcome couldn't be more dramatic. Either we will become as gods or we be obliterated. One way or another, the prophecies promise that planet earth will never be quite the same again.

Of course, other questions remain which we'd love to see answered. What we can conclude at this point is that *many peoples, both ancient and contemporary, testify to the same destinies.* Our fate is dead ahead. The clock is ticking. We have to make choices. According to all of them, we must realign ourselves to spiritual values or we are doomed. However, exactly what those values are remains unspoken. And as we study the history of those who channeled entities from another time and place, we should fear that *some of these values are far from noble.*

For while some prophecies state *the gods* will help us – others question whether we can we trust these gods. Are these gods divine guides, alien astronauts who nurtured us, or demonic deceivers? Perhaps this answer will become clearer as we continue the story of pagan religions and ancient wisdom. There are other voices to examine which *share a common cosmology – a particular method of understanding reality.* Moreover, like the Native Americas of ancient time, they too emphasize the knowledge of the stars, calendars, and the power that comes from such things. We turn to them now.

Notes

[1] A "stele" is an engraved stone tablet the ancients set upright as a monument marker commemorating special events or providing history for future generations.

[2] The Sun moves one degree in procession about every 72 years. The size of the Sun itself is one-half of one degree. Depending upon the width of the rift (assuming it is also about one-half of one degree as seen from the earth), the Sun could come into contact with this spot and move across it over a period of about 36 years (it is calculated). Hence, the galactic alignment is a period of over three decades, not just one day. In theory, the perfect eclipse would be exactly half-way through this period, or about 1999-2000. This is important. December 21, 2012 isn't the date of the true eclipse.

[3] The notion of how humans *know* and *conceive* of mental ideas begins with Plato and his concept of 'heavenly ideal ideas.' Plato put forth the philosophy of knowledge as follows: We know about a chair because 'in the heavenlies' there is a perfect 'idea of a chair' what I call an 'ideal idea.' In the 20th century, Rudolf Steiner, a German mystic put forth the occult concept that these ideas are 'alive' in the 'spirit world.' (Steiner - according to Trevor Ravenscroft, *a student of Steiner* – was a white magician. Hitler considered him his most threatening enemy as Steiner could detect what Hitler was doing telepathically), *"Steiner advocated a form of ethical individualism, to which he later brought a more explicitly spiritual component. He based his epistemology on Johann Wolfgang Goethe's world view, in which 'Thinking ... is no more and no less an organ of perception than the eye or ear. Just as the eye perceives colours and the ear sounds, so thinking perceives ideas.'"*

See *http://en.wikipedia.org/wiki/Rudolf_Steiner*. Objects whether animate or inanimate have spiritual counterparts, *doppelgangers*, in the spirit realm. We would be tempted to think about these as the *'bizarro universe'* of Superman. This mirrors Terrence McKenna's Dr. Doolittle experience of 'talking with the animals' (more precisely, insects) in mental trance-like states. We will pick up this theme in the discussion of the *Spirit of the Antichrist* later in the book.

4 *Pagan* is an offensive word, but there isn't a good synonym less offensive. I could use "heathen" but it seems worse. Pagan means "all religions that aren't connected to the God of the Bible." Non-pagan religions are Judaism, Christianity, and Islam. It is akin to the Hebrew term, *Gentile in the sense of "grouping" one class of people excluded from one other*. In Judaism, there are two types of people, Jews and Gentiles. Gentiles are non-Jews. It too is an offensive term although its usage through the years has reduced the insult that once was associated with it. My use of "pagan" isn't necessarily meant to be "insulting" but it is meant to identify a common, ancient "world-wide religion" that is prevalent amongst all ancient cultures. It intends to distinguish this religion from the three monotheistic religions based upon the God of the Bible. As one Seattle witch noted to one of my Jewish friends, monotheistic religions see God "outwardly"; all others, Hinduism, Buddhism, New Age, etc., see God "inwardly."

5 Andrews and Andrews, *2012: An Ancient Look at a Critical Time*, Penguin Books, New York, 2008, page 43, 44.

6 Jenkins, John Major, *Maya Cosmogenesis 2012*, Bear & Company Publishing, Rochester, Vermont, 1998, pp. 321,322.

7 Additionally, a popular "cult" movie from the year, 2009 (*cult* in the sense of 1970's classic, *The Rocky Horror Picture Show*), was *Paranormal Activity*.

8 Daniel Pinchbeck, op. cit., pg 109.

9 Ibid, pg. 110.

10 Jenkins is a rare breed, an author focused on 2012, but not a new age enthusiast.

11 Jenkins, op. cit., page 211, 212.

12 "Modern Bwiti is syncretistic, incorporating animism, ancestor worship and Christianity into its belief system. Bwiti use the hallucinogenic root bark of the *Tabernanthe iboga* plant, specially cultivated for the religion, to induce a spiritual enlightenment, stabilize community and family structure, meet religious requirements and to solve problems of a spiritual and/or medical nature. The root bark has been used for hundreds of years as part of a Bwiti coming of age ceremony and other initiation rites and acts of healing, producing complex visions and insights anticipated to be valuable to the initiate and the chapel."

See *http:// en.wikipedia.org/wiki/Bwiti* for more information.

13 This could be a reference to Sumeria, today's Iraq and Iran, and its arcane knowledge including astrology

Chapter 7:
Circular Revelations in England

You know I wanted to be a spaceman
That's what I wanted to be
But now that I am a spaceman
Nobody cares about me
Say, hey! You mother earth
You better bring me back down
I've taken just as much as I can
But around and around and around and around
Is the problem of a spaceman

Harry Nilsson

Roundabouts – Learning to Drive in the Mother Country

Roundabouts weren't new to me. I did my fair share of driving when I worked in Boston for five years, commuting 47 miles each way from my home in New Hampshire.

I made my way from Nashua through Chelmsford, Massachusetts, then Carlisle, Concord, and finally Cambridge. It was a great commute in the fall when the leaves were changing. Nevertheless, the ugliness of the "roundabouts" almost outweighed the great views.

Traffic was heavy and Bostonians are notoriously crazy drivers. Nevertheless, for five years I made the commute and never had a fender bender despite venturing those traffic circles in Cambridge every day. "Round and round you go, where you stop, nobody knows." Believe me, the last thing you want to do is stop in a roundabout. You miss your exit; best go *'round* one more time!

A few years later, I found myself with my family in London celebrating Christmas with some English friends. As part of the stay, I learned to drive *on the wrong side of the road* to transport my family, staying at the London Marriott, across the Thames (by *Big Ben*) to where our friends lived near Heathrow Airport. What really demanded my attention was navigating the roundabouts. The frantic circle with cars whizzing every which way was truly daunting.

No doubt, the English invented the roundabout. Merry old England is just brimming with these not-so-merry-go-rounds.

Bright and early on a cold, crisp but sunny morning a day or two before Christmas, my good friend Gordon gave me "English driving lessons." We motored cautiously around Parliament, St. James Park, and Buckingham Palace, made our way through many roundabouts (*always going backwards* as far as I was concerned) and finally found our way to the highway.

The roundabouts were a challenge to say the least. Gordon instructed, "As you enter, veer left. Remember cars in the roundabout have the right-of-way. He who hesitates is lost. Goose it!"

Fortunately, for me, my friend was an excellent teacher and I managed. Later that night, driving solo (without my teacher), we made it safely out to their home and back, enjoyed a great "old English dinner," and as it turns out, we weren't too frightened by many a roundabout. I had much to be thankful for that Christmas, including my acquisition of the skill necessary to drive safely in London – *though there are residual effects to this day*. Now every time I enter a roundabout here "in the States," I'm thinking to myself, "Which way do I turn as I enter the circle? Who has the right-of-way? Can I get out once I get in?" *Roundabouts* – what a way to go!

Having thoroughly disparaged them by my remarks, I must nonetheless admit that in some cases the roundabout is a much better tool than a traffic light to keep the buggies bustling. Furthermore, I've concluded in the past ten years, there are other types of circles in Britain requiring even more attention. Not only does their confusing nature surpass the roundabout, as we will soon see, *these circles can be decoded providing startling data about the end of days*.

Circles and Henges – What Was Their Real Purpose?

Long before the Maya or the Olmecs were observing the stars in the Americas, there were pagan priests doing astronomy in England and Western Europe. Eight million visitors verify this fact ever year when they come to Stonehenge in Wiltshire, England. The crowds gather to view the greatest European artifact of the Megalithic period. Tourism peaks during the summer solstice when visitors witness how these great ancient *standing stones* align to this very event. Tourists leave enthralled, but virtually no one realizes how their brief astronomical education barely scratches the surface of the great mysteries these calendric circles hold, scattered as they are throughout western, central, and northern England.

Indeed, it may be a surprise to some that there are many other henges in England besides Stonehenge. Yet, despite their number, these circles share the same pagan religious significance – each site was unquestionably a burial ground for thousands of ancient worshippers. Additionally, these circles were the heart of these pre-historic communities. The *keepers of the circle* were priests who maintained calendars to determine planting times. By predicting heavenly events like solar or lunar eclipses, they displayed their astronomical skills, leveraging this expertise into leadership. In effect, *the circles provided the means to accredit these priests promoting them to the head of the community.*

Since Stonehenge dates to about 3000 BC, surprisingly it may in fact be a *latecomer to the circle forming business in pre-historic England.* According to various scholars, the Thornborough henges are likely 500 to 800 years older, dating from around 3500 - 3800 BC. This distinctly ancient time of origin lends itself to some fascinating possibilities.

In late 2009, authors Christopher Knight and Alan Butler published an amazing book about these many henges. Entitled *Before the Pyramids: Cracking Archaeology's Greatest Mystery,* the book builds upon their earlier work, *Civilization One.* Despite the fact that, *Before the Pyramids,* is a 250-plus-page work of non-fiction, I managed to devour it in a few hours during an otherwise crowded 24-hour period. I found it *that* fascinating.

Knight and Butler do their best to overturn most of the orthodox views regarding what these formations mean.

First off, we wonder who built them. Most folks suppose the *Druids* were responsible, a strange pagan religious people *who worshipped nature.* With averred mystical and esoteric qualities, the Druids have given rise to ample historical speculation and colorful fictional works. They even impressed Julius Caesar. In his annals, he discusses their astronomical intelligence and

FIGURE 25 – STONEHENGE IN WILTSHIRE, ENGLAND

knowledge of the earth's dimensions.

However, were the Druids the originators of the *henges*? Most historians, including Knight and Butler doubt it. The Druids established themselves in England perhaps 3,000 years *too late* to claim responsibility.

Knight and Butler make a second iconoclastic assertion: The true purpose of the henges was not just astronomical, but *metrological*. Metrology is the study of *standards* or as we might say, "weights and measures." While not yet accepted by Academia as this hypothesis is barely one-year old, the theory is breathtaking in its ability to explain the phenomena in a new and highly scientific way. Knight and Butler take us on an amazing journey of exploration (both mental and physical) in which they share with us, step-by-step, how they stumbled across this insight. It has some far-reaching repercussions as we shall see.

FIGURE 26 - THORNBOROUGH HENGE – NORTH YORKSHIRE, ENGLAND

The Megalithic Yard

The key element necessary for their discoveries was the work of Alexander Thom (1894-1985).

Thom was an engineer who spent his free summers exploring various megalithic ruins across England and France, taking measurements, and postulating that humankind from this period had developed an astounding measurement system – the *Megalithic Yard*.

Thom sought to demonstrate that many people shared this system of "standards" across a wide span of geography at a time long before historians regard humankind to know such things. Experts so far dismiss his findings as inconsequential and unproven. Nevertheless, Knight and Butler may have the data now to alter Academia's opinion. With their discovery, Thom may now measure up.

First, the key measurements:

- The key standards appear to be the "MEGALITHIC YARD" (MY), "INCH" (MI) and "ROD" (MR).

- The MY (megalithic yard) is 2.722 feet (about 32.67 inches).

- The MI (megalithic inch) is 1/40th of the MY (about 7/8's of an inch)

- The MY is 60% of the MR (megalithic rod) (about 55 inches).

One might think that *metrology* is the most boring subject one can imagine. However, it turns out not to be the case. Sir Isaac Newton became the head of England's *Weights and Measures,* a job he coveted, just after the year 1700. He held this post for quite some time. Why so much interest in how things are measured? Because in understanding how ancient man measured things, we uncover just how vast was the knowledge ancients possessed.

Measures turn out to be one means by which we uncover *ancient wisdom* alluded to earlier. Not only did Newton seek this knowledge, but Francis Bacon and other famous scientists of this period also searched endlessly for the same.

Knight and Butler unexpectedly achieved their first breakthrough when they decided to measure a circular-shaped edifice by an 18th century architect, John Wood. *The King's Circus* in Bath was the building of interest. Knight and Butler knew Wood was a founding Freemason in his region and a founder of a newly formed Druid Society there. That was their first clue. Putting the two facts together in a mental leap, they decided to test the Megalithic Yard by using it to measure Wood's structure. They accomplished the measurement quickly using a software application on the Internet, *Google Earth*. In a few brief moments, they were able to measure the building's proportions and were stunned to find it "exact" in megalithic yards (symmetrical in this regard). In other words, the measurements *came out even*. It dawned on them that they had stumbled upon the usage of the megalithic system by an 18th century architect suffused in Masonic secrets.

Knight and Butler then used their knowledge of the Megalithic Yard and *Google Earth* to measure various *circle sites* in England. As they calculated each one, they found the correlation was exact across the board. In his lifetime, Thom hadn't been able to measure such large structures precisely. However, with this new technology, Knight and Butler could do it easily, quickly, and with accuracy. Therefore, the authors had demonstrated that the megalithic distances developed by Thom *perfectly measured the English henges.*

To be specific: Knight and Butler calculated that King's Circus circumference is 732 MY. Afterwards, they discovered that Thornborough has a circumference of 732 MY as well. The diameter of each is 233 MY. 233 MY multiplied by π is 732 MY (731.993), twice 366 MY. This number is highly significant because seldom are circumferences whole integers. Plus, the measure betrays the fact that *the ancients knew how to calculate the size of a circle using π ("Pi"- an irrational, non-repeating number, often represented simply by 3.1416.)*

Suddenly, a completely new possibility loomed. As they continued to see the relationships in these measures, they caught a glimpse of just how sophisticated and important the henges were for the ancients. They posed a theory that this knowledge could unlock the dimensions of the earth. If true, Knight and Butler would prove that this kind of ancient wisdom existed almost 4,000 years before Christ. This would truly be astounding.

Measuring the Circumference of the Earth

How did Knight and Butler verify the ancients knew the size and shape of the earth? The story is fascinating but lengthy. We can do little more than touch on the highlights here.

To begin, Knight and Butler theorize that the ancients were able to determine that while the earth makes an annual rotation around the sun in 365 days, (the sun rises and sets 365 times), at the very same time, *stars rise and set 366 times*. Scientists call this a *sidereal day*. (See the figure below for a graphical explanation.) A sidereal day is 236 seconds less than a solar day. *This differential adds up over a year and accounts for the distinction between a solar year and a sidereal year*. The difference owns to the fact that the earth rotates around its axis at the same time it orbits the sun. Knight and Butler postulate that ancient astronomers determined that the earth itself is a sphere (a planet) within a metaphorical "sphere" (our outward view of the sky) that should be divided or partitioned into 366 sections (each section is an *arc or degree* – 366 degrees instead of 360, because the Megalithic Circle had 366 degrees). In effect, these authors indicate that the ancients ascertained these things from very meticulous measurements of the movement of stars at night. That's where the *henges* come in.

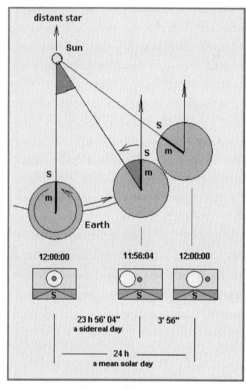

FIGURE 27 - A SIDEREAL DAY
AUTHOR: FRANCISCO JAVIER BLANCO
GONZÁLEZ, MODIFIED BY J.G. SAVARD
SEE EN.WIKIPEDIA.ORG/WIKI/
FILE:SIDEREAL_TIME_EN.PNG

Initially, the henges were just large circular mounds of dirt built up with a corresponding circular ditch dug beneath the mounds. The grounds keepers filled the ditches with water to help reflect the light in the night sky. The horizon in these areas of England is unusually flat (especially for most landscapes in Western Europe). So star watchers can see (virtually) horizon to horizon, witnessing stars rise and set throughout the night. The *mounds* perfect this.

Observers, by placing themselves in the center of the circle and placing rods into the mounds at the exact points that stars arise, measure from one night to the next, how the sky changes.

In effect, *the ancients were creating an "artificial horizon."* They did this in order to create a set of measures, with which they would measure the size of the earth. Furthermore, they could pass down these standards through the ages within family lines. This esoteric knowledge enabled a caste of priests to exploit this secret knowledge from generation to generation – elevating them and maintaining their power over the masses. When one considers that Francis Bacon sought the same hidden knowledge, it gives a completely new meaning to his famous quotation: "Knowledge is power." *This knowledge was very powerful indeed.*

Furthermore, as we will see, it's this knowledge that may be a key portion of the hidden knowledge that has been secretly shared through the ages by secret fraternities such as the Freemasons.

How did the priests accomplish these measures in ancient times? I'll offer a brief explanation here (see the sidebar below on how to create a *MEGALITHIC MEASURING BOB*).

The Megalithic Yard (MY) is determined by comparing the count of swings measured against a stellar movement in the sky. Keep in mind that no matter the speed the pendulum swings, as long as the length of string is the same, it takes the same amount of time for one completed swing. The *length of a pendulum* accounts for *how long the interval is*. By establishing a constant measurement, like the time it takes for Venus to move from point A to point B in the sky (measured by the distance set between two poles), the astronomer establishes a standard length that will be constant from place to place on earth, and from one millennium to the next.

As the ancients innovated further, they created henges with stones to elevate the artificial horizon and to improve upon the precision of their measurements creating the stones with perfectly flat tops. Stonehenge was a then *modern upgrade* to Thornborough (built several hundred years later). The use of the higher and more symmetrical horizon also made it possible to shrink the sizes of the henge while maintaining accuracy. It turns out, Stonehenge's circumference is 366 MY – exactly half that of Thornborough.

Knight and Butler describe in detail how with the help of engineering friends and other scholars, they were able to postulate that ancient man proved the circumference of the earth with just these naked eye observatories. Knight and Butler also field-tested their hypotheses. They proved that the circles at Thornborough connected with other circles nearby (within 10 kilometers or so) – showing that ancients were able to verify the length of one degree or arc of latitude. By multiplying this length by 366, ancient humankind could measure the circumference of the earth!

Therefore, we can surmise that the ancients knew the earth was round and it rotated around the sun. This seems odd to us since we know all too well the story of the medieval church and its false belief in an earth-centric model. It castigated and/or excommunicated Copernicus, Kepler and Galileo who rightly knew otherwise. Similarly, we have supposed (incorrectly) that our knowledge base is *progressively built, always growing into more and more enlightened views.* In reality, our forebears learned much in times past that was lost. We've had to re-discover information previously learned, but forgotten or destroyed through the ravages of time. For instance, we can only begin to imagine how much knowledge the ancients had recorded in the vast library of Alexandria, Egypt. When this library burned, much of our ancient heritage went up in flames. Thus, civilization lost vast amounts of ancient wisdom (only an enlightened few kept smatterings of it alive through their priesthood and later through secret societies). A few other shocking conclusions in Knight and Butler's book:

- There is a tight correlation between the henges and the Pyramids. The Egyptians may have leveraged early English know-how when building the Pyramids at least 1,000 years later.

- The layout of Thornborough demonstrates exact consistency with Orion's Belt. This correlation equates to Robert Bauval's conjecture in *The Orion Mystery.* In fact, the authors consulted Bauval and recorded their extended conversations. Generally, he concurred with their findings.

- The location of the Thornborough circles is exactly 1/10th earth's north/south latitude from the true North Pole (1/10th the polar circumference). Is this just another coincidence?

- Knight and Butler point out, there are no less than six super-large henges "in this part of the world, and their presence in so small an area tends to add up to the feeling that this area of Britain was considered in some way very special by those who labored to dig the ditches and throw up the banks."

- There are strong correlations between the megalithic system and the metric system. The book argues that the connection goes all the way back to *Sumerian* times (the beginning of civilization according to secular anthropologists and archeologists). The authors conjecture the Sumerians may have originated the metric system (and not the 18th century French!)

- As to the Freemasons, the second portion of their book analyzes the measurements of Washington DC; constructed and dedicated by the Freemasons (its primary architect was Pierre Charles L'Enfant who was a Mason as was George Washington and many other founders of the United States). The distance between the many circles in *Washington DC,* are "even numbers" in Megalithic Yards. This clearly implies *the secret knowledge of Freemasonry includes these megalithic measures.*

CREATING A MEGALITHIC PENDULUM MEASURING "BOB"

Below, cited from *Wikipedia* (and the author, Christopher Knight), a detailed explanation for the procedure to establish a "standard measure for the length of the pendulum cord" and thus create a measure capable of use worldwide and through time. *Knight outlines a procedure for Neolithic astronomers to make a Venus Pendulum. Trace a circle on the ground using megalithic **pi** (732/233).*

1. Mark off one megalithic degree of azimuth on the circumference using megalithic **pi**.

2. Place two poles on the ends of the degree and a sighting pole in the circle's center.

3. Standing at the sighting pole, observe Venus's motion between the marker poles.

4. As Venus moves through the megalithic degree, swing a pendulum and count the beats.

5. The goal is to count 366 beats during Venus's transit of the poles from start to finish.

6. Adjust the length of the cord if too many or few beats are counted, and recount until 366 are counted

7. The length of a pendulum calibrated this way is 0.5 MY at 60° N with an error of 0.002%.[2]

Mathematically a megalithic degree is 1/366 part of a Venusian day, which is the time for Venus to trace one complete circle across the sky. At maximum retrograde Venus is moving slower than the background stars so a Venusian day is slightly longer than a sidereal day and a megalithic degree of the Venusian day lasts 236.2486 seconds. Into this measure of time, 366 beats of 0.5 MY Venus pendulum fit very precisely. Venus' retrograde motion was determined by Neolithic astronomers in Megalithic observatories such as Newgrange in Ireland, which uses three interlocking carved spirals to perform astronomical calculations by geometric methods. Anecdotally, a number of small weights are present at all megalithic sites which may be discarded pendulum bobs."

See *http://en.wikipedia.org/wiki/Megalithic_yard.*

- The symmetry of the system has many stunning properties. The ratio of the earth's circumference to the moon is 366:100. The ratio to the sun is 366:40,000. Every 10,000 days the moon turns 366 times in relation to the stars. There are temperature ratios too: If the freezing point of water is set to zero (like a Celsius thermometer), and the boiling point is established at 366° – then absolute zero (the coldest temperature possible in the universe) is exactly 1000° below zero. Comparisons with metric weights and sizes are often symmetrical too.

Knight and Butler don't go so far as to connect distances or measurements to the Maya structures in the Americas. No doubt, this would be a fascinating study to attempt.

What if the Mayan structures were built in concert with the megalithic system? The implication would be just as profound if not more so, as the link inferred between them and the Egyptian Pyramids (given the distances involved, or more specifically the wide oceans between them) would prove beyond any doubt the common source of this building program. We expectantly await the sequel.

English Crop Circles – The Mowing Devil

One of the most controversial subjects over the past thirty years is the formation of large circles in the grain fields of England. These exotic designs often appear overnight. Known as *Crop Circles*, these contemporary formations are as mysterious as the pre-historic henges.

As we will soon see, these formations may have much more in common with the ancient henges than just "circles whose meaning has hitherto been unknown." Various parties have documented a great deal of research and expressed strong opinions. This includes views by the popular scientist, Carl Sagan. However, the debate isn't new.

In *1678,* an English pamphlet published via woodcut displayed the mysterious formation a farmer discovered on his property – *speculating the Devil had something to do with it* (See below). Likewise, the January 2000 issue of *Journal of Meteorology* republished another report of Crop Circles from **July 29, 1880** (*Nature*, Vol. 22, pp. 290-291). The article describes investigations made a few days before by amateur scientist John Rand Capron. We read:

FIGURE 28 - WOODCUT, THE MOWING DEVIL 1678

The storms about this part of Western Surrey have been lately local and violent, and the effects produced in some instances curious. Visiting a neighbour's farm on Wednesday evening (21st), we found a field of standing wheat considerably knocked about, not as an entirety, but in patches forming, as viewed from a distance, *circular spots*....I could not trace locally any circumstances accounting for the peculiar forms of the patches in the field, nor indicating whether it was wind or rain, or both combined, which had caused them, beyond the general evidence everywhere of heavy rainfall. They were suggestive to me of some cyclonic wind action... (Emphasis mine).[1]

The research shows that most of the time, the circles are either plainly formed by human beings (intentionally so), or can easily be attributed to human activity. Given enough time and the right instruments, smart people can make any formation. But who created these circles centuries ago? Who or what designs them today? Are the forces in play then the same ones now? Perhaps the most frequent perspective is the correlation made between sightings of UFOs and the appearance of these decorative field formations, employing circles in various fashions.

However, not everyone is certain aliens are at work. If natural causes are exclusively responsible, all circles must be the work of human beings. But are *all* Crop Circle designers *human*? The (1) complexity of some and the (2) speed with which many appear certainly challenge the *purely human* theory of their origin. Additionally, *the sophistication and size of the circles continues to evolve year after year*. And the critical element is not just skill but how quickly a few are created out of the blue.

As illustrated in the "409 Circles at Milk Hill" (see the figure adjacent), to create these designs requires a gargantuan level of effort. Then you must factor in the degree of difficulty of actually cutting them into grain so the grain isn't destroyed – just wilted at selected heights to cause the stalk to fall. Some even require cutouts that take into account unleveled ground and assume their viewing at heights requiring a helicopter (hardly discrete) to observe if the design is in fact flawless. The genuine item always is. Finally, many of these formations are made in the dark with some completed in an hour or less. Mel Sanger notes:

Most crop circles materialize overnight, while only a few have appeared during the day. One rather intricate pattern, literally across the road from Stonehenge, is known to have formed in under an hour, in broad daylight. Spread over hundreds of square miles, as many as 30 arrays, some being as wide as 4000 feet, have appeared in one night. No small accomplishment, considering it is all done in the dark. The hoaxers, who claim to be the master designers, could only produce their inferior circles in the light of day. Many separate case studies show that, indeed, it is common for a farmer to leave his field intact at dusk and return to find a work of crop art impressed in his field the next morning.

Therefore, there are numerous reports of Crop Circles that appear to transcend human resourcefulness (given the exacting detail as well as such rapid creation). This implies some sort of super-human effort is required for their formation. But what kind of "super-human" are we talking about? A word of warning: From this point forward, *things are about to get very strange.*

FIGURE 29 - 409 CIRCLES AT MILK HILL, ENGLAND, 2001

The Crabwood Glyph

In 2002, a striking Crop Circle appeared that seemed to respond to an over-the-top website. This site, the "Watcher Website," discusses the possible connection between (1) aliens, (2) pre-historic accounts of giant beings (the *Nephilim* who lived upon the earth prior to and along with our current species of human beings since the time of Adam forward – see Genesis 6:4), and (3) the *Roswell event* (a crash of an unidentified aircraft or UFO in 1947). This subject matter also links to (4) the unusual structures on the surface of Mars known as *Cydonia* that some suppose "intelligence of the extraterrestrial type" sculpted. The whole discussion is very much in line with Eric von Däniken and his theory of alien astronauts made famous in his 1968 bestselling book, *Chariots of the Gods.*

The "Watcher Website" focuses on who could have formed the *Cydonia* (spelled with a "C") Martian monuments and the possible relationship to *Sidonia* (spelled with an "S") aka Sidon – ancient Lebanon where the *Baalbek* ruins are located. Like certain Crop Circles, some regard the massive and intricate nature of the Baalbek ruins beyond the creative ability of human-kind. Complicating the analysis is the conclusion by the experts that the builders of Baalbek accomplished this project many thousands of years ago, even prior to the Pyramids.

Watcher's *Webmaster* created an icon (on the left, see figure below), to advertise his small business in 1996. The Crop Circle (to its right) appeared several years later on August 15, 2002.

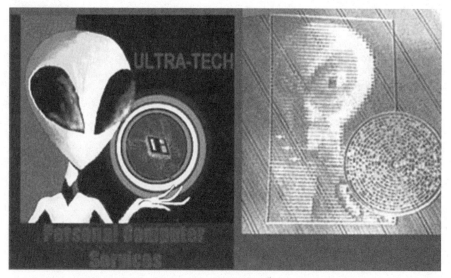

FIGURE 30 - THE CRABWOOD GLYPH COMPARED TO THE WATCHER ICON

Is it a stretch to see the Webmaster's icon parodied in a crop circle from 2002? To be sure, the correlation and the details of the circle created quite a firestorm. The Crabwood Glyph even left circle debunkers scratching their heads.[2] However, there's much more to the story than just the image which appears to mimic the icon. The level of detail included in the circle went beyond any other Crop Circle produced to that point in time.

Here are some of the details:

- The design is separated into two images, a rectangle and a circle.

- The rectangle mimics the resolution of a TV screen with 59 lines of resolution. The image is created with varying widths of "grain" used for black lines and inverse "croping" of the crops to create white lines. The effect creates a "gray scale." (By the way, the glyph appeared in a field near a television station).

- The circle uses 33 lines of information. There is a message in the circle created with ASCII characters ("ones and zeros").

- The message is an odd one:

- Beware the bearers of false gifts and their broken promises.   Much pain but still time. Believe. There is good out there. We oppose deception. Conduit Closing. (Bell Sound).

- [Bell sound? Think of Leroy Anderson and his quaint classical work, *The Typewriter*. **Ding!**]

But the numerical facts are even more intriguing:

- 59 lines of resolution in the rectangle.
- 33 lines in the disc message.
- 26 words in the disc message.
- ASCII characters in the disc, 151.
- ASCI "bits" of information, 1,208.
- 59 – 33 = 26
- 59 X 33 = 1947, the year of the Roswell event.
- 33 X 59% = 19.47, a fractal of the year of the event.
- 59 – 26 = 33, the latitude of Roswell.
- 33 x 3.141592 (π) = 103.67, the longitude of Roswell.

That's a lot of information packed into a tight little circular message built with the raw stuff of *Cheerios®*. So, did these messengers target those who follow the Website? Who are the messengers? Why did they state, "There is good out there" and "We oppose deception"? Were they responding to their accusers? Finally, were they confirming that Roswell was part of their "handiwork" as well?

The 2012 Crop Circle

On July 8, 2008, near the Avebury henge, one circle provides the most direct correlation between the meaning of the Crop Circle phenomenon and the prophecies by the Maya, vis-à-vis, the importance of the date December 21, 2012 (see *Figure 33*).

In the formation, all nine (traditional) planets of our solar system circle the sun in their locations precisely where they will be on that specific date (unfortunately, our picture of this glyph is limited). Solar software confirms the precision of the planet's locations (see the chart below the picture). Upon analysis, the level of precision is amazing. Is it just another hoax? If so, the formation is extravagant, taking a great deal of planning and precision in its creation. How many people, over what duration and with what special equipment, are required to build a formation like this?

However, there are other reasons besides *degree of difficulty* and *peculiarity of measure* to consider a non-human cause for the strange appearances of these circles, so often found in the areas near to the old circles (i.e., the "henges").

FIGURE 31 - THE CRABWOOD GLYPH OF AUGUST 15TH, 2002

Indeed, the old circles and the new ones have traits in common. First, they occupy the same areas (more about that shortly). Secondly, the purpose of the henges had pagan religious significance. Moreover, the paganism thousands of years ago may have tarnished the areas, marking them as ground given over to paganism.[3]

Daniel Pinchbeck spends a considerable amount of space in his book, *2012: The Return of Quetzalcoatl* to try to understand the meaning of such circles. As noted earlier, Pinchbeck is characteristically inclined to "experience it first and ask questions later." He has attended conferences and walked these fields season after season to determine what Crop Circles mean. He describes the strong sensations he and his friends have experienced when standing in the circles. Many who experience this phenomenon for the first time faint or are knocked down by the sounds and the psychic presence they encounter. For Pinchbeck, something deeply spiritual is transpiring in those circles that are clearly not human in origin. They are a place to encounter other-worldly phenomena.

Are Crop Circles Mandalas?

Mandalas are used in Hindu and Buddhist rituals to aid in meditation and to encourage a trance state. They are primary circular in nature, and are intended to represent the cosmos or the universe. They may include images of large stars or deities at their center. Jung believed they could help him understand more about the inner emotions of his patients. Supposedly, they help the person who focuses on them to merge his/her consciousness with the cosmos. As such, they are deeply spiritual. Given both their design and their purpose, is it possible that Crop Circles are meant to create a similar affect? Consider this definition of Mandalas which speaks to their essential purpose:

FIGURE 32 - MANDALA,
THE HOUSE OF COMMONS,
FOR THE VISIT OF THE DALI LAMA

Mandalas are commonly used by tantric Buddhists as an aid to meditation. More specifically, a Buddhist mandala is envisaged as a "*sacred space,*" a "Pure Buddha Realm," and also as an **abode** of fully realized beings or **deities**. While on the one hand, the mandala is regarded as a place separated and protected from the ever-changing and impure outer world of *samsara* [*the life cycle of life with emphasis on suffering*] and is thus seen as a **"Buddhafield"** or a **place** of Nirvana and peace...[4] (*Emphasis mine*)

In her book, *Yoga: Immortality and Freedom*, scholar Mircea Eliade explains that the mandala is also important for spiritual warfare:

At the periphery of the construction there are four cardinal doors, defended by terrifying images called "guardians of the doors." Their role is twofold. On the one hand, the guardians defend consciousness from the disintegrating forces of the unconscious; on the other, they have an offensive mission – in order to lay hold upon the fluid and mysterious world of the unconscious, consciousness must carry the struggle into the enemy's camp and hence assume the violent and terrible aspect appropriate to the forces to be combated. Indeed, even the divinities inside the mandala sometimes have a terrifying appearance... The guardians of the doors and the terrible divinities emphasize the initiatory character of entrance into a mandala...[5]

Just exactly what do *henges*, the grain fields' *Crop Circles,* and Mandalas have in common? The answer appears to be that they are all means for humans to open themselves to higher levels of consciousness, specifically, *methods to encounter non-human entities.* Pinchbeck ultimately draws the same conclusion too, that Crop Circles and Mandalas share this spiritual element.[6] Perhaps it's not overstating things to say that *Crop Circles* are *Mandalas* drawn by *the space brothers* to create another means to meet them.

Crop Circles and the Meta-Conscious Mind

This mandala-like affect is parodied through an intriguing experience. Colin Andrews in his book with partner Synthia Andrews (*2012: An Ancient Look at a Critical Time*), explores the Crop Circle experience from many angles. Colin Andrews literally wrote the book on Crop Circles and coined the term eventually accepted in the Oxford English Dictionary in 1997. Andrews brings a great deal of research to the table (he has studied about 2,500 circles). Thus, he's a noted authority (perhaps the *most* noted authority) on the subject. Financed in 1999 by the Rockefeller Foundation to investigate the fraudulent aspect of Crop Circles and publish his findings, Andrews estimates 80% of the circles are unequivocally of human origin. Nevertheless, *Andrews remains a firm believer in an* **ultra-dimensional cause** *for the other 20%*.

He continues his explanation of the phenomenon linking it with the advancement of human consciousness. In this way, he harmonizes (or to use the New Age word, *resonates*), with other Mayan authorities that believe the goal is *the transformation of consciousness.*

Andrews compares what he calls *meta-consciousness* with Jung's collective unconscious. He contends that our minds are interconnected. He also believes human minds link to a higher level of consciousness. This collective intelligence is somewhat autonomous yet remains influenced by what we imagine.

For instance, Andrews recounts how he visualized an object (a Celtic cross) and then the next day (for the first time ever), discovered the image had just appeared in a nearby Crop Circle formation. His imagining seemed to make it come into being. Was this an action of the meta-conscious mind, only a simple case of "mind over matter?" It certainly amounts to a lot more than bending spoons. He confirms that Crop Circles are associated with the henges and with other ancient locations like *Silbury Hill*, the largest ancient manmade *mound* in the world (a sacred site to those of the *Druid* persuasion).

Quoting Andrews:

> We know that the formations occur quickly, in some cases within a few seconds. Eyewitnesses report the plants suddenly oscillate, moving back and forth wildly, then simply collapse to the earth. Dowsing ["Water witching"], a technique used to detect earth energy, demonstrates the formations are linked to ley lines, or lines of *k'ul*, as the Maya would say. Ley lines is the term used by modern people for the lines of energy across the planet... Interestingly, the ley lines also link the formations to ancient sacred sites such as Stonehenge and Avebury. Are the circles activating these ancient sites as Mayan Elder Hunbatz Men says will happen?[7]

Elaborating, Andrews speaks of magnetic activity and the disruption of compasses within a Crop Circle. He indicates also how an iron residue is present within an authentic Crop Circle (*ultra-dimensionally created*), a residue that is of a purity not found in nature (surely these aren't Fullerenes too!) Moreover, he talks about a "chirping sound" that he and others have witnessed, tape-recorded, and analyzed. According to Andrews, the sound is verifiable, but to date no one knows what the sound is or what it means.

His most fascinating story relates a visit by an 87-year-old Aztec Elder named *Tlakaelel* and his guide, Burt Gunn. They arrived at the Andrews' office in Guilford, Connecticut on May 23, 1994.

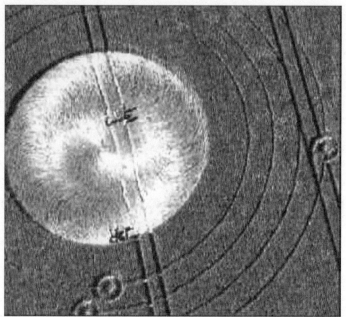

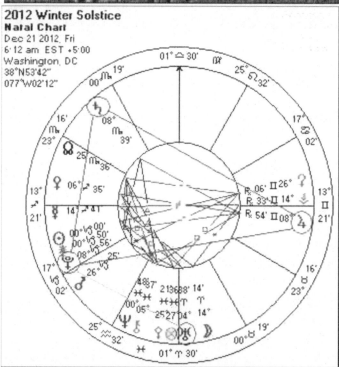

FIGURE 33 - CROP CIRCLE WITH SOLAR SYSTEM AND
THE POSITIONS OF THE 9 PLANETS ON 12-21-2012

The Elder Tlakaelel offered a drawing he had frequently envisioned and asked Andrews if he had ever seen the design before. Andrews had not. They went through many designs together. However, no one design pictured the image.[8]

As the meeting ended, Tlakaelel and Gunn got into their car and began to drive away. At that very same moment, the fax machine awoke and Andrews received a fax from Reg Presley of the musical group, *The Troggs*, a friend to Colin. The second page displayed an amazing design of a Crop Circle (a scorpion) just recently formed there. As you might guess, it was the very design that Tlakaelel had been describing. Additionally, its location in England was in a field where the ancients held ceremonial (pagan religious) dancing. What did this infer? Was it only an interesting synchronicity?

One year later, Tlakaelel joined the Andrews at Silbury Hill where the scorpion circle first appeared. The mood was reverent. The Elder quietly pointed to several spots on the landscape where there was "energy" – Andrews recognizing that each location noted by Tlakaelel was where a Crop Circle had been previously. As they walked to a site called the West Kennett Long Barrow, a man looking all of 18, appeared on a bicycle seemingly out of thin air. Suddenly he stopped and looked directly at Tlakaelel and said, "My ancestors respect and welcome you and thank you for coming." The two talked for several minutes about the importance of the land. Then the young man disappeared as mysteriously as he had appeared. In the months that followed, Andrews indicates that many Crop Circles began featuring Mayan symbols. Additionally, several of the designs reflected 2012 themes and predictions. What an amazing tale! The story resembles an episode on *The X-Files*.

Given such strange goings-on, what can we conclude? The connection of paganism from the henges of England, to the Pyramids of Egypt, to the structures and glyphs of Mesoamerica, all *seem to tell a universal story*. We discern a connection to an expansion of human consciousness, to intelligence in our ancient ancestors, and to beings of celestial origin. The cosmology of circles and spheres, of planets and suns, of human and divine beings, all seem coded in monuments and messages originating from 5,000 years ago, right up to today. And they all testify to a cohesive religious worldview, which I have called paganism. Please be mindful that my label is not, in and of itself, meant to pour scorn upon this viewpoint. At this stage, I am merely connecting the dots, illustrating how there is a singular, unified earth religion that is "as old as the hills"[9] or henges as the case may be.

So is there a single explanation for the origin of these common traits in all these phenomena? Is there *meta-consciousness* at work that ties all these formations to human activity, either physical or spiritual?

On the other hand, are UFOs involved? Did ancient alien astronauts teach our ancestors how to look at the skies and measure the earth? Could humans have figured this out by themselves? If non-human sources are involved, should we assume they are extraterrestrials?[10]

Alternatively, could these beings be what we call *demons*? Is there a diabolical scheme of spiritual deception at work in these circles? What might it tell us about decoding Doomsday? Did the ancients encounter the spirits in the circles they created? Were the circles necessary to cause the spirits to materialize and allow their worshippers to encounter them?

Joni Mitchell's song, *The Circle Game*, seems to include some insight about these phenomena I'm sure she didn't intend, but it's a fascinating poem when considering these special circles nonetheless:

> *Though (our) dreams have lost some grandeur coming true*
> *There'll be new dreams, maybe better dreams and plenty*
> *Before the last revolving year is through*
> *And the seasons they go round and round*
> *And the painted ponies go up and down*
> *We're captive on the carousel of time*
> *We can't return, we can only look behind*
> *From where we came*
> *And go round and round and round*
> *In the circle game*

33 Degrees of Separation

David Flynn is a fascinating researcher and author. We will refer to him several times. He has a knack for identifying fascinating numerical coincidences. In the case of Crop Circles, what does Flynn have to say that we might find interesting and helpful? His book, *The Temple at the Center of Time*, spends a small but provocative bit of space on the crop circle topic.

Flynn's primary thesis in *The Temple at the Center of Time* is that the Jewish temple, a design given directly by Yahweh to Solomon, *is a uniquely architected building and a stunning revelation*. The Temple in Jerusalem not only is at the center of time, it's also at the center of *space* – specifically the space we live in, the earth.[11]

134

Flynn points out how many fascinating parallels exist between space and time, particularly when measuring distances from the Temple mount in Jerusalem and linking them to the prophecies of the Bible.

Flynn also affirms that authentic Crop Circles strongly correlate to the *henge areas*. Flynn suggests that modern occurrences of Crop Circles seem to arise beginning around 1980 from Avebury in Wiltshire through to Yorkshire (in the north where Thornborough resides).[12] While they may appear worldwide, they seem especially prevalent in this location.

Furthermore, he proposes a fascinating correlation to the number 33 (utilized in the Crabwood Glyph). As we will see, the number 33 is a particularly intriguing number. Throughout the Bible, three is a number associated God and the number 33 often connects to Jesus Christ.[13] If one assumes for a moment that Lucifer exists and is the enemy of God as the Bible contends, it would follow that he is eager to take the place of God "every which way" he can. It's also logical to suppose he seeks to co-opt the number of God to represent symbolically his intention to usurp God's place in the grand scheme of things.

According to Flynn, this number also connects to Satanism, Demonology, and even UFOs (the *Grays* typically stand 3 and $1/3^{rd}$ feet tall according to many researchers – I don't know this firsthand as I've yet to see one). Since many experts of both phenomena often link the two together, it isn't far-fetched to consider the correlation.

Let's trace his *circular argument (pun intended)*: Visualize taking a compass and drawing two arcs across the map of England. Picture placing the sharp point of the compass at the Temple Mount in Jerusalem – then extend the pencil end the equivalent of 1980 nautical miles in England. The first arc begins (intersects) in the middle of Hampshire in the south and runs through the middle of Lincoln in the north. Create the second arc 33 miles further west, 2013 nautical miles from the same point in Jerusalem, beginning in the east/west middle of Dorset in the south arching through the middle of Yorkshire in the north. Between those arcs, you've created a swath that tightly correlates to the areas of the henges and Crop Circles. Besides being interesting dates in their own right (*1980* for the year crop circle interest began and *2013*, 1 off 2012), *they also reflect the number 33 once again*. First, note the swath is 33 miles wide. Although contrived by the directions I've given, according to Flynn, these distances are highly significant. 1980 miles from the Temple is equivalent to 30° of the earth's circle, while 2013 is 33.33° of that same-sized circle.[14]

Flynn is suggesting, because these phenomena collectively line up at precise distances tied to key dates and the number 3, UFO activity and paganism, are *leaving a calling card for us to decode.*

However, is this just another mathematical coincidence? Perhaps it is nothing more than that. But if you keep adding up all of these phenomena, there comes a point where you must conclude that **coincidence** *is a much more fantastic explanation than believing* **the fantastic** *is the most probable explanation.*

Similarly, the circle has often symbolized the infinite nature of God. In contrast, the circle frequently symbolizes the sun. Moreover, the notion of the *Sun God* (Apollo, Horus, Osiris) has been established as the manner of worship most antagonistic (and repugnant) to the God of the Bible.[15]

So, circling back, is there a connection between henges, Crop Circles, UFOs, and 2012? We know that the Maya worshiped many gods, including the Sun. We can assume, without anticipating much debate, that the ancient creators of the henges likely had the same basic theology as the Maya. If Knight and Butler are correct in their interpretation of the meaning of the henges, the knowledge developed in England over 5,500 years ago, may have seeded the pyramid building in Egypt. Could it have been the ancient intelligence behind the Mayan pyramids as well? On the other hand, is all of this speculation so astronomical to be unbelievable? Lastly, *are these connections part of decoding Doomsday?*

Chapter Summary

We have covered astounding if not unsettling material in this chapter. The following points are worth summarizing here:

- Ancient humankind saw in the stars information that disclosed a great deal about the earth, its size, and its place in the Solar System. Ancient humans identified that the earth circled the Sun, was a sphere, and could determine the circumference of the earth with precision. Circles were of the essence of the creation and the mode the creator used to build his universe.

- Measurements in ancient times correlate to sightings of the stars, their movements, and the timing from location to location in the sky. From the information gathered, ancient humans in England (and Mesoamerica) learned astounding and technical astronomical information such as the *precession* of the earth (aka the progression of the equinoxes).

- The ancient henges in England were astronomical (and probably astrological) centers of knowledge. Their builders used these structures to facilitate highly accurate measurements of the movements of the heavens and to establish a "global" means to measure distances and seasons. They discovered the secret of the circle by learning about π.

- Other ancient builders such as the creators of the Egyptian Pyramids may have used this knowledge gained at the "henges" of England, which may have pre-dated the Egyptian works by as much as 1,000 years (assuming the traditional dates are right). The pyramid according to some breaks the code of how to "square the circle" and may be an advancement of sorts from this perspective.

- The "modern" metric system (constructed and adopted in France in 1791) may in fact be thousands of years older, as the megalithic systems has many stunning symmetries with the metric system.

- The secrets of Freemasonry appear to include awareness of the megalithic measurements utilized in ancient structures such as the henges. We know that Pierre Charles L'Enfant, the architect of Washington DC, along with George Washington, were strong Masons. Washington DC's "layout" aligns in a stunning way with megalithic measurements proving they were taken into account by these architects and that they used this method of measuring.

- The Crop Circles, a public phenomenon since the 1980's is actually much older, dating back to events in the 17th and possibly 16th century. The association of the "devil" with Crop Circles arises at the very beginning of the phenomena.

- While the majority of Crop Circles may be human in origin, the experts believe that at least 20% of the formations aren't "human creations" given the circumstances (particularly given how quickly these circles are created).

- Some of the Crop Circle formations seem to encode knowledge in intricate detail about circumstances of 2012, such as the pattern that expresses the precise locations of planets on the date of December 21, 2012. This suggests this date might be important to its designers. Or, it may merely be another deceptive means to promote 2012 to the "already convinced."

- There is a strong connection between the pagan activity of the henges with the ancient religion of Egypt and the pre-historic Americas. The location of the Crop Circles strongly correlates to the number 33, a key number in the Bible, Freemasonry and various Luciferian schools of thought. This suggests that there is an ominous spiritual connection.

- There appears to be a message encoded in the very location of the Crop Circles that may have implications for decoding Doomsday. This message connects to the future appearance of aliens, a Buddhist Christ, or other spiritual beings. As such, traditional Jewish or Christian sources suggest that the whole phenomenon is a deceptive ploy of the Judeo-Christian God's ultimate archenemy – *Satan*.

The discoveries covered in the past two chapters demand we consider substantial ties between 2012 predictions and supernatural phenomena. For readers who consider themselves naturalists (all causes and effects can be explained by *natural* persons or things), perhaps we may have uncovered enough empirical facts to cause you to reconsider your worldview. *There is much more to come along these lines.* We have seen how revelatory information, both trivial and profound, emanates from entities outside the mundane realm. The experiences often have observable results – be they embossed in grain fields or images revealed to our conscious minds; be they willfully requested by taking drugs to induce trance states or be they observed with our mere physical senses. However conveyed, these disclosures challenge our traditional modern mental model of how the world works. I hasten to add, from a practical standpoint, it matters little whether the source of these disclosures is ultra-dimensional or extraterrestrial. In the final analysis, at issue isn't whether such realities exist, but *whether they can be trusted.* Are such beings benign or are they evil?

It's as if there are footsteps in the house and we can't help but feel our heart beat a little faster. Perhaps it's time we open the door to find out who's lurking on the other side – if we dare to look.

Notes

1 *http://en.wikipedia.org/wiki/Crop_circle.*

2 Daniel Pinchbeck, who has spent a great amount of time investigating crop circles, talks about one of his most skeptical friends who was finally convinced that something non-human was at play when they witnessed and walked through the Crabwood circle firsthand.

3 To coin a phrase, "Once a *pagans' pasture,* always a pagans' pasture."

4 *http://en.wikipedia.org/wiki/Mandalas.*

5 Tom Horn, *Apollyon Rising 2012,* Crane, Mo. Defender, 2009, pp.259, 260. Citing Mircea Eliade and Willard R. Trask, *Yoga: Immortality and Freedom,* Princeton, N.J., Princeton University, 1970, pp. 221, 222.

6 I arrived at this insight before reading Pinchbeck's book and was somewhat startled that he drew the same conclusion. It was either an intriguing synchronicity or "great minds working in the same channels." Of course, we could both be wrong.

7 Andrews and Andrews, op. cit., pg. 233. Most intriguing too is the fact that the ley lines relate to 366 virtual degrees dividing the earth and not 360. The rose line in Paris used to reflect the first meridian as does today's Greenwich. It is tied to 366. Other alignments with ancient cities follow these same lines too, another evidence of the ancient world-wide religion. This is discussed in *The Knights Templar Revealed.*

8 See Andrews's photographs at his web site: *http://www.colinandrews.net /Circles Over Years002.html).*

9 Classical literature is a sophisticated cover for demonism and paganism. Erasmus said this concerning classical studies: "Under the cloak of reviving ancient literature, paganism tries to rear its head, as there are those among Christians who acknowledge Christ only in name but inwardly breathe heathenism." Quoted from *Apollyon Rising 2012,* Thomas Horn, Defender Books, Craine, MO., 2009.

10 Benjamin Crème (a New Age leader we will meet again in the next chapter), is a strong advocate for the coming of the Buddhist Christ, known as *Maitreya,* who he believes is alive and living in the world today. He shares his provocative point of view about Crop Circles and UFOs: "The crop circles are there to draw attention to the fact that the *Space Brothers* are there. They are amazing constructions. They are made in seconds by the 'ships' of the Space Brothers. They are complex and beautiful constructions which cannot be made in any other way. They appear all over the world but the majority are in the south of England. Why? Because Maitreya is in London." See *http://en.wikipedia.org/wiki/ Benjamin_Creme.*

11 In making this point, Flynn is reflecting the orthodox Jewish view, a perspective also held by Sir Isaac Newton. We will look at this theory in more depth later.

12 Flynn's suggestion that 1980 marked the "beginning" of the crop circle phenomenon is not accurate according to Colin Andrews who, as I noted, literally "invented the term "Crop Circle" in 1985. His book on the subject was entitled, *Circular*

Evidence, co-authored with Pat Delgado in 1989. Flynn would be more accurate if he were to state that crop circles began to be a public phenomenon around 1980.

[13] Jesus may have lived to be 33 years old, may have died in 33 AD, ministered between the 30th and 33rd "parallels latitude," taught between 30 AD and 33 AD, and performed 33 different miracles recorded in the gospels.

[14] We'll see how the number 33 pops up again in other UFO / occult topics we've yet to cover.

[15] We will pick up this theme again when we discuss the Freemasons and the findings of Thomas Horn in his recent book, *Apollyon Rising 2012*.

Chapter 8:
Esotericism, UFOs, and the Last Days

Everyone is helpful, everyone is kind
On the road to Shambala
Everyone is lucky, everyone is so kind
On the road to Shambala

Three Dog Night

What's Old is New Again

C.S. Lewis, Christianity's most famous apologist of the 20th century said, "Just because the shoe fits, this doesn't mean it's a new shoe." Lewis wasn't speaking about Nikes, Uggs, or whatever famous brand was contemporary to his time. He reminds us that just because an emerging religion is fashionable, that doesn't make it original. Anyone who's been around long enough knows that it's not just style but religion too, where *renovation* is more popular than *innovation*. Ecclesiastes teaches, "There is nothing new under the sun." Today we might say, "What's old is new again."

In context, Lewis was speaking of *Pantheism*. A recurring religion, it winds its way in and out of style down through the centuries. We see it underpinning eastern philosophies and belief systems (e.g., Hinduism, Buddhism). Upon analysis, we can trace its system of belief all the way back to ancient *Babylon*.

Pantheism is actually a *mystical misnomer*, a word that *sounds like something it's not*. The word is composed of two elements, "pan" (referring to the Greek god of nature), and "theism" (the belief in a *personal* God). Even the movie *Avatar (2009)*, features blue creatures resembling classic pictures of Peter Pan or Puck from a *Midsummer Night's Dream* (Shakespeare), who sports pointed ears and a tail. Likewise, the *Avatar world* is **Pan-dora**. It's no accident that this world is "alive" with plants and trees seemingly conscious and animated. This is a key element of the story and part of the movie's sensational appeal.

When the two elements of the term Pan-theism are put together, it connotes a personal God "assimilated into nature," where nature is not only divine, but *conscious, willful, and self-directed*. This idea exceeds what we infer by "personifying nature" with the term, "Mother Nature," an attribution which implies little more than "laws that guide natural processes." When we invoke this phrase, we don't think of nature as a living person on the same level of humans. Yet the "mysticism" embedded connotatively in the word *pantheism*, seems to inflate *nature* into something *that is intentional and goal-directed.* This is romantic, but highly unscientific, even to the most mystical of scientists influenced by such books as *The Tao of Physics,* Fritjof Capra's popular 1975 book on how modern physics mirrors eastern mysticism.[1]

Another 20th century apologist, Francis Schaeffer, pointed out that a more accurate term for this concept should be "pan-everything-ism" in an attempt to extract the *person* out of the term. The Judeo-Christian tradition strongly contrasts its belief in a personal God who, while existing everywhere throughout His creation (an attribute known as His *omnipresence*), is nonetheless *distinguished from that creation.* This is to say that God is more than nature – He transcends it.

The New Age Movement

In the 1980's, the *old shoe became new again.* Pantheism shape-shifted and assumed its 20th century form: *The New Age Movement.* Here, we encounter yet another misnomer. The New Age is *anything but new.* The New Age viewpoint builds its not-so-systematic thinking on top of Theosophy (our next topic), which itself is based on Hinduism and Tibetan Buddhism. Its thought leaders did little more than take an arcane version of esotericism and "Americanize" it. Through a well-regarded book, *The Aquarian Conspiracy* written by Marilyn Ferguson in 1980, the *open conspiracy* was widely disclosed documenting the literally dozens of organizations, authors, shamans, foundations, counselors, and various pop-culture self-help books and periodicals characterizing this pseudospiritism movement. The New York Times called Ferguson's book, the "Bible

FIGURE 34 - *THE AQUARIAN CONSPIRACY* BY MARILYN FERGUSON

of the New Age Movement." This acclamation was a bit overstated since the book laid out little in the way of spiritual truth – it was more about *reporting* – documenting how widespread the ideas of the New Age were, infiltrating virtually every spiritual organization that wasn't expressly Christian, Jewish, or Islamic.

For many evangelicals, the book awakened concerns that elite esotericists and upper class pagans were winning the spiritual battle at the end of the 20th century. However true (or not), it was stunning how many identified with what Ferguson advanced. Why, all-of-a-sudden (in the words of Kipling), did "East meet West?" How could this happen? What was the catalyst?

If we study American intellectual history, we see that the change emerged because (1) America had forfeited the "moral high ground" it held following World War II, as well as (2) losing its national self-esteem resulting from the debacle known as *Vietnam*. Additionally, (3) the liberal mainline denominations offered little spiritual substance to the masses other than watered down theology – aka naturalism spruced up with a few religious terms. This was due to a 1960's theological retreat by mainstream Protestants known as the "God is dead" movement. Various books by domestic theologians acquainted American "mainstream Protestants" to progressive European neo-orthodox and liberal theologies then dominating Europe and widely adopted there for the previous 100 years.[2]

As far as budding young intellectuals at U.S. colleges were concerned, (1) the *American Church* (both Catholic and Protestant), (2) *University Regents and Administrators* throughout *Academia*, as well as the (3) *Federal Government*, were seen *as failing institutions*, part of the old generation's *system* that could no longer be trusted. American youth declared war on the *Establishment*. Upon Nixon's resignation after the scandal we call *Watergate*, all that was bad about America seemingly proved to be true. Disillusioned, young idealists searched for a new way forward.

In popular culture, the wind of change commenced in the 60's with the Beatles visit to India during their *mystical phase*, searching for answers to life's tough questions. Soon popular culture was overrun with rampant drug usage (highlighted by Timothy Leary's LSD experiments), hippies and "free-love," rock-and-roll, and the counter-culture's greatest moment, *Woodstock*. As mentioned at the book's outset, this was the *Eve of Destruction* – in more ways than one.

The change continued in the 70's with Transcendental Meditation[3] and radical, intense massage therapies like "Rolfing." Ouija (weegee) boards, séances, and channeling aliens became discussion subjects in the media as well as a popular replacement to fill the spiritual vacuum experienced by so many. In essence, *spiritism* replaced *materialism*. Pop-religion transformed spirituality into esotericism. Personal piety and good works, trademarks of 19th century Christianity in America, faded into the background. Spirituality was all about "personal experience" and *mysticism* in particular.[4]

Not long after Ferguson's "Aquarian conspiracy" was acknowledged, Shirley MacClaine went *out on a limb* in her 1983 book by the same title. "The book received both acclaim and criticism for its candor in dealing with such topics as reincarnation, meditation, mediumship (trance-channeling), and even unidentified flying objects (UFOs). This book made Shirley MacClaine the butt of many a joke, especially by the late-night comedians."[5]

Today, the concepts and ideas of the New Age Movement continue to be popular themes of many self-help books. Perhaps the most well-known is *The Secret* published in 2006. Expressly directing its adherents to "name it and claim it" – to visualize what you want and watch it happen – *The Secret* generated so much interest it was even made into a movie.[6] Nevertheless, like so many other New Age self-help works, the emphasis was heavy on self and light on altruism. Underneath the esoteric mysticism lay a self-obsessed commercialism. "It's all about me."[7] Consequently, *The Secret* drew its fair share of criticism and mockery in the name of more traditional, tried-and-true worldviews,

FIGURE 35 - RHONDA BYRNES' *THE SECRET*

which championed philanthropic pursuits as essential to *true spirituality*.

So where did these oh-so-foreign notions of spirituality originate? To discover their headwaters, we must head *east* and pick up the trail of early westerners who went the way of the *Swami*.[8] It turns out that if the West hadn't met the East – as if to spite Kipling – the East's spiritual approach might have faded away, merely road-kill on the highway to modernism.

Madam Blavatsky, Theosophy, and Nazi Anti-Semitism

Americans are noteworthy for borrowing a good idea and making the most of it. After World War II and going forward, if America sanctioned *something*, from nuclear reactors to hula-hoops, it went golden worldwide. When we give something *the thumbs up* – the world adopts, if not adores, whatever we approve. We are market makers for wacky ideas, goofy products, and even trite television shows. If you can make it in America, you can make it anywhere. It's no different in spirituality.

To the Aryan Theosophical Society of New York. With H.P.B.'s & H.S.O.'s good wishes London, October, 1888.

FIGURE 36 - BLAVATSKY AND OLCOTT, LONDON, 1888

Around the turn of the 19th century (1901), Eastern religions appeared to be in their twilight, casualties of the enlightened mind. As it turns out, their death sentence was overturned. Several Europeans and Americans came to the rescue, breathing life into Hinduism and Buddhism. Occidental (western) adaptation of the old oriental ways reinvigorated these religions and made them vital again. The two most notable figures in this restoration were *Madame Helena Petrova Blavatsky* (Russian born, 1831 – most frequently referred to in esoteric circles as HPB, a self-imposed nickname), and Henry Steel Olcott, a lawyer, agriculturalist, and a journalist "hack" that covered the *Spiritualist* phenomenon (born in New Jersey, 1832). The two met in 1874. In 1875, they founded the *Theosophist Society* in New York City. They quickly became New York City's first and most famous *odd couple* – at least at the end of the 19th century.

The following summarizes what Theosophy attempts:

> The Theosophists (combine) spiritualism and science to investigate the supernatural reflected the society's desire to combine... religion and reason and to produce a rationally spiritual movement. This "occult science" within the Theosophical Society was used to find the "truth" behind all of the world's major religions. Through their research, Olcott and Blavatsky concluded that Buddhism best embodied elements of what they found significant in all religions.
>
> Olcott utilized Western scientific reasoning in his synthesis and presentation of Buddhism... Notably, his efforts represent one of the earliest attempts to combine the scientific understanding and reasoning of the West with the Buddhist religion of the East. The interrelationship he saw between Buddhism and Science paralleled his Theosophical approach to show the scientific bases for supernatural phenomena such as auras, hypnosis, and Buddhist "miracles."[9]

Some admirers regarded Olcott to be a *bodhisattva*, a Christ-like figure, reincarnated from the Third Century. Many throughout southern Asia considered him a reformer of Buddhism and additionally saw him as a prominent figure in the history of Ceylon, today's Sri Lanka, where he spent considerable time.[10]

However, in Europe and America, the more influential of these two is HPB, through two voluminous but highly influential books – *Isis Unveiled* (1877) and *The Secret Doctrine* (1888). Although erratically penned, they remain significant in esoteric circles even today, despite their negative impact in the 1920's and 30's. Like Mayan enthusiasts who downplay the most notorious characteristic of the Mayan religion – *human sacrifice* – New Age authors seldom acknowledge the horrific heritage of Theosophy contributing as it did to German National Socialism, aka *Nazism*.

HPB's writings were thinly disguised anti-Semitism. She proclaimed the superiority of the *Aryan* race, the fifth "root race" of seven supposed races. Furthermore, as if she hadn't already gone too far, she insisted the Aryans descended from the survivors of Atlantis, destroyed 850,000 years ago. *Yes, that's correct, 850,000 years ago.* Quite a different timeline from what Plato offered and what alternative historians propound today (12,000 years ago). HPB indicated that the Jewish race was from "inferior stock" – an offshoot of the Aryan race.

According to her, there are many modern non-Aryan peoples inferior to the Aryans. Frequently, she contrasts Aryan with Semitic culture (denigrating the latter), contending that Semitic races have become "degenerate in spirituality and perfected in materiality."[11] Clever wording, but highly racist.

HPB's grandfather was a *Rosicrucian Mason* who maintained a large library of occult works. He also once belonged to a German secret society that supposedly had contact with "unknown Superiors" (presumably *spirit guides*). Like her Grandfather, HPB developed her own superiors – the "Great White Brotherhood" in *Isis Unveiled* – a book she claimed was "dictated to her by a tall Hindu who came every day as she sat down to write. *HPB did not suffer from writer's block.*"[12] HPB also indicates that she spent time in Tibet with "the Brothers" becoming a Tibetan adept (which scholars doubt is true contending she couldn't sneak past the British into Tibet – the Brits feared she was a Russian spy, a worry not without merit).

So just how important was Blavatsky to the Nazi movement? Heinrich Himmler, the head of the SS, built his case for Aryan superiority firmly upon HPB's writings. Himmler sent his scientists and adventurers off to Tibet, prior to World War II, in an attempt to prove the theory regarding the superiority of the Aryan race.[13] The Third Reich built its *natural* science squarely on these *supernatural* myths.

Christopher Hale, who studied the infamous Nazi expeditions to the Himalayas, draws these conclusions:

> The *Secret Doctrine* made an especially powerful impression in Germany and Austria. Olcott had even considered moving the Theosophical Society headquarters from India to Germany [*yet another relocation following London*] after the English Society for Psychical Research had exposed Madame Blavatsky as a fraud (she was caught out writing the letters which she claimed were 'precipitated' by her mahatmas). Some fifty years later, after 1933, Theosophy would become even more popular as Germans were encouraged to turn away from Christianity and embrace faiths that were considered to be more Aryan. For many, *The Secret Doctrine* appeared to reconcile science and belief, nature and myth, and in Germany, it catalyzed a much older intellectual tradition...[14]
>
> All over Europe, and in India itself, theosophy became a cult. Its disciples were not the hungry masses who poured into spiritualist meetings and séances desperately seeking solace; they were intellectuals, diplomats, philosophers, and even scientists. United under the Tibetan symbol of the swastika, they infested the salons and laboratories of Europe. As in *The Secret Doctrine* itself, science and occultism lay happily side-by-side in a fetid embrace.[15]

According to Trevor Ravenscroft, an historian of the Third Reich,[16] Dietrich Eckhart (aka the intellectual father of Nazism), was heavily influenced by Blavatsky and *The Secret Doctrine*.[17]   In 1919, members of the German Workers Union determined that what they needed was a young bachelor with esoteric interests, attractive to women, who could mesmerize audiences with his speeches. After searching for the right person, they determined that a young private in the army, Adolf Hitler, would fill the bill. Hitler later acknowledged Blavatsky and gave Eckhart a *shout out* for making him what he was. No doubt Eckhart's instruction in Black Magic ritual was instrumental in Hitler's reliance upon occult empowerment to fulfill what he saw as his sacred destiny: To defeat Christianity and Judaism, restore the purity of German blood, and conquer the world.

Alice Bailey and the Externalization of the Hierarchy

One of the most bizarre themes of occult philosophy and religion is the insistence that there are a series of "masters" who live in remote places and guide what happens in our world. HPB's *Great White Brotherhood* was an update to her grandfather's "unknown Superiors." This tradition continues with the most important disciple of HPB, Alice Ann Bailey (1880-1949), typically nicknamed *AAB* by her followers. Bailey, while born in England, lived most of her life in the United States.

Like Blavatsky, Bailey was a *channeler*, claiming to take telepathic dictation from a supernatural source she identified as *Djwhal Kuhl*, aka DK, the *Tibetan*. She wrote over 20 books, from 1919 to 1949 acting as his agent, commenting to the effect that she didn't always agree with DK, but what he said was exactly what she put down on paper. She knew her supernatural superiors as the *Masters of Wisdom*, of which Jesus was but one (and according to her *not* the supreme Master). In the *Externalization of the Hierarchy,* Bailey indicates that the time is soon coming when the "Hierarchy of ancient Masters" will disclose themselves to all humanity. A prayer given to her by DK, known as the *Great Invocation,* is a prayer to call upon the Masters to leave their "hidden ashrams" and live in the cities of the World. For Bailey, the *Christ* is a collective title for these various spiritual gurus. The "Return of the Christ" is the culmination of *the divine plan* realized through these spirit guides.

All scholars of merit connect the teachings of Bailey and Blavatsky.[18] There is strong evidence to support this conclusion. When controversy emerged over who would lead Theosophy and the New Age movement, Bailey and her husband, Foster Bailey, a 32ⁿᵈ degree Mason, led a "Back to Blavatsky" movement to counter her rival Annie Besant. To this day, there remains a debate among Theosophists as to whether Bailey was true to HPB.

Nevertheless, Bailey is by far and away the most prominent mastermind of the New Age. We can see this in the numerous organizations she founded with her husband. To name but a few: *The Arcane School, The Group of New World Servers,* and *Lucis Trust,* originally known as *Lucifer Trust.*[19] After Alice Bailey died in 1949, Foster Bailey took over Lucis Trust and continued to lead it until his own death in 1977.

As with the other pagan (world) religions both past and present, Bailey placed a strong emphasis on transformation, reincarnation, and Karma. Like the Freemasons, there is an emphasis on the mystical powers of *Venus* and *Sirius*. As with HPB, there is frequent mention of Shamballa (spelled, *Shambhala* in Buddhist references), the divine seat of power for *Sanat Kumara* who is, according to Bailey, the ruler of this world and a focal point for occult power and *eternal life.*[20]

Like Blavatsky, Bailey was strongly anti-Semitic, believing that the Jews "have bad Karma," blame the Gentiles for all their problems, and "require the best for their children no matter what the cost to others." She talked frequently about "the Jewish Problem" and claimed after World War II, that the occupants of the concentration camps were 80% other races and only 20% Jews. From a practical standpoint, she was a holocaust denier.

One Rabbi said this of her teachings regarding Judaism:

> Bailey's plan for a New World Order and her call for "the gradual dissolution—again if in any way possible—of the Orthodox Jewish faith" revealed that "her goal is nothing less than the destruction of Judaism itself... This stereotyped portrayal of Jews is followed by a hackneyed diatribe against the Biblical Hebrews, based upon the 'angry Jehovah' theology of nineteenth-century Protestantism. Jews do not, and never have, worshipped an angry vengeful god..."[21]

This brings us to another prominent but often questioned end-times issue: *The worldwide conspiracy of the rich and powerful,* to foist *democratic socialism* upon all the peoples of the world, ending individual nation states and creating a single one-world government.

There is little debate that Blavatsky's teaching heavily influenced National Socialism in Germany through Himmler. But will history repeat itself? Could we see this happen in the 21ˢᵗ Century? Almost every ultra-conservative speculates that "the elite families of the world" are working behind the scenes to bring world government to flower. Furthermore, many conservative authors argue that the spiritual teachings of Alice Bailey and the ascended Masters have and continue to sway these elites.

Obviously, it doesn't help efforts to *controvert this conspiracy theory* when Lucis Trust, the organization Alice and Foster Bailey founded, boasts members like David Rockefeller and Henry Kissinger, typically key figures in the supposed conspiracy.

George H.W. Bush, a renowned member of *Skull and Bones*, the secret society at Yale, only threw more fuel on the fire when he called repeatedly for a "new world order of the ages,"[22] the very same language used by Bailey. Conspiracy theorists call attention to how Freemasons have affected America from its inception, including directing the creation of the Great Seal of the United States, with its "All Seeing Eye," the unfinished Pyramid, and the motto, *Novus Ordo Seclorum* (Latin for "New Order of the Ages," often translated, *New World Order*). Putting his money where his mouth is, Bush (41) has given over one million dollars to Freemasonry.

Despite all these details, can we conclude the conspiracy is real? I'm reminded of what C.S. Lewis said about any *good* conspiracy theory: "It takes the *undeniable*, and transforms it into the *unbelievable*." As with the conspiracy we discussed surrounding Denver International Airport, it may or may not be true, but it's no longer possible to easily brush it aside. We all know how to finish the truism, "Where there's smoke..."

In an important book that we will reference throughout the remainder of this chapter, *The Stargate Conspiracy*, authors Clive Prince and Lynn Picknett document the many elusive ties between various elements of this grand conspiracy, which appear to even include an eager CIA that's seeking to obtain the capability of *remote viewing* – the ultimate means to gather intelligence anywhere at any time (past or present):

> Most conspiracy theorists (we are not denying that we fit the description ourselves) tend to think in terms of one identifiable group behind every plot and hidden agenda. Unfortunately for such theorists and romanticists alike, real life is not so simple. Where conspiracies exist they are likely to involve various individuals and groups who have a vested interest in a particular outcome. It may be that the Stargate conspirators include CIA operatives, Freemasons, politicians and their wealthy backers, who believe they have something to gain by creating this belief system, or fear they have something to lose if it does not happen. This conspiracy is bigger than one group or set of individuals.

What is clear is the nature of the conspiracy's objective. It is to push a particular system of belief on as many levels as possible, from the general public to genuine dyed-in-the-wool New Agers. 'They' are after all of us – hearts, minds and souls.[23]

Alice Bailey died in 1949. However, her ideas continue to influence the "Stargate Conspiracy" as we shall see.

Benjamin Crème and Flying Saucer Cults

The legacy of Blavatsky and Bailey continues today in the life and work of Benjamin Crème. Crème, born in 1922 in Scotland, presently runs *Share Magazine*. Crème's magazine documents numerous instances where his organization has accomplished "good works" by directing its charitable activities toward impoverished areas throughout the world. Additionally, a number of noteworthy personages have published articles in *Share*, such as Prince Charles of England. Finally, for good measure *Share Magazine* also regularly contains *channeled material*, although admittedly one can be sure the author of the channeled articles isn't on the payroll, thus avoiding social security payments.

Crème is known best for his prediction that the *Maitreya* is destined to reveal himself in our time. This Maitreya is the Buddhist Christ – the next incarnation of an ascended master.

Crème claims that Maitreya manifested himself through (or *overshadowed*) Jesus 2000 years ago, that Maitreya resided in the Himalayas, and in 1977 he descended from his ancient retreat in the Himalayas and took an airplane to London. He took up residence in the Indian-Pakistani community of London in the Brick Lane area. He has been living and working there, seemingly as an ordinary man, his true status known to relatively few. Maitreya has apparently been emerging gradually into full public view so as not to infringe humanity's free will.

In 1982, Crème and his organization the *Tara Center*, took out a full-page ad in many newspapers around the world proclaiming that the Christ was soon to appear. However, in a contradictory progression of this story, Maitreya requires the cooperation of a human subject to become visible. Unfortunately, for Crème and company the human subject set to host this incarnation (supposedly living in London) apparently *changed his mind* – he wouldn't allow his body to be the vehicle for this transformation. Therefore, "Christ" delayed his appearance. Consequently, Crème's followers began to drift away. Not in the least bit flummoxed, in 1997 Crème once again predicted a television appearance of the Christ. For a second time, Maitreya was a no-show.

Like Bailey and Blavatsky before him, Crème claims he receives his messages *telepathically from a spirit guide.* This has led him to channel large volumes of written material. If one thing seems certain about all of these spirit guides – *they have no gift for brevity.*[24]

When Crème began his career in the 1950's, he helped spur a new trend for Theosophy. Crème was a member of an early UFO religious group, *The Aetherius Society*, founded in London by a George King, who claimed to have spoken with an alien who used the name, *Aetherius.* Crème eventually disagreed with King and went his own way.

Various UFO religions have come and gone too. We mentioned the *Brotherhood of the Seven Rays,* the subject of the book *When Prophecy Fails,* another 1950's cult that broke apart after aliens repeatedly failed to land the ship as predicted by Dorothy Martin and her followers. The *Heavens Gate Group* was also a UFO-based group, mixing New Age concepts with science fiction and the Christian apocalypse, concluding in a disastrous outcome.[25]

But what is it that these flying saucer cults believe? Here's a summary belief statement derived from materials published by *The Aetherius Society:*

1. Jesus, Buddha, Krishna and other great religious leaders were of extraterrestrial origin and came to Earth to help humankind.

2. In this sense, all major religions are similar in nature and all religious paths lead towards the same ultimate end.

3. Karma and reincarnation are considered two natural, all pervasive laws of God.

4. There is advanced, intelligent life on other planets. Unidentified flying objects really are intelligently controlled extraterrestrial spacecraft visiting this Earth.

5. Extraterrestrials are friendly and are here to help humanity in its development.

6. A belief that humankind, and all of life, is a divine spark of the Creator, our God, and that Earth is a classroom on the evolutionary ladder of life.[26]

With these principles laid out, it's easy to homogenize Theosophy and Flying Saucer cults into a singular, *New Age worldview.* If the goal of this over-the-top teaching was nothing more than personal transformation, whether poppycock or not, it might not transgress our sensibilities. Unfortunately, the ultimate objective of these enlightened teachers is far more menacing.

Where is All This Heading?

Throughout the theosophist literature, the fundamental goal is implementation of what the enlightened ones call, "The Plan."

The key to *The Plan* is overcoming the obstacle of *monotheistic religion*. The Plan's proponents teach that its advocates can only make progress on the goal of *human transformation* when this esoterically advanced spiritual regime guts Judeo-Christian-Islam religions of their *dualistic* and *legalistic* essentials.[27]

Other New Age thinkers like David Spangler and Barbara Marx Hubbard, teach that there will be a selection process – there are "keepers" and then, *there are those to be tossed*. The language isn't subtle – those that aren't compliant will be re-educated through placement in special concentration camps. Hubbard indicates, "People will either change or die. That is the choice."[28]

The Hierarchy will eliminate religious freedom and replace it with a single, world-state religion. Alice Bailey states, "It is this revelation which lies behind all the activities which now engross the attention of the Hierarchy."[29] Mel Sanger comments:

> Unlike the East, where these pagan teachings are familiar, in Western society there is a need to break down traditional monotheistic (and/or athe-istic) resistance to them. To ease penetration, New Agers encourage "light encounters," psychic experiences which seem to carry the individual be-yond normal consciousness into a new realm of spiritual sensation. Also known as, "a doorway to higher consciousness," the suitably impressed person will be encouraged to seek this experience on a regular basis. The only way to achieve it, however, is through passivity and a willingness to submit one's mind to outside control of a "guide."[30]

Unmistakably, not only is *someone* asking us to let go of our religious convictions, but also our volition – our "will" or "control of self." *Someone* is insisting we relinquish personal freedom to achieve spiritual perfection. This is a rather fascinating principle to ponder: Spiritual growth comes from the *elimination* of our personal choice. Needless to say, such backward advice flies in the face of the worlds' most venerated religious teachers from Confucius to Christ. Members of the New Age clearly aren't advocates of existentialism.

So why can we believe such a thing? Who is this someone calling for the diminution of our individualism? Who's pulling these strings at the other end?

Without hesitation or apology, the New Agers tell us who. David Spangler indicates its humanity's old friend *Lucifer*. Furthermore, if we really want to get saddled up with the New Age, we must submit to a *Luciferic Initiation*. This process he promises will "set us free." ? ?

> ...the angel of man's evolution, will *(progress us on our)* journey to "god-hood" at the new level, which includes a personal experience of the "knowledge of good and evil." New Agers confirm that this knowledge is what Lucifer offered to Eve in the Garden, and it's being offered again today. Only it's been misunderstood, due to fear inherited from the superstitious Judaic/Christian religion. Since God has both a good and an evil side, and one cannot attain complete godhood with only one side, Lucifer comes to give us the final gift of wholeness. If we accept it, then he is free and we are free. That is the Luciferic initiation. It is one that many people now, and in the days ahead, will be facing, for it is an initiation into the New Age.[31]

How reminiscent of other promises made by Lucifer! Making a guest appearance in the Garden of Eden as the talking snake, Lucifer said to Eve, "Eat the apple, then you will be as gods." Given the trouble that his advice got us into in the first place, I for one, am rather reluctant to adopt any more of his bright ideas.

Of course, the majority of smart people strongly doubt such dramatic shifts in spirituality and religious freedom would happen here in America. And for good reason. This course of action leads to a radical assault on the U.S. Constitution, which protects the right of religious freedom. Additionally, there are too many fundamentalists scattered about to protest and prevent it.[32] It's no wonder the goal of the New Age luminaries has been frustrated – so far.

Nevertheless, let's consider the unthinkable for a moment: What circumstances could cause this to change? What would have to happen to abridge these freedoms? How could we possibly embrace Lucifer, rehabilitated or not, as the source of spiritual transformation?

There are two ways this unbelievable scenario could come about: First, a *massive re-evaluation of the nature of God*. Monotheistic religions could falter *if* there is compelling and overwhelming evidence for the idea that many gods, rather than one, shaped our humanity. Secondly, the unbelievable could occur *if* something or someone removes the *hindrance* to change – namely, those who believe in the Bible's infinite personal God.

Neither of these occurrences seems likely. But what if both of these *game changers* take place within the same play? What if, in one amazing event, many gods suddenly appeared to help set our world right and at the same time, *instantly*, those who believe in a singular, personal God of the Bible, were eliminated as hold outs to society's reclamation? The world certainly wouldn't be the same.

Close Encounters of the Ultimate Kind

One of the most noteworthy figures in today's New Age blend of Ufology, Pyramidology, and Theosophy is Dr. J.J. (James) Hurtak, PhD from the University of Minnesota.

A former professor at California State University at Northridge and a genuine *polymath*, Hurtak is founder of the *Society for Future Science* and author of *The Keys of Enoch*. He also holds the title, *Research Director, Great Pyramid of Giza Research Association*.

Picknett and Prince point out that Hurtak flits between two different groups, the so-called *pyramidiots* like Robert Bauval and Graham Hancock (who are academically oriented, resembling true archeologists), and the channelers such as Andrija Puharich,[33] Alice A. Bailey, and the infamous magus Aleister Crowley (aka "the Great Beast" – a name he fondly adopted). Their point: Hurtak demonstrates a chameleon quality. In the first group, he's a serious academic. In the second, he's an extraordinary visionary and prophet. He cloaks his *group two* speculative ideology with his *group one* credibility layer, owing to his associations with empirically oriented research of the Pyramids.[34]

Hurtak is particularly famous for bringing to the attention of our modern world the actual identity of the ascended masters – the so-called "Council of Nine" – purportedly the ancient *nine gods of the Egyptian Ennead*.[35] The "Nine" speak through a single entity that takes the name, "Tom," most likely a modern nickname for A-Tum, chief of these gods (even spirits have a sense of humor). Tom communicates substantial information through his channelers in the book, *The Only Planet of Choice*. In this book, "Tom" recommends Alice Bailey and follows her racist lead. According to Tom, he bases his racism upon the "fact" that some human races have alien DNA and some don't. Should we guess which races are supposedly smarter? Picknett and Prince comment:

> There are thousands of enthusiastic believers in the (Egyptian) hypotheses... They do not, as a whole, realize that they are also tacitly opening themselves up to the spiritual message of James Hurtak, which in essence also means that of Alice Bailey. This prompts a worrying thought: Will the Bailey/Hurtak *The Keys of Enoch* become the Bible of the new Millennium? ... it is this aspect of the whole issue of the Council of Nine that is, in our view, by

far the most important. For while the objective reality – or otherwise – of the Nine is a fascinating subject, surely it is far less important than an analysis of their spiritual message. After all, it is their teaching that drives their followers, and their actions, in turn, could impinge upon us (all)... [36]

In Hurtak's *Keys of Enoch,* he describes a divine program that will commence with house cleaning or cleansing. The *Forces of Light* will battle the *Forces of Darkness.* The Forces of Light are certainly advocates of Hurtak's message. But who comprise the evil doers? Of course, it's those stick-in-the-mud Jews, Christians and Muslims. However, it's not just the *monotheistic bigots* – also included in the force of darkness are those atheists too focused on history, science, and facts to see the bigger picture. For those who aren't working with the *Light*, Hurtak warns, "it will be a time of Great Tribulation." In a great reversal, Hurtak predicts Doomsday is coming *to Bible believers.* Using words like "cleansing" and "selection," if in charge these intellects could foment a second holocaust.

Jacques Vallèe, a noted UFOologist for three decades, compares the ideology of the "Nine" with the Nazis. Contactee propaganda undermines the image of human beings as masters of their own destiny, according to Vallèe. It attempts to convince us that there are "higher races" implying that "lower races" should be eliminated.[37]

Hurtak sugarcoats the racial cleansing of *the Plan* by twisting more biblical language and names for his purpose:

> The conclusion of a 'divine program' after which there will be an upward spiral into the new 'master program' from the Father-Spirit Initiative. The increasing of inner 'Peace' and blessings of 'Joy' that will come with the pouring of the gifts of the Holy Spirit Shekinah upon spiritual mankind who will perceive the knowledge of the Most High God and use the wisdom of the 'Sons of Light,' to prepare for Government in the Name of YHWH.[38]

Picknett and Prince believe even the "non-esoteric" work of Robert Bauval and Graham Hancock is part of the esoteric game plan: "What is clear is that the essential message in their books – from *The Orion Mystery* to *The Mars Mystery* – fits the same overall agenda, bringing it to a much wider, global audience and helping to pave the way for the acceptance of Hurtak/the Nine's ideology."[39]

Picknett and Prince quote Bauval and Hancock to underscore those authors' *millenarian tone*:

The millennium is rushing in. There is much work to do for all who feel part of the same quest, namely to bring about a new and much needed spiritual and intellectual change for this planet. Giza, without a doubt, has a major role to play. [*Bauval*]

Poised on the edge of a millennium, at the end of a century of unparalleled wickedness and bloodshed in which greed has flourished, humanity faces a stark choice between matter and spirit – the darkness and the light. [*Hancock*][40]

Prince and Picknett caution that all is working together to create a coordinated tapestry of deception and ultimate doom through *the teachings of occult activists*, from Blavatsky to Bailey, from Crème to Spangler, from Hoagland to Hurtak, and finally, to a future world religious leader who will personify their ideology. "Could the early years of the twenty-first century see the emergence of a new Jesus or a new Moses to make sense of our puny, worthless lives and hand down from above a new set of commandments? Will the prophesied 'return of the Great initiate' [*SDW: perhaps Quetzalcoatl?*] become a reality, thanks to some carefully contrived stage management?"[41] What would trigger this? Prince and Picknett speculate *some sort of major event* – a rollout of *prima facie* evidence,[42] that the God of the Bible is either *dead or passé*. In essence, He is an outdated figure that the New Agers insist we "rise above."

The possibility must be seriously considered that the conspirators are preparing the ground for some kind of major occurrence, a revelatory event that will suddenly, dramatically, and radically change the world forever. What form this might take is uncertain – a carefully stage-managed 'return of the gods' to Giza before a mass audience, perhaps – but what is certain is that these people have the resources and technology to present such an event... As the stories of Hitler's Germany and countless other examples from history prove beyond doubt, ordinary decent folk can only too easily be persuaded to commit atrocities against their fellow man if they truly believe it is part of a grand design... [43]

Indeed, today speculation arises from many pundits that the authorities are preparing us for such a mind-blowing revelation. We saw the British Government release their UFO files in 2008. In America, the freedom of information act has opened the file on *Roswell* (at least to a meager extent), demonstrating just how much experimenting the U.S. Air Force did out west since World War II. No wonder there was (and continues to be) much speculation about UFOs.

Not that we can legitimately doubt the reality of UFOs any longer. As Dr. I.D.E. Thomas says in his book, *The Omega Conspiracy*, UFO researchers *can bury us in evidence*. The issue is, "What, or who, are UFOs?" Not "do UFOs exist."

Debating their existence might have been a good discussion in the 1980s; but today, UFO's are a *fait accompli*.[44] The real message of the British closing their files was that UFOs happen all the time, they just haven't proven to be a credible threat.

Perhaps the loudest "shot across the bow" was with the Catholic Church's announcement in 2009 that we shouldn't "fear the aliens" because we all originate from God's creative act. The Catholic Church recognizes just how potentially destructive *an alien appearance could be to the faith of their flock*. They appear to be setting expectations to reduce the trauma in the event it comes to pass.

> **Vatican City** – ET phone Rome. Four hundred years after it locked up Galileo for challenging the view that the Earth was the center of the universe, the Vatican has called in experts to study the possibility of extraterrestrial alien life and its implication for the Catholic Church. "The questions of life's origins and of whether life exists elsewhere in the universe are very suitable and deserve serious consideration," said the Rev. Jose Gabriel Funes, an astronomer and director of the Vatican Observatory. Funes, a Jesuit priest, presented the results Tuesday (November 10) of a five-day conference that gathered astronomers, physicists, biologists and other experts to discuss the budding field of astrobiology – the study of the origin of life and its existence elsewhere in the universe. [45]

In 2008, Funes was quoted in the Vatican Newspaper, *Observatore Romano*. Here he said:

> Just like there is an abundance of creatures on Earth, there should also be other beings, even intelligent ones that were created by God. That doesn't contradict our faith, because we cannot put boundaries to God's creative freedom. As Saint Francis would say, when we consider the earthly creatures to be our "brothers and sisters," why couldn't we also talk about an "extraterrestrial brother?" He would still be a part of creation.

Amazing advice coming from the Catholics. But is it the right message? Admitting that *aliens may exist* is one thing; but embracing them merely as God's creatures may be more than misleading. Perhaps we should heed the biblical admonition, "Brethren, test the spirits, for not all spirits are from God."[46] As Captain Kirk would say, "Raise the shields Sulu, full strength!" Caution suggests that now is not the time to drop our guard. Given that pagan religion from the past beats the same drum as the New Age of today, it's a portentous warning. "Lock and load! Something insidious is preparing to attack!" Tom Horn, an author who has researched and written about the

UFO/ET/New Age connection in several notable books, made these comments when interviewed in *Vision Magazine*, Nov. 2009, (pg. 15):

> On December 23, 2002, I was interviewed on **American Freedom Network News**. Rick Wiles had read an editorial I wrote about the role that popular films were playing in conditioning culture for a new religion, an ET religion and New Age universalism that would eventually displace traditional Christianity. Toward the end of the one-hour broadcast, Rick asks what would happen if the leaders of the world walked out into the well of the United Nations with ET and made *formal official disclosure*. His opinion was that it would shake organized Christianity from its foundations and open the door for Antichrist. I agreed, and pointed out how the leaders of the Church, including those I respected and worked with, had their heads intentionally in the sand and were refusing to seriously calculate the theological and philosophical ramifications, leaving their adherents at risk. (*Emphasis mine*)

Raising the specter of a pending ET announcement is a quick way to lose credibility – unless, of course, it turns out to be true. Nevertheless, *predicting the behavior of "the evil one" who Jesus called "a liar and father of lies" is a losing proposition*. As we have seen throughout the history of UFO groups, *deception is the rule, not the exception*. "There's just no telling what he will do." And whatever Satan says he will do is usually the last thing he would.

Therefore, I won't boldly predict it *must* happen; only that it *could* happen. The trend line of the data merits this possibility as *the logical outcome* of what we've learned thus far about what appears to be a well-laid-out plan in the making for ages. Whether we are talking about Crop Circle encryptions, Theosophist promises of transformation, or supposed Mayan prophecies of the end of the world, *all appear to point to the same outcome*.

Will this disclosure be in 2012? Will it be a few years later? One thing is for sure: It won't be long before we find out.

Let me emphasize that you don't have to fully subscribe to what I'm proposing. At minimum, "take it into advisement." No matter who may be making the introduction, if the *official disclosure* does happen as Tom Horn and many others believe it will, recall my warning: It's unlikely ET is who he says he is. He may in fact be none other than who the Bible calls *Antichrist*.

Sir Isaac Newton asserted that it's our duty to endeavor to know who Antichrist is in order to avoid him... "A duty of the greatest moment... lest in so degenerate an age (we be) dangerously seduced and not know it."[47]

Jesus told his disciples ahead of time this deception would be so stunning, that if it were possible even the "elect" would be deceived.

> *For there shall arise false Christs, and false prophets, and shall shew great signs and wonders; insomuch that, if it were possible, they shall deceive the very elect. Behold, I have told you before.* (Matthew 24:24, 25)

As my daddy taught me, being forewarned is being forearmed.

Notes

[1] The inspiration for the book came to him during a psychedelic session.

[2] This theology proved vacuous by the failure of the European Church, leading up to World War II, to offer any meaningful resistance to Nazism and Fascism. Dietrich Bonhoeffer, a noted German Theologian, was a prominent exception, martyred for his participation in a plot to assassinate Hitler. Bonheoffer spent considerable time in America, teaching at Union Theological Seminary in New York City. He resigned his post there after sensing that there was "no theology here" – liberalism had transformed the school unacceptably to his way of thinking. That is why many considered liberalism in theology thoroughly bankrupt.

[3] TM® was itself an "American remake" of ancient eastern mysticism, brought to the U.S. by Maharishi Mahesh Yogi. If you can't make it in the East, do so in the West. It's a much bigger market.

[4] Mysticism is defined as "a system of religious belief or practice that people follow to achieve personal communication or union with the divine."

[5] See *http://en.wikipedi.org/wiki/Out_on_a_Limb_ (Shirley_ MacLaine_ book)*. Before David Letterman beat up Sara Palin nightly in his monologue, he thoroughly rattled Shirley's cage to the point of her (and everyone else's) exasperation.

[6] *The Secret* was the latest incarnation of American positive thinking, a distinctly American phenomenon that has been part of the American spiritual scene for over 200 years. The most well-known is Norman Vincent Peale's *The Power of Positive Thinking*. But the Unity School, Church of Religious Science, and several others all spring from American Transcendentalism of Ralph Waldo Emerson, and more specifically "New Thought" which was much newer in the early 19th Century than is the "New Age" in the 20th. See Mitch Horowitz, *Occult America*, New York, Bantan Books, 2009, 290 pages, for the history of this distinctly American philosophy.

[7] A stark contrast to Rick Warren's opening in his best seller, *The Purpose Driven Life*: "It's not about you."

[8] A Swami is a teacher of respect for a Hindu teacher or Saint. It would be roughly equivalent to "Rabbi" in Hebrew or "Father" in Catholicism.

[9] See http://en.wikipedia.org/wiki/Henry_Steel_Olcott

[10] Mitch Horowitz indicates that Olcott served his country during the civil war doing what we would call forensic accounting today, uncovering schemes to cheat the government. Edwin Stanton the Secretary of War for Abraham Lincoln recognized Olcott's service and indicated that it was as important as "winning a battle." He was also the leader of the first crime team pulled together to investigate Lincoln's assassination and his team made the first arrests when chasing John Wilkes Booth. (Horowitz, op. cit., pg. 44). However, some would say that his ability to detect fraud apparently failed him when he did his due diligence on HPB.

[11] *The Secret Doctrine, the Synthesis of Science, Religion and Philosophy*, Vol.II, p.200. The world religion consistently exudes anti-semitism, yet another strong argument (since there is a common thread) that it's heritage is at odds with the God of the Bible, namely personified in Lucifer who originated it.

[12] Hale, Christopher, *Himmler's Crusade*, Edison, NJ, Castle Books, pg 23.

[13] The movie, *Seven Years in Tibet*, starring Brad Pitt, also provides some insight into this story, although it does not go into much depth, as does Hale, regarding Himmler's occult motivation for the expeditions.

[14] Hale, op cit., pg 26.

[15] Hale, op cit., pp. 29,30.

[16] See Ravenscroft, Trevor, *The Spear of Destiny*, 1973. First American Edition, 1982 by Samuel Weiser, York Beach, ME. 353 pages.

[17] "A fictionalized, female version of Eckart (Dietlinde Eckhart) appeared as the main villain and head of the Thule Society in the 2005 anime movie, *Fullmetal Alchemist the Movie*. In part 4, Phase 1 of the 2000 ad (comics) story 'Zenith (comics)' by Grant Morrison and Steve Yeowell Eckardt is referred to and depicted as the poet and mystic who initiated a German army corporal (Adolf Hitler) into the occult group called the *Cult of the Black Sun* after recognizing his potential as a medium. Eckardt and Haushofer put Hitler in contact with the *Great Old Ones* with ther [sic] goal of helping the Nazis engineer superhuman bodies that could act as physical vehicles for these Dark Gods." See *en wikipedia.org/wiki/Dietrich_Eckart*.

[18] See Lewis, James R. and J. Gordon Melton. *Perspectives on the New Age*. SUNY Press. 1992.

[19] Lucis Trust continues operating today closely associated with the United Nations. Members include such interesting individuals as George Schultz, Henry Kissinger, David Rockefeller, and Paul Volker. Food for conspiracy to be sure.

[20] Shamballa was also the city Marco Polo tried to find that contained the fountain of youth, or the "tree of life."

[21] *http://en.wikipedia.org/wiki/Alice_Bailey#cite_note-Gershom-149*

[22] Ominously, Bush (41) gave the "Toward a New World Order" speech on 9-11, 1990. 911. Conspiracy theorists love synchronicities like this.

[23] Picknett and Prince, *The Stargate Conspiracy*, New York, Berkley Books, 1999, pp. 317, 318.

[24] A second certainty we repeatedly see: The "Masters" or "Nine" – use deception to mislead and ultimately ruin the credibility of their followers as their predictions generally fail. Uri Geller refused to channel them, saying they were "cosmic clowns."

[25] This group of 39 individuals committed mass suicide in March 1997 to ready themselves for an alien space ship "pick up." The aliens supposedly followed the Hale-Bopp comet.

[26] See http://en.wikipedia.org/wiki/Aetherius_Society.

[27] *Dualistic* in the sense that God is distinct from humans, *legalistic* in the sense that the basis of biblical spirituality is moral and ethical laws governing behavior of individuals and society.

[28] Hubbard, Barbara Marx, *Happy Birthday Planet Earth*, Ocean Tree Books, 1986, p.32, quoted by Sanger, Mel, Mel, *2012 – The Year of Project Enoch?* Rema Marketing, 2009, Part II, Page 13.

[29] Bailey, Alice, *The Externalization of the Hierarchy*, Lucis Trust, 1983, Section IV, p 543.

[30] Sanger, Mel, *op. cit.*, Part II, Page 17.

[31] Spangler, David, *Reflections on the Christ*, p.37, quoted by Sanger, op cit., pg 12, 13.

[32] Perhaps some members of the American Civil Liberties Union (ACLU) will still be active. If so, we may finally see a good purpose of their efforts!

[33] Puharich was a medical and para-psychological researcher, medical inventor, and author, who's best known for bringing Uri Geller to the U.S. for scientific investigation. Some suggest he also had strong connections with the CIA. Recently, I discovered a good friend of mine is his nephew. He was able to confirm many aspects of what Picknett and Prince discuss – and many other fascinating stories!

[34] Opinions about him seem to suggest that he is made of *Teflon* – nothing bad sticks – which makes him especially dangerous.

[35] The Ennead, a group of nine deities in Egyptian mythology worshipped at Heliopolis consisting of the sun god *Atum*, his children *Shu* and *Tefnut*, their children *Geb* and *Nut* and their children *Osiris, Isis, Set* and *Nephthys*.

[36] Picknett and Prince, op. cit., pg 321.

[37] Jacques Vallèe, *Messengers of Deception*, pg. 217, quoted from Picknett and Prince, op. cit., pg. 332.

[38] Hurtak, J.J. *The Keys of Enoch*, pg. 585, quote taken from Prince and Picknett, op. cit., pg. 322.

39 Prince and Picknett, op. cit., pg 328.

40 Ibid, pp. 326, 327.

41 Ibid, pg. 332.

42 *Prima facie* evidence is *proof at first glance.* It is obvious and sufficient to establish a legal case or fact until disproved. If aliens were to land on the White House lawn, that would be *prima facie evidence* that intelligent life exists elsewhere. It would however, not prove *they are actually extraterrestrials.* It might only be what they want us to believe.

43 Ibid, pp 329, 300.

44 An accomplished fact – already done, already decided.

45 David, Ariel, November 10th, Associated Press.

46 I John 4:1.

47 "And therefore it is as much our duty to indeavour to be able to know him that we may avoyd him, as it was theirs to know Christ that they might follow him. Thou seest therefore that this is no idle speculation, no matters of indifferency but a duty of the greatest moment. Wherefore it concerns thee to look about thee narrowly least thou shouldest in so degenerate an age be dangerously seduced & not know it. Antichrist was to seduce the whole Christian world and therefore he may easily seduce thee if thou beest not well prepared to discern him. But if he should not be yet come into the world yet amidst so many religions of which there can be but one true & perhaps none of those that thou art acquainted with it is great odds but thou mayst be deceived & therefore it concerns thee to be very circumspect." (Sir Isaac Newton, *Untitled Treatise on Revelation,* Section 1.1).

See *www.newtonproject.sussex.ac.uk/view/texts /normalized /THEM00135.*

Chapter 9:
Nostradamus and His Predictions for the Last Days

I figure lots of predictions is best.
People will forget the ones I get wrong and marvel over the rest.
Alan Cox

Never make predictions. Especially about the future.
Casey Stengel

The First Prophet to Make a Profit

M*ay you live in interesting times.* More often a curse than a blessing, this Chinese proverb is familiar to most of us. Indeed, we intuitively recognize that "peace and quiet" can be rather dull – war and noise are much more energizing, creating lots of excitement and, of course, lots of stress.

General Omar Bradley, who kept his colleague General George Patton in line during World War II, defined the essence of war, "as endless periods of utter boredom, punctuated by brief moments of sheer terror." Interesting times, exciting though they be, can be harmful to your health.

Michele de Nostredame, known by his Latinized name, *Nostradamus*, lived in such times.

- Born in 1503, he was a contemporary with King Henry VIII (the famous English king with six wives, predecessor to daughter Queen Elizabeth I); 11 years after Columbus sailed to America.

- When Nostradamus was 14, Martin Luther nailed his 95 "theses" (points to debate) on the "Wittenberg door" – a blog posting of sorts, more accurately "nail mail," that put the Catholic Church on notice that reforms must be made to the Church. Luther's posting eventually ignited the Protestant Reformation.

- The Black Death (Bubonic Plague) ravaged France repeatedly, in and around the years, 1525, 1537, and 1546 which profoundly affected his life as we will see.

- In 1541, when Nostradamus was 38, John Calvin established a very strict form of Protestantism in Geneva, Switzerland.

- Six years later, in 1547, Ivan the Terrible crowned himself "Tsar" of Russia and began his expansionist empire shaping the Russia we all have come to know and suspect.

Nostradamus' times were remarkable. They were a crossroads for the institutions of *church and monarchy*, vastly reshaping politics and religion, as well as setting the stage for the modern world.

But who is Nostradamus? Today, he is popularly regarded as the world's most accomplished "seer," whose predictions have tantalized prophecy buffs for the past five centuries. Even during his own time, he was well-known and held in high esteem by his primary patron, Catherine de Medici, an Italian orphan, who had become the *unpopular* Queen of France – being neither French nor noble.

We associate Nostradamus with his book of prophecies. In 1555, he published his first section of *The Prophecies*. Ultimately, he would make 1,000 predictions through four-line poems (known as *quatrains*). Nostradamus organized his book into ten centuries, each with 100 quatrains (one quatrain per prophecy). *(Note: My references to his "verses" make use of 'C' for Century # and 'Q' for Quatrain #).*

Nostradamus first gained fame by warning Henry II, King of France, that he would experience a painful death in single combat, through two injuries experienced in one blow.

> *The young lion will overcome the old one*
> *On the field of battle in single combat:*
> *He will put out his eyes in a cage of gold:*
> *Two fleets [wounds] one, then to die a cruel death.[1] (CI:Q35)*

Despite the warnings and the urgings of those who knew about the prophecy, the King decided to fight in a joust, purely as an exhibition, in 1559. Both Henry, and his younger jousting partner, sported *a lion on their shields*. However, during the bout, the younger's jousting lance, targeting Henry, shattered upon striking Henry's armor, plunging two large broken fragments of the lance into his head. The first entered through Henry's face cover (the "golden cage" of Nostradamus' prophecy) into his eye and brain, while a second fragment tore through Henry's throat. After suffering ten long days of pain and agony, the King mercifully met his maker.

Queen Catherine knew of Nostradamus' prediction before the event. So, after the King's death (which mirrored the prediction in so many details), she called Nostradamus to her Court. He explained to her that his predictions came from an innate skill he possessed, perfected by his grandfather during his youth, and had nothing to do with a conspiracy against the King. Satisfied, she requested that Nostradamus predict the future of all her sons; thereupon, he received a pension from the Queen and continued to consult with her for the remainder of his life (Nostradamus died in 1566, at age 62, another death he would accurately predict). Keep in mind that Nostradamus didn't need royal support; he was doing quite fine financially through his own efforts.

Nostradamus had first published his annual *Almanac* in 1550 and then, as stated above, his first collection of *The Prophecies* in 1555. His publishing business, run from his home in Provençal (southern France), wasn't only dealing with the future, however. Nostradamus was a trained medical doctor, an apothecary (pharmacist or *chemist* as the Brits say), and a manufacturer of cosmetics. He even published a cookbook specializing in jams and jellies for medicinal purposes.

Nevertheless, today he's known as a modern-day prophet for his many predictions, mostly far off into his future (particularly the 20th century) with an emphasis upon his native country, France.

Dr. No was also an astrologer, although experts say *not a particularly good one*. His astrological charts are frequently flawed according to scholars and his math could have used some proofing. Despite this, as we will soon see, he was uncanny in getting his predictions right – *most of the time*. Without question, his accuracy was due in part upon his proclivity for vagueness. Fearing repercussions from the politicians, priests, and kings about whom he prophesied, Nostradamus cloaked his predictions in symbols, anagrams, and especially by (apparently) *publishing his predictions in no particular chronological order*; thus, making it very difficult for anyone to hold him accountable for what he foresaw.

Nostradamus was committed to the Catholic Church. He was no Protestant sympathizer. But he was wary of his church because he knew that his methods were unorthodox, *literally*. He cleared his upper room attic and turned it into his esoteric study, filled with his astrologer's *astrolabe* (to calculate the positions of planets and stars in the future or past), and his *scrying* bowl (a large pot of water, to "presage" images of the future whose reflections would be presented there during his late night scrying sessions).

But before the orthodox gather virtual wood to burn his memory at the stake, we should note that Nostradamus was an *extraordinarily compassionate person*. He left medical school early to treat victims of the Plague in 1525. Again in 1537, he "dropped everything" once again to walk the countryside and tend to the sick. He lost his first wife and two children to the disease. But instead of souring him on life, it galvanized his commitment to relieve suffering whenever he could.

Furthermore, his sense of medical treatments reflected modern techniques. He realized the dangers of throwing the sick in a room together. By most accounts as an apothecary, he was adept in using plants and herbs effectively. Thus, despite his emphasis upon fortune telling, he was no witch doctor. Medically, he was ahead of his times.

Neither was he a hermit or pauper as many mad prophets are often stereotyped. He was sophisticated and did well financially in the prophecy publishing business. We could say he was the first renown and respected *prophet to make a profit* using his most unusual gift.

His fame continues to expand today as his name seems consistently connected with *all-things-doomsday*. We see this especially today, due to the success the *History Channel enjoyed* with their 2009 series, *The Nostradamus Effect*, along with other special documentaries purportedly demonstrating his fulfilled prophecies.

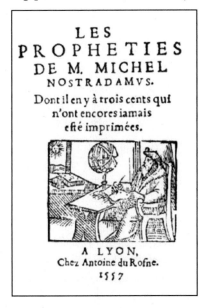

FIGURE 37 - 1557 PRINTING OF LES PROPHETIES

Encoding Predictions in the Quatrains

The Prophecies of Nostradamus were published in three separate offerings between 1555 and 1566, culminating in a total of 942 four-line predictions (58 quatrains are missing from the 7th "Century"). Because the quatrains were organized by *Centuries*, this literary device misleads the reader into believing that there is a clear chronological order to the quatrains. With only one or two exceptions (one which we will study later), most scholars say this turns out not to be true. The experts assert the predictions are jumbled, showing no particular sequence that the non-scholar could detect.

However, this timeless technique was only part of Nostradamus' encryption strategy.

Since the codes typically used in the Bible were already widely known in the Catholic Church, Nostradamus couldn't use a biblical form of encryption as did John the Revelator (see below). He had to invent his own style of cryptography. For instance, names of cities and countries were usually not spelled out, nor were the names of people. They were identified by something symbolic that students of history or geography could use by which to identify them. Likewise, dates were seldom given. Instead, Nostradamus would use astrological coordinates, indicating when a particular planet or planets would appear within a specific constellation. Precise locations were occasionally included, but because he wasn't too exact with his astrolabe, Nostradamus might get the latitude wrong when he provided it. Most of the time, he gave us no more than a symbol or image that tradition associated with a location. When it comes to people, Dr. No would muddle the letters of a name or create a name based upon a spelling of the sounds. We will see some examples when we look at his predictions about the Antichrist. Given all the tricks he employed, it's amazing we can make any sense of his prophecies at all. But with a capable scholar who knows Nostradamus' encryption techniques, we can decode *Les Propheties*.

This is not to say that interpreting Nostradamus is easy. As I said earlier, Nostradamus is an expert at *obfuscation* – he makes the plain and simple, complex and challenging. Consequently, there is much that is lost in translation, not just from Provençal French to English, but from *prophetic symbolism* to *literal meaning*. No doubt Dr. No would consistently astound us if we could understand more of what he was setting forth. But as we will see later, there is another strong reason why his prophecies were made intentionally vague.

While the apostle John in his apocalypse also hides his message, the key to decoding his cryptology is to understand the Old Testament. Seldom are the images and allusions incorporated into Revelation original; they generally refer to images and allusions previously employed by the prophets of the Hebrew Bible. Likewise, the numerology John incorporates into his book is consistent with numerology used throughout the Bible. Later, we will see this mainly when we compare Revelation to the Book of Daniel. In summary, while

Revelation is a hard book to grasp, we break its code simply by "knowing our Bible."

In retrospect, it's perfectly clear Nostradamus felt threatened. But in seeking to protect himself, he hid his *Easter eggs*[2] too well. In the final analysis, we would be right to complain that Nostradamus makes us work far too hard to unlock his codes. By doing this, he invites excessive speculation and encourages misunderstanding.

In essence, we simply don't benefit as much from his predictions as we would had he chosen a less cryptic way to communicate. Nevertheless, there is still much we can learn and many predictions that should astound even the most dubious skeptic.

Nostradamus and the Three Antichrists

One of the special contributions of Nostradamus to decoding Doomsday is his view that there would be *more than one Antichrist*. While the Apostle John in the New Testament prophesied only one antichrist in Revelation 13,[3] in his epistles John indicated that there are many antichrists that have gone out into the world. Likewise, Jesus warns his followers that there will be many false Christs. In contrast, the Apostle Paul was clear that there would be only one antichrist. We see this implicitly in his descriptions of "the coming lawless one" in I and II Thessalonians. What is the answer? Are these views inconsistent? Can they be harmonized?

We discussed earlier how the Syrian King, Antiochus IV Epiphanies, fulfilled many aspects of the mission of Antichrist when he stopped the daily sacrifice of the Hebrews and committed the "abomination of desolation" in 167 BC. While Jesus Christ certainly understood this very same history, he nonetheless indicated that the final days would be revealed by yet another abomination of desolation, "foretold by Daniel the Prophet." Jesus warned, "When you see the Abomination of Desolation, flee to the hills. The Temple will be destroyed. Not one stone will be left unturned." In 70 AD, Titus stopped the sacrifices and the Temple was destroyed just as Jesus had predicted. Scholars generally agree that this happened before John's Revelation was committed to writing, which logically implies yet another antichrist will come on the scene in the future, specifically the Beast of Revelation 13, who will desecrate a yet-to-be-built Temple in *the last days*, and thus fulfill the prophecy of Daniel *for a third time.*

The Bible illustrates history repeats itself – particularly prophetic history. When Christians consider that each of the seven major feasts of Moses (such as Passover, Yom Kippur, Rosh Hashanah, Pentecost, etc.), appear to point to an event that has been (or will be) fulfilled in the life of Jesus Christ, they readily conclude that this pattern of repetition is *intentional*. The Bible doesn't mind repeating itself. Indeed, this repetitious pattern is seen throughout.

Therefore, let me summarize what appears to be the Bible's methodology: *Step One*, identifying an "archetype" in a vision or dream; Step *Two*, witnessing one or more fore-types transpiring in space-time; and finally, *Step Three*, concluding with the real thing – an ultimate fulfillment of the prophecy that answers every detail.

We see countless examples of this, but to name a few (coming from the Christian perspective):

- The Tabernacle of Moses preceded the Temple of Solomon, both of which contained the presence of God through the Ark of the Covenant. These foreshadowed the incarnation of God in man, Jesus Christ, in whose flesh the "fullness of deity dwelt in bodily form."

- The Passover lamb of the Jewish Seder meal pictured the sinless Lamb of God, Jesus, that took away the sin of the world;

- The ascension of Jesus Christ ("in the clouds") foreshadows the rapture of the Church;

- The Feast of the First Fruits (following the Passover) foreshadows the resurrection of the dead. And so on…

That's why the notion that Nostradamus could foresee *three* antichrists isn't a contradiction to conservative biblical scholarship. The *spirit of Antichrist* is an ongoing reality, apparently incarnating itself, or possessing a strong leader from time to time, throughout history. This pattern is underscored by Nostradamus in his vision of multiple personages of evil that punctuate the history of this past millennium. Let's look at the relevant quatrains.

Napoleon

Because Nostradamus was living in France, the majority of his prophecies are associated with France. The first Antichrist that Dr. No talks about is homegrown, lives 200 years future to Nostradamus' time, and is a tyrant who shall reign for 14 years (Century VII, Quatrain 13). His name was Napoleon. Napoleon was born in *Corsica*, previously an Italian island, only becoming part of France one year before Napoleon was born.

We read a clear prediction that reflects these historical facts:

> *An Emperor will be born near Italy,*
> *Who will cost the Empire very dearly.*
> *They will say, when they see his allies,*
> *That he is less a prince than a butcher. (CI:Q60)*

His name is an anagram, based on sounds, and mixes the second sound with the first. *Pau Nay Loron* becomes *Nay Pau Loron*, and if you say it fast, it becomes *Nā.pō.leōn.* Additionally, his Corsican name, according to Scarlett Ross (one of the sources studied, see the Bibliography), was *Naupoleone*, which also reinforces the "look alike, sound alike" anagram game Nostradamus played.

> *Pau, Nay, Loron will be more of fire than blood, To*
> *swim in praise, the great one to flee*
> *to the confluence (of rivers). (CVIII:Q1)*

> *He began as a soldier, but became emperor,*
> *exchanging his short cloak for a long robe,*
> *much to the distress of the Catholic Church:*
> *From simple soldier he will attain to Empire,*
> *From the short robe he will grow into the long.*
> *Brave in arms, much worse towards the Church,*
> *He vexes the priests as water fills a sponge.*
> *(CVIII:Q57)*

FIGURE 38 - NAPOLEON BONAPARTE, THE 1ST ANTICHRIST

Napoleon would march a half-million troops into the Russian winter, only to desert his troops, giving his chief adversary, Alexander I (the Russian Czar) the victory. His troops faltered and died in the snowy white territory of the Russian landscape:

> *Ready to fight one will desert [faint or disappear],*
> *The chief adversary will obtain the victory;*
> *The rear guard will make a defense,*
> *The faltering ones dead in the white territory. (CIV:Q 75)*

Nostradamus goes on in CX:Q24, to talk of Napoleon's captivity and escape from Elba. In CII:Q66, he points out how his fortune changed and Napoleon leads his army again, only to be ultimately defeated at Waterloo on June 18th, 1815. Nostradamus also calls Napoleon "the old destroyer" (CIV:Q82), which is important, because the name *Napoleon is related to Apollo*, the son of Jupiter, and frequently referred to as *the destroyer*. The Antichrist himself is identified as "the destroyer" in the Revelation of John (*Abaddon* in Hebrew and *Apollyon* in Greek). We can easily see **N.Apolo.eon** is an Italian and French transliteration of *Apollo*. We will review this in depth in a later chapter.

Napoleon concerned Nostradamus greatly because he was a Frenchman and he would do great harm. However, he is only the first of three antichrists. The next two bring even greater catastrophes upon the people of our planet.

Hitler

Nostradamus is at it again with a play on words to identify his second predicted antichrist. The Rhine and Danube, the two great rivers, identify the area from which this antichrist is to arise. The Lower Danube was known as *Ister* or *Hister* by the Romans. Hitler is of course derived with a single letter: Change an "l" out for an "s" then transpose the "t" and the "s." Next, Venus is sometimes the name Nostradamus uses for Venice (another "sound alike"). The extent of the antichrist's power will be to both Africa and to Asia. And, for good measure, we know that Hitler ordered the bombing of Malta.

FIGURE 39 - ADOLF HITLER, THE 2ND ANTICHRIST

In the place very near not far from Venus
The two greatest ones of Asia and of Africa,
From the Rhine and "Hister" [Lower Danube]
they will be said to have come,
Cries, tears at Malta and the Ligurian side [Genoa]. (C IV:Q68)

Another quatrain appears to pinpoint the Antichrist coming from central Europe (the very depths of the West). He will be born of poor parents and through his tongue he will seduce many. His fame will be regarded toward Asia (Russia and perhaps Japan who allied with him – although the Russian pact would be broken by Hitler shortly after the conflict in Europe began).

From the very depths of the West of Europe,
A young child will be born of poor people,
He who by his tongue will seduce a great troop:
His fame will increase towards the realm of the East. (CIII:Q35)

Another quatrain, usually quoted by television programs associated with Nostradamus, is seen by some referring to images of tanks driving through rivers. Additionally, in this quatrain, it appears that *Hister* (Hitler) will be "one against many" – all others in the region will oppose him. But he is stubborn and learns nothing from the battles he loses. (*The Great One* some speculate may be Franklin Delano Roosevelt).

Beasts ferocious from hunger will swim across rivers;
The greater part of the region will be against the Hister,
The great one will cause it to be dragged in an iron cage,
When the German child will observe nothing. (CII:Q24)

Another prophecy related to World War II appears to speak of the *Maginot Line*, a series of trenches and bunkers designed by the French to keep the Nazis from invading France. The river was divided precisely in 15 parts just as the prophecy states. But the *line* was not effective. In a few short days, the Germans bypassed it, and soon marched down the *Champs d' Elysees* in Paris.

Near the great river, great ditch, earth drawn out,
In fifteen parts will the water be divided:
The city taken, fire, blood, cries, sad conflict,
And the greatest part involving the coliseum. (CIV:Q80)

But there is more about the second Antichrist:

It will be at this time and in these countries that the infernal power will set the power of its adversaries against the Church of Jesus Christ. This will constitute of the second Antichrist, who will persecute that Church and its true Vicar, by means of the power of three temporal kings who in their ignorance will be seduced by tongues which, in the hands of the madmen, will cut more than any sword. The said reign of the Antichrist will last only to the death of him who was born at the beginning of the age... (Epistle to Henry II)

There is debate about who "the three" are: Hitler, Mussolini, and perhaps Stalin are generally proposed, but so are Pope Pius XII (who may have supported fascism), and even Roosevelt. But given that the focus is on persecution of the Church, the third *king* seems unlikely to be the Pope or FDR.

There is yet another quatrain tied to the antichrist that mentions the *three*:

> *The antichrist very soon annihilates the three,*
> *Twenty-seven years his war will last.*
> *The unbelievers are dead, captive, exiled;*
> *With blood, human bodies, water and red hail cover the earth. (CVIII:Q77)*

The question here is whether the *27 years* disqualifies this quatrain from referring to the second antichrist. However, if we recognize that the Second World War began with the excessive war reparations called for by the Treaty of Versailles in 1919, this could suggest that the antichrist's war of 27 years began at that time, continuing until 1945. Could this be the proper interpretation? Perhaps, but many Nostradamus buffs believe this quatrain refers to the third antichrist and the length of the third antichrist's term.

There are many other quatrains that refer to World War II, but we don't have the space to cite them all. However, one in particular seems worthy of bringing to the reader's attention. It appears to predict the two atomic bombs dropped on Japan:

> *Near the gates and within two cities*
> *There will be two scourges the like of which was never seen,*
> *Famine within plague, people put out by steel,*
> *Crying to the great immortal God for relief. (CII:Q6)*

Mabus

Many Nostradamus scholars believe that the third antichrist is known as Mabus. We see his name in Century II, Quatrain 62:

> *Mabus then will soon die, there will come*
> *Of people and beasts a horrible rout:*
> *Then suddenly one will see vengeance,*
> *Hundred, hand, thirst, hunger when the comet will run. (CII:62)*

John Hogue is a frequently cited authority on Dr. No. He recently published a book on Nostradamus and the three antichrists. He speculates that as with the first two antichrists, the third is likewise to be named through the use of an anagram. From Hogue's perspective, *Mabus* is the code name of Antichrist number three. Hogue speculates that **Mabus** could be identified as one of several contemporary figures. He proposes: (1) **Osama** bin Laden; (2) George W. **Bush**; (3) **Yassar** Arafat; (4) Barak **Obama**; and (5) **Saddam** Hussein.

Of course, as of 2010, Bush is out of power, Arafat and Hussein are dead, and Osama bin Laden may be too. But through various letter shifting and inversion of the shapes of letters, one can derive *Mabus* from any of these above

names. The flip side of this exercise is how it points out the typical wild speculation spawned when one seeks to decode the proper name of the Antichrist.

Additionally, I find Mabus' "soon death" to be inconsistent with the
rest of the allusions to the nature of this third antichrist. As we see in Nostradamus' comments below (from his Epistle to Henry II), Mabus' quick
death runs counter to his explicit statements about Antichrist, which follow
very closely to what the Apostle John has to say about his *beast*.

For these reasons, I'm not convinced *Mabus* actually refers to the antichrist.

> Then the great Empire of the Antichrist will begin where once was At-
> tila's empire and the new Xerxes will descend with great and countless
> numbers, so that the coming of the Holy Ghost, proceeding from the 48th
> degree, will make a transmigration, chasing out the abomination of the
> Christian Church, and whose reign will be for a time and to the end of time.
>
> This will be preceded by a solar eclipse more dark and gloomy than
> any since the creation of the world, except that after the death and passion
> of Jesus Christ. And it will be in the month of October that the great trans-
> lation will be made and it will be such that one will think the gravity of the
> earth has lost is natural movement and that it is to be plunged into the
> abyss of perpetual darkness.
>
> In the spring there will be omens, and thereafter extreme changes, re-
> versals of realms and mighty earthquakes. These will be accompanied by
> the procreation of the new Babylon, miserable daughter enlarged by the
> abomination of the first holocaust. It will last for only seventy-three years
> and seven months.
>
> After that Antichrist will be the infernal prince again, for the last time.
> All the Kingdoms of Christianity will tremble, even those of the infidels, for
> the space of twenty-five years. Wars and battles will be more grievous and
> towns, cities, castles and all other edifices will be burned, desolated and de-
> stroyed, with great effusion of vestal blood, violations of married woman
> and widows, and sucking children dashed and broken against the walls of
> towns, by means of Satan, Prince Infernal, so may evils will be committed
> that nearly all the world will find itself undone and desolated. Before these
> events, some rare birds will cry in the air: Hui, Hui [Today, today] and
> sometime later will vanish.
>
> After this has endured for a long time, there will be almost renewed
> another reign of Saturn, and golden age. Hearing the affliction of his peo-
> ple, God the Creator will command that Satan be cast into the depths of the
> bottomless pit, and bound there. Then a universal peace will commence be-
> tween God and man, and Satan will remain bound for around a thousand
> years, and then all unbound. (Epistle to Henry II)

In this description, Nostradamus talks of the third antichrist as *Xerxes*, the King of Babylon, from the same general area as *Attila* the Hun (both connected to southwest Asia). This suggests that the antichrist may come from Babylon or southwest Asia. This seems to be corroborated by another quatrain:

> *The year 1999, seventh month,*
> *From the sky will come a great King of Terror:*
> *To bring back to life the great King of the Mongols,*
> *Before and after Mars to reign by good luck. (CX:Q72)*

Many interpret this quatrain to refer to the attack on 911 although the date is off by two years.[4] Some say 1999 is an anagram for 911. The important point here is coming from the sky, this *King of Terror*, brings back to life the King of the Mongols, which could be easily interpreted as Genghis Khan, from the 13th century, who conquered southwest Asia as far as Babylon. Another quatrain often associated with the third antichrist refers to Hannibal and to Babylon. Hannibal was the great warrior from Carthage (in Northern Africa) who used elephants to attack the Romans in the Alps, no less, during the 3rd century BC.

> *One who the infernal gods of Hannibal*
> *Will cause to be reborn, terror of mankind*
> *Never more horror nor worse of days*
> *In the past than will come to the Romans through Babel. (CII:Q30)*

In both of the last two quatrains, the word *terror* stands out and suggests that the reign of the third antichrist, will be *a reign of terror*. It also infers that Babel (Babylon) brings great terror to the Romans (to the Italians or more broadly, Europe). Lastly, another quatrain often related to 911, provides similar imagery.

> *At forty-five degrees the sky will burn,*
> *Fire to approach the great new city:*
> *In an instant a great scattered flame will leap up,*
> *When one will want to demand proof of the Normans. (CIV:Q97)*

Is this a reference to New York City, the *new city*? Does this depict the image we awoke to on the morning of 9-11-01? We know that New York is not exactly at 45° (it's 41° – possibly Nostradamus' incompetence with the Astrolabe again). Plus, it's true that U.S. officials sought French intelligence to help prove that Osama Bin Laden was behind the attacks. So the quatrain could be linked to 911.

In summary, from my vantage point, Nostradamus sought to provide additional images of the end times leading up to the millennium of 1,000 years of peace, in which Satan would be bound, just as described in the Apocalypse of John. It appears he intended that his predictions not conflict with the Bible's, but supplement them. The notion the Antichrist comes from Babylon or Assyria is a clear theme among many prophecy mavens today. Therefore, it would be a prediction consistent with how many commentators interpret the Bible.

However, are these interpretations of the quatrains irrefutably true? Hardly. As I said at the outset, Nostradamus disguises his visions so thoroughly it's very difficult to be certain about anything. Taken altogether, it appears that he makes specific predictions relating to real facts about historical figures. Nevertheless, given the limited evidence that we can amass, it's difficult if not impossible to thoroughly satisfy even the most open-minded skeptic.

The Missing Book of Nostradamus, Is it Authentic?

But, hold everything. There is apparently, another whole level of mystery to Nostradamus' message that no American author has brought to the foreground. It's found in the writing of *Ottavio Cesare Ramotti*, an Italian expert on Nostradamus. If his findings are correct, the Nostradamus popularly understood is *not the essential Nostradamus* at all. His prophecies are encrypted far more deeply than American scholars report. Apparently, what we read in the quatrains are just "crumbs" and not the actual message Nostradamus intended that adepts would derive from his works *in the last days*. Ramotti says,

> Interpreters who persist in focusing on the quatrains, which are actually a form of hermetic *charade*, without intuiting their development and solution through decryption into clearer statements, will gather only crumbs of the Nostradamic vision. The result of what I call the "crumb-hunters" interpretations is that they bring a lack of credibility to bear on the great seer himself. By such random interpretations of his prophecies they end in failure, which, curiously, never reflects on them but always on Nostradamus, who prophesied that they would bring him, for a time, to "complete ruin." (*Emphasis mine*)[5]

Ramotti appears to have discovered two separate keys to interpreting Nostradamus. The first he laid out in his first book, *The Keys to Nostradamus*, which deciphered the chronology of the quatrains, meaning that *there is a specific sequence, jumbled though it may be,* to help interpret their meaning. As we said earlier, Dr. No randomly published his quatrains. He didn't disclose a chronological sequence to the reader; nonetheless, it appears he ordered them according to a particular cipher Ramotti discovered in the 1990's.

From the Publishers' "Foreword" to *Nostradamus: The Lost Manuscript*, we obtain a succinct statement regarding the significance of Ramotti's discoveries:

> (Ramotti) has now unearthed in the Italian National Library in Rome a previously lost manuscript written in the hand of Nostradamus. This manuscript contains eighty illustrations by the master prophet himself further corroborating Ramotti's previous ordering of the prophetic quatrains.

This manuscript was featured on the History Channel's two-hour documentary, *Nostradamus: The Lost Book*, aired in 2009. However, that program focused only on a dozen or so of the watercolors printed therein. *But, as it turns out, the documentary did not discuss the truly important elements of the book.*

Therefore, let me highlight here why the so-called *Lost Manuscript* is so important:

- It confirms a sequence for the ordering of the "plates" (the watercolors) which verifies the same sequence Ramotti discovered elsewhere for how to order the quatrains.

- This sequence provides strong evidence that the *Lost Manuscript* was indeed authored by Nostradamus.

- The *Lost Manuscript* focused primary attention on the succession of Popes from 1631 forward to the 21st century.

- This papal succession validates (corroborates) the same succession prophesied by Saint Malachy (to be discussed shortly).

The first cipher technique brings to light Nostradamus' quatrains detailing the Popes from the "Restoration of the 19th century" through World War II. Ramotti's explanation of the decoding is complex (combining quatrains in the *Centuries* with those in the *Almanacs*, referred to unfortunately by Ramotti as "Prophecies" adding to the confusion). For those interested, I suggest you directly review Ramotti's book. Space won't allow for me to cover it here.

However, I offer a simple explanation as follows: Ramotti develops a *sine curve* using the specific way that Nostradamus *signed his initials*. This consists of four ciphers. The first relates to the specific century number, the second the first number of the quatrain, the third, the second number of the quatrain, and the fourth, the page number of the *Lost Manuscript*. It actually connects quatrains from the *Prophecies* to the related illustration in the *Lost Manuscript* to amplify their meaning!

The sequencing for his elaboration on the Papacy, in the *second half* of the 20th century, follows a similar technique, but also is much too complex to cover here.

To recap, it's this numerical decryption method, based upon Nostradamus' initials, which allows us to understand what he predicted for the papacy hundreds of years into the future. Indirectly, this implies a time limit before "the world as we know it" is concluded. We'll see this too in the pages ahead.

The Succession of Popes

First, let's do a quick review of the salient aspects of what Nostradamus predicted regarding several Popes, from the second half of the 20th century (and into the 21st). For our purposes we will look at only the following Popes (Pope Benedict began his reign in 2006, well after Ramotti published his books). The Latin names are from the Prophecy of St. Malachy, his abbreviated nicknames. (We will discuss the relevance of this Prophecy to Nostradamus at the end of this chapter.) The Popes from 1963 to 2005 are listed as follows:

- 1963 — Pope Paul VI, *Flos Florum*, reigned 15 years
- 1978 — Pope John Paul I, *De Medietate Lunae*, reigned < 1 year
- 1978 — Pope John Paul II, *De Labore Solis*, reigned 27 years

Quatrains for Pope Paul VI, begin with the following:

He who bears the great cape will be troubled
By grave scandal as the reds march on.
The family of the dead man will be almost prostrate
But reds to reds add more red still. (C8:Q19)

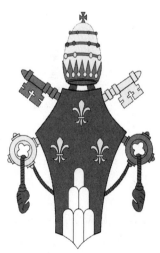

Pope Paul VI (Montini) attempted to come to the aid of the kidnapped Aldo Moro, President of the Christian Democrats in Italy. The two were very good friends. The kidnapping was carried out by the *Red Brigade* (an Italian/ communist/ terrorist group). Eventually, the Red Brigade was defeated and disbanded, but only after both Moro and Montini, the Pope, were dead. In the prophecies of St. Malachy, Pope Paul VI is known as *Flos Florum*, a flower among flowers, and his coat of arms showed three flowers (or *fleur-de-lis*, "lis" being

FIGURE 40 - POPE PAUL VI,
COAT OF ARMS

French for "Lilly," see the figure above). Three more quatrains cited below connect these actual historical facts to Nostradamus' predictions regarding this Pope:

> The exit of Flora will be the cause of his death
> Hatched over time in plots both old and new,
> Such is the fate to befall the three lilies
> For their mistaken fruit and their rotten pulp. (C8:Q18)

> Rain and wind, the hour of the hysterical barbaric band has come.
> Supplies, munitions, and soldiers pass through Tyrrhenia,
> Cross over Siene, reduce the successes of FLORA.
> The two will be killed, united in friendship. (19 Prophecy, 8 18 October)

> Where the great man comes to be put to death,
> Unimprisoned, his loyal friend stands in his square:
> After six months the Trojan hope will die stillborn.
> When the Sun is elected, ice fills the rivers. (C6:Q52)

The next Pope, *John Paul I*, Albino Luciani, was regarded as a sensitive and gentle soul. He reigned for only 33 days before he died. Rumors persist that he discovered a financial conspiracy within the Vatican and was *poisoned* for threatening to reveal it. We cite three quatrains that speak to these details (remember, Nostradamus made these predictions 400 years earlier):

> Elected Pope, his election is mocked,
> Provoking sudden strong emotion in this timid man.
> Too much goodness and sweetness lead him to death,
> A gentle guide extinguished on the night he departs. (C10:Q12)

> The Arabs shall be deprived of their weapons:
> Their greatest quarrels shall increase.
> Thunderstruck Albino, generous Father,
> Seven corrosives will strike to the marrow. (2 Prophecy, 54 September)

> Those who will undertake to subvert
> The reign of equal name, invincible and powerful
> By night, by fraud, will cause all three to fail,
> The greatest at his bench, reading in his Bible (C5:Q83)

In 1978, the Palestinians surrendered their weapons to their enemies during the "lunar interval" (his reign lasting a little more than a lunar month). Albino's name is mentioned. His papal name, John Paul, was equal to his successor (Pope John Paul II) who was "invincible and powerful". Frauds, or conspiracies, impact all three Popes of 1978 (aka the year of "three Popes"). Many ultra-orthodox Catholics believe it is because all three Popes sought to implement the mandates of Vatican II in 1965, principles which traditionalists regarded as heretical.

Finally, we come to *Pope John II*, (Karol Józef Wojtyła), perhaps the strongest and most influential Pope in our times. Polish in origin (one of few non-Italian Popes during the past 100 years), he stood strong against communism at the time that Lech Wałęsa (leader of *Solidarity*, a greatly revered labor movement), was exerting pressure upon the Polish communist regime.

He traveled considerably more than most Popes and also suffered an attempted assassination from a Turkish terrorist, *Ali Agca*. His Papacy was dedicated to the Virgin Mary (note the *M* in the coat of arms).

**FIGURE 41 - POPE JOHN PAUL I,
COAT OF ARMS**

Let's study several quatrains that likely pertain to John Paul II:

> *Roman Pontiff you must not approach*
> *The city that reddens two rivers.*
> *It is there one will come to spill your blood,*
> *Yours and your beloveds' when the red rose blooms (C2:Q97)*

**FIGURE 42 - POPE JOHN
PAUL II, COAT OF ARMS**

The two rivers, the *Bosporus* and the *Horn of Gold*, border the city of Constantinople on the north (the city of two rivers), in Turkey. The Pope visited the City in 1979, reddened by two bloodthirsty sultans, in a vain attempt by the Pope to reconcile two warring sects. Ali Agca escaped from a prison in Constantinople and later would wound the Pope (along with several others of the Pope's entourage), in Rome's St. Peter's Square. The time of this event is predicted to be when, "the red rose blooms," which may refer to the French Socialists gaining power in France, who employed the symbol of a *red rose in a fist*. This occurred in 1981. Likewise, it was on May 13, 1981, that Ali Agca attempted the assassination of Pope John

Paul II. The Pope made a pilgrimage to the grotto of Lourdes, August 15, 1983 (the location of the *Vision of Fatima*), to thank the Virgin Mary for protecting his life during the assassination attempt. We read:

> *Surrounded by the Pyrenees Mountains, a great crowd*
> *Of foreign peoples follow the new made king*
> *By the River Garonne to the mountain's great temple,*
> *When the shy Roman patriarch walks to the water. (C6:Q01)*

> *Solar man from Polonia, seized as he entered*
> *The goat herder's cavern, pulled forth by the beard,*
> *Overseen like some low beast,*
> *Is taken across the Pegourdans to Tarbes. (C10:Q29)*

Pope John Paul II is known as the *De Labore Solis*, the sun laborer, in the prophecy of St. Malachy. There are many reasons for this, which we will cover momentarily. The Pope visited the city of *Tarbes*, specifically mentioned in the last quatrain. And we remember that the Pope was Polish. He walked with President Mitterrand from the city's temple, built centuries after the prophecy was published, to the spring in the cavern where Bernadette (one of the three children seeing the [supposed] image of the Virgin Mary) tended her goats. After the assassination attempt, the Pope would be watched over ("overseen") carefully by his security team.

In this recap of Ramotti's take on Nostradamus, we haven't referred to the corresponding images of the Popes and related circumstances from the *Lost Manuscript*. But these pictures do appear to corroborate what we read in the quatrains. However, let's look at one plate (watercolor) that seems to refer to Pope John Paul II.

In the picture following, we can see a number of symbols that may help to identify this "picture prophecy" as a reference to Pope John Paul II:

- There is a sun prominent in the background that may be the clue to link this pope to *De Labore Solis*.

- There is a Madonna and child contained within the Pope's staff (his papacy being dedicated to the Virgin Mary).

- There is a Saracen sword being welded by a knight in the lower left hand corner, typical of a Turkish or Muslim warrior. We know that the Turkish assassin attempted to strike a fatal blow.

- The rooster on the Pope's crown, most likely relates to the French, as the "cock" often is a symbol used by Nostradamus for France. Apparently, this symbol says the Pope's mind is very directed to the French. This could be for reasons seen in the story concerning the Vision of Fatima at Lourdes.

- The three coins on the book may speak to financial conspiracies in the Vatican which his predecessor was ready to condemn, but this Pope simply "carried these circumstances" with him, deciding not to make it an issue.

- The horse at the lower right may symbolize the Pope's many travels. A lion attacking the horse may symbolize the Vatican's bureaucracy taking advantage of the Pope's travels to strengthen their hold on the institution. ("While the cat's away, the mice will play!")

Ramotti spends the better portion of his book analyzing the various plates and connecting them to the Quatrains to which they appear to coincide. The presentation is compelling. However, the other discovery that occupies the second half of his book is much less so.

Ramotti's *second discovery* is a *cryptic key* inscribed by Nostradamus upon a stone in Turin, Italy, that allows for hidden messages buried in the quatrains (Italian messages buried in the Provençal French). Apparently, Nostradamus developed a skip letter sequence similar to what we've seen in the *Bible code.* However, instead of an "equidistant letter skip sequence," Nostradamus built a skip sequence based upon the year he first published his Prophecies, 1555. Ramotti explains this cipher and illustrates how it's used to uncover more meaning to Dr. No's quatrains.

I'm leaving this discovery out of our discussions for two reasons: First, we don't have space. Secondly, I don't find it particularly compelling. The additional information is confusing, a bit contrived, and in my mind, subject to even greater debate.

However, before we depart Ramotti, we must note that he provides one additional piece of information, which is crucial to understand the context of Nostradamus' prophecies and the timing of the end of days, at least from Nostradamus' perspective.

FIGURE 43 – DE LABORE SOLIS FROM *THE LOST MANUSCRIPT*

When Does Nostradamus Predict His Prophecies Conclude?

Commentators on Nostradamus often point out that Dr. No stated his ability to see into the future was limited to the year 3797. This date appears in his letter to his son, César. However, Ramotti says of this date, that it's "*nothing other than a simulated date made up to satisfy the concrete thinking of his contemporaries.*" Using a method of addition in numerology (which Ramotti apparently believes to be valid), he suggests 3797 actually equals "8" or "infinity." If so, this suggests that Nostradamus could see *up to the end of time.*

In his letter to Henry II, Nostradamus makes it clear "there shall be restored almost another reign of *Saturn* (Saturn often refers to Western nations in the quatrains) and a golden age: Satan "captured, bound, and thrown into the abyss" at which point his prophecies will have been mined (exhausted or concluded). This appears to correspond exactly to what John prophecies in Revelation. We read a pertinent confirming statement in C1:Q48, which states:

> *When twenty years of the reign of the Moon have passed*
> *For seven thousand years another will hold the throne,*
> *When the Sun takes up the days he left behind,*
> *Then my prophecy is mined and done.*

After the thousand years are finished, time ends and eternity begins. But what does the 7,000 years refer to? Ramotti proposes that "20 years of the Moon" equals 7,000 solar years. His calculation is 29.1 x 12 x 20 = 7,000. Following the pattern of Daniel (one day for one year, *according to Ramotti's interpretation*), a lunar month is about 29.1 days times 12 months, which equals one lunar year or 349.2 solar years; this number times 20 lunar years, equals 6,984 solar years, rounded to 7,000.

Ramotti quotes an American psychic, *Solara* (from her book, *The Opening of the Door*, Noesis, 1995), who indicates that the catastrophic prophecies of Nostradamus "'will no longer be valid when humanity becomes conscious of itself.' According to Solara, we have precisely twenty years, from January 11, 1992, to December 13, 2011, to cross through the dimensional door that leads to liberation from physical bonds and to (our) birth of an era of joy."[6]

Here, the important point isn't whether we are at the end of this 7,000-year period, whether 20 lunar years equals 7,000, or whether Solara (and Ramotti) are right to believe in a window of time through which humanity must pass to liberate its consciousness.

The key issue is that 3797 as a date may not be relevant. Nostradamus' prophecies may be concluded at the same time the Bible's prophecies are, as his direct statements state in his letter to Henry II. If true, this makes Nostradamus' prophecies *align* rather than *conflict* with the traditional Biblical interpretation.

Furthermore, what Solara and Ramotti may believe about *consciousness and extraterrestrials* is not contained within Nostradamus' prophecies either.

Finally, as to 2011 (Solara's date which approximates 2012), it's *not* a date contained within Nostradamus' quatrain, but may be another example of 2012 enthusiasm urging proponents to read into his prophecies. My point being, many conflicts between the prophecies of Nostradamus and the end of days, *as the Bible depicts them*, may not be conflicts at all. Nostradamus may be much more orthodox in his prophetic scenario of the end times than his supposed experts typically allow.[7]

The Prophecies of the Popes *Evelyn*

Nostradamus was extremely interested in Papal succession. We see this in the "Lost Manuscript" of watercolor paintings where it's a dominant theme.

What is fascinating is that it corroborates what is known as "the Prophecy of the Popes" or the Prophecy of St. Malachy (alluded to earlier).[8] The correspondence is so precise that some have proposed the St. Malachy prophecy is really *a product of Nostradamus* and not the 11th-century *Bishop of Armagh in Northern Ireland* to which it's attributed.

The prophecy was first published in 1595 by a Benedictine historian, Arnold de Wyon, in his book, *Lignum Vitæ*. However, it's significant that Bernard of Clairvaux wrote a biography of the Bishop, but makes no mention of the prophecy. Since Bernard wrote this work in the 12th century, logically it suggests that no prophecy existed then.

Nevertheless, as John Hogue points out (Hogue has also written a book on the St. Malachy prophecy), it makes no difference whether St. Malachy or Nostradamus set forth the predictions; the prophecies are valid if history proves them true. 112 popes were predicted. So far, 111 predictions out of 111 appear to be correct. Only the final pope, number 112, who the prophecy identifies as *Peter the Roman*, remains to be verified.

According to the prophecy, the final five popes are: (5) the "flower of flowers" (*Flos Florum*, Paul VI); (4) "the midst of the moon" (*De medietate lunae*, John Paul I); (3) "from a solar eclipse" (*De labore solis*, John Paul II); (2) "glory of the olive" (*Gloria olivae*, Benedict XVI); and (1) "Peter the Roman" (*Petrus Romanus*, yet to be determined). We must look into the names and the rationales for why these names historically match the prophetic titles.

John Paul I (*De medietate lunæ* – the midst of the moon or from the half-moon):

- He reigned for 33 days, died before the new moon, and was born on the day of the half moon, October 17, 1912.

- His name, *Albino Luciani* refers to "white light," as *Albino* relates to white and *Luciano*, relates to "lucius" and "lux."

John Paul II (*De labore solis* – "from a solar eclipse" or "of the labor of the sun."

- Was born on the day of a partial solar eclipse over the Indian Ocean (May 18, 1920), and died on the day of a rare double eclipse over the southwest Pacific and South America (April 8, 2005). This appears to be the most convincing argument.

- John Paul II, Karol Wojtyla, labored "in the sun" in a quarry during World War II.

- His special admiration is for the Virgin Mary, known as the *Woman of the Sun* in Revelation 12 (one depiction of her).

- Traditional Catholics view Catholicism, post-Vatican II, as "the great apostasy" and see this time in which Pope John Paul I and II reigned as "the eclipse of the sun."

- John Paul traveled around the world many times, following the path of the sun.

Benedict XVI (*Gloria olivæ*– "glory of the olive") is the last short phrase on the list (which refers only to a name for a Pope).

- The symbols of the order of St. Benedict include the olive branch. The Pope is not Benedictine, but chose the name Benedict.

- Benedict XVI hopes to reunite the Greek and Russian orthodox churches, by "extending an olive branch." Also, Greece is frequently symbolized by the olive.

- Some point to the Olivet Discourse of Christ in Matthew 24, which speaks to the end times. Olivet refers to the Mount of Olives. Those who profess this view believe this Pope will be the Pope who sees these final events come to pass.

- The Pope himself indicates the name relates to the legacy of Pope Benedict XV, who was known for *diplomacy* and conservative theological views. Others suggest his intent is to lead a "counter-reformation" returning to more traditional Catholic principles practiced prior to Vatican II.

While the last Pope, *Peter the Roman,* is sometimes dismissed as a later forgery, the only extant version of de Wyon's publication includes the phrase of this final prediction. It reads:

> *Peter the Roman, who will nourish the sheep in many tribulations; when they are finished, the city of seven hills [SDW: Rome] will be destroyed, and the fearsome Judge will judge His people. The End.*

There is a fascinating correlation to the foundational Jewish book of the Kabala, known as the *Zohar,* which is dedicated to the mystical study of the Torah. The *Zohar* predicts the destruction of the City of Rome when the leaders of the world are gathered there during the last days. The Zohar supplies the Jewish year when this destruction happens: 5773. Guess what year that is in our contemporary calendar? That's right: *2012.*

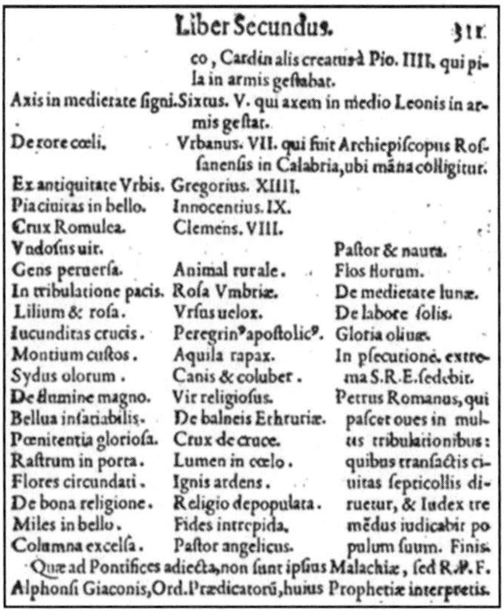
Liber Secundus. 311.
co, Cardinalis creatus à Pio. IIII. qui pila in armis gestabat.
Axis in medietate signi. Sixtus. V. qui axem in medio Leonis in armis gestat.
De rore cœli. Vrbanus. VII. qui fuit Archiepiscopus Rossanensis in Calabria, ubi mãna colligitur.
Ex antiquitate Vrbis. Gregorius. XIIII.
Piaciuitas in bello. Innocentius. IX.
Crux Romulea. Clemens. VIII.
Vndosus uir. | Pastor & nauta.
Gens peruersa. | Animal rurale. | Flos florum.
In tribulatione pacis. | Rosa Vmbriæ. | De medietate lunæ.
Lilium & rosa. | Vrsus uelox. | De labore solis.
Iucunditas crucis. | Peregrin⁹ apostolic⁹. | Gloria oliuæ.
Montium custos. | Aquila rapax. | In psecutioné extrema S.R.E. sedebit.
Sydus olorum. | Canis & coluber. |
De flumine magno. | Vir religiosus. | Petrus Romanus, qui pascet oues in multis tribulationibus: quibus transactis ciuitas septicollis diruetur, & Iudex tremẽdus iudicabit populum suum. Finis.
Bellua insatiabilis. | De balneis Ethruriæ.
Pœnitentia gloriosa. | Crux de cruce.
Rastrum in porta. | Lumen in cœlo.
Flores circundati. | Ignis ardens.
De bona religione. | Religio depopulata.
Miles in bello. | Fides intrepida.
Columna excelsa. | Pastor angelicus.
Quæ ad Pontifices adiecta, non sunt ipsius Malachiæ, sed R.P.F. Alphonsi Giaconis, Ord. Prædicatorũ, huius Prophetiæ interpretis.

FIGURE 44 - FINAL PART OF PROPHECY OF ST. MALACHY IN LIGNUM VITAE, 1595, P. 311

J.R. Church, of *Prophecy in the News,* discovered this reference in the *Vaera* (section 9 volume 3, section 34) verses 476-483. According to the *Zohar,* the *Mashiach* (Messiah) will appear late in 2012, signaling the time of Jacob's Trouble, or what Christians refer to as "The Great Tribulation" (a period to last either 3.5 or 7 years) which culminates with the Battle of Armageddon.

The timing of the publication of the *Prophecy of the Popes,* in 1595, allows for the possibility that Nostradamus did in fact originate these prophecies. It's noteworthy also that symbols used in the paintings of *The Lost Manuscript* correspond, as we have seen, to the names used in the St. Malachy prophecy. Given that Nostradamus created his works in 1555-1566, the timing of de Wyon's publication in 1595 allows that Nostradamus could have created it (i.e., if de

Wyon had published it in 1495, it would prove otherwise). We also know that Nostradamus wouldn't have wanted any blame for predicting negative outcomes for the Papacy that could be tied directly to him. Using the same logic in reverse, we could see how these predictions further confirm my thesis – *Nostradamus' true prophetic approach correlates to the Revelation of John much more than the Nostradamus experts acknowledge.* Based upon the information we've cited, it's probable that Nostradamus saw his predictions concluding in the 21st century, timed with the last Pope, *Peter the Roman*, not in 3797.

Therefore, did Nostradamus make these papal predictions? We may never know for sure. But as John Hogue suggests, the predictions have proven out 111 times before. If there is only one Pope after Benedict XVI, Rome may be destroyed as the prophecy warns. If this turns out to be correct (and hopefully for those who live in Rome this doesn't happen), my bet is the next Pope will indeed be the last to wear "the shoes of the fisherman."

Notes

[1] Nostradamus, *Les Prophecies*, (Centuries I, Quatrain 35), 1555.

[2] Today, *Easter Eggs* refer to something hidden in a DVD, which if you uncover it, will open up an entirely unadvertised feature.

[3] Technically, John predicts two beasts, one who is known as Antichrist, the other, the False Prophet. One is from the sea, the other from the earth. The second beast demands the whole world worship the first beast. Along with the Devil, they comprise a "Satanic Trinity."

[4] Once again, we can see how this dating error, it if is an error, may have been due to Dr. No's imprecision with his astrolabe (when certain celestial objects would be located where). An accurate reading may have resulted in 2001.

[5] Ramotti, O.C., *Nostradamus: The Lost Manuscript*, Rochester, Vermont, Destiny Books, page 75.

[6] Ibid., pp. 114, 115.

[7] Of course, this does not mean his techniques are orthodox or acceptable.

[8] This section utilizes extensive information from Wikipedia on "The Prophecy of the Popes." See *http://en.wikipedia.org/wiki/Prophecy_of_the_Popes*.

Chapter 10:
Sir Isaac Newton, the Temple, and the End of the World

*As far as the laws of mathematics
refer to reality, they are not certain,
and as far as they are certain,
they do not refer to reality.*

Albert Einstein

The World's Greatest Thinker

If we sought to identify the greatest mind which had proved itself worthy of the title, *The World's Smartest Mind*, who would we choose? Several obvious names would come to mind. Albert Einstein would be a popular choice. Johann Sebastian Bach and Wolfgang Amadeus Mozart would be likely musical entrants. In Philosophy, perhaps we would choose St. Thomas Aquinas or René Descartes. In Art, we would likely pick Leonardo Da Vinci. If we focused on *wisdom* as the primary criteria, Confucius would receive some votes, as would King Solomon, traditional author of the *Book of Proverbs* in the *Bible*.

FIGURE 45 - SIR ISAAC NEWTON
BY SIR GODFREY KNELLER 1689

What candidate would I nominate for this title? Without hesitation, my choice would be Sir Isaac Newton.

As a mathematician, Newton invented *Calculus*.[1] As an historian, he wrote a treatise on ancient kingdoms and developed a highly detailed chronology of early historical events which challenges much of academic thinking today. As a physicist, he discovered the *laws of gravity* (for which he and that falling *apple* are most famous). Few realize however, that he was the first scientist to discover the *particle nature of light*. Additionally, Newton was fluent in many languages, not only reading but also writing Latin, Greek, and Hebrew. As a chemist, he accumulated what may have been the world's great library on Alchemy (which in that era *was* chemistry if one excises its esoteric aspects).[6]

When we speak of a true Renaissance man, Sir Isaac Newton outshines all others of the enlightenment era. Newton even served as President of the famed *Royal Society*[2] from 1703 until his death in 1727. The Royal Society itself, in 2005, voted Newton ahead of Einstein as the physicist who contributed the most to science. In Michael Harts, *The 100: A Ranking of the Most Influential Persons in History*, Newton finished second only to Mohammed.[3]

What is of most interest to our study, however, is the fact that Newton knew the Bible intimately and was conversant with many aspects of theology. The well-known English philosopher, John Locke, wrote of him, "Mr. Newton is really a very valuable man, not only for his wonderful skill in mathematics, but in divinity also, and his great knowledge is the Scriptures, wherein I know few his equals." [4]

The Search for Ancient Wisdom

As mentioned early in our study, the great minds of the enlightenment searched diligently for *keys* to wisdom – ways to discern the unity in the knowledge of all things. Those who quested for this ancient wisdom called it *prisca sapientia* – pristine or sacred knowledge. They believed God originally gave humankind this pure and uncorrupted understanding of nature and the universe.[5]

Their search began with the essential elements of knowledge – language and numbers. Ancient Hebrew, sometimes called "proto-Hebrew," was the first alphabet with symbols *based on sound*. Some biblical scholars suppose that Moses developed (perhaps through God's direct revelation), a language based on *sonic* characters as opposed to pictures (hieroglyphs) characteristic of other ancient languages such as Sumerian, Egyptian and Mayan.[6] Other Bible experts believe that God gave the alphabet to humankind prior to the Flood of Noah.[7] They boldly assert that the language of Adam and Eve was Hebrew.

FIGURE 46 - ANKH (LIFE)

Newton, and other enlightenment thinkers, believed God had hidden *prisca sapientia* even in the letters of the language; such knowledge decrypted the natural world.

David Flynn's wonderful book that takes up these subjects, *Temple at the Center of Time*, discusses John Dee's singular mark of *Hermes* (aka Mercury and Thoth, the *god of writing, the messenger*). Dee, Queen Elizabeth's astrologer, believed that he wrote what God gave him to write (perhaps an early example of *channeling*, assuming that God wasn't actually the source of Dee's *inspiration*). Dee believed this symbol to be the most ancient mark of the divine. Hebraic sages believed the mark to be a combination of the last letter of their alphabet, the "*tawv*," (resembling our lower case "t"), with a word meaning *promise* or *oath*. They believed this was the mark placed on Cain by God to warn others not to harm him, lest Cain be avenged sevenfold at their expense (see Genesis 4:10-15). The Greek version of this symbol was the combination of their "**T**" (the Tau) plus the "**Ω**" (Omega). This resembles the Egyptian glyph "ankh" closely. Taken together, this symbol placed on the forehead of Cain represented God's oath to Cain to "preserve his life."[8]

Three principal ancient civilizations of the known world, the Phoenicians (occupying today's Lebanon and Syria), the *Hebrews*, and then the *Greeks*, shared the basic characteristics of this earliest language – no doubt necessitated by the extensive trade carried on amongst these civilizations *after* the Exodus from Egypt and *before* the Babylonian captivity of the Jews (ca. 1500 BC to 600 BC).

Indeed, the earliest form of Greek is a mirror image of the earliest form of Hebrew.[9] Likewise, the Phoenician alphabet follows the same structure as proto-Hebrew and appears to have been derived from it. In fact, the Phoenicians sound-based language is where we derive many of our words associated with sound and communication:

- *Phonetic* – symbols that represent the sounds of speech.
- *Phonemes* – the smallest unit of sound that carries meaning.
- *Phonics* – a method for teaching reading based upon sounds.
- *Phone* – relating to speech, the basis for telephone.

Newton was also an expert in *Cryptography* – the science of codes or encryption. Newton wrote to another brilliant mind, the German Gottfried Leibniz, encrypting certain sections of his method of Calculus to keep it from falling into the hands of others who might have claimed this discovery as their own. Newton's fascination with cryptography also motivated him to seek out "God's encryption." In John Maynard Keynes[10] biography of Newton, he makes this point:

> (Newton) regarded the universe as a cryptogram set by the Almighty – just as he himself wrapped the discovery of the calculus in a cryptogram when he communicated with Leibniz. By pure thought, by concentration of mind, the riddle, he believed, would be revealed... He did read the riddle of the heavens. And he believed that by the same powers of his introspective imagination he would read the riddle of the Godhead, the riddle of past and future events divinely foreordained.[11]

Newton believed, as did Francis Bacon and many others, that the Bible contained such a code; it could disclose universal truths about God and nature. Energized by the prospect of the soon return of Jesus Christ (as we noted previously, predicted by many in the year 1666), Newton studied the Bible in earnest looking for this code as part of his analysis of Bible prophecy.

Newton's study of the *Temple of Solomon* was of particular interest. Newton believed that God designed the Temple and gave this design to David, the blueprints from which Solomon then built. Because it was God's own design, Newton supposed he might find many hidden truths within its architecture. It's no wonder that ancient traditions of esotericism see the Jewish Temple as the focus of *prisca sapientia*. Indeed, the primary allegory at the center of Freemason initiation describes the death of the (supposed) chief architect of Solomon's Temple, Hiram Abiff.[12]

Newton understood the linkage between time and space. While not discovering time as a dimension, he indicated it was impossible to know time except through space, and in particular, motion through space. Newton was careful to distinguish his notion of God from the creation. He believed God was eternal, but not eternity. God was everywhere – substantially, not just virtually – yet God was not a *created thing* (which would include, to the detriment of New Age depictions, the idea that *God equals energy*, since energy is a created *thing*). Neither was Newton a deist although experts would often interpret his lasting influence this way.

Although the laws of motion and universal gravitation became Newton's best-known discoveries, he warned against using them to view the Universe as a mere machine, as if akin to a great clock. He said, "Gravity explains the motions of the planets, but it cannot explain who set the planets in motion. God governs all things and knows all that is or can be done."[13]

The name of God, known as the *Tetragrammaton*, (the four letters **YHWH**, often pronounced by the non-Orthodox Jew as *Yahweh* or *Jehovah*), means "God was, God is, and God will be."

In these matters, Newton followed the thinking of the great rabbinic teacher, *Maimonides* of the 12th century. Indeed, Newton was a devout Christian, believing in Jesus Christ as God's divine and only Son; but Newton did not believe the doctrine of the Trinity to be necessary or even accurate in explaining the nature of the Godhead. Newton was a staunch monotheist in every respect. Fearing the inquisition of the Church, Newton kept all of his theological writings unpublished until after his death.

Metrology and Numerology

Newton became *Warden of the Mint* of England and later *Master of the Mint*, positions he held from 1696 to his death in 1727. As such, he was the head of English *weights and measures*. Although this position was generally a *sinecure* (a paid job requiring little to no work), Newton took it seriously.

One of Newton's works connected his official position to his biblical studies; the treatise he wrote on the concept of the *Sacred Cubit*.[14] Like most *measures and standards*, the cubit ties to *human* proportions. The language of measures readily discloses this origin:

- "Foot," (an English foot of 12 inches close to the Roman foot),

- "Digits" (aka "inches" and in Roman terminology unicæ),

- "Palms" (the size of the hand, 3.6 modern English inches),

- "Cubits" (the length of the forearm from elbow to fingertip of the middle finger, equals 6 palms in the common cubit),

- "Rod" or "reed" typically the height of a man (and composed of three "common" cubits).

Ancient cultures demonstrate very similar units of measure. The cubit ranged from about 21 inches to more than 25 inches. Newton discusses the cubit in relationship to several ancient structures including the Temples of Sumeria and the Pyramids of Egypt. Deducing measurements from historical records, Newton concludes his treatise demonstrating that the sacred cubit was very close to 25.60 inches.[15] However, Flynn points out in his study that Newton believed the sacred cubit to be precisely 25.20 inches. This conclusion seems very plausible, as we shall see.

Newton saw the *common cubit* equaling six palms and the *sacred cubit* seven palms, each palm equaling 3.6 inches, based upon Ezekiel 40:5, where Ezekiel uses a "rod" to measure the temple.

The 7-palm cubit would stand out as sacred due to its relation to the number 7. Seven is the only cardinal number that does not divide evenly into 360. The sacred number, 2520 (100 times the sacred cubit) is also the result of 360 x 7.[16]

Nonetheless, we might ask, "Why is the number 2,520 'the sacred number?'" This is where David Flynn's biblical sleuthing possibly *decrypts Newton's surprising view.*

One of the most famous stories of the Bible is the "Handwriting on the Wall" when the last King of the Babylonian Empire, *Belshazzar,* suddenly sees a hand and finger writing a series of characters on the wall of his palace during a decadent banquet, one in which the King used the Hebrew Temple implements as serving dishes and décor. The image was so frightening that the account says, "The king's knees smote together and gave way" (and infers he may have required a change of undergarments). At the recommendation of the king's mother, the King called the retired governor and the head of the *Magi,* Daniel, to the banquet.[17] The inscription read, "MENE MENE TEKEL UPARSIN." Daniel interpreted these words, "God has numbered your kingdom and finished it. You are weighed in the balance and found lacking. Your kingdom is divided and given to the Medes and Persians."[18] Later that night, the Medes and Persians conquered, without contest, the supposed impregnable city of Babylon just as Daniel had prophesied.

	Gerahs
MENE	1,000
MENE	1,000
TEKEL	20
MENE DIVIDED	500
Total:	2,520

FIGURE 47 - THE SACRED NUMBER

Flynn points out that Newton, as head of the mint and expert in ancient languages, would easily have recognized these words to be equivalent to *monetary values.* Why is this so? First, we must know that the *gerah* was the lowest denomination of money in Chaldean times (think of it as our penny, referenced once again in Ezekiel, in relation to the future Temple). Twenty gerahs equaled a shekel (TEKEL). One thousand gerahs equaled a MENE. UPARSIN was the dividing of the MENE in two (1000 divided by 2 equals 500 gerahs). From this, the number 2,520 results, a *number written by the very hand of God.* The only other circumstance in which the hand of God writes something for others to read is, of course, the recording of the Ten Commandments, "by the finger of God." So, the very few instances are special indeed.

This number becomes a key to interpreting not only the prophecy of the "handwriting on the wall," but also important in understanding the *Apocalypse of John* (the *Book of Revelation*), the prophecies of Daniel, and surprisingly, the geometry of the creation of God. Flynn states, "…the number 2,520 is the key to Newton's hidden prophetical direction, and the metaphysical design of prophecy and time itself. It is a theory of the prisca sapientia that Newton intuitively believed existed, but did not have the resources or data to investigate. He did, however, anticipate that the means for its proof lay in the future."[19]

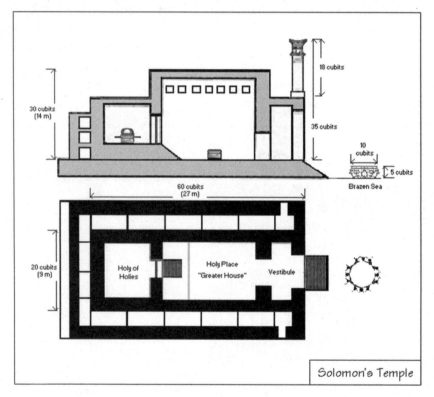

FIGURE 48 - SOLOMON'S TEMPLE, AS MEASURED IN CUBITS

Of course, the *sacred cubit* is a fractal of 2,520 (25.20). This sacred cubit was the measure God gave to Moses and it was the measure used to size the *Tabernacle*, the *Ark of the Covenant*, and the *Temple of Solomon* (and the far more massive future temple of Ezekiel, Chapters 40-48). Ironically, the Ark of the Covenant's description culminates in *Exodus 25:20.* When we combine other divine numbers (frequently used in the prophecies of Daniel and John), with the sacred cubit, a collection of fascinating measures result. But before we examine those measures, here's a quick lesson on the most basic *numerology* of the Bible to set the stage.

The numbers **7** and **3** are regarded to be divine numbers:

- The number **7** is considered *full* and *complete*. 7 is used throughout Revelation: 7 Lamp stands, 7 Spirits of God, 7 Seals, 7 Bowls of Wrath, etc. 7 is generally associated with 'perfection' or 'completion.'

- The number **7** dominates the Hebrew account of creation and Hebrew laws.

- The 7th day is the Sabbath. There are 6 years, then a Sabbath Year. There are 7 x 7 (49) years, then comes the Jubilee Year (50th year).

3 is the number of the Trinity. **33** is the number of Christ. **33** is also associated with the Temple of God.

Then, there is the number **6**:

Circle	Divisor	Dividend
360	1	360
360	2	180
360	3	120
360	4	90
360	5	72
360	6	60
360	7	51.428571
360	8	45
360	9	40

- **6** is the number of man.

- **666** is the number of the Beast of Revelation 13.

- Goliath, a fore type of the Beast, had **6** fingers on each hand, and **6** toes on each foot. He was **6** common cubits tall (10'8").

- There are **6** days for humans to accomplish their tasks, and the 7th day is the Sabbath, a day to reflect on God's good creation.

Only **7** divided into **360** yields a non-whole repeating decimal. 7 times 360 equals **2,520**.

FIGURE 49 - SPECIAL QUALITIES OF 360

360 is a special number too, as the adjacent table illustrates. This is why the symmetry between the sacred numbers, **2520**, **3**, **7**, **33**, **360**, and **Pi** (π) is so fascinating. The proportions of the sun, earth, and moon show clear correlations to these numbers and their interrelationships.

Newton believed God gave the Hebrews these methods of measurement – *they were not the invention of humans* – therefore, the measurements have divine sanction. *They are His numbers,* not ours. Consequently, His *prophecies* and His *creation* are meaningfully interpreted by using His *numbers.* Furthermore, upon tracing their history, it's clear that English measurements of nautical and statute miles stem from these standards. Thus, measurements are meaningful in depicting relationships and proportions in the mind of God – they reflect upon the manner in which He made the world.

Flynn points out numerous symmetries (summarized here):

- One day equals 360 degrees. 7 days is 7 x 360 or **2,520** 'degrees'.

- Earth's average diameter is **7,916.813** statute miles which is:

- (7 x 360) or **2,520** x π (3.14159) recently verified by NASA within .666 of a mile.

- **7,916.813** x π equals **24,873.493**... the earth's average circumference.

- Our Moon's diameter is (6 x **360**) or 2,160 miles.

- The average distance from the Earth to the Moon is **234,888** statute miles.

- This can be calculated by taking **77.77** x *pi* x *pi* x *pi* x *pi* x *pi* x *pi* x *pi* (**77.77** times *pi* seven times).

- The Moon's apogee (furthest point) is **252,000** statute miles (**2,520** times 100).

- The Moon's circumference, **6,785.8401** miles, subtracted from the Earth's diameter, 7,916.8134 equals 1,130.9733 miles.

- **1,130.9733** divided by π equals **360**.

- The Sun's mean diameter is (**2,520 x 7 x 7 x 7 + 1,260**) or **856,620** statute miles.

While these symmetries are fascinating, what do they mean? Do they prove that God is the creator of the heavens and the earth? Certainly, to those persuaded by intelligent design, or *teleology*, they do. Measures such as these encourage the Freemason's view that God is "the *Ancient Geometer*," inspiring them to assert that, when God is construed in this way, His reality becomes demonstrable and a universal concept *acceptable to all religions*.[20] God as designer becomes a least common denominator that we all can embrace.

The Temple at the Center of Time and Space

David Flynn's controversial thesis is that the *location of Temple Mount* and specifically, the founding stone where the Ark of the Covenant rested (in the Holy of Holies) is the *center of the time and space* (from the standpoint of relevance to God's providential plan for humankind). This is the view shared by the ancient Hebrew sages. According to Flynn, it was expressly the view of Sir Isaac Newton.

However, Newton didn't have the ability to undercover what appears to be an amazing relationship between *time* (the *year* that key events occur to the Hebrew people) and *space* (related to those Kingdoms detrimentally impacting the Hebrew people – and the respective *locations of these various Kingdoms on the globe*).

Flynn attempts to prove this correlation by pointing out how the *distance from the Temple Mount* (Jerusalem) to various capital cities of relevant Kingdoms *equals the year in which such Kingdoms most influenced the nation of Israel*. Generally, Flynn proposes these distances in *statute* miles (before Christ) and *nautical* miles (after Christ). In some cases, they correlate to standards like English *yards*. I will only mention a few instances here (and leave it to the reader to go directly to Flynn to study his argument). Flynn points out:

- Babylon destroyed the Temple of Solomon in **587** BC. The city of Nippur, the religious center of Babylon's religion is **587** statute miles from the Temple Mount.

- The Media-Persian Empire conquered Babylon and continued to rule the Jews. The handwriting on the wall appeared October 12, **539** BC. Babylon is **539.86** statute miles from the Temple Mount.

- Queen Ester withstood the evil advisor to the King, Haman on the banks of the river of *Ulai*, in Shush, Iraq. *Ulai* relates to our word, *evil*. This location is **666** miles from the Temple Mount.

- The black *Kabba Stone* of Islam, the center of religious worship in Mecca, is **666** miles from the Temple Mount.

- The Temple Mount of Jerusalem (Mount Zion) is **2,520** feet above sea level (according to Flynn).

- The *Ark of the Covenant,* Flynn believes, may be located **25.20** miles east of the founding stone of the Temple, on *Mount Nebo*, at an altitude one-half the sacred number, **1,260** feet above sea level.

- The number of 360-day, prophetic years, from the destruction of Solomon's Temple in **587** BC to the Roman Destruction of the Temple of Herod in **70** AD, was **666** prophetic years. The calculation:

587 BC (temple destroyed by Babylon) +
70 (temple's destruction by Rome) = 657 solar years
657 x 365.25 = 239,805 solar days.
239,805 / 360 = **666** prophetic years (of 360 days).

While Flynn's thesis is fascinating conjecture, his argument eventually leads to the conclusion that there are many different calculations that decode *Doomsday in the year 2012*. We will come back to that point in a later chapter to consider such arguments and the wisdom of asserting 2012 as a relevant date for Bible prophecy.

Newton's Prediction of 2060 as the End Date

Newton wrote more about theological and biblical topics than he did natural science. Some examples: He wrote on a *Historical Account of Two Notable Corruptions of Scripture*. Newton also wrote a treatise on the language of prophecy and a commentary on common elements in the Prophecies of Daniel and John the Revelator (*Observations on the Prophecies of Daniel and the Apocalypse of St. John*).

Since the zenith of English apocalyptic fervor in 1666, the possibility of decoding Doomsday fascinated Newton. However, after 40 more years of study (and maturity), he decided to develop only a *timeframe* for when the Apocalypse would occur, without *identifying a precise date*. Why did he undertake this? Newton was convinced that it was "not for us to know times and seasons." He offers his pre-

FIGURE 50 - BANNER OF THE HOLY ROMAN EMPIRE

diction " …not to assert when the time of the end shall be, but to put a stop to the rash conjectures of fanciful men who are frequently predicting the time of the end, & by doing so bring the sacred prophesies into discredit as often as their predictions fail. Christ comes as a thief in the night, it is not for us to know the times & seasons which God hath put into his own breast."[21]

Newton based his calculations upon a widely held belief from the days of the early Church Fathers forward (second and third centuries), that the Antichrist will lead a confederacy of nations representing a "revived Roman Empire." History tells us the date of the fall of the Roman Empire was 476 AD. Newton believed that it was *revived* with the coronation of Charles the Great (*Charlemagne*) on Christmas Day 800 AD. With Charles, the *Holy Roman Empire* commenced. The Empire lasted for slightly more than 1,000 years, until *Napoleon Bonaparte* forced its dissolution on 6 November 1806. Newton believed that with the advocacy of the new Emperor, the Pope then represented the supreme power in the world and, being an Anglican, was destined to become *the Beast* of Revelation 13.

Newton applied the sacred number of **2,520** and its half, **1,260** (both used frequently in the prophecies of Daniel and St. John), as years instead of days. By simply adding the 1,260 to 800, he arrived at **2060**. Newton believed that this date was *the earliest date* that the Apocalypse could happen. By adding 1,260 years to the date of *Pope Gregory VII's* death in **1084**[22] (a Pope who "changed the dates and seasons" from the old Julian to the today's *Gregorian* calendar – one of the characteristics of the "little horn" of Daniel[23]), Newton calculated the date of **2,344**. However, he arrived at a still later date by adding 2,300 years (2,300 being another set of days in Daniel) to the date of the destruction of the Temple by Rome (the Kingdom of the "little horn") in 70 AD. He then suggested **2370** was the latest date of Christ's return. This is how Newton created a bracket of time from 2060 to 2370, within which the world would witness the Second Coming.

Newton's Importance to Decoding Doomsday

What should we make of Newton's predictions? Does he provide meaningful assistance in decoding Doomsday? Unlike Nostradamus, Newton didn't have visions and didn't seek to prophesy by means of spiritual inspiration or through methods (such as *scrying*) that the Church would denounce as *esoteric if not demonic*. Alchemy fascinated Newton and no doubt, he was an Alchemist (at least to some extent). He may have gone as far as holding a belief that Alchemy preserved a form of ancient knowledge. However, Newton stopped well short of seeing in Alchemy a philosophical or theologian solution to the spiritual needs of humankind. Alchemy, as a religious system, was not this Englishman's cup of tea.

In distinct contrast to Alchemy, Newton believed in the authority of the Bible and in the supernatural inspiration of the prophecies of the Bible. His view of the Bible was especially orthodox.

For instance, perhaps for more than one thousand years, Church scholars treated the prophecy of the Bible as history or allegory. Newton, like many believing Christians in his day and ours, disagreed. *He believed the prophecies of the Bible would literally come true in the future. Jesus' return would be in **space and time.*** There would be a literal, physical kingdom of God upon this earth. Furthermore, Newton likely believed that God had chosen to encrypt some of his truths in the Bible and in the architecture of the Jews. Newton's emphasis upon the Hebrew Temple suggests that he believed God had hidden *prisca sapientia* in its architecture. However, we can't find record in Newton's writings of any specific discoveries about the Temple that provided added weight to the truthfulness of God's revelation. Nevertheless, if Newton were alive today, he would likely be the first to use a personal computer and *Bible Code* software in an attempt to understand what God has encoded in the Torah.

Newton's attempt to predict a range of time in which Jesus Christ would return to earth, makes use of the same techniques that many have attempted before – in his example, to treat *days as years* – and to select a date he deems significant, adding those years to this date and arriving at a speculative conclusion about when Doomsday will happen. The number **2,520** is significant. However, we've seen how many, including the Jehovah's Witnesses, have used this number in decoding Doomsday, to an unfortunate outcome.

Some might argue that the sheer genius of Newton adds strength to the argument that Bible prophecy must be true. After all, if one of the world's smartest minds believed in it, we shouldn't scoff. However, this logic is a double-edged sword. Newton also believed in many facets of Alchemy that modern science would refute. His belief in the Bible's prophets doesn't add weight to the veracity of the Bible any more than it proves what Alchemy contends – that with the *philosopher stone*,[24] one can turn lead into gold.

David Flynn's speculations on the *relationship between time and space* are fascinating in their own right. However, we could criticize Flynn for confusing the reader regarding what Newton *believed* in contrast to what Flynn *proposes*. Most of Flynn's calculations and speculations are his own. They are fascinating and worthy of review, but they aren't necessarily what Newton would have concluded. Furthermore, Flynn asserts that he has *decoded* Newton – he believes his documented evidence is sufficient to prove that

Newton found *the code* that unlocks many hidden meanings in the prophecy of the Bible. While the number, **2,520**, is one interpretation of God's hand-writing on the wall, we should remember it wasn't what Daniel expressed. Both interpretations could be true, but Newton nowhere comes right out and says that this number is the key to his understanding of the Bible's prophecies. Consequently, Flynn's conclusion is logical and appealing, but probably *not certain* given that he bases his conjecture mostly upon *inferences* and not actual quotations from Newton's writings. However, I still applaud his undertaking.

On the other hand, Newton did find biblical numerology important and a key to interpreting the meaning of what the Bible's prophets declare. This is crystal clear from his writings. *Biblical numerology is a consistent means by which the Bible conveys its message.* If God has truly inspired the Scripture, this numerology is important and logically reflects on the mind of the divine author and His message. As we will see later when we study Daniel and John on the subject of the Antichrist, this numerology is incisive to *make heads and tails* of what these writers prophesy.

Therefore, we can say the following in summary about Newton's help in deciphering Doomsday:

- Newton believed that the Bible was supernatural revelation to humankind from God and should be searched for understanding our future;

- The prophecies in the Bible will be fulfilled in history – they aren't simply allegories or past history;

- The Bible's prophets, Daniel and St. John, should be read together as they interpret and reinforce each other's message;

- Biblical numerology is crucial to correctly interpret Bible prophecy.

And finally, we could also recall that Newton elected not to predict a specific date, since he asserted that to predict such a date and miss it, brings criticism not only upon the decoder but upon the message of the Bible.

Sir Isaac Newton was among the first layman to study prophetic matters in his spare time. He was also quite modern in asserting how Bible prophecy will be *literally fulfilled* (the words by which Evangelicals primarily convey that prophecy will come to pass *in the space-time world*). Newton would just need to lay low on the matter of the *Trinity*. But as the world's smartest man, he wouldn't need this advice. He knew when to hold his peace.

Notes

[1] Gottfried Leibniz published his Calculus first in 1684, however, Newton had completed his work in 1667, but chose not to publish until his conflict with Leibniz forced him to do so. In fact, Newton was reluctant to publish much until 1704.

[2] The *Royal Society of London for the Improvement of Natural Knowledge, known simply as the Royal Society,* boasts the longest active scientific journal, first published in 1665. Early in his reign, Charles II formalized *The Society* with a charter. Prior to this, members like Francis Bacon and Christopher Wren, associated with a number of other great English minds in the so-called "Invisible College."

[3] Hart, Michael H. *The 100: A Ranking of the Most Influential Persons in History.* New York: Carol Publishing Group/Citadel Press, 1978. Influential is of course very different from smartest.

[4] Quoted by David Flynn, *Temple at the Center of Time,* pg. 15, from Franz Kobler, *The Jewish Frontier;* March 1943, "Newton on the Restoration of the Jews," pg. 21.

[5] During the 15th and 16th centuries, most scholars still believed in the truthfulness of the Bible as God's revelation to the human race. Many Bible scholars believe the language of humankind before the Flood was "proto-Hebrew."

[6] "Pictograms" are the basis for the Chinese and Japanese "alphabets" whereas Korean characters are phonetic.

[7] Perhaps more the substance of legend than Biblical fact, *Enoch,* the son of Methuselah, supposedly was the inventor of language. The book bearing his name indicates that the Nephilim called him "the scribe" and attributed to him the creation of language. Many mystery religions talk of "Enochian" knowledge, and consider Enoch the originator of *prisca sapientia.* According to Flynn, the name Enoch means, "initiate." The Bible says, "Enoch walked with God and God took him." (Genesis 5:24) The Book of Hebrews (11:5) indicates it was because of Enoch's great faith that God favored him and he did not experience death.

[8] We are familiar with the "mark" of the beast, 666, also placed on the forehead or forearm of those pledging an oath to Antichrist during the "Great Tribulation" described in Revelation 13. However, the author contrasts this mark to God's mark placed on the foreheads of those God promises to protect and preserve. It is most interesting that the Hebrew version of this mark resembles only the lower case t – which resembles a simple cross. *Could the mark of the cross have been the original "mark" of God to preserve the life of Cain?*

[9] Flynn, op. cit., pg. 90.

[10] Keynes is the famous economist whose theories of economics (Keynesian) are followed by our present President, Barak Obama.

[11] John Maynard Keynes, *Newton, the Man* (New York: Meridian Books, 1956), pg. 36, quoted by Flynn, op. cit., pg. 21).

[12] This Hiram was likely referenced in I Kings 7:13, 14. Josephus, in his *Antiquities of the Jews* (Chapter 3:76) indicates that Hiram was an Artificer (a skilled worker – not specifically the architect), "Now Solomon sent for an artificer out of Tyre, whose name was Hiram: he was by birth of the tribe of Naphtali, on his mother's side (for she was of that tribe); but his father was Ur, of the stock of the Israelites." The Freemason Allegory is a "loose interpolation" of the Bible – but not very well supported.

[13] Tiner, J.H. (1975). *Isaac Newton: Inventor, Scientist and Teacher*. Milford, Michigan, U.S.: Mott Media

[14] Newton distinguished the sacred cubit from the "common cubit."

[15] Sir Isaac Newton, *A Dissertation upon the Sacred Cubit of the Jews*, Hebrew University, The Newton Project, 10 pages.

[16] Sir Isaac Newton, *Prolegomena to a Lexicon Propheticumbe*, Yahuda mss 14.f The Newton Project. Quoted by Flynn, op. cit., pg. 87.

[17] Daniel was the head of the "wise men" aka the Magi. His influence continued through the centuries as it is the wise men of Persia who seek out the Hebrew Messiah, which Daniel predicted. Our word, *magic*, derives from 'magi.'

[18] Daniel 5:26-28.

[19] Flynn, op. cit., pg. 43.

[20] I do not mean to confer a favorable and supportable view of the Masonic notion of God. It does appear that God created the heavens and the earth with impeccable symmetry; thus, He is a God who is mindful of geometry and the importance of symbolism. But as a theist, I believe God is also personal and much more than just a "watchmaker" as the Deist supposes.

[21] Sir Isaac Newton, Yahuda MS, 7.3g, f. 13v. The Newton Project – University of Sussex, East Sussex London: 2007. See *www.newtonproject.sussex.ac.uk*.

[22] This Pope's death is now determined as May 25, 1085.

[23] Pope Gregory was also famous for ending the manner in which the laity, known as the Investiture Controversy, appointed Catholic clergy. This led Henry IV of Germany, then Emperor, to call for the Pope's removal.

[24] The so-called *philosopher stone* is most commonly regarded as a substance that Alchemists believed to be the essential, if not a magical element, that would catalyze the process and transform lead into gold.

Chapter 11:
The Knights Templar, Freemasonry, and America's Role in the Apocalypse

Whoever dares our cause reveal,
Shall test the strength of Knightly steel;
And when the torture proves too dull,
We'll scrape the brains from out his skull
And place a lamp within the shell
To light his soul from here to hell.

Dr. George W.L. Bickley
Founder, Knights of the Golden Circle, 1854

Dan Brown, Pop Historian of the 21st Century

Dan Brown didn't intend to be an alternative historian. No doubt, he set out to write great suspense novels and use little known facts about religion and history to thicken his plots. In his break out work, *Angels and Demons*, and his second book, *The Da Vinci Code*, Brown focuses on European Christian history. But in his latest book, *The Lost Symbol*, Brown goes domestic, highlighting the behind the scenes story of how Freemasons built our republic and literally architected our nation's capital.

In all three books, Brown leverages several proven story-telling enticements to great effect captivating his many readers. His works involve conspiracy theories, international destinations, religious controversy, political intrigue, and action-packed chase scenes. However, the lasting influence of all his books is how his alternate history (which for the most part he believes is true), creates anxiety among the unsuspecting masses. Specifically, his iconoclastic perspectives shatter many of our cherished assumptions about *secret societies*.

We once believed such shadowy groups were the object of paranoid delusions; *usual suspects* that "discontents" (pop-history delinquents with too much idle time and too many madcap opinions), regarded as the puppet masters pulling the strings as it were, *behind the curtain* in our world. But after Brown's books, we aren't so sure this derogatory assessment of conspiracy theorists continues to stand its ground. As the saying goes, *just because you're paranoid, doesn't mean they aren't watching you*. Although unintended, Brown has made conspiracy theorists much more respectable.

206

In *The Da Vinci Code*, we encounter a group known as the *Priory of Sion*, supposedly a cabal of notable historical figures like Leonardo Da Vinci, Sir Isaac Newton, and Victor Hugo, who maintained a clandestine organization and secret tradition concerning the truth about Jesus Christ and his unique relationship with Mary Magdalene, his closest patron (and supposed wife).

During the wild chases, we come across other figures, notably Sir Leigh Teabing,[1] an expert in the Priory and their military arm, the Knights Templar – a band of nine French knights (from the province of Champagne in northern France), who traveled to the Holy Land on the pretense to protect pilgrims during the first Crusade (early in the 12th century).[2]   As the story unfolds, we learn the Templars had other motives, including searching out great wealth under the *Temple Mount in Jerusalem* (aka Mount Moriah and to Jews, Mount Zion).[3] In the story, the Templars return to Europe with great wealth (and perhaps the Ark of the Covenant to boot!) Soon they become the first international bankers of Europe (true predecessors to the Rothschild's).

FIGURE 51 - SEAL OF
THE KNIGHTS TEMPLAR

Their official story lasts for 190 years, from 1118 to 1307, when in October of that year, on Friday the 13th,[4] their largest single debtor, the King of France (Phillip the Fair), rounded them up from across his country throwing them all in prison. Making good use of the inquisition and its tools of torture, Phillip IV and the Pope Clement II spent several years seeking to pin charges of heresy, blasphemy, and even sodomy on the Templars, mostly to no avail.

Ultimately, Phillip and the Pope allowed many Templars to recant and go free; however, not before they burned several leaders at the stake including the Grand Master, *Jacques de Molay*[5] who refused to admit to any wrongdoing, either personally or in regards to his Templar Knights.

In the first of Dan Brown's notable books, *Angels and Demons*, the secret society of interest is *The Illuminati*. The premise of Brown's story is the conflict between science and dogmatic religion raging over the past 400 years. Science is represented by an 18th century secret society known as *the Illuminati*, a Bavarian group founded in 1776 by Adam Weishaupt. This group asserted that human *reason*, not religious dogma, should guide human society, particularly government. Moreover, it's not coincidental that it was founded just as the American Revolution was getting in full swing.

The Illuminati were the radicals of the enlightenment. By 1785, fearing their revolutionary message, the Bavarian government outlawed this Order. In Brown's story, this enlightened group lies dormant for 225 years, biding its time, planning for the right moment and opportunity to get its revenge on the Catholic Church. Finally, as the old pope dies and the College of Cardinals prepares to vote for a new Pope, they spring into action. What's their plan? The four most likely to be considered for the Papal vacancy, the *Preferiti*, are kidnapped, purportedly by the Illuminati. One by one, they are murdered in gruesome ways. Each bizarre murder connects in some way to one of the primordial elements in Aristotelian science: Air, water, earth, and fire. Eventually Brown's hero, Robert Langdon saves the day, cunningly using his knowledge of symbols and Italian art. However, as the story ends, we are told that the Illuminati didn't really exist after all and hadn't for two centuries. This covert clan from the 18th century was merely being used as a sinister cover by the former Pope's murderer. What's relevant to us is that Brown's conclusion, while perhaps more reasonable than his story, simply isn't true to fact.

In the most recent Brown thriller, *The Lost Symbol*, Brown once again lands Robert Langdon in a great city filled with symbolism – Washington D.C. Langdon comes to D.C. on a false pretense, being misled into believing he is helping his good friend and 33rd Degree Freemason, Peter Solomon. He quickly learns that it's a villain, Mal'akh, who is seeking Langdon's help to discover "the Lost Symbol" within the District of Columbia. Mal'akh believes this symbol is the key to unspeakable power. However, as in the other stories, the deadly path the protagonists follow to uncover the truth is burdened with hidden messages, puzzles, and cryptography. In particular, we learn about the cryptographer's mind-bender, the *magic square*. Langdon and Katherine Solomon – the heroine of the story and Peter's daughter – race down this shadowy path as they seek clues to the lost symbol. Along the way, Langdon educates Katherine (and us) on the history of Freemasonry and its impact upon D.C.

As we've noted earlier, both George Washington and Pierre Charles L'Enfant were Freemasons. They were "designing men" planning Washington's streets and building locations, hiding deep Masonic symbolism throughout, such as: Occult pentagrams, Masonic compass and squares, mystical circles, and astrological connections to constellations such as Virgo and Orion. There are some who dispute this history, believing the initial building program just wasn't that imaginative. But to a growing number of historians it seems evident these *builders made use of many Masonic symbols.*

As Brown is inclined to do, even the names of his characters are related to the important background points. For instance, King Solomon (Peter's namesake) is the supposed originator of many Masonic secrets. Likewise, Mal'akh has one alias, last name *Abaddon*, which refers to "the Destroyer," as explained in the Book of Revelation (*Apollyon* is Greek and *Abaddon* is Hebrew, but both are actually alternate names for *Apollo*, aka, the Sun God).

We see in Brown's book how the Washington Monument, an Egyptian obelisk, plays an important role disclosing the lost symbol. Brown's lost symbol, however, may leave the reader a bit disappointed. The irony is that *there is a real lost symbol* of which Dan Brown is *not* apparently aware. Ironically, it too has much to do with the Washington Monument. *Truth is stranger than fiction* as we will see. As we study these clandestine groups, we will disclose what the real lost symbol is. *Mr. Brown: Please pay attention.*

These Secret Societies are All Intertwined

If we take what Dan Brown asserts at face value, we would likely conclude every one of these secret societies is independent from the others. While we know that the *Order of Knights Templar* was once a historical reality, after its official dissolution in the 14th century many scholars believe its ongoing influence is unimportant. Most believe the *Priory of Sion* never existed but was an elaborate hoax.[6] On the other hand, all experts agree that the *Illuminati* did exist but most doubt its existence today. The only secret society that appears undeniable and influential today is the *Freemasons.*

What's at issue (in our 21st Century), is *whether these former cabals had any consequential impact on Freemasonry* – such that we should lay awake nights wondering what this elderly Order is up to today. It seems though if we mount even the slightest study, we quickly discern that the connections between these organizations are many, are historically verifiable, and fascinating (if not foreboding) for their potential implications to our 21st Century world. Furthermore, when it comes to decoding Doomsday, understanding the relationships between these secret societies is *one of the important codes we must break.* By breaking this code, *we will see precisely how America figures into the Apocalypse.* The key: Understanding the connections between the Templars, Illuminati, Freemasonry, and the many ancient sources of wisdom we've previously discussed such as Alchemy, mysticism, and particularly Egyptian mythology.

The obvious question then is, "Are these many groups and belief systems really linked?" More specifically, "Are the Freemasons more than a social club with funny hats and bling-covered aprons 'round their waists'? Are their secrets worth dragging out into the open?" To answer these questions, we must do some painstaking historical inquiry – a quest if you will, reminiscent of the search for the Holy Grail – for the facts surrounding *the secrets of these secret societies.*

What Really Happened to the Knights Templar?

The first matter of importance is determining the destiny of the Knights Templar. What happened after Friday the 13th, 1307?

As discussed above, many of the French Templars were imprisoned by King Phillip on that date. It's speculated that the secret raid of King Phillip was leaked to some Templars beforehand. Most scholars believe that these Templars escaped with much of their fabulous treasure loaded on their many ships. The largest group of Templar ships sailed around the west coast of Ireland, escaping English blockades, and circled back across the northern-most parts of Ireland and Scotland, landing on the eastern shores of the Scots. The Scottish King, Robert the Bruce – at odds with the English King, Edward II – welcomed the Templars. He provided sanctuary for the Knights. In turn, they provided him substantial military prowess.

The same authors that brought us *Holy Blood, Holy Grail,* Michael Baigent and Richard Leigh (the book that originated Dan Brown's thesis in *The Da Vinci Code*), document a number of important historical and empirical facts in another book, *The Temple and the Lodge.* First, they provide photographs of a number of apparent Templar settlements including one graveyard in particular, which contains 80 or more Templar graves, complete with Templar symbolism and the Masonic symbols of *square and compass.* Likewise, several buildings also display the Templar and Masonic symbols.

Secondly, Baigent and Leigh believe there is strong circumstantial evidence for the presence of the Templars. They cite accounts of a famous border battle between English King Edward and Robert the Bruce: The *Battle of Bannockburn in 1314.* Edward had amassed over 20,000 English warriors and 500 knights at the Scottish border. Bruce had less than half that many in the field. At the height of battle, a fresh force appeared on the horizon coming to the aid of

Bruce and his floundering army. The authors indicate that whoever the force was, it put "the fear of God into them" (my words, not theirs). Their appearance caused the English to bolt. They left their silver, gold, armor, and many of their weapons lying in the field. Thereupon, the Scots won a great victory. Baigent and Leigh speculate that the recently settled Templar Knights (donning

their long white tunics sporting the bright red Templar cross), ominously appeared riding across the horizon with their long flowing beards whirling in the wind. Considered by far the best fighting force in all of Christendom, at the very first sight of the Templars the English turned tail and fled with nary a second thought.

Thirdly, we encounter the famous Church featured at the end of *The Da Vinci Code*. Here's what we know about it: In the city of Roslin, William Saint-Clair (Sinclair) built *Rosslyn Chapel* circa 1454. Earlier, Catherine Saint-Clair had married the first Grand Master of the Templars, Hugues de Payens. Saint-Clair was also a descendent of Marie Saint-Clair who was the second Grand Master. Also, it's not inconsequential that the floor plan of the Chapel is laid out to match the ancient Temple of Solomon in Jerusalem. While a

FIGURE 52 - AMERICAN MAIZE IN ROSSLYN CHAPEL?

supposed Christian Church, the symbols throughout the Chapel aren't Christian at all; indeed, they're nothing if not bizarre. One symbol in particular has provoked another fantastic theory, which if true, lends further credence to the theory that the Templars were present in Scotland and undeniably, the founders of Freemasonry.[7]

On some arches in the Chapel, American maize (i.e., corn) appears to be imprinted. This wouldn't be *amazing* (pun somewhat intended) except for the fact that Columbus didn't sail to America for another 50 years and such corn doesn't grow naturally in Europe. So just how did Saint-Clair know about American maize?[8] The theory set forth: Not all ships sailed to Scotland. The treasures and the ships were split into two groups, one heading to Bruce's Scottish sanctuary while the other went to the New World.

Additionally, there's strong evidence that someone did some serious, deep digging in Nova Scotia, apparently hiding something valuable there. Though no treasure has yet been discovered, many a modern treasure hunter has probed beneath the surface there, finding layer upon layer of wooden platforms appearing as though a series of stacked rooms were built to hold something of value. However, as each layer is uncovered it floods, making each successive layer more inaccessible.

Additionally, another artifact appears in Newport, Rhode Island. There a building of great age exists that some speculate to be Templar construction from the 14th century. Apparently, on a Spanish map from the early 15th century, there's a note that indicates a "Norman (French) settlement" existed there. If the Templars built a colony and resided there for some number of years, no doubt (like the Pilgrims of Plymouth Rock fame), they learned about corn and its cultivation from the natives. Could this explain the symbols on the arches of Rosslyn Chapel?

Then there is the plain fact that the Scottish Rite of Freemasonry indicates *its origin is Scotland* (which seems logical, given its chosen name). The accounts of its history, in one or two speeches delivered in the 18th century by noteworthy individuals, appear to provide another line of corroborating evidence.

In 1737, Royal Society member and Mason, Andrew Michael Ramsey delivered a speech to Freemasons in Paris, later known as *Ramsey's Oration*.[9] Ramsey indicated, "Our Order formed an intimate union with the Knights of St. John of Jerusalem" (which inherited the Templar assets, bestowed by Pope Clement V). In this same speech, Ramsey indicated that Freemasonry was connected to the ancient mystery schools of the Greek goddess Diana and *the Egyptian goddess Isis (emphasis mine)*.[10]

According to Baigent, Leigh, and Lincoln: A German Mason, *Baron Karl Gottlieb von Hund*, joined the Frankfurt Masonic Lodge in 1751. He possessed a list of Templar Grand Masters dating from his time back to the early days in Scotland. Hund founded another secret society, an extension of the Scottish Rite – *The Order of the Strict Observance* – after taking an oath of unquestioning obedience to *mysterious and unseen superiors*. The authors indicate that the list was virtually identical to the members of the Priory of Sion, the supposed secret society featured in *The Da Vinci Code*. The authors contended this second list corroborated the *Dossier Secretes* of Jacque Plantard which he claimed he found in the National Library in Paris. In any event, "they felt this provided strong support for the belief that both the Priory and Freemason Hund [*The Order of Strict Observance*] were directly tied to the Knights Templar."[11]

Illuminati – Radical Republicans of the 18th Century

What of the Illuminati? How do they figure into the Masonic story? As already mentioned, the Illuminati were radical revolutionaries out to destroy the Church and the Monarchy. It's usually asserted they had only a mild affect upon America's revolution, while they had an enormous impact upon the French version. At issue is the reality of an *infiltration of the Illuminati into the Masonic organization*; perhaps, into the highest levels of its leadership. Some academics judge this notion a by-product of an overactive imagination. While it's a favorite of conspiracy theorists, the facts nonetheless seem to point to its genuineness.

One particularly telling piece of literary history provides a summary judgment. John Robison, a Mason invited to join the Illuminati in late 18th century (100 years after the founding and supposed dissolution of the secret society of Illuminism), wrote a book with a not-so-succinct title, *Proofs of a Conspiracy Against All the Religions and Governments of Europe Carried on in the Secret Meetings of the Free Masons, Illuminati, and Reading Societies.*[12] Robison, a professor at Edinburgh University, quoted from one of Weishaupt's letters to his fellow Illuminati:

> The great strength of our Order lies in its concealment. Let it never appear in any place in its own name, but always covered by another name, and another occupation. None is fitter than the three lower degrees of Freemasonry; the public is accustomed to it, expect little from it, and therefore takes little notice of it.[13]

Of particular import was a 1782 Masonic convention at Wilhelmsbad in Hesse. According to historian Nesta Webster, it was at this order that both

Illuminism and the *Order of Strict Observance* (mentioned briefly above), apparently were covertly merged into the Freemasons. For neither was publicly noticed from that time forward. Jim Marrs comments:

> With divisive issues settled and the Illuminati safely hidden away within the Freemasons, the Convent [sic] of Wilhelmsbad proved a turning point for the order. Although attendees were sworn to secrecy, the Count de Virieu later wrote in a biography, "The conspiracy which is being woven is so well thought out that it will be... impossible for the Monarchy and Church to escape it." "From the Frankfurt Lodge, the gigantic plan of world revolution was carried forward," [William] Still wrote. "The facts show that the Illuminati, and its lower house, Masonry, was a secret society within a secret society."[14] "Even though the Illuminati faded from public view, the monolithic apparatus set in motion by Weishaupt may still exist today," Still commented. "Certainly, the goals and methods of operation still exist. Whether the name Illuminati still exists is really irrelevant."[15]

Masonic historians bear witness to the same. Manly P. Hall wrote that "Freemasonry is a fraternity within a fraternity – an outer organization concealing an inner brotherhood of the elect... The invisible society is a secret and most august fraternity whose members are dedicated to the service of an... *arcanum arcandrum* [a sacred secret]. Likewise, Albert Pike agreed that Freemasonry has "two doctrines, one concealed and reserved for the Masters... the other public..."

Because members of the hidden fraternity have taken an oath of secrecy, Masons regularly and strenuously deny that any hidden agenda exists. But is this denial part of the deception? We may never know. Motivating this nay saying sentiment may not be intention, but *ignorance*. Even the famous *Casanova*, himself a Mason, stated that one could be a Master Mason for 50 years and still not know the real secrets of the fraternity.[16]

Furthermore, many speculate that at the heart of Freemason doctrine is a belief in secret knowledge or *gnosis* (the Greek word for knowledge), another candidate for the true meaning of the Masonic "**G**"), which was provided in ages past and learned by the Templars during their adventures in Palestine. This theory suggests to some that the Templars learned many secrets shattering their orthodox Christian faith. After coming to terms with the truth, they obtained extant copies of Gnostic documents and then blackmailed the Church. Obtaining the Papal endorsement so early in their Order's history (at the Council of Troyes, 11 years later in 1129), lends support to the idea that the Templars knew something which threatened the Pope. It may also explain why the

Church reacted with such rage when the tables could be turned against the Templars.

With the Crusades concluded (a dismal failure by any account), the Order's *raison de être* vanished and their effectiveness waned. It didn't help matters that their piety had dissolved too. Today, we describe a crew infused with alcohol to be "drunk as sailors." Back then, the phrase was "drunk like Templars." In respect and in wealth, their reversal of fortune is historically unrivaled.

Freemasonry and Egyptian Paganism

Assuming we've offered sufficient proof and explanation as to how these secret societies are connected, the next pertinent issue is, "What does Freemasonry believe?" Furthermore, "How do the doctrines of Freemasonry motivate the organization today?" In short, we know that overthrowing Monarchy and Church isn't today's agenda. So what is?

Typical political conspiracy theorists, as mentioned earlier, connect the proposal of "one-world government" with George H.W. Bush's advancement of a *new world order* – a means to reduce world conflicts and eliminate wars, famines, and other challenges we humans face. Masons, along with many others similarly inclined, may seek to diminish brazen nationalism to inspire a singular world government in hopes of bringing about a brighter future.

But conspiracy theorists claim the globalist ambition includes much more than politics – *esoteric spiritual goals* also lie behind this hidden agenda. Beliefs about mysticism, the order of the cosmos, and humankind's relationship to "The Great Architect of the Universe" (TGAOTU) propel Freemasonry to seek particular spiritual objectives too.

However, upon a closer look we see many of these notions *aren't so noble*. Indeed, as distinguished as the concept of a single, world socialist government may be to most progressives today, the spiritual scheme behind it all is truly old-school – astonishingly unsophisticated – advancing myths of the most ancient and archetypal kind. In essence, *the symbolism of Egyptian mythology is at the heart of Freemasonry*. Indeed, we can rightly say the fundamentals of Freemasonry are tied to *the paganism of ancient Egypt*.

From a treatise, "The Great Work in Speculative Freemasonry," The Dormer Masonic Study Circle in 1930 offered this commentary:

> It is now generally acknowledged by those competent to judge, that of all *the ancient peoples the Egyptians were the most learned in the wisdom of the Secret Doctrine*; indeed, there are some who would have it that Egypt was

the Mother of the Mysteries, and that it was on the banks of the Nile that the Royal Art was born. We can affirm, without entering into any controversy on the matter, that the wisest of philosophers from other nations visited Egypt to be initiated in the sacred Mysteries; Thales, Solon, Pythagoras and Plato are all related to have journeyed from Greece to the delta of the Nile in quest of knowledge; and upon returning to their own country these illumined men each declared the Egyptians to be the wisest of mortals, and the Egyptian temples to be the repositories of sublime doctrines concerning *the history of the Gods and the regeneration of men*.[17] (*Emphasis mine*)

We've encountered allusions to this "secret doctrine" many times in our exploration here, but most notably in the works of Madame Helena Blavatsky. What's truly at the heart of *the Secret Doctrine*?

In the early dynasties of ancient Egypt, the obelisk was known as the *ben ben* stone. It was a monument to the sun god, *Ra*. Later Pharaohs dedicated their obelisks to *Osiris*, the brother of *Isis*. Osiris was the god of this world, the underworld, and supposedly the afterlife. The Egyptian myth revolves around the conflict between Osiris and Seth, Osiris' evil brother. Seth kills Osiris, but Osiris is resurrected by his son Horus. This resurrection is facilitated by "the lion's grip." In the symbolism of Freemasonry, this same grip is used to "raise to life" the initiate in the Third Degree ceremony. The scholars of Freemasonry agree *the story of Osiris' resurrection is essential to the lessons of their Order*. We use the phrase, "giving someone the third degree," inferring we are giving someone a difficult time. Little do we realize the phrase relates to Masonic initiation, to the more intense process to achieve the rank of Third Degree Freemason. Even less do we recognize that upon receiving the Third Degree, the initiate has taken part in a ceremonial resurrection from the dead that's at the heart of Freemasonry. Masonry isn't just a social club.

Of equal or surpassing stature, is one of the Masons' most important symbols, *the obelisk*, which connects directly to this legend.

One scholar, Martin Short (not the comedian!), points out in his book, *Inside the Brotherhood*, "If, as some Masonic historians claim, Hiram Abiff is really Osiris reborn, there could be no greater proof of Masonic ascendancy in the modern world than Egyptian obelisks thrust by Masons into the heart of the West's greatest cities." Michael Bradley, in his book, *Secrets of the Freemasons*, explains:

An obelisk was erected in the Place de la Concorde in Paris in 1833 under the supervision of the Minister of Public Works, Louis Thiers, a Freemason. The London obelisk, now known as Cleopatra's Needle was like the French obelisk, a gift from the Viceroy of Egypt, Mohammed Ali, in 1819. But it wasn't transported from Egypt until 1877 when an eminent Mason, General Sir James Alexander shipped it to London, with financing by another Mason, Dr. Erasmus Wilson, at a cost of £20,000. In the same year, its twin was given to America and once again it was Masons who organized and financed the transportation from Egypt. According to Martin Short, "The prime mover was a New York editor named William Hulbert, the benefactor (to the tune of $75,000) was William J. Vanderbilt, and the sailor was Lt-Cmdr Henry Gorringe. All were Freemasons."

To confirm its importance to Freemasonry, the erection of the cornerstone in Central Park in 1880 "was a brazenly Masonic affair," says Short. "Nine thousand Freemasons marched with bands through the streets to Greywacke Knoll where Jess Anthony, the Grand Master of New York Masons, laid the 7-ton cornerstone." Finally, when the Washington Monument was completed, Short describes the dedication ceremony which took place in February 1885 as "another dose of fraternal self-congratulation. One prominent brother spoke of Masons now as builders of human society." [18]

Albert Mackey, in his book *A Manual of the Lodge*, admits that Freemasons join with most pagans through the ages *as worshipers of the sun*. Furthermore, as the emphasis on the obelisk bears witness (a not-so-subtle symbol of the phallus), Freemasons (almost all, *unsuspectingly* and *unwittingly*) participate in a fertility cult. Even the simple circle "with a dot in the middle" is a symbol signifying "the phallus" to Freemasons. Mackey states, "The point within the circle is an interesting and important symbol in Freemasonry... The symbol is really a beautiful but somewhat abstruse [puzzling] allusion to the old Sun-Worship, and introduces us for the first time to that modification of it, known among the ancients as the worship of the phallus."[19] It's unexpected to say the least.

Albert Pike would correct Mackey inasmuch as he believed that Masons worship not the sun-god, but the god behind the sun, the bringer of light, or *Lucifer*. According to Marrs, "Pike wrote that *Adonai*, one of the biblical names for God, was the rival of Osiris, the Egyptian sun-god, a prominent figure in Masonic Traditions... "Thousands of years ago, men worshipped the sun... Originally they looked beyond the orb [our solar system's sun] to the invisible God... The

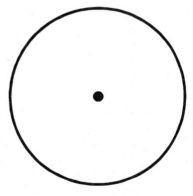

FIGURE 53 - MASONIC SYMBOL OF SUN AND PHALLUS

worship of the Sun [the invisible God] became the basis of all the religions of antiquity." [20] But their invisible god didn't use the same name as the Hebrew God (Adonai). To sharpen Pike's point: *Lucifer good, Adonai bad.* Certainly, Pike would decry any charge of Satan worship. He considers the Masonic teaching "Luciferian" and not Satanic. However, should we take comfort in Pike's qualification?[21] The Bible warns its adherents "And no marvel; for Satan himself is transformed into an angel of light" (II Corinthians 11:14). "*Luciferic truth*" **is** *the very disguise that Satan hand picks.* Pike's denial is in reality an admission that opponents' allegations are right on target.

As we dig further, we find even more unsettling ties to Alchemy and Hermetic science[22] embedded within Freemasonry. Mackey wrote, "There can be no doubt that in some of what are called the [Masonic] High Degrees there is a very palpable infusion of a Hermetic element. This cannot be denied." Marrs says, "The mythical and magical practice of alchemy was passed down from the Egyptians." Then he quotes Picknett and Prince who explain: "The [Hermetic science] practice embraced a fine web of interlinking activities and modes of thinking, from magic to chemistry, from philosophy and hermeticism to sacred geometry and cosmology. *It also concerned itself with what people today call genetic engineering and methods of delaying the aging process, and of trying to attain physical immortality*"[23] (emphasis mine).

We can amass considerable evidence that at the highest levels in Freemasonry hides belief in the practice of ritual magic and knowingly paying homage to Lucifer. The "beast" – Aleister Crowley – was a 33rd Degree Freemason. Foster Bailey, head of Lucis (formerly Lucifer Trust), was a 32nd Degree Mason also. Indeed, if you seek out the dark side of ceremonial magic, virtually all of those in that clandestine school will be members of a Masonic lodge.[24] Paying homage to the dark side appears to be the crowning achievement of the inner circle.

Perhaps we should ask the question from old radio program, *The Shadow*, "What evil lurks in the heart of man?" Given that most Masons know next-to-nothing about this, the answer still may be, "nothing particularly diabolical." Indeed, many would counsel that we shouldn't make too much of it. Then again, it's the true-believers, just as in any group, that *steer the course for everybody, whether they've disclosed the destination or not.*[25] Certainly they don't broadcast their deep mystical beliefs – that is obvious – and it's clearly their intention not to do so. Even Jesus advised, "Don't cast your pearls before swine." Nevertheless, it's the adepts who are "in the loop." It's these about which we *do* have to wonder.[26] And wonder (if not worry), we should.

When encountering this information, Masons (who profess Christianity) must question whether associating with an organization built on such speculative philosophy and occult mysticism (at its core), is consistent with their Christian faith.

My father, William Woodward, a 32nd Degree Freemason, finally walked away from the organization when he considered that *its secrecy and ritual* were at odds with his personal beliefs and Christian commitment. His attendance at a Masonic funeral with its *pomp and circumstance* finally caused him to consider that the two different belief systems weren't compatible. Understand, my Dad isn't a theologian and he's less likely than most to overreact. Nevertheless, for him, Freemasonry no longer passed the sniff-test.

The Plan for America

Francis Bacon is one of the most fascinating figures in history.[27] Many literary geniuses believe he was the author behind all Shakespearian plays (this list includes Samuel Clemens [Mark Twain], Walt Whitman, Henry James, Sigmund Freud, and Ralph Waldo Emerson). Bacon may also have been Queen Elizabeth I's illegitimate son. Despite a public quarrel, she knighted him in 1603. Bacon was England's Grand Chancellor under King James I (of King James Bible fame). He was also founder of the *Invisible College*, which was transformed into the *Royal Society* after Cromwell was no longer "protecting England" and repressing free thought amongst the Academia. Bacon is considered by many to be the father of Freemasonry in England[28] and experts believe he was at the center of the more esoteric "Order of the Rosy Cross" (Rosicrucianism). In fact, Michael Baigent and Richard Prince indicate that Rosicrucianism, Freemasonry, and Bacon's Royal Society had virtually identical membership rolls – the only difference being that the Royal Society met publicly

FIGURE 54 - FRANCIS BACON

and the other groups met in secret.

Bacon wrote The Wisdom of the Ancients and The New Atlantis. The latter work laid out a plan for a utopia in the New World based upon Platonic ideals and Masonic aspirations. America would be the site to fulfill the Mason's Great Plan, building a New Atlantis (originally, Atlantis was one of the planned names for Washington D.C.). It's no coincidence that the Virginia Company, founded in 1606 and which launched the colony of Jamestown in 1607, was financed in part by Francis Bacon.

Earlier, Sir Walter Raleigh had led a failed colonization effort on Roanoke Island, North Carolina, in 1584. This failure diminished broad interest in the New World until *The New Atlantis* was published after Bacon's death in 1626. Manly P. Hall, Masonic historian indicates that the reason *The New Atlantis* was published posthumously was that Bacon "gave away too much." [29] He contended that the goal of secret societies for thousands of years (since the Tower of Babel forward), had been to create an ideal commonwealth in the *political world* with enlightened leadership at the helm. It's quite true that Bacon's book was instrumental in moving this New World program forward; but obviously not without a great deal of help.

Hall believes that all but one of the 56 signing members of the Declaration of Independence were Masons (non-Masonic historians admit to no more than 15). But clearly, the list of Masons we can confirm is a "Who's Who" of the American Revolution: George Washington, Alexander Hamilton, James Madison, Ethan Allen, Henry Knox, Patrick Henry, John Hancock, Paul Revere, John Marshall, and of course, Benjamin Franklin. While there's no record of Thomas Jefferson's initiation, most believe there is little doubt he was a *member in good standing* too. His near blind support for the French Revolution is telling in this regard.

An interesting sidebar for advocates of capitalism: While Jamestown was considered a failed colony, not long afterwards, the *Puritans* of Thomas Bradford (so named because they sought to *purify* entirely the Church of England from any taint of Catholicism), created their "city on a hill" in Plymouth, Massachusetts. Interestingly, according to historian William Still, one of the keys to their success when compared to Jamestown's failure, was Bradford's decision to stop holding all property (notably land) in common as was done in Jamestown (it being driven by Platonic, *utopian* ideals),[30] in order to parcel out the land to each family so they could maintain their own property and grow their own food. After this was done, the colony flourished.

Many conservative American's might protest this emphasis upon Freemasonry and American's past. Most likely they would argue we should credit the *Pilgrims* and not the *utopians* for the formation of America and to set us on the right path to achieve the formidable position of America in the 20th and 21st Centuries. Adding to this debate is the adaptation (or better, obfuscation) of *Christian intentions with Masonic ambitions*. Hall, himself a 33rd Degree Freemason, explains in his book, *The Secret Destiny of America*,

> The rise of the Christian church broke up the intellectual pattern of the classical pagan world. By persecution of this pattern's ideologies it drove the secret societies into greater secrecy; the pagan intellectuals then re-clothed their original ideas in a garment of Christian phraseology, but bestowed the keys of the symbolism only upon those duly initiated and bound to secrecy by their vows.

America's Symbols Disclose the Religion of the Founders

As in Jesus' parable of the "wheat and tares growing together," it's nigh unto impossible to distinguish between the influences of Freemasonry and Christianity and give credit where credit is due. The "American Experiment" relies upon both (1) the separation of church and state and (2) freedom of religion. Neither principle is inherently Christian; yet, American Protestants of all flavors are among the first to laud the wisdom of this governing philosophy. (Like capitalism, all of these principles are thoroughly pragmatic and highly

FIGURE 55 - THE WASHINGTON MONUMENT - AN EGYPTIAN OBELISK

effective, but not essentially biblical). Furthermore, even most conservative Evangelicals *denounce any form of theocracy, Christian or not*, knowing the excesses of religion when it attempts to govern a secular population. This doesn't mean that our forefathers were without faith in God. However, when we examine objectively the source of our forefathers' beliefs, it's rather clear that their ideology and intentions were *suffused with Egyptian mysticism*.

At the risk of upsetting American patriots and suggesting a thorough rewriting of our American History textbooks, it's also perfectly plain that many of our famous forefathers *weren't particularly Christian*. Take George Washington for instance. He went to church every week. But he would never confirm he believed in the deity of Christ. Christian virtues were extolled, but biblical theology wasn't. As stated before, when we examine the evidence the commitment of many if not most of the Founding Fathers was to a strange mixture of reason and *classical paganism*. Many historians have disputed that the layout of the symbols and streets of Washington reveal the hand of Masonic design. But more and more scholars are changing their minds.

Even David Ovason who became a Mason after he wrote *The Secret Architecture of our Nation's Capital: The Masons and the building of Washington, D.C.,* "argues effectively that the city's layout intentionally incorporated the esoteric belief system of Freemasonry, especially as it involved astrologically aligning the capital with the constellation Virgo (Isis)."[31] And this is before scholars give consideration to the newly discovered evidence covered in an earlier chapter regarding Washington D.C.'s megalithic measurements. That evidence is conclusive regarding Masonic intent.

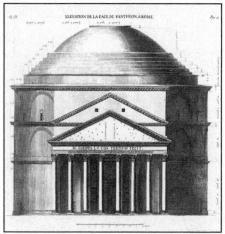 

FIGURE 56 - COMPARISON OF CAPITOL TO PANTHEON

The Washington Monument, as previously discussed, is plainly an Egyptian symbol of *Osiris* (aka *Apollo* in both Roman and Greek mythology). Even the front of the capital building is distinctly related in design to the *Pantheon* in Rome (built by Emperor Hadrian in 126 AD).

The Pantheon, with the stunning *oculus* featured early in Brown's *Angels and Demons*, is a monument to "every god." This comparison is obvious when looking at the U.S. Capitol in an 1846 photo with the dome under construction[32] (see below). If the Washington Monument is a phallic symbol, isn't it obvious what the dome of the Capitol represents? If the obelisk is a symbol of Osiris, isn't the dome a symbol of Isis (Venus/ Virgo)? [33]

While this connection may first appear far-fetched, the coincidence of three major monuments connecting Osiris and Isis (Apollo and Virgo), demonstrate that it's no Freudian slip. The fact is the *Vatican Basilica is also designed with the Pantheon in mind*. And the dome of the Vatican was closely followed in the creation of the dome of the U.S. Capitol. Furthermore, it's no coincidence that *an obelisk stands directly in front all three buildings*. Fool one once, shame on you. Fool my twice shame on me. *Fool me three times and I'm clearly not paying attention.*

We should also remember that the reason our Nation's Capitol Building is spelled *Capitol* and not *Capital*, isn't just to trip up 5th graders on a spelling test, but because our Founders wanted to call attention to Washington's emulation of Rome, where *Capitoline* Hill figured prominently in that city's story. That's why Tom Horn argues in his book, *Apollyon Rising 2012*, that the *real lost symbol of Masonry is the vital connection of Osiris and Isis* (Apollo and Venus/Virgo), epitomized in these structures. The symbols of male and female – the acknowledged signs of a fertility cult – are prominently and unashamedly displayed. A reasonable person should conclude that *our leaders consciously intended the erection of these symbolic structures*. They didn't choose Judeo-Christian symbols; they choose esoteric Egyptian symbols to epitomize the underlying belief system upon which to build the new republic.

The Great Plan and the Great Seal of the United States

The myth of Osiris is a story of resurrection. This legend discloses the most essential meaning to the symbols on the *Great Seal of the United States.* Certainly, I expect many naysayers will express doubt that the symbols on our *Great Seal* have much to do with anything other than recognizing the 13 original colonies and a hope for God's blessing upon our nation. But most Masons agree that the facts (and the pictures) speak for themselves.

In 1846, a 33rd Degree Freemason (and author) James D. Carter confirmed this when he said that Masonic symbolism is clearly identified whenever "an informed Mason examines the Great Seal."[34]

Running through the many symbols on the Seal:

- It's interesting, but perhaps not sinister, that there are so many 13's: The stars above the eagle, arrows in his left claw, leaves on the olive branch, stripes in the shield, steps on the uncapped pyramid, and letters in *annuit coeptis*. 13 is a power number in the occult, but still, we *did* begin with 13 colonies.

- 1776 was when the Illuminati were formed, but it was also the date our republic declared itself independent from England.

- It's a bit more intriguing that there are 32 feathers in one wing of the Eagle and 33 on the other (possibly calling attention to the two highest degrees in Freemasonry?)

- While the bird is a bald eagle, the original design by Thomas Barton was a *Phoenix*, a distinct bird of superiority and importantly, *immortality*. The Phoenix symbolizes resurrection. It too is part and parcel of Egyptian mythology (a bird that supposedly appears in Egypt only once every 500 years).

FIGURE 57 – THE GREAT SEAL OF THE UNITED STATES

Here, however, is where the ambiguity of the symbols ends. The uncapped pyramid and its "all seeing eye" above (aka the Eye of Providence or the *Eye of*

Horus) can only be regarded as "not Masonic" if we are being disingenuous. These symbols are peculiarly Masonic and obviously Egyptian.[35]

Manly P. Hall eloquently elaborates on the many facets of the meaning of the Great Seal:

> Here is represented the great pyramid of Gizah, composed of thirteen rows of masonry, sowing seventy-two stones. The pyramid is without a cap stone, and above its upper platform floats a triangle containing the all-seeing eye surrounded by rays of light... The Pyramid of Gizah was believed by the ancient Egyptians to be the shrine tomb of the god Hermes [Mercury] or Thot[h], the personification of universal wisdom. No trace has ever been found of the cap of the great pyramid. A flat platform about thirty feet square gives no indication that this part of the structure was ever otherwise finished; and this is appropriate, as the Pyramid represents human society, imperfect and incomplete. The structure's ascending converging angles and faces represent the common aspiration of humankind; above floats the symbol of the esoteric orders, the radiant triangle with its all-seeing eye...
>
> The combination of the Phoenix, the pyramid, and the all-seeing eye is more than chance or coincidence. There is nothing about the early struggles of the colonists to suggest such a selection to farmers, shopkeepers, and country gentlemen. There is only one possible origin for these symbols, and that is the secret societies which came to this country 150 years before the Revolutionary War... There can be no question that the great seal was directly inspired by these orders of the human quest, and that it set forth the purpose for this nation as that purpose was seen and known to the Foundering Fathers. The monogram of the new Atlantis reveals this continent as set apart for the accomplishment of the great work – here is to arise the pyramid of human aspiration, the school of the secret sciences.[36]

Perhaps no single action in the last century was more telling that *the game is still afoot*, than the move by Vice-President Henry Wallace and Franklin Delano Roosevelt to place The Great Seal on the one dollar bill in the days of *The New Deal* leading up to World War II. Both were no less than 32nd Degree Freemasons.

Horn comments, "Both men were fascinated with the concept of a new breed of people – new Atlanteans for the New Atlantis similar to Hitler's contemporaneous exploration for the Aryan supermen – led by an earthly messiah." Wallace opens the kimono with a clear statement that foreshadows the words of George H.W. Bush ("41" – member of *Skull and Bones* and contributor extraordinaire to Freemasonry): "It will take a more definite recognition of the Grand Architect of the Universe before the apex stone [capstone of the pyramid] is finally fitted into place and this nation in the full strength of its power is in position to assume leadership among the nations in inaugurating 'the New Order of the Ages.'" [37]

As Vice-President Wallace discloses, the Plan for America and the Great Work of Freemasonry were connected long ago. For those of us who consider themselves Christians and patriots, we must come to terms with the fact that the driving force (or "forces") for national greatness is no longer related to the creation of the "shining city on the hill" (Pilgrim leader Thomas Bradford's comment that Ronald Reagan affirmed in his view of American destiny). The impetus for American leadership has shifted; it's now in the hands of those who believe and promote the Secret Doctrine – from Bacon to Bush (41 and 43) – that drive America's taking charge – inaugurating the New Order of the Ages.[38]

This new order may very well catalyze the transformation of human consciousness predicted by the Maya and promoted by Novelty Theory, Hermeticism, Illuminism, Ufology, Esotericism and the New Age Movement. However, it's the vital connection with classical pagan mythology that shines the brightest light revealing *The Plan*" and the personage responsible for its implementation.[39]

Just when you thought the plot couldn't grow any thicker, we come upon information that will likely require the reader's suspension of disbelief until – by chapter's end – we present a complete and compelling set of facts. Take a deep breath and prepare yourself.

The Resurrection of Apollo, the Coming of Antichrist

We've discussed before, the association of Apollo and the Antichrist. What we must reveal here is the staggering possibility that the coming Antichrist could be an American leader, *a resurrection of Apollo*, fulfilling the prophecies inherent in (1) the motto, *Novus ordo seclorum*; (2) the symbols of Osiris and Isis; (3) the rising of the Phoenix; (4) the *all-seeing eye of Horus* (Osiris' son), floating above the (5) tomb of Osiris (aka *Pyramid of Giza*). In short, *this future American leader may be the protagonist spearheading the fulfillment of "the Great Work."*

Tom Horn takes us step-by-step through the facts.[40] Charles Thompson (a great friend to the Masons and admirer of Benjamin Franklin's Philosophical Society) created the mottos on the Great Seal of the United States. First, the motto **ANNUIT COEPTIS** (*"He approves [our] undertaking"*) derives from Virgil's *Aeneid*, in which is said, *"Juppiter omnipotes, audacibus annue coeptis"* (*"All-powerful Jupiter favors [the] daring undertakings"*). Likewise, **NOVUS ORDO**

SECLORUM, was inspired by Virgil's Eclogue IV: *Magnus ab inegro seclorum nascitur ordo* (line 5). The original Latin reads: "And the majestic roll of circling centuries begins anew."

This phrase belongs to the *Cumaen Sibyl* – curiously but hardly coincidentally – *the prophetess of Apollo*, ironically portrayed in Michelangelo's Sistine Chapel paintings (who honored her as a divinely inspired prophet – See FIGURE 59 adjacent).[41] From this poetic line he derived, *novus ordo seclorum*, "new order of the ages." The complete prophecy reads:

> *Now the last age by Cumae's Sibyl sung*
> *Has come and gone, and the majestic roll*
> *Of circling centuries begins anew:*
> *Justice returns, returns old Saturn's reign,*
> *With a new breed of men sent down from heaven.*
> *Only do thou, at the boy's birth in whom*
> *The iron shall cease, the golden race arise,*
> *Befriend him, chaste Lucina; 'tis thine own Apollo reigns.*
> *He shall receive the life of gods, and see*
> *Heroes with gods commingling, and himself*
> *Be seen of them, and with his father's worth*
> *Reign o'er a world...*

The prophetess communicates that a new breed of men would be sent down from heaven. The son of Jupiter, *Apollo*, would be given new life when the god Saturn (the Bible's Satan) returns to reign over the earth in a new Pagan Golden Age. Horn comments:

> Accordingly, the name Apollo turns up in ancient literature with the verb *apollymi* and *apollyo* (destroy), and scholars including W. R. F. Browning believe the apostle Paul may have identified the god Apollo as the "spirit of Antichrist" operating behind the persecuting Roman emperor, Domitian, who wanted to be recognized as "Apollo incarnate" in his day. Such identifying of Apollo with despots and "the spirit of Antichrist" is consistent even in modern history. For instance, note how Napoleon's name literally translates [to] "the true Apollo."

While this explanation seems fantastic, consider how this coincides with the prophecy in Revelation 17:8 (incidentally, one of the most obscure prophetic passages that Bible scholars try to interpret):

> The beast that thou sawest was, and is not; and shall ascend out of the bottomless pit, and go into perdition: and they that dwell on the earth shall wonder, whose names were not written in the book of life from the foundation of the world, when they behold the beast that was, and is not, and yet is.

Isn't it interesting also, that the facsimile of the ancient coin we included earlier, showing the image of *Antiochus IV Epiphanes*, the Syrian-Greek Antichrist of the 2nd century BC, displays the image of *Apollo* on the reverse side? (See Figure 8 on page 42) Perhaps you are thinking, "You can't be serious. The Antichrist, an American President?" Wasn't that the plot line in *Omen III*?[42] Yes, but just because it was a bad movie doesn't mean its inspiration was off-base. There is a distinct possibility this nightmare could come true. With more than a few remarkable little-known facts from the founding of America, the possibility fits with the rest of the puzzle pieces like it was designed from the beginning. Who's to say that it wasn't? The "wheat and tares" have grown together for over 400 years. As the Judeo-Christian emphasis in America has diminished over the past 100 years, it seems more than logical that the esoteric underpinnings of our great nation now move front-and-center to occupy our attention and dominate our future direction. *The lost symbol and our secret destiny may soon become incarnate for all to behold.*

Manly P. Hall provides us with the "smoking-gun" to reinforce this intended stratagem:

> The outcome of the "secret destiny" is a *World Order ruled by a King with supernatural powers*. This King was descended of a divine race; that is, he belonged to the *Order of the Illumined* for those who come to a state of wisdom then belong to a family of *heroes-perfected human beings*.[43]

Or, as Sibyl indicated in her prophecy (via the writing of Virgil), his rule will be an example of *"Gods and heroes, commingling."* In the words of John's Revelation, *"The resurrected beast: who was, is not, and is to come."* Osiris, aka *Apollo* is resurrected, in the final chapter of the play to bring Francis Bacon's *New Atlantis* to fruition, create the *New Order of the Ages,* and fulfill the *Great Work*. This is the ultimate meaning of *The Secret Doctrine* and *The Plan*.

The Timing of the Masonic Messiah

But the story isn't finished quite yet. We still have the question of "when." As it turns out, the timing when the Masonic Messiah makes his appearance may also be predicted by certain Masonic ciphers. Any bets in what year this messiah is to appear? While I find the evidence compelling that Masonry looks to America to lead *The Great Work* forward, as soon as dates are offered, I confess *my enthusiasm wanes.* Nevertheless, let's consider Tom Horn's worthy analysis. To break the code, apparently, we must return to *The Great Seal – the "Trestle-Board" for the Great Work.* Hall indicates that the unfinished pyramid is the "trestle-board setting forth symbolically the task to the accomplishment of which the U.S. Government was dedicated from the day of its inception."[44] What is a trestle-board? *The Masonic Dictionary* says this:

> In Operative Masonry, the Trestle-Board is of vast importance. It was on such an implement that the genius of the ancient Masters worked out those problems of architecture that have reflected an unfading luster on their skill. The Trestle-Board was the cradle that nursed the infancy of such mighty monuments as the cathedrals of Strasburg and Cologne; and as they advanced in stature, the Trestle-Board became the guardian spirit that directed their growth...In the Masonic Ritual, the Speculative Freemason is reminded that, as the Operative Artists erects his temporal building in accordance with the rules and designs laid down on the Trestle-Board of the Master Workman, so should he erect that spiritual building, of which the material is a type, in obedience to the rules and designs, the precepts and commands, laid down by the Grand Architect of the Universe in those great books of nature and revelation which constitute the spiritual Trestle-Board of every Freemason.[45]

In other words, the plan for the *Great Work* is made plain by its trestle-board, symbolized by the various elements of the *Great Seal.* Horn makes this additional clarification, "...it is the drawing board for the destiny of America and is branded by 1) the identity of the Great Architect to whom the work is dedicated; and 2) the date on which the work was started and is to be completed."[46] Horn quotes Paul Foster Case, writing about the Great Seal in 1976, who noted the probability that the 13 steps symbolized 13 time periods:

> Since the date, 1776, is placed on the bottom course of the pyramid, and since the number thirteen has been so important in the symbolism of the seal, it is not unreasonable to suppose that the thirteen courses [rows] of the pyramid may represent thirteen time periods.[47]

However, Case didn't speculate on what the length of the 13 periods might be. The insight disclosing the likely meaning comes from John Kehne, whom Horn cites, coupling the Great Seal's date of 1776 with the Mayan ending date of 2012:

FIGURE 58 - CUMAE SYBIL OF MICHELANGELO, SISTINE CHAPEL

This Seal shows a thirteen-step pyramid with 1776 in Roman numerals... [The year] 1776 was not only the year that the Declaration of Independence was signed, but was also a special year in the Mayan calendar. Just as the last katun in the Great cycle is "katun 2012," the first katun in the cycle of thirteen was "katun 1776." [When the first katun ended] In fact, the katun ended thirty-three days before the signing. So 1776 is the bottom level of the pyramid, where the date is actually inscribed – the top of the pyramid is therefore 2012.[48]

Therefore, we have *"come full circle"*. The Mayan 13 katun cycle of 19.7 years per katun, can be matched – literally step-by-step – to the pyramid as seen on the Great Seal above. Horn also quotes an academic, Richard N. Luxton who suggested the katun cycles of the Maya coincide with the Christian doctrines of "the last judgment." In his translation of the prophecies of 16th century Mayan prophet, *Chilam Balam*, Luxton connects his prophecies to real dates and counts connected to the katun cycles, the *Colonial Count* katun of 1776, commencing a series of events leading up to an apocalyptic conclusion in 2012.[49] Horn indicates whether the periods of time are precisely 19.7 years or 20 years (reflective of our Gregorian calendar), the 13 steps conclude in the time of great expectation – 2012-2016.

Horn speculates, built upon the Christian expectation of a seven-year tribulation period (tied to Daniel's final seven years – aka one week of years or a "Jewish Decade"), that 2012 represents the beginning of the seven-year period and 2016, the "midpoint" when the Antichrist reveals himself, half-way through the Tribulation period as predicted by the prophet Daniel.

FIGURE 59 – THE TIMING OF THE GREAT WORK

Horn's attempts to strengthen his assertion that *the Masonic Messiah debuts during this 2012-2016 period*, through an elaborate analysis of the Freemasons' 1st Degree Tracing Board, (which is different than a trestle board – see Figure adjacent). Horn contends that the astronomical positions of the sun, moon, and the Pleiades (as illustrated on the Tracing Board) are as they will be in December 21, 2012. At the Winter Solstice, the sun at its Zenith will be directly in front of the seven (visible) stars of the Pleiades. But is Horn's conclusion warranted?

My review of the materials suggests that Horn *may* be making too much of the *locations of these orbs* as illustrated on the tracing board. The key assertion is that the sun in the upper left is "lying in the dark rift" of the Milky Way,[50] which I don't believe is clear from its picture on the Tracing Board. Furthermore, lectures I reviewed on the purpose and information of the Tracing Board certainly provide no hint that this was intentional such that it would reinforce his spine-tingling conclusions.[51] Nevertheless, Horn's insights regarding (1) the implied resurrection of Apollo from the many symbols of Masonry, (2) the secret plan for America as articulated by Manly P. Hall, and (3) America's leadership to implement the *Great Plan,* appear substantiated from all the information we're reviewed (and from much more data Horn presents in his outstanding book). No doubt very few Freemasons would come to the same conclusions as Tom Horn, even after a careful review of the subject matter by many other authors and scholars (that's not just plentiful but overwhelming). This lack of concurrence, however, more likely

FIGURE 60 - 1ST DEGREE TRACING BOARD

stems from *partisan skepticism* than an objective interpretation of the data.

It's instructive that Winston Churchill used a consultant (one *Dr. Walter Johannes Stein*), who was thoroughly conversant with Adolf Hitler's occult beliefs and Hitler's reliance upon the black arts, Stein having spent considerable time with Hitler during his early twenties, thus able to better predict Hitler's behavior. However, Churchill demanded this matter be kept secret because no one outside of Germany would believe just how committed Hitler was to the *Secret Doctrine*. Trevor Ravenscroft in his fascinating book, *The Spear of Destiny*, comments:

> The failure of the Nuremberg Trials to identify the nature of the evil at work behind the outer façade of National Socialism convinced him that another three decades must pass before a large enough readership would be present to comprehend the initiation rites and black magic practices of the inner core of the Nazi leadership... He understood why a unanimous agreement had been made among the Judges to treat the accused as though they were an integral part of *the accepted Humanist and Cartesian system of the Western world*. To have admitted even for an instant what their defeated enemies were really like, to have lifted the veil to reveal the real motives for such an astonishing reversal of values, might have opened millions of people to the risk of a terrible corruption... It was thought expedient to speak in dry psycho-analytical terms when considering the motives for incarcerating millions of human beings in Gas Ovens rather than to reveal that such practices were an *integral part of a dedicated service to evil powers* (emphasis mine). [52]

Sometimes truth – no matter how malleable it has become, softened, if you will, by copious as well as compelling citations – still remains *just too hard to swallow*.

Summary and Conclusions

The topic of Knights Templar and the secret societies connected through shared history is a fascinating and controversial subject which Dan Brown has done his best to bring to our attention (and to generate a handsome profit no doubt!) His stories have exposed an ancient mythology that may lead to a surprising scenario in which America (through a Masonic Messiah energized by the resurrected spirit of Apollo), moves the world toward an apocalyptic conclusion.

- Brown infers that there are no connections between the various secret societies he introduces in each of his three most recent books, other than the Templars and the *Priory of Sion*, a secret group featured in *The Da Vinci Code*, which has been demonstrated to be a hoax in the past few years.

- However, the linkage between the Knights Templar and Freemasonry is direct and substantial; after driven underground, the Templars assume the identity of Freemasons. As such, the many traditions of the Templars (and much of what they discovered while crusading in the Holy Lands), was incorporated into Freemasonry.

- Freemasonry and its "secret doctrine" are derived from Egyptian mythology, specifically Hermeticism, and in particular the story of Isis, Osiris, Seth, and Horus. The story emphasizes the promise of resurrection based upon recognizing these Egyptian deities and possessing arcane knowledge about the manner of this resurrection. *Resurrection is at the heart of Freemasonry.* Freemasonry isn't the Kiwanis or Rotary Club.

- Other secret societies from the 18th century appear to have deepened the clandestine knowledge embedded in Freemasonry. These groups included the *Illuminati*, the *Order of Strict Observance* (and *Rosicrucianism*). The first two were merged into Freemasonry before the 19th century began.

- America has been the focus of Freemasonry for hundreds of years. America is at the center of the Masonic "Great Plan" to lead the world to a single government and religion in the name of brotherhood and enlightenment. Most of our key Founding Fathers were Masons. Many were not particularly Christian.

- The lost symbol of the Freemasons relates to the meaning inherent in the fertility symbolism of the obelisk and dome, prominent in Washington and Rome. Freemasons have been instrumental in situating Egyptian monuments in London, New York, and Washington DC. They fervently believe in the power of symbols.

- Masonry describes God as "The Great Architect of the Universe" (TGAOTU). The Masonic historians, Albert Pike, Albert Mackey, and Manly P. Hall, have articulated that the god of Freemasonry is dualistic, containing both an evil and a good nature. The good nature they define to be *Luciferic*. As such, these assertions are theologically at odds with the Judeo-Christian concept of YHWH. [53] This has also opened Masonry to the charge of worshipping Satan, a charge they vehemently disallow. But in their denials they actually affirm what they deny.

- America's symbols, including the Great Seal of the United States, were heavily influenced by Masonic ideals. Even the mottos that appear on the Great Seal are derived from Virgil and his quotations of the Cumaen Sybil – *the prophetess of Apollo.* Sybil's full prophecy underscores the prospect for the coming of a *new breed of man*, whose nature is comingled with the gods, to rule the world.

- There is a strong association between Apollo (Osiris) and the Spirit of Antichrist. The symbols of Freemasonry and the commentary of Masonic historians emphasize that the expected Masonic Messiah will, in some manner, represent *the Spirit of Apollo*. Apollo has many aspects; however, the Bible decodes his name as "destroyer" leading to the identification of this Messiah with the Antichrist of Revelation (see chapters 9, 13, and 17). Previous foretypes of the Antichrist demonstrate a distinct association with Apollo.

- The timing of the appearance of this Masonic Messiah could be decoded in the Great Seal of the United States. Tom Horn has showcased how the 13 steps of the Giza Pyramid (which also represent the tomb of Osiris), may correspond to the Mayan calendric 13 katuns (of 19.7 years), which began in 1756 (the first katun ending in 1776) and lead up to December 21, 2012.

Keep in mind: While the 2012 prophecies barely have 20 years of research to expound their meaning, the Bible has over 2,000 years of commentary. Therefore, what the Bible has to say may surprise some readers, since it provides explicit details about what happens on Doomsday as well as the many personalities and events leading up to it – which no other source is even marginally aware.

Notes

[1] Leigh Teabing refers to authors Richard Leigh, Michael Baigent, and Henry Lincoln, authors of the 1982 book, *Holy Blood, Holy Grail* – the "alternate history" investigation into the *Priory of Sion*. Teabing is an anagram for Baigent, while Leigh is the last name of Richard Leigh. Brown thought he was honoring the authors by incorporating their names into the story. In turn, they sued him for copyright infringement, a suit Brown won.

[2] Jerusalem was captured by the 1st Crusade in 1099 and held for 88 years until it fell to the famous Muslim general, Saladin, in 1187. For another 120 years, the Templars would wage war to win the Holy City back but were mostly on the defensive in several other cities and castles in the Holy Lands during the last 75 years of this period.

[3] The nine Norman Knights from Champagne probably had many other motives too. They likely were related to the Merovingian's, the noble family line producing Frankish and other kings during the 4th through 8th centuries. This family line was superseded by the Carolingians upon the ascendancy of Charlemagne as Emperor in 800 AD. According to Butler and Defoe in *The Knights Templar Revealed*, these families may connect all the way back to the "Salt line families," the Essenes, and the Minoans. The insinuation of these authors is that their Christianity was little more than "skin deep." Their heritage reached well beyond the time of Christ. The families felt displaced and saw in the Crusades a chance to gain power, prestige, and to restore their fortunes. It's fascinating conjecture to be sure.

[4] Most scholars believe this event is why Friday the 13th, in Western traditions, is a day of bad luck.

[5] The personage from whom *The Demolay Society for Boys*, obtains its name.

[6] But conspiracy theories die hard. Clive Prince and Lynn Picknett in their 2006 book, *The Sion Revelation: The Truth About the Guardians of Christ's Sacred Bloodline*, "accepted that the pre-1956 history of the Priory of Sion was a hoax created by Plantard, and that his claim he was a Merovingian dynast was a lie. However, they insist that this was part of a complex red herring intended to distract the public from the hidden agenda of Plantard and his 'controllers.' They argue that the Priory of Sion was a front organization for one of the many crypto-political societies which have been plotting to create a 'United States of Europe' in line with French occultist Alexandre Saint-Yves d'Alveydre's synarchist vision of an ideal form of government."

From *http://en.wikipedia.org/wiki/Priory_of_Sion*.

[7] In their book, *The Templar Revelation*, Clive Prince and Lynn Picknett wrote: "We now could be certain, without any shadow of a doubt, that the starting place for Freemasonry was the construction of Rosslyn Chapel in the mid-fifteenth century." Pg. 313, cited by Marrs, *Rule by Secrecy*, New York: Harper, 2000, pg. 245.

[8] The gospel of Luke records that Christ and his disciples plucked ears of grain on a Sabbath and ate them, angering the Pharisees who witnessed this, complaining it was another example of Christ breaking the Sabbath. The point: Ears of grain (corn?) appeared to have existed in the Middle East and thus, this "grain" may have been brought back from Palestine by the Templars. America was perhaps not the only solution to the maize mystery. Either way, however, it would indicate the Templars were in Scotland.

[9] This public admission may have led one year later, in 1738, to a Papal Bull by Pope Clement XII outlawing Freemasonry, condemning it as pagan and unlawful, and threatening any Catholic who joined this society with excommunication.

[10] Ibid., pg. 246.

[11] Ibid., pg. 247.

[12] Reading societies, included *The Thule Society*, which was very influential in the Nazi movement as has been documented earlier.

13 Adam Weishaupt, *Die neuesten Arbeiten des Spartacus und Philo in dem Illuminate-nOrder*, 1794. Cited by Marrs, op. cit., pg 238. Weishaupt used the name Spartacus as his code name. One wonders what this name signified to him. My supposition: He saw himself a slave attempting to free other slaves from the tyranny of monarchy and ecclesiastical control.

14 Marrs, op cit., pg 241. Citation of Still from William T. Still, *New World Order: The Ancient Plan of Secret Societies* (Lafayette, LA: Huntington House Publishers, 1990.

15 Marrs, op.cit, pg 242. Citation of Still, op. cit., pg. 81.

16 Ibid, pg. 248.

17 See *http://www.mt.net/~watcher/greatwork.html*, pg. 1.

18 Michael Bradley, *TheSecrets of Freemasons*, New York: Barnes and Noble, 2006, pg. 163.

19 Ibid., pg. 164.

20 Marrs, op. cit., pg. 263.

21 Indeed Pike and other Masons believe that God has a good and bad side. Lucifer is the good side. Even if Christians don't react to the Lucifer assertion, they would strongly disagree that the God they worship *has a bad side*. Christians may be accused of having a *Manichean* theology (*Mani*, a 3rd Century Persian believed that there is a good god and a bad god – this was embraced in *Gnosticism*), but they do have a reasonable explanation for evil in the world. Eastern thought believes in the Ying and the Yang, the black and white symbol, of which the Masonic symbol of the black and white checkerboard is actually a parody. The meaning: God is both good and evil. Christians must repudiate a theology that maintains this perspective. At the very core, Masonic theology is *Gnosticism*. Very few Masons would embrace Gnosticism if they knew their organization believed it. But it's true nonetheless.

22 Hermeticism is defined as a combination of the Greek God *Hermes* and the Egyptian God, *Thoth*. There are pseudo-graphical writings of a Hermes Trismegistus. The combined god is considered a god of knowledge, writing, and magic. Trismegistus means "thrice great" and may be dated from Egypt in the third century BC.

23 *Ibid, pg. 264.* Citations of Picknett and Prince, *Templar Revelation,* pg., 113. Mackey, op. cit., pg 329.

24 All those who surrounded Hitler were members of a reading society such as the *Thule Society*, a Masonic Lodge, or avowed Rosicrucianists. I rest my case.

25 Just consider political parties: It's the extremists that push the Democrats and Republicans to the left or right. The rest of us moderates have to live with the nominees they put in front of us.

26 In studying the rise and fall of the Third Reich, it is startling how few serious ideologues it took to capture the mind and hearts of the German nation. Of course, when we dig deeper we find out how much Black Magic influenced Adolf Hitler. The powerful affect of non-human entities, summoned by ritual magic, can't be ruled out in how Na-

zism ascended so quickly and powerfully. Trevor's Ravenscroft's *The Spear of Destiny*, brings this convincingly to light.

[27] This brief synopsis is culled from Jim Marrs recital, op. cit., pp. 227-232.

[28] England's first initiation was in 1641 when Sir Robert Moray became a Mason. In 1717, the English Grand Lodge formed, bringing four separate Masonic lodges together into one organization.

[29] Hall – never discouraged to postulate the fantastic – indicates, "Time will reveal that the continent now known as America was actually discovered, and, to a considerable degree, explored more than a thousand years before the beginning of the Christian era... The true story was in the keeping of the Mystery Schools, and passed from them to the Secret Societies of the medieval world. The Esoteric orders of Europe, Asia, and the Near East were in at least irregular communication with the priesthoods of the more advanced Amerindian nations... Plans for the development of the Western Hemisphere were formulated in Alexandria, Mecca, Delhi, and Lhasa [Tibet] long before most European statesmen were aware of the great Utopian program." Cited by Marrs, op. cit., pg. 230, from Still, op. cit., pg. 49.

[30] The leadership of Jamestown was Mason unlike the Puritans at Plymouth.

[31] Thomas Horn, *Apollyon Rising*, Crane, Mo., 2009, pg. 111.

[32] The original design used in all three buildings was based upon the Temple of Veiovis, on *Capitoline Hill*, built in the 200 BC. The Roman God Veiovis was related either to the Greek god of healing, Asclepius, or to the god *Apollo*. My bet is on Apollo. Most of this temple is destroyed. Mussolini excavated a portion of it in 1939. If true, all three buildings are replicas of the *original Temple of Apollo*.

[33] Constantino Brumidi was the painter of choice for the Vatican to refresh its many frescoes early in the 19th century. He painted a number of frescoes in our Capitol, notably "The Atheosis of Washington" which means "Making Washington a God," featured on the inside of the Dome.

[34] Horn, op. cit., pg. 128.

[35] "The Solar Eye [on the Great Seal of the United States] was called the eye of Apollo... the sacred and mysterious Eye of the Most High of the gods... Thus it is held in the highest estimation by all Royal Arch Masons." Charles A. L. Totten, *Our Inheritance in the Great Seal of Manasseh, the United States of America,* quoted by Horn, op. cit, pg. 145.

[36] Manly P. Hall, *The Secret Destiny of America*, Chapter 18, cited by Horn, op. cit., pp. 127,128.

[37] Henry A. Wallace, *Statesmanship and Religion* (New York: Vanguard, 1948), pg. 116, cited by Horn, op. cit., pg 131.

[38] This is not to call them "Nazis" – but to point out they are either being oblivious, unsophisticated, or disingenuous as to from whence their ideology springs.

[39] Is Freemasonry innocuous? Perhaps quoting Adolf Hitler will point out that it isn't without its sinister aspects. "But there is one dangerous element which I have cop-

ied from them. They have developed an esoteric doctrine, not merely formulated it, but imparted it through the medium of symbols and mysterious rites... That is to say without bothering their brains but by working directly on the imagination through the symbols of a magic cult. All this is the dangerous element I have taken over. Don't you see that our Party must be of this character? An Order that is what it has to be. An Order, the hierarchical Order of a Secular Priesthood." Cited by Ravenscroft, op. cit., pg 175.

[40] Horn, op. cit., information selected from pp. 138-140.

[41] "In the Middle Ages, both the Cumae Sibyl and Virgil were considered prophets of the birth of Christ, because the fourth of Virgil's *Eclogues* appears to contain a Messianic prophecy by the Sibyl, and this was seized on by early Christians as such—one reason why Dante Alighieri later chose Virgil as his guide through the underworld in *The Divine Comedy*. Similarly, Michelangelo prominently featured the Cumae Sibyl in the Sistine Chapel among the Old Testament prophets, as had earlier works such as the Tree of Jesse miniature in the Ingeberg Psalter (c. 1210). Virgil may have been influenced by Hebrew texts; according to, amongst others, Tacitus. Constantine, the Christian emperor, in his first address to the assembly, interpreted the whole of *The Eclogues* as a reference to the coming of Christ and quoted a long passage of the *Sibylline Oracles* (*Book 8*) containing an acrostic in which the initials from a series of verses read: "Jesus Christ Son of God Savior." This is the same acrostic famous in Christian symbol of the Fish and the Greek word for fish, pronounced, *"Ic-thuse."*

See *http://en.wikipedia.org/wiki/Cumaean_Sibyl.*

[42] Starring Sam Neal as the Antichrist and would-be American President.

[43] Hall, *Secret Destiny.*, pg. 26, cited by Horn, op. cit., pg 246, 247.

[44] Hall, *Secret Teachings*, pg. 91. Cited by Horn, pg 247.

[45] See http://www.masonicdictionary.com/trestleboard.html.

[46] Horn, op. cit., pg. 255.

[47] Paul Foster Case, *The Great Seal of the United States,* 10th ed., Los Angeles, Builders of Adytum, 1976, pg. 29, cited by Horn, op. cit., pg 272.

[48] Horn, op. cit., pg. 272, Cited Kehne from *http://www.december212012.com.*

[49] The Book of Chumayel: The Counsel Book of the Yucatec Maya 1539—1638, Richard N. Luxton, trans., Series: "Mayan Studies 7", Laguna Hills, CA: Aegean Park, 1995), pg. 307, cited by Horn, op. cit., pg. 271.

[50] Horn, op. cited, pp. 274-277.

[51] See the lecture by Gary Kerkin at *http://www.freemasons-freemasonry.com /first-degree-tracing-board.html.*

[52] Ravenscroft, op. cit., pp. xiii and xiv.

[53] *"This then is the message which we have heard of him, and declare unto you, that God is light, and in him is no darkness at all." (I John 1:5) and "Every good gift and every perfect gift is from above, and cometh down from the Father of lights, with whom is no variableness, neither shadow of turning." (James 1:17)*

Chapter 12:
The Spirit of the Antichrist

What is good? All that enhances the feeling of power, the Will to Power, and
power itself in man. What is bad? All that proceeds from weakness...
The weak and the botched shall perish: first principle of our humanity.
And they ought even to be helped to perish.
What is more harmful than any vice? Practical sympathy with all the botched and the
weak Christianity... The problem I see in this work is... what type of man must be
reared, must be willed, as having the highest value, as being the most worthy of life and
the surest guarantee of the future... and in these a higher type certainly manifests itself:
something which... represents a kind of **superman**.

Friedrich Nietzsche, *The Antichrist*

Blessed are the poor in spirit, for theirs is the kingdom of heaven.
Blessed are those who mourn, for they shall be comforted.
Blessed are the gentle, for they shall inherit the earth.
Blessed are those who hunger and thirst for righteousness, for they shall be filled.
Blessed are the merciful, for they shall obtain mercy.
Blessed are the pure in heart, for they shall see God.
Blessed are the peacemakers, for they shall be called the children of God.

Jesus of Nazareth, The Christ (*Matthew 5:3-11*)

A Philosopher Prophet of the Modern World

Friedrich Nietzsche is the single most incisive "philosopher prophet" for
the *spirit of our times*, a world-spirit the German philosophers called, the
Zeitgeist. Perhaps in a morbidly poetic way, he died in an insane asylum
in 1900, just as the new century he envisaged began. He made many bold assertions – the most memorable of which is from his book, *Thus Spoke Zarathustra*; the would-be epitaph of God, announced through the words of a madman, "God is dead." We may recall the work by the same name by Richard
Strauss that served as the overture to Stanley Kubrick's *2001: A Space Odyssey*,
our cultures' first exposure to the notion that extraterrestrials guided life on
earth (the featured magical black monolith responsible for our growth) and
takes us to the next level, when the *Star Child* returns to earth.

Debate continues today whether Nietzsche's madness should be blamed on
his nihilist perspectives. There is also a considerable debate whether his many
iconoclastic statements should be taken literally: "Is God really dead? Is Christianity really the enemy? Are the Jews really a race we should blame for the

240

'devaluation of man?' Will a *superman* emerge as the doorway to our future? Can humans really establish their own values to live by?"

There were many intellectual sources that German National Socialism (Nazism) drew upon as they assembled their diabolical beliefs. Adolf Hitler often turned Nietzsche's best sound bites into his own. For on the one hand, we could define *Nietzsche's philosophy as Nietzsche meant it to be understood;* on the other hand, we could discuss *how the Nazis promoted it.* It's true that the two views would be distinct. However, the vital question is whether this distinction – what becomes a defense of Nietzsche – is really warranted. No doubt he was misquoted and his name misused by the Nazis. Then again, Madame Helena Blavatsky (HPB) could muster a defense for Theosophy on the same grounds. *Theosophy* dramatically influenced both Hitler and Himmler. As a result of "the Secret Doctrine," each sought occult powers in order to strengthen the Third Reich. But does that mean that HPB should be held accountable for the actions of Hitler and Himmler? Wouldn't HPB and Nietzsche alike abhor Auschwitz? Consequently, shouldn't we declare them free of any responsibility?

FIGURE 61 - FRIEDRICH NIETZSCHE IN 1882

Regardless of whether Nazism followed their precepts carefully, the final assessment of Nietzsche's philosophy (or HPB's for that matter), is the legacy of their intellectual contribution to society and their lasting impact which make things better or worse. Given that rather obvious basis for rendering a verdict, surprisingly *many* experts nonetheless continue to defend these intellectuals, especially Nietzsche. Even in the introduction to the Barnes and Noble edition to *The Antichrist*, Dennis Sweet argues that Nietzsche hated "the Church" and not Christianity. The enemy wasn't the *Jewish race*, but Jewish *religion*. The downtrodden shouldn't be literally eliminated, they just shouldn't be extolled. God isn't really dead, just our ideas of God are outdated. And so on.

All enlightened protests aside, do Nietzsche's own words really clear him from the allegation that he was voicing the Spirit of Antichrist? A careful study of the underlying motivations and passions of his words do indeed clarify the matter. In studying Nietzsche "in his own words," (noting the epigraph at the outset of this chapter), the stark contrast between his vitriolic proposals and the sublime message of Jesus Christ is obvious. In fact, we plainly see a vivid description of what the Bible means precisely by *the spirit of Antichrist*. Furthermore, when we contemplate the nature of the "man of sin" who is still hiding behind the curtains (perhaps soon to be revealed), we gain critical clues from Nietzsche regarding the personality and *operating procedures* of the coming Antichrist.

We have discussed the "Antichrist types" of such seers as Nostradamus. In this chapter, our purpose is to appreciate the descriptive portrait painted by the Jewish prophets in both Old and New Testaments. We begin by reference to John, the prophet and author of the *Book of Revelation*, who most scholars today believe was John the Apostle as well as the author of the gospel that bears his name.

First off, we must make note that John is the Bible's only prophet to use the term, *antichrist*. John says in his letters to his flock:

> *Beloved, believe not every spirit, but try the spirits whether they are of God: because many false prophets are gone out into the world. Hereby know ye the Spirit of God: Every spirit that confesseth that Jesus Christ is come in the flesh is of God: And every spirit that confesseth not that Jesus Christ is come in the flesh is not of God: and this is **that spirit of antichrist,** whereof ye have heard that it should come; and even now already is it in the world. (I John 4:1-3).*

> *For many deceivers are entered into the world, who confess not that Jesus Christ is come in the flesh. This is a deceiver and an antichrist. (II John 1:7)*

It's interesting that John doesn't use the term, *Antichrist*, in his *Apocalypse* (what we call the *Book of Revelation*), probably penned ten years before his epistles. There his description of the Antichrist is, *The Beast*. Interestingly, while John's prophecy speaks so definitively about the personage of Antichrist, he seeks to make clear – it's the *spirit* of Antichrist that's *our persistent enemy through all ages*. That spirit is already *in the world*. Many false prophets are inspired by this dangerous force. It seems that every generation has its brush with this spirit. Certainly, "the greatest generation" confronted it as it was embodied in Adolf Hitler.

However, in this chapter I wish to expose how his final incarnation will be distinctively different and *much more subtle* in style, albeit in the end *more destructive*. This encounter is enormously consequential, for this battle between the forces of Antichrist and the true Christ, is history's central theme. It's no small matter.

John makes this point plain when he points out the primary purpose for the *incarnation* (God becoming man). John described it this way, *"For this purpose the Son of God was manifested, that he might destroy the works of the devil."* (I John 3:8b) Furthermore, whether we are aware of it or not, the prophets of the Bible don't back away from the fact that the war rages still. The Apostle Paul counseled his church at Ephesus:

> *Put on the whole armour of God that ye may be able to stand against the wiles of the devil. For we wrestle not against flesh and blood, but against principalities, against powers, against the rulers of the darkness of this world, against spiritual wickedness in high places. (Ephesians 6:11, 12)*

Paul intimates that the forces are many, are *not monolithic* (they are diverse – there isn't just one devil); they are highly organized and living in an unseen world surrounding us.

The Wizard of Oz said to Dorothy, "Pay no attention to that man behind the curtain." But the Bible counsels that the "man behind the curtain" is really the collective sinister force *behind all the evil that we encounter in the empirical world.* Forgetting who's behind the scenes weakens our ability to stand firm against this power. To arm ourselves properly, we must first remember who we're up against. When we encounter push back, it's a good time to stop and recall that our struggle isn't against mere mortals and human institutions. There are many other players on the field that we can't see, but best consider whether we're playing offense or defense.

The Two Faces of Evil

One of the premises of Nietzsche's philosophy is the mythological interplay of two differing sides to this spirit, the means through which personality (and potentially evil) actualizes and presents itself – known as the *Apollonian and Dionysian* personas or facades.[1]

In the Greek myths, Apollo and Dionysus (Bacchus in Roman myth) are the two sons of Zeus. Apollo is the god of *the sun, of poetry, and of music.* Dionysus is the god of *wine, ecstasy, and intoxication.* "In the modern literary usage of the concept, the contrast between Apollo and Dionysus symbolizes principles of wholeness versus individualism, light versus darkness, or civilization versus primal nature."[2] To amplify, Apollo represents the *rational*, Dionysus the *irra-*

tional. The Apollonian way is one of control. The Dionysian way is one of abandon. The first is "ordered;" the second "chaotic." One is more easily led toward *materialism* (in this philosophical sense, i.e., *naturalism or rationalism*); the other toward *spiritualism* (i.e., *mysticism or spiritism*).

While the two aren't rigid rivals or exact opposites, one or the other may dominate our behavior at any particular point in time. Freud's psychological theory of mental health suggested that both impulses of the "Id" and the "Super-ego" must be acknowledged and properly integrated into our personality or neurosis would result. *Apollo* (perhaps the "Super Ego") mustn't forever repress the passionate drives of *Dionysus* (clearly the "Id"). A healthy person allows both "gods" of the psyche to find expression. If either is left unchecked by the other, *if the Ego allows one or the other to dominate,* extremes result. Either extreme can become evil personified.

This inner struggle finds outward expression too. The "world spirit," the *zeitgeist,* also can be characterized in one of these two "polar personas." Indeed, these inner impulses impact the world in dramatic and (all-too-frequently) detrimental ways.

Consider the following characterization: The Antichrist spirit of the 20th century was mostly *Dionysian,* driving Adolf Hitler toward the mystical, the chaotic, the passionate, and the use of brute force to eliminate the opposition. His personality was petulant (and often perverse); his speeches were at best emotional and exuberant; at worst raging with rancor and spewing acrimony. Myths and legends dominated Hitler's *Weltanschauung* (worldview). His pursued black magic, sought higher levels of consciousness for selfish purposes, and encounters with spirit entities. He learned rituals through his occult handlers to control these spirits, employing their power to his ends. Indeed, he achieved and maintained power through the realm of the spirit. His form of fascism was energized by dark esotericism. His destructiveness wasn't solely "madness." It was infused with evil.

In contrast, I predict the Antichrist spirit of the 21st century will be *Apollonian* (thereby connecting to the material we reviewed in the previous chapter). When the Antichrist appears, perhaps in the years just ahead, he may first take charge by establishing order in the name of peace. Much of his appeal will be based on offering new answers to intractable dilemmas. His arguments will not be based on myth or legend. He will likely extol technology and science as the philosophy to guide his solutions. His manner and methods will seem rational and pragmatic. He will identify the ultimate enemies of humankind. One will be parochial politics, particularly *nationalism*. The boundaries of nation states must be softened. Next, he will decry divisive *narrow-minded religion.* He will argue (without much debate from me) that too many wars have been fought "in the name of God" at the expense of peace and prosperity. Tolerance will be the by-word of his speeches. But tolerance will only go so far. In the final analysis, *the intolerant will not be tolerated.*

The *Weltanschauung* of the apollonian Antichrist will be the achievement of a "New Order of the Ages." For this Antichrist, *hegemony* is crucial to his administration. He will seek totalitarian control. His supremacy will sometimes be achieved through ubiquitous systems employing technology (as we see depicted in Revelation 13, with the "Mark of the Beast"). His edicts, even those most damaging to human rights, will be justified in the name of what's best for the majority. Personal liberty will be sacrificed. Intrusive rules and restrictions will be the warp and woof of society. His fascism will be enforced by his own malevolent and omnipresent image, a three-dimensional replica watching over humankind demanding obedience and promising retribution for any form of defiance. The specter of "Big Brother" overseeing our every move will become a daily reality when the "false prophet" causes everyone to receive *the mark of the beast* and to worship his image. Fearing the excesses of the left, once again society's reaction will be to swing far right. Fascism will arise once more – this time driven by our "Western Cartesian system" but blended with a technically sophisticated appreciation for the mystical. Black magic will be out; while white magic will be revered. ET will feel he's already home.

Another key element driving the Beast will be what Nietzsche called, "The Will to Power." What did Nietzsche mean by this idea?

Nietzsche's philosophy of a "will to power" can best be grasped by contrasting it to the teaching of an earlier German philosopher, Arthur Schopenhauer, who proposed that the motive behind animal behavior (including ours) can be best summarized as a "will to live." Schopenhauer asserted that throughout the universe is a force driving creatures to procreate and avoid death at all costs. However, Nietzsche saw Schopenhauer's notion oversimplified and much too benign. Nietzsche believed that creatures are driven to control their environments even to the point of excessive self-preservation. Life is best safeguarded when threats are eliminated. Creatures are willing to risk life to achieve such power. The male lion establishes his supremacy over other males to win his right to the lionesses with no thought for the well-being of his defeated rivals. Only the most powerful prevail. Evolution mandates the survival of the fittest. Only "the best genes in the genetic pool" should have the right to procreate. As Genghis Khan said, "It's not enough that I win; everyone else must lose!" We can detect this principle in the heroes of folklore: They sought glory much more than gold. And they would risk life and limb to achieve it. When warriors faced certain death, such as the 300 Spartans at Thermopylae, it was the promise of *glory* that inspired courage. To them, glory meant *immortality*.[3]

It's true that the *will to power* isn't inherently wicked, but if it's applauded as the highest virtue (to the exclusion of all others), evil outcomes are predictable. ("When the elephants dance, the grass suffers.") Nietzsche coined the term, "herd mentality." The *superman* will not be driven by religion or social norms. He will overcome the herd – he will become the "overman." The needs of the many will diminish the place for the individual. The mantra will become "Peace and stability at all costs." We've seen many totalitarian regimes before, most recently in the Soviet Union and in China. But the ultimate totalitarian regime may be ready to reveal itself soon – this time with an intelligence service far more severe than the KGB. And if the conclusion of the last charter turns out to be correct, the ultimate totalitarian regime will be right here in what was formerly the homeland for democracy and liberty.

The Beast From the Sea

The description of the Beast from John's Apocalypse has been the focus of commentary for almost 2,000 years in Christendom. My "exegesis" here and throughout our study of Judaic and Christian scripture will be to provide the perspective regarded as the most biblical by the greatest number of today's scholars. Additionally, many difficulties in interpretation will be avoided by simply cross-referencing the *Apostle John* to *the Prophet Daniel*. Furthermore, additional clarity is easily achieved by seeking an explanation of the symbols employed *within the body of the same text*. That's to say, what a symbol means in Revelation is often disclosed by simply finding its definition in a nearby passage. It's not as obscure as it seems.

In Revelation Chapter 13, John describes the terrifying vision of the apollonian Antichrist:

[1]And I stood upon the sand of the sea, and saw a beast rise up out of the sea, having seven heads and ten horns, and upon his horns ten crowns, and upon his heads the name of blasphemy.

[2]And the beast which I saw was like unto a leopard, and his feet were as the feet of a bear, and his mouth as the mouth of a lion: and the dragon gave him his power, and his seat, and great authority.

3And I saw one of his heads as it were wounded to death; and his deadly wound was healed: and all the world wondered after the beast.

4And they worshipped the dragon which gave power unto the beast: and they worshipped the beast, saying, Who is like unto the beast? who is able to make war with him?

5And there was given unto him a mouth speaking great things and blasphemies; and power was given unto him to continue forty and two months.

6And he opened his mouth in blasphemy against God, to blaspheme his name, and his tabernacle, and them that dwell in heaven.

7And it was given unto him to make war with the saints, and to overcome them: and power was given him over all kindreds, and tongues, and nations.

Our first priority to understand the meaning of John's Apocalypse, is to *identify the key symbols he uses and their meaning.* To begin with, who is **the dragon**? The devil, you say? John identifies him as such earlier, in Chapter 12, verse 9, *"And the great dragon was thrown down, the serpent of old who is called the devil and Satan, who deceives the whole world."* There is no mystery here.

Next, we come to **the beast**. The beast comes out of the sea displaying *ten horns, seven heads,* and *ten diadems* [crowns]. Previously, in Chapter 12, John also identified the dragon with the same words, *"Then another sign appeared in heaven: and behold, a great red dragon having seven heads and ten horns, and on his heads were seven diadems."* We see that both the dragon and the beast possess the same attributes. This emphasizes that "the [force] behind the curtain" is really who's pulling the strings. The beast is the physical, empirical realization of the invisible spirit being – Satan.

But what are *the horns and heads with blasphemous names?* In Chapter 17, John identifies them this way:

9And here is the mind which hath wisdom. The seven heads are seven mountains, on which the woman sitteth…

12And the ten horns which thou sawest are ten kings, which have received no kingdom as yet; but receive power as kings one hour with the beast.

13These have one mind, and shall give their power and strength unto the beast.

Prophecy pundits debate *the seven mountains reference.* Those familiar with classical literature know that Rome is the "City of Seven Hills;" hence, the reference most likely refers to Rome. However, in Jewish literature Rome can represent any western city antagonistic to Judaism.[4] The ten horns are defined as ten kings who have a very brief reign with the Beast. Referring to Revelation 13:5, we are told that his empire is short-lived, only 42 months (3.5 years). Daniel confirms this as well (see Daniel 9:27). Hence, John uses the small period of "one hour" to emphasize their reign is very brief indeed, especially in terms of *biblical time*.

As to the kings themselves, they are most often understood as ten nations *related to the Roman Empire of old*. Today, some speculate that these nations might be the ten regional (geographical and worldwide) spheres as espoused by the members of the Treaty of Rome (signed, by the way, on Rome's *Capitoline Hill*), who established this plan in the 1950's. The formation of Europe with its own currency, the EURO, was step one. Today, Africa is being reorganized into a single monetary and trading sphere under Muammar al-Gaddafi of Libya. North America too is moving toward consolidation of Canada, Mexico, and the U.S., into a single trading group (through NAFTA). We also see this in South America. Thus, the Dollar could eventually give way to the "AMERO" – a currency for the entire Western Hemisphere. That's if the EURO experiment succeeds. At this moment in 2010, it's on the brink of failure.

Conversely, most experts believe the ten kings refer to ten sovereign nation states, most likely European nations; while an emerging theory speculates that the ten nations could be composed of ten sovereign nation states surrounding Israel such as Syria, Iraq, Iran, Saudi Arabia, etc. (*the eastern leg* of the old Roman Empire). America's role in Iraq may inadvertently facilitate Iraq's taking the lead in the years ahead in this region of the world (perhaps with its headquarters in Babylon – literally fulfilling what John prophesies regarding "mystery Babylon"). However, the issue of whether Babylon will be "revived or not" also remains a major debating point on the table. The majority report still suggests that Europe, possibly including the United States, comprises this 10-nation consortium (and eventually turns against Israel in a colossal act of betrayal). Given our previous study, the inclusion of America in this group may be inevitable.

The beast of Revelation has characteristics of all the previous kingdoms that the Old Testament prophet Daniel describes, including those of a leopard, bear, and lion. Daniels' vision in Daniel, chapter 7, mirrors John's vision in many ways as we read below:

²Daniel spake and said, I saw in my vision by night, and, behold, the four winds of the heaven strove upon the great sea.

³And four great beasts came up from the sea, diverse one from another.

⁴The first was like a lion, and had eagle's wings: I beheld till the wings thereof were plucked, and it was lifted up from the earth, and made stand upon the feet as a man, and a man's heart was given to it.

⁵And behold another beast, a second, like to a bear, and it raised up itself on one side, and it had three ribs in the mouth of it between the teeth of it: and they said thus unto it, Arise, devour much flesh.

⁶After this I beheld, and lo another, like a leopard, which had upon the back of it four wings of a fowl; the beast had also four heads; and dominion was given to it.

⁷After this I saw in the night visions, and behold a fourth beast, dreadful and terrible, and strong exceedingly; and it had great iron teeth: it devoured and brake in pieces, and stamped the residue with the feet of it: and it was diverse from all the beasts that were before it; and it had ten horns.

⁸I considered the horns, and, behold, there came up among them another little horn, before whom there were three of the first horns plucked up by the roots: and, behold, in this horn were eyes like the eyes of man, and a mouth speaking great things.

Daniel begins with an allusion to "the great sea" from which his four beasts arise. Scholars believe the symbol of the sea refers to the thrashing and turmoil of global political dealings. Isaiah the Prophet said, *"The nations shall rush like the rushing of many waters; but God shall rebuke them, and they shall flee far off, and shall be chased as the chaff of the mountains" (Isaiah 17:13a).* From the clamor and chaos, continuous throughout the ages, order finally arises through a single, most-powerful world government with the *Beast* at its helm.

Daniel's lion is regarded as the first great and powerful kingdom, *Babylon* and King Nebuchadnezzar. The second, a bear, referred to the Media-Persian Empire – led by Cyrus the Great – who conquered Babylon in 540 BC. The third creature, a leopard, referred to Alexander the Great, who built his Greco Empire circa 321 BC; lasting until Pompey and Julius Caesar overcame it in the first century BC.⁵ Once again, we see the use of the symbol, "heads" referring to the four separate portions or divisions of the Greco Empire, formed by the four generals of Alexander: Ptolemy, Lysimachus, Cassander, and Seleucus. The final great and terrible beast, "dreadful and terrifying and extremely strong… [With] large iron teeth," once again refers to the ten nations as described by John. This is the imperial empire of Rome. Also, we see the use of "horns" (which is a sign of "holding onto power," akin to our saying of "taking the bull by the horns"), when mentioning the Roman confederation. These correlations are so plain, that many modern scholars assume Daniel was written just before the time of Christ's advent, when Daniel could recite history through a literary method, "apocalyptic writing." This conclusion is, of course, driven by those who see "foretelling" and "visions" as the fruit of a demented mind or a fraud. (But as Jesus remarked, "Wisdom is known by her children").[6]

Then Daniel gives us another name for the beast – "the little horn" (verse 8). The *Little Horn* had the eyes of a man, uttering great boasts. John reinforces the same trait in Revelation 13:6, *"And he opened his mouth in blasphemy against God, to blaspheme his name, and his tabernacle, and them that dwell in heaven"* who are those *"whose names are written in the Lamb's Book of Life"* (as the Spirit of God dwells within them). Paul the Apostle expands on this point, calling the Antichrist the "man of sin" and the "lawless one." The Antichrist *"Who opposeth and exalteth himself above all that is called God, or that is worshipped; so that he as God sitteth in the temple of God, shewing himself that he is God."* (II Thessalonians 2:4). Paul's adds further information for us to consider: The Antichrist will claim authority *as a divine being.* Furthermore, with a flair for the dramatic, he will make this pronouncement in the "Temple of God."

Daniel adds, "The Little Horn" *pulls out three of the other horns in order to gain ascendancy.* Scholars agree that seven nations of the ten nation confederacy support the *beast,* while three oppose him and are removed in his final step to secure power.

Perhaps the most puzzling statement by John regards *the fatal head wound that was healed.* In this statement, we must ask, "Has John switched the intent of his symbol, no longer referring to a nation, but to a physical head?" When the *head is healed,* the event amazes the whole world and causes everyone to worship the beast and the dragon that empowers him (who presumably resurrects the beast from the dead). Because of its dramatic impact, it seems more likely that this physical restoration to life is exactly what John intends. A rebirth of a nation is intriguing, but it wouldn't cause the whole world to "wonder after the beast." In fact, many experts believe this action is a satanic "copycat" maneuver – resurrecting the beast as a parody to the resurrection of Jesus Christ. More detail on this subject upcoming.

With the symbols interpreted (mostly by cross-referencing John to his own explanations or by comparing John's symbols with Daniel just as Newton advised), we can develop a summary of the *apollonian Antichrist* and his ascension to world domination.

- From a tumultuous political environment, the Antichrist will appear, promising order in the midst of global chaos.

- Ten leaders of sovereign nation states (or ten "regional governors" from around the world, perhaps trading groups), pledge support to this singular figure to lead the world forward.

- To accomplish his rise to power, he must overthrow three of the ten leaders who challenge his leadership.

- An assassination attempt, a fatal wound to his head, is miraculously healed. The world is amazed. His resurrection proves that he is no ordinary politician. The world acquiesces to his leadership and pledges support to the power behind this leader.

- His empire has attributes of all the great kingdoms of the Bible, from the time of Daniel (circa 550 BC) forward. Great glory, power, prestige, ruthless force, cunning, and speed in conquest are all exhibited by the beast and his confederacy.

- The leader seeks to establish his authority based upon his amazing rise to power and apparent resurrection from the dead. In the Temple (presumably rebuilt in Jerusalem), He claims to be a divine being or demigod.

- His speeches are filled with claims to a new future, to the potential of the world without God as extolled by the Bible. His proclamation is that we have no need of useless traditions of a "Hebrew tribal deity" – God has no place in his "brave new world."

- While the beast will reign supreme, his reign will last only 1260 days (3.5 years) according to both John and Daniel. In Chapter 9 of Daniel, as discussed before, the final seven years of his 70 weeks occurs. The week begins with a covenant between the 10 nations. Half-way through the week, the Antichrist is unveiled, betraying the nation of Israel, and overcoming 3 kings who oppose him. The "time of Jacob's trouble" or the Great Tribulation begins. As we will see in the next chapter, this time will culminate in the Battle of Armageddon and the coming of Messiah.

Nietzsche and the Übermensch

Nietzsche's most famous contribution pointing the way to humanity's destiny is disclosed through the birth of the "superman" or "*übermensch*." The term is not an easy one, but getting it right will help us to understand more about *the future füehrer*. A discussion from an article in Wikipedia is quite helpful to "*get*" his meaning:

The first translation of *Thus Spoke Zarathustra* into English, was by Alexander Tille, published in 1896. Tille translated Übermensch as **Beyond-Man**. In his translation published in 1909, Thomas Common rendered Übermensch as "Superman"... George Bernard Shaw... did the same in his 1903 stage play *Man and Superman*. Walter Kaufmann lambasted this translation in the 1950's for failing to capture the nuance of the German *über* and for promoting an eventual puerile [silly] identification with the comic-book character *Superman*. His preference was to translate Übermensch as "overman." Scholars continue to employ both terms, some simply opting to reproduce the German word.

The German prefix *über* can have connotations of superiority, transcendence, excessiveness, or intensity, depending on the words to which it is prepended. *Mensch* refers to a member of the human species, rather than to a man specifically.[7]

Hitler's "supermen" in the 1936 Olympics, supposedly the product of genetic engineering, conveyed a vulgar misunderstanding of Nietzsche's iconic idea. And as Jesse Owens demonstrated (Owens, the black American gold medalist of this Olympics who whipped the German supermen in several key *track and field* events), the supermen were still half-baked.[8]

Nietzsche's concept was based first and foremost on the proclamation that "god is dead." Since there is no God, according to Nietzsche, the only alternative is for man to overcome the death of God and go beyond what man previously assumed were his finite, human limitations. Man must become "overman." Without God – neither our fate nor our meaning enjoys any guarantee. *We must provide our own values.* These values can no longer be based upon the sentimentality of Christianity or outmoded Hebraic laws. Man must find his own way and become the measure of all things.

However, to which man is Nietzsche referring? Is this as man is now or man as he may become, perhaps *after* he has been re-engineered or revived by, as some suppose, an alien form of DNA?

One of the great secrets of the time immediately before World War II was that the whole western world was concerned about "eugenics" – not just Germany. The Microsoft dictionary defines *eugenics* this way, "the proposed improvement of the human species by encouraging or permitting reproduction of only those people with genetic characteristics judged desirable." George Bernard Shaw, the English playwright, can be seen in an old film discussing his idea that every human should appear before a tribunal annually to justify his or her existence. He declares that if we have nothing to offer society, we should be eliminated. Few realize that *Planned Parenthood* was originally formed to attack the problem of "low brow" individuals out-populating the "high brows." The organization sought to teach birth control to the poor and the undereducated, in order to reduce the underperforming population, thereby increasing the number of persons with a higher IQ and those with an opportunity to get a "good education" and become contributors rather than a burden on society. Even the Queen of England conspired with the Australian Government to kidnap "white" orphans in England (or orphan "suspects"), ship them off to Australia, and have them "out populate" the aborigines. The Church of England in Australia was complicit in this project and as NBC's documentary on the subject showcased a few years ago, many unspeakable abuses resulted. (In recent years, *supposed* Australia orphans finally located their living English parents and siblings, which made for some awkward but often amazing reunions.)

The movie, *Mediocracy*, starring Luke Wilson, talks about a future world populated exclusively by the illiterate with low IQ's. Wilson, possessing a very average IQ hovering around 90, time travels to this world and becomes the leader of the entire world. It's analogous to a familiar aphorism, "In the land of the blind, the one with the weak eye is the leader." [9]

In the TV series, *Andromeda*, certain characters called *"Nietzscheans,"* utilize selective breeding, genetic engineering, and even nano-technology to alter their nature. They are transformed into a race called *Übermenschen*. Their opponents deride them as the "Ubers."[10]

Today, we are hearing more and more discussion about altering the genetics of the human race, to improve our faculties, whether its eye-sight, hearing acuity, foot-speed, or intuitive skills. The mixing of human and animal DNA is already an established fact in the lab. Is the Nietzschean concept of Übermensch ready to become reality?

In a May 2000 paper by Richard Hayes, "The Politics of Genetically Engineered Humans"[11] we learn how eager scientists are (unfettered by a biblical God who would condemn it); to create a human that transcends what nature (or God) has made. Hayes warns,

> ... The prospect of genetically engineering the human species is categorically beyond anything that humanity has ever before had to confront. People have trouble taking these issues seriously – they seem fantastical, or beyond the pale of anything that anyone would actually do or that society would allow. As a consequence there exist no self-identified constituencies of concern, and no institutions in place to effectively focus that concern.

Just how committed are scientists to create the *Übermensch*? *Very.* Consider these comments:

> And the other thing, because no one has the guts to say it, if we could make better human beings by knowing how to add genes, why shouldn't we? What's wrong with it? . . . Evolution can be just damn cruel, and to say that we've got a perfect genome and there's some sanctity to it? I'd just like to know where that idea comes from. It's utter silliness. – *James Watson, Nobel Laureate, Discover of DNA*

> "Making babies sexually will be (come) rare," [Arthur] Caplan speculates. Many parents will leap at the chance to make their children smarter, fitter and prettier. Ethical concerns will be overtaken, says Caplan, by the realization that technology simply makes for better children. "In a competitive market society, people are going to want to give their kids an edge," says the bioethicist. "They'll slowly get used to the idea that a genetic edge is not greatly different from an environmental edge." – Hayes, quoting from, *abcnews.go.com /ABC2000 /abc2000living /babies2000*.

> Biotechnology will be able to accomplish what the radical ideologies of the past, with their unbelievably crude techniques, were unable to accomplish: to bring about a new type of human being... within the next couple of generations ... we will have definitively finished human History because we will have abolished human beings as such. And then, a new *post-human* history will begin. – Francis Fukuyama, George Mason University, author of *The End of History*.

Just for good measure, how about we throw in a new type of class warfare in the future too? The differentiation will be based on those who have "*uber*-DNA" and those that don't. Lee Silver of Princeton University shares numerous incisive comments we best not ignore:

> The GenRich – who account for 10 percent of the American population – all [will] carry synthetic genes. All aspects of the economy, the media, the entertainment industry, and the knowledge industry are controlled by members of the GenRich class . . . Naturals work as low-paid service providers or as laborers . . . [eventually] the GenRich class and the Natural class will become entirely separate species with no ability to cross-breed, and with as much romantic interest in each other as a current human would have for a chimpanzee. [12]

Silver continues:

> Many think that it is inherently unfair for some people to have access to technologies that can provide advantages while others, less well-off, are forced to depend on chance alone... [But] American society adheres to the principle that personal liberty and personal fortune are the primary deter-

minants of what individuals are allowed and able to do. Indeed, in a society that values individual freedom above all else, it is hard to find any legitimate basis for restricting the use of repro-genetics... [I] argue [that] the use of reprogenetic technologies is inevitable... whether we like it or not, the global marketplace will reign supreme.[13]

Apparently, even our enterprising American capitalism can't be trusted in the days ahead. The free market will force us down the path to alter human DNA. According to this line of thinking, it's time we re-engineer our gene pool, bring order to the chaos of creation, and take up the rationalistic goal of making our human genome bullet-proof.

So what would our plan be to accomplish this makeover of the human race? First, we must unshackle medicine from old-fashioned mores that block the advancement of humanity. Then, we must redefine human perfection, no longer based on what is natural or absent of mutation. In summary, we must corrupt the natural in order to achieve a new kind of human perfection – the *Übermensch*.

George W. Bush (43) in his January 31, 2006, State of the Union address called for legislation prohibiting the creation of "human-animal hybrids, and buying, selling, or patenting human embryos." Yet, no relevant laws exist today.

H.G. Wells, who was so prescient in this regard, based his novel *The Island of Doctor Moreau* on these most perplexing issues. *The Chimera is not a legend, but a future certainty.*[14] Huxley's *brave new world* has arrived! It's Orwell's *1984*, all over again.

It doesn't take a crystal ball to see the apollonian Antichrist's agenda becoming crystal clear.

Genetic Reengineering in the Bible

The Bible suggests that genetic reengineering isn't new to the human race. In fact, one of the earliest records of this phenomenon may be recorded in Genesis 6:4: *"There were giants (Nephilim) in the earth in those days; and also after that, when the sons of God came in unto the daughters of men, and they bare children to them, the same became mighty men which were of old, men of renown."* The Nephilim are sometimes translated "giants" and sometimes "beings who came down from above." The writer of Genesis (tradition teaches it was Moses), relates that these "gods" were the cause for the tales in ancient mythology regarding the interplay between "the gods" and humankind.

We've already encountered this same idea in many different sources – that humankind was *engineered* by extraterrestrials. The Bible's account suggests that both before and after the Great Flood, angels came to earth and "took wives," begetting a race of part-human, part-angel beings. It's a fantastic assertion to be sure. But there is considerable evidence that this is exactly what the Bible teaches. Moreover, it's not a peripheral issue.

In fact, it appears that (1) it was the express reason for God to send the flood upon the earth; and (2) the reason that Noah's family was selected to survive the flood – because Noah's family tree didn't include these demigods. Noah and his sons were "unblemished" from the heavenly human hybrid. *"These are the generations of Noah: Noah was a just man and **perfect in his generations**, and Noah walked with God"* (Genesis 6:9). The *Book of Enoch*, a non-canonical book quoted in the *New Testament*, confirms the same, indicating that 200 "watchers" (aka, *angels* in the Book of Enoch and the Book of Daniel) descended on Mount Hermon, in the days of Jared (the Father of Enoch, who was 800 years old when Enoch was born).[15] The Bible goes on to describe the Rephaim numerous times. The Rephaim inhabited the land of Canaan, destined to be the land of Palestine and Israel.

We are familiar with the phrases, "wilderness wanderings," "wandering Jew," "forth years in the wilderness," and perhaps the campaign led by Moses and Joshua to conquer this territory, that led to the slaughter of the people living in the land (by the Israelites), where previously Abraham and the other patriarchs lived.[16] Perhaps we aren't so familiar with the fact that the reasons the Jews wandered in the wilderness was due to their unwillingness to conquer the holy land. What was the reason for their reluctance? They feared the *Nephilim*, the giants who lived there. 12 spies were sent into the land to spy and gather intelligence. 10 of the spies said, "No go." Their report is located in Numbers 13:33, *"And there we saw the giants, the sons of Anak, which come of the giants: and we were in our own sight as grasshoppers, and so we were in their sight."* The minority report came from Joshua and Caleb who said in the words of today, "So there are giants. So what? We will still take them down because the Lord is with us." These words are almost the same as David used when going against Goliath with only five smooth stones and a slingshot. We are told that Goliath was a Nephilim or Rephaim as well:

> Then said David to the Philistine, Thou comest to me with a sword, and with a spear, and with a shield: but I come to thee in the name of the LORD of hosts, the God of the armies of Israel, whom thou hast defied (See I Samuel 17:45).

Clearly, the Bible isn't bashful in relating stories about giants. Some of its most famous stories and plot lines require acknowledging this amazing history as crucial both to the meaning of the passage and the underlying theology. Far from being a peripheral issue, this fantastic topic turns out to be *a central feature of the Bible's story of redemption*. It's stunning how few know this and even fewer in the Bible-believing world are willing to admit it.

Demon Seed and the Antichrist

The movies have had a field day with the idea that the Antichrist would be the physical offspring of Satan. We saw this in *Rosemary's Baby*. The *Omen* series is based explicitly on this premise too. Many other horror stories talk about the *incubae* and *succubae* (the male or female demon spirit that copulates with humans).

Furthermore, Tom Horn indicates that St. Augustine wrote of this type of demonology as well as Renaissance theologians who believed that the "return of the Nephilim" would result in the resurrection of Antichrist. Horn quotes Fr. Ludovicus Maria Sinistrari de Ameno (1622-1701): "To theologians and philosophers, it is a fact, that from the copulation of humans with the demon... Antichrist must be born." Horn also quotes Louis Paulwells and Jacques Bergier in *The Morning of the Magicians* that this was the express plan of Hitler:

> Hitler's aim was neither the founding of a race of superman, nor the conquest of the world; these were only means towards the realization of the great work he dreamed of. His real aim was to perform an act of creation, a divine operation, the goal of a biological mutation which would result in an unprecedented exaltation of the human race and the "apparition of a new race of heroes and demigods and god-men." [17]

Likewise, Trevor Ravenscroft goes into great detail about the legends of the search for Holy Grail, much of the literature written in the 13th century in reference to certain persons in the 9th (the key characters being Klingsor and Landulf II, adepts in Black Magic, sexual rituals, and the conjuring of sexual demons). Hitler saw himself as the reincarnation of one or more of these evil characters.[18]

In contrast to the notion that Dan Brown puts forth, the Holy Grail isn't necessary the blood line of Christ (which appears to be a concept springing from the south of France); instead it's the seeking of a new bloodline, *a bloodline altered and infused with the new genetics of the gods*. The search for the Grail fascinated Richard Wagner, who wrote the opera *Parsifal* based upon a 13th century poem.[19] At one time Wagner was Nietzsche's best friend until they came to a parting of the ways not long before Nietzsche went insane. Wagner's influence was the main reason that the nephew of Sir Neville Chamberlain,[20] Houston Steward Chamberlain, relocated to Germany. It's astonishing to learn that it was Chamberlain, an Englishman, who was considered the intellectual successor to Nietzsche, and another primary contributor to Hitler's vision.

Ravenscroft says:

> With a stupendous erudition which mesmerized the German intellectuals, he [Chamberlain] contrived to synthesize the opposing doctrines of Richard Wagner and Friedrich Nietzsche... he developed and expanded Wagner's doctrine of the Aryan Master Race... With one stroke of the pen, he eradicated the whole idea that a noble race needed to decline and decay with the force of natural law. For it was at this point in the extension of Wagner's thinking that he cunningly incorporated Nietzsche's belief that a "higher Race" could be bred. [21]

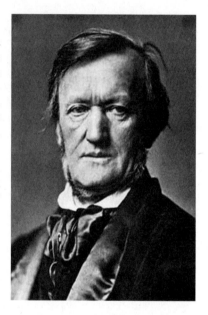

FIGURE 62 - RICHARD WAGNER

Where did Chamberlain get such ideas? According to Ravenscroft, it was well known among the leaders of the German military prior to World War I that he wrote "most of his works in a condition of trance in which hierarchies of evil spirits manifested themselves before his gaze. And that he never knew when or where his very soul would be seized by demons who drove him on into the feverish continuation of his work, leaving him later like an exhausted shell, frequently in near hysteria or on the point of collapse."[22]

But was Hitler specifically influenced by the Nephilim notion? Apparently he was. The founder of *The Thule Society* in Bavaria, one Rudolf Glauer, along with Dietrich Eckhart (another notorious handler for Hitler we've previously mentioned), was also heavily influenced by Madame Blavatsky, creating his Thule mythology directly from her writings. Ravenscroft explains:

Glauer himself was entirely lacking in spiritual faculty. He simply transposed Blavatsky's grotesque descriptions of the magical conditions prevailing in the vanished civilization of 'Atlantis' to give a pre-historical background to the mythological world of the Edda in which Gods, giants, men and beasts were engaged in a bloodcurdling struggle for survival. In respinning the age-old legends of Niflheim [Nephilim?][23] … he introduced Theosophical ideas about the magical relationship between cosmos, earth and man. He predicted that the latent powers and faculties slumbering in the blood of the Aryan race would unfold in the twentieth century when "Supermen" would reappear on earth to awaken the German people to the glories of their ancient heritage and lead them in the conquest of the world.[24]

Ravenscroft quotes Paulwells and Bergier (from *The Morning of the Magicians*), in talking about the "land of Thule" that was:

"…like Atlantis… thought to have been the magic centre of a vanished civilization. Eckhart and his friends believed that not all the secrets of Thule had perished. *Beings intermediate between Man and other intelligent Beings from Beyond,* would place at the disposal of the Initiates a reservoir of forces which could be drawn on to enable Germany to dominate the world again and be the cradle of the coming race of Supermen which would result from mutations of the human species. One day her legions would set out to annihilate everything that had stood in the way of the spiritual destiny of the Earth, and their leaders would be men who knew everything, deriving their strength from the very fountainhead of energy and guided by the great one of the ancient world. Such were the myths on which the Aryan doctrine of Eckhart and Rosenberg was founded and which these 'prophets' of a magic form of Socialism had instilled in the mediumistic mind of Hitler (*emphasis mine*). [25]

Therefore, we can conclude with a high degree of certitude that the *Spirit of the Antichrist* correlates to the notion of the Nephilim – the *human-god hybrid, the Übermensch* – and their reawakening.

The Mark of the Beast

The second half of Revelation, Chapter 13, tells us of a second beast, generally known as *The False Prophet,* who most biblical experts speculate will be a religious world leader, forcing everyone in the world to worship the image of the first beast. This beast comes from the earth rather than the sea. As the *third character* of the story, most scholars through the ages consider him the reflection of a false *Holy Spirit – the third member of the trinity of Satan.* We read:

[11]*And I beheld another beast coming up out of the earth; and he had two horns like a lamb, and he spake as a dragon.*

[12]*And he exerciseth all the power of the first beast before him, and causeth the earth and them which dwell therein to worship the first beast, whose deadly wound was healed.*

¹³*And he doeth great wonders, so that he maketh fire come down from heaven on the earth in the sight of men,*

¹⁴*And deceiveth them that dwell on the earth by the means of those miracles which he had power to do in the sight of the beast; saying to them that dwell on the earth, that they should make an image to the beast, which had the wound by a sword, and did live.*

¹⁵*And he had power to give life unto the image of the beast, that the image of the beast should both speak, and cause that as many as would not worship the image of the beast should be killed.*

¹⁶*And he causeth all, both small and great, rich and poor, free and bond, to receive a mark in their right hand, or in their foreheads:*

¹⁷*And that no man might buy or sell, save he that had the mark, or the name of the beast, or the number of his name.*

¹⁸*Here is wisdom. Let him that hath understanding count the number of the beast: for it is the number of a man; and his number is Six hundred threescore and six. (Revelation 13:11-18)*

It's postulated that the reference to the "horns of the lamb" implies that this leader would masquerade as a Christian leader given that Jesus is the *"lamb of God who taketh away the sin of the world."* Jesus is clearly referenced as this lamb in John's Revelation.

Making the image of the beast "come alive" and demanding that everyone worship the image of the beast may involve holographic technology – we can't be sure. But what is most fascinating is his insistence that all must be marked with a number of the forehand or forehead – *the infamous 666.* This technology links to a world financial system, providing an identification number for everyone in the world. To participate in the world system of the beast, this mark is indispensable. The number is THE *method to control the populace.*

But what specifically is the mark? Its nature is the most captivating puzzle preoccupying Bible authorities throughout the 2,000 years since this was first prophesied by John. It's the ultimate doomsday code. And it's a code that's been difficult to break. Explanations include everything from the simple to the exotic. The most straightforward explanation was offered by Hal Lindsey years ago: Three sixes refer to the number of God – "3" – and the number of man – "6." Three sixes would simply mean "man making himself god." This is perfectly consistent with verse 15.

Others relate the "three sixes" to a numerological coding technique called *Gematria.* Since Roman and Greek numerical systems used their alphabets (their "letters"), rather than "Arabic characters" and "powers of ten" such as our decimal system, a word or name *has a numerical value.* Names are frequently translated into a Greek or Roman equivalent and the values added together. For instance, Caesar Nero added up to 666. But then, so does Henry Kissinger in Greek. Depending upon what is included in the name and that something isn't added or lost in translation, it's not that difficult to wind up with 666. It's a contrived method, but frequently put to work nonetheless in an attempt to break the code of the Beast.

Then there are the technological explanations. The Universal Product Code (UPC), aka the bar code, uses three sixes to calibrate the product specific code. Is this the mark of the beast? Its technology is a possible candidate. It's certainly odd that those who developed the "UPC" saw to it that *three sixes* should be the numbers to distinguish product (or personal?) identities. I doubt the irony of this decision was lost on them.

Those that speculate the Antichrist may be Muslim, point out that the Arabic characters for Allah resemble 666 in Arabic. That adds some fuel to their growing fire which proposes the Antichrist will be "the Assyrian" described in Isaiah and several other Old Testament prophetic passages.[26] In Latin (using the Roman alphabet and "Roman numerals," the numbers would be: **VIVIVI.** Does this suggest a solution to the enigma? Where's Robert Langdon (Tom Hanks' character in the Dan Brown novels) when you need him?

The most exotic explanation is also the most intriguing and pertinent to the foregoing discussion on genetics. Could the mark of the beast be a *genetic marker of some kind?* Tom Horn proposes this possibility. Could receiving the mark mean accepting some manner of trans-human gene splice that changes the DNA of the recipient? What makes this particularly foreboding is an assumption *that someone who is not purely human can no longer be saved by the death of Christ.* This conclusion is derived from the supposition that the primary reason fallen angels sought to contaminate the human race by *intermarriage* was to eliminate the possibility that the Messiah could be the perfect and obedient *son of Adam* and therefore, no longer qualifies to redeem all sons of Adam (see Romans, Chapter 5). In like manner, receiving this mark may temporarily preserve your earthly life, but accepting it destines you to eternal doom. Then again, beheading was invented to keep the body from its being eligible for "rising from the dead" (and I'm rather sure God is able to overcome the problem of putting heads and bodies back together, since even one DNA molecule contains the entire coding scheme for a human being – should that be a factor and I'm not sure that it is).

But just what are the consequences for those that "opt out?" Horn quotes George Annas, Lori Andrews, and Rosario Isasi from their article in the *American Journal of Law and Medicine*, "Protecting the Endangered Human: Toward an International Treaty Prohibiting Cloning and Inheritable Alterations."

> The new species, or "posthuman," will likely view the old "normal" humans as inferior, even savages, and fit for slavery or slaughter. The *normals*, on the other hand, may see the *posthumans* as a threat and if they can, may engage in a preemptive strike by killing the posthumans before they themselves are killed or enslaved by them. It is ultimately this predictable potential for genocide that makes species-altering experiments potential weapons of mass destruction, and makes the unaccountable genetic engineer a potential bioterrorist. [27]

The Resurrection of the Spirit of Apollo

The *Egyptian Book of the Dead* quotes Osiris (Apollo) saying, "I am Yesterday and I am Today; and I have the power to be born a second time." Manly P. Hall proclaims, "Osiris will rise in splendor from the dead and rule the world through those sages and philosophers in whom wisdom has become incarnate." Additionally, Horn quotes Hall from *The Secret Teachings of the Ages*, in which he says, "The Dying God shall rise again! The secret room in the House of the Hidden Places shall be rediscovered. The Pyramid again shall stand as the ideal emblem of solidarity, inspiration, aspiration, resurrection, and regeneration."[28]

Interestingly, Edgar Cayce, *the Sleeping Prophet*, predicted in the 1930's that a secret room known as the *Hall of Records* would be discovered within the Egyptian Sphinx. This room would provide proof of the Antediluvian civilization of Atlantis and provide the history of the world before the Flood of Noah. So far, it remains undiscovered although Egyptian archeologists are slowly probing for it. Given that it would ruin the notion the Egyptians built their own pyramids, we can assume the Egyptians may continue to drag their feet. Does the Bible confirm that Osiris (Apollo) shall rise again?

The answer appears to be *yes*. This resurrection is spoken of in Revelation Chapter 17:1-13. It's part of the passage describing *Mystery Babylon*. We read:

> *¹And there came one of the seven angels which had the seven vials, and talked with me, saying unto me, Come hither; I will shew unto thee the judgment of the great whore that sitteth upon many waters:*

²With whom the kings of the earth have committed fornication, and the inhabitants of the earth have been made drunk with the wine of her fornication.

³So he carried me away in the spirit into the wilderness: and I saw a woman sit upon a scarlet coloured beast, full of names of blasphemy, having seven heads and ten horns.

⁴And the woman was arrayed in purple and scarlet colour, and decked with gold and precious stones and pearls, having a golden cup in her hand full of abominations and filthiness of her fornication:

⁵And upon her forehead was a name written,

> MYSTERY,
> BABYLON THE GREAT,
> THE MOTHER OF HARLOTS AND
> ABOMINATIONS OF THE EARTH.

⁶And I saw the woman drunken with the blood of the saints, and with the blood of the martyrs of Jesus: and when I saw her, I wondered with great admiration.

⁷And the angel said unto me, Wherefore didst thou marvel? I will tell thee the mystery of the woman, and of the beast that carrieth her, which hath the seven heads and ten horns.

⁸The beast that thou sawest was, and is not; and shall ascend out of the bottomless pit, and go into perdition: and they that dwell on the earth shall wonder, whose names were not written in the book of life from the foundation of the world, when they behold the beast that was, and is not, and yet is.

⁹And here is the mind which hath wisdom. The seven heads are seven mountains, on which the woman sitteth.

¹⁰And there are seven kings: five are fallen, and one is, and the other is not yet come; and when he cometh, he must continue a short space.

¹¹And the beast that was, and is not, even he is the eighth, and is of the seven, and goeth into perdition.

¹²And the ten horns which thou sawest are ten kings, which have received no kingdom as yet; but receive power as kings one hour with the beast.

¹³These have one mind, and shall give their power and strength unto the beast.

We've already covered most of the symbols discussed in this passage from John's Apocalypse. The critical new information is the mention of seven kings, five who have already fallen, one who currently is, and another that has not yet come. The final one that comes will remain "only a little while." The *Beast* is this final one, who is also, therefore, an *eighth yet related to the seventh*. After his reign is finished, he will go to destruction. While the language seems rather convoluted, scholars believe that the mystery of the seven kings can be decoded by reciting those kingdoms that have dominated the Hebrew peoples through its history. These kingdoms would be as follows:

1. **Egypt** – Who held the 12 Tribes of Jacob (Israel) until Moses.

2. **Assyria** – Through Sennacherib who destroyed the 10 Northern Tribes of Israel in the 8th Century BC.

3. **Babylon** – That took the remaining two tribes into Captivity.

4. **Media-Persia** – Cyrus and Darius that conquered Babylon.

5. **Greece** – Alexander that conquered Babylon (an empire split into four parts, corresponding to the four generals of Alexander).

6. **Rome (Ancient)** – Pompey and the Caesars until 135 AD.

7. **Rome** (during the Apocalypse) – To be determined.

8. **Antichrist,** who is of Rome (7).

Conceived this way, the prophecy seems easily explainable. These seven kings (five of whom are historical) are distinct from the ten kings that haven't yet received a kingdom (who remain future). They will reign with the beast and will give their authority to him. Therefore, we see there are two references; one to ten kings and a separate reference to seven kings. Verses 12 and 13 make it very clear that they aren't the same. This leaves us with the mystery of verse 8: *"The beast that you saw was, and is not, and is about to come up out of the abyss and go to destruction."* This Beast is plainly represented as a resurrected being. *It's the only example of reincarnation in the Bible.* He's certainly the same Beast as already explored in Chapter 13. *He was but is not, but will come out of the abyss.* Another name for the abyss is "perdition" and the Greek word closely related to *Apollyon* – *Apoleia* – is also used to name the Spirit of Antichrist, *Apollyon or Abaddon*, in Revelation chapter 9. In fact, it's the very same word is used in Revelation 13:8. Paul teaches that this man, the lawless one, is the *son of perdition*. He says in II Thessalonians 2: 2-4:

[2] That ye be not soon shaken in mind, or be troubled, neither by spirit, nor by word, nor by letter as from us, as that the day of Christ is at hand.

*3 Let no man deceive you by any means: for [that day shall not come], except there come a falling away first, and that man of sin be revealed, **the son of perdition;***

4 Who opposeth and exalteth himself above all that is called God, or that is worshipped; so that he as God sitteth in the temple of God, shewing himself that he is God.

Paul indicates that the Antichrist is the son of one coming from *perdition*, the son of *Apoleia*.

The *Book of Enoch* indicates that the *Watchers*, the angels who spawned the Nephilim, have been bound and kept in this perdition and won't be released for 70 generations until they are set free to be thrown into an chasm of fire (what John refers to as "the lake of fire"). But is there an "in-between" period where they roam the world again before their final judgment?

Enoch 15:9-10 prophesies, "The spirits of the giants... shall be concealed, and shall not rise up against the sons of men, and against women; until they come forth during the days of slaughter and destruction." Could the prospects of a zombie-like appearance of spirits from the underworld, freshly reborn, during the last days, actually be a possibility? This nightmare, as unbelievable as it seems, appears prophesied in this passage in Enoch. And it's consistent with what John teaches.

Yeats and His Poem, The Second Coming

William Butler Yeats is considered one of the most seminal English language poets of the 20th century. Perhaps his most famous poem, *The Second Coming*, he penned in 1921. The themes he touches on reinforce the troubling message of this chapter:

Turning and turning in the widening gyre
The falcon cannot hear the falconer;
Things fall apart; the center cannot hold;
Mere anarchy is loosed upon the world,
The blood-dimmed tide is loosed, and everywhere
The ceremony of innocence is drowned;
The best lack all conviction, while the worst
Are full of passionate intensity.
Surely some revelation is at hand;
Surely the Second Coming is at hand;
The Second Coming! Hardly are those words out
*When a vast image out of **Spiritus Mundi** [Spirit world]*
Troubles my sight: somewhere in sands of the desert
A shape with lion body and the head of a man,

A gaze blank and pitiless as the sun,
Is moving its slow thighs, while all about it
Reel shadows of the indignant desert birds.
The darkness drops again; but now I know
That twenty centuries of stony sleep
Were vexed to nightmare by a rocking cradle,
And what rough beast, its hour come round at last
Slouches towards Bethlehem to be born.

Like so many other intellectuals at the turn of the century, Yeats was heavily influenced by Theosophical thought. He joined *The Ghost Club* in 1911 and participated in paranormal research. He indicates in his own words that magic played an important role inspiring his creativity. He indicated that without it, he couldn't have accomplished some of his best work, especially his writing on the great mystic author and artist, William Blake.

FIGURE 63 - WILLIAM BUTLER YEATS BY GEORGE CHARLES BERESFORD, 1911

W. H. Auden, an Englishmen-cum-American citizen, another of the greatest English-language poets of the 20th century, downplayed the lasting effects of the occult and mysticism on Yeats' contribution, commenting that his fascination with mysticism was a "deplorable spectacle of a grown man occupied with the mumbo-jumbo of magic and the nonsense of India." Bully for him! Spoken like a true English naturalist. Nevertheless, Yeats, like so many others early in the century, *found meaning in the metaphysical.* This poem possesses a few of the most frequently quoted and memorable lines in modern poetry:

Things fall apart; the center cannot hold; Mere anarchy is loosed upon the world.

Scholars as they are wont to do, have attempted (mostly unsatisfactorily), to fathom Yeats' inscrutable meaning. Many suggest the poem is a commentary on the twilight of European culture. Others suppose Yeats possessed a genuine sense of a coming Apocalypse, perhaps in his time. Because he had just lived through World War I when he wrote this poem, did he simply foresee another World War?

> *"Twenty centuries of stony sleep were vexed to nightmare by a rocking cradle, and what rough beast, its hour come round at last slouches towards Bethlehem to be born."*

Did Yeats foresee an Antichrist emerging from the *Spiritus Mundi* (spirit world)? Is it pedestrian to understand Yeats in a more literal way? Is his yet another voice, predicting a diabolical visitor soon to be born? Was this vision summoned from his own experimentation in the occult? One thing appears certain: Yeats' poem has its own foreboding imagery that mirrors the biblical themes we've studied in a profound and prescient way.

If we stop to take a look back, it's staggering to realize how so many scholars early in the 20th century *turned to spiritualism and the occult to find meaning and direction*. It seems that the personal Judeo-Christian God *may have died just as the madman proclaimed*. But his survivors couldn't stand the prospects of a *world without spirit*. They frequently conjured unfathomable and frightening images which should have caused these intellectuals to shrink back in fear. Although perilous, the prospect to create the *Über-mensch* was a temptation too enticing to abandon.

In conclusion, we sometimes talk about experiencing *hell on earth*. But in so saying, we never consider that the expression could literally come true. After contemplating the nature of the Antichrist spirit, the history of those who sought to incarnate it before and its renewed goal of creating a genetically enhanced person – "men and heroes (demigods) co-mingling" – perhaps we must acknowledge the inevitability of the Sybil's prophecy. A true *transhuman* could emerge, a demigod designed to mastermind our destiny and lead us to its realization. If so, the finale is far more incredible than we've imagined up to this time.

The story of Dr. Frankenstein and his monster, Mary Shelly's masterpiece, was no casual horror story penned merely to sell books. It intended to heighten our sense of what happens if we attempt to play God. Let it stand as a final word of warning: We best become aware of the manner of beast we unleash upon our unsuspecting world should we allow what Jesus called the *abomination of desolation **and its offspring*** to become a reality in the days ahead.[29] That is the exactly what the Spirit of the Antichrist seeks. Can this destiny be averted?

Notes

¹ These two sides of the same orange are true of both human and "fallen" spiritual forces.

² See *http://en.wikipedia.org/wiki/Apollonian_and_Dionysian*.

³ Unfortunately, in our media-managed world, we also award fame to those seeking power through acts of cowardice. Assassins seek notoriety by claiming their "15 minutes of fame" at someone else's expense. The *nobody* becomes *somebody* when they strike down "a somebody we admire." Who would remember John Hinckley if he hadn't taken shots at Ronald Reagan?

⁴ This information comes from my friend, Rabbi Daniel Lapin, who is an expert in Hebrew and Hebraic literature.

⁵ For a more extensive of these Kingdoms see my first book, *Are We Living in the Last Days?* – Chapter 11.

⁶ A much more politically correct way of saying what Forrest Gump stated, "Stupid is as stupid does."

⁷ See *http://en.wikipedia.org/wiki/%C3%9Cbermensch*. Then there is the Yiddish take on the term, which I recently learned from Rabbi Lapin, in which a *Mensch* connotes an 'outstanding guy.' In this respect, it's a real complement!

⁸ Interestingly, *Superman* originally was an *evil* character in the comic books, and was based on Nietzsche's concept.

⁹ Today, we hear frequent discussion regarding demographics, tax revenues, and how in America over 50% of the population pays no income taxes. With this trend "growing worse" it's possible to foresee how eugenics could be a solution a future fascist government unloosed from the moorings of humanism and individualism might seek to help "balance the budget."

¹⁰ See *http://en.wikipedia.org/wiki/%C3%9Cbermensch*.

¹¹ See *http://www.loka.org/alerts/loka.7.2.txt*.

¹² This state of affairs doesn't sound like much fun to me. I'm quite sure that my wife would rather not see the death of romance announced so blithely. But would she consider it in the name of furthering science? I seriously doubt it.

¹³ Quoted by R. Hayes, source: Lee Silver. *Remaking Eden: How Cloning and Beyond Will Change the Human Family*, New York: Avon Books, 1997, pp. 4-7, 11.

¹⁴ Tom Horn provides a superlative discussion of this subject in his chapter, "Will Modern Science Play a Role in the Coming of Apollo?" in *Apollyon Rising 2012*. One amazing quotation from his book, "When describing the benefits of man-with-beast combinations in his online thesis, *Transhumanist Values*, Bostrom [*www.nickbostrolm.com*] cites how animals have "sonar, magnetic orientation, or sensors for electricity and vibration," among other extra-human abilities. He goes on to include how the range of sensory modalities for transhumans would not be limited to those among animals, and that there is "no fundamental block to adding say a

capacity to see infrared radiation or to perceive radio signals and perhaps to add some kind of telepathic sense by augmenting our brains." (Horn, op. cit., pg 203).

15 This location today is the Golan Heights in Syria. It is also the Mount of Transfiguration where Jesus appeared to his disciples with Moses and Elijah. What does this say about the meaning of this particular mountain? Some scholars are willing to speculate that it's a special and perhaps unique doorway into the spirit world. I can't easily agree, but find it fascinating to consider.

16 The idea that the inhabitants of Canaan were tainted with angelic DNA provides a reasonable explanation why YHWH would demand their total annihilation, as a number of scholars have proposed. While humankind would still regard such destructiveness savage, it's no longer a random act of violence without rationale.

17 Ibid., pg 214. Paulwells and Bergier: *The Morning of the Magicians*, Paris, 1960, pg. 68.

18 Hermann Goring indicated that Hitler believed himself to be the reincarnation of Landulf II and Count Acerra (the probable historical figure behind Klingsor of the Opera), and he thought himself to be the reborn Tiberius (Caesar). Hitler could never be accused of modesty. See Ravenscroft, op. cit., pg. 186.

19 "*Parsifal* is an opera in three acts by Richard Wagner. It is loosely based on Wolfram von Eschenbach's *Parzival*, the 13th century epic poem of the Arthurian knight Parzival (Percival) and his quest for the Holy Grail." See *http://en.wikipedia.org/wiki/Parsifal*.

20 Sir Neville Chamberlain was the Prime Minister of Britain before World War II (who falsely proclaimed "peace in our time" through pacifying Hitler by giving away territory for Hitler's "lebensraum" strategy [land as a buffer to safeguard the "father land"]. Chamberlain was one of the 'bad guys' whose name is generally associated with appeasement.

21 Ravenscroft, op. cit., pg 115.

22 Ibid., pg. 119.

23 Niflheim was part of a Norse myth - an ancient abode of men and demigods amidst darkness and dense mist. Might it have taken its name from the Nephilim? I propose the two are connected conceptually and linguistically. Proving this would be another matter, with facts most likely lost in the *mist* of time.

24 Ibid., pg 159.

25 Ibid, pg. 160.

26 The Assyrian is most likely a reference to Nimrod, who many sources believe is the true historical figure behind Osiris. He was the ruler over Babylon at its inception. Many Masonic historians believe that the Tower of Babel, not the Temple of Solomon is the true "Temple" in which Masonry first dawned, with Nimrod the first Mason. In this way, the Antichrist could be the resurrected "Assyrian" although in his present incarnation, he may be American, European, or another race. Chuck

Missler believes that the first Antichrist was Nimrod and so shall the second one be also. It's important that the notion of "the Assyrian" could be symbolic in this manner. It's not essential that the Beast be truly from Iraq – just that he's "Nimrod."

[27] Horn, Op. cit., pg 207, quoting the *American Journal of Law and Medicine*, Vol. 28, Nos. 2 and 3 (2002), 162.

[28] Horn, op. cit., pg. 211, citing Hall, *The Secret Teachings of the Ages*, pg. 104.

[29] Daniel Pinchbeck in *The Return of Quetzalcoatl* delves into the "Grays" of UFO fame and what their purported genetic experiments (on their spacecraft after abduction) might mean. It's a fascinating discussion. The many statements of Grays to Abductees are consistent in explaining that they seek to create an alien-human hybrid. But for what purpose? Pinchbeck suggests that they are emotionless, boring beings who are attracted by our energy, exuberance, and vitality. They are trying to horn in on our manner of life. Pinchbeck quotes John Major Jenkins (as did I) on the matter of what their sinister intent might actually be. Pinchbeck doesn't speculate, as I do, that should these visions are *actual* encounters (and not just mind-bounded nightmares), the Grays are trying to contaminate human DNA infecting it with their own. Are they trying to improve their race? Christian cosmology would speculate that they aren't really worried about their legacy or progeny. They are simply out for themselves. They are deceptive and full of mischief. What they do is destructive and playing the part of the spoiler. Furthermore, if the conclusions of many authors who discuss the Nephilim and their motives are correct, the Grays are still seeking to destroy the chance for humanity to be redeemed by the blood of Jesus Christ. I don't hold out much hope for their mission to be achieved.

PART THREE:
COUNTDOWN TO
DOOMSDAY

Chapter 13:
The Three Wars of World War III

*"That land of hallowed memories is yet to receive again its
ancient tenants and to yield its teeming riches to the old age of the people whose infancy
was nurtured on its maternal bosom... The olive and the vine shall again spread their honors over the mountains once delectable, now desolate; the corn shall laugh in the valley
where the prowling Bedouin pitches his transient tent, and joyous groups of children, the
descendants of patriarch fathers, shall renew their evening sports in the streets of crowded
cities, where now the ruinous heaps tell only of a grandeur that has passed away."*

George Bush, Professor of Hebrew
New York City University, 1844

The Valley of the Dry Bones

Tracking our ancestors has become an obsession for some. But based on personal experience, what we uncover about our forebears may some-times best be buried again as quickly as possible!

However, in the case of Presidents George H.W. Bush (41), and George W. Bush (43), they can find some honor in an ancestor by the same name of George, who is akin to a first cousin, perhaps five times removed. This George Bush was a professor at New York City University when he wrote a proof for the return of the Jewish people to the land of Palestine.[1] Writing almost exactly 100 years before the nation state of Israel was re-born, Bush fashioned an "attempted proof" from Ezekiel Chapter 37:1-14, known among those familiar with the Bible as Ezekiel's "Vision of the Dry Bones." His short book of 60 pages, *The Valley of Vision: or the Dry Bones of Israel Revived,* was published by Saxton & Miles in 1844. The sampling of prose in the epigraph shows Dr. Bush knew how to add flowery meta-phors to his message.

I studied a theological book review of Bush's work prepared at Prince-ton Theological Seminary for their July 1844 theological journal. General-ly, Professor Bush was applauded for his treatise. The commentary con-sidered whether the passage in question referred to a (1) literal restoration of Israel or merely a (2) "symbolic restoration" – specifically, predicting the conversion of Jews to Christianity – which up to that time had been the position of the Christian Church (for about 1750 years!) [2] The reviewer noted that the Professor was staking an unusual claim in professing a view of the physical reestablishment of the Jewish nation, when most everyone else derived a figurative interpretation.[3]

Dr. Bush believed the outcome might entail both, but that the prophecy clearly referred to a future event, not to the prior restoration of the Hebrews from Babylon in 538 B.C.[4] This was a break from the theological interpretations of the past and was anticipating the millenarian position then in the making (remember, this was when William Miller was gathering his troops out West). According to the reviewer, Bush's position on the political/ national *nature* of this restoration of Israel was overly dogmatic. The primary criticism of his book, from the Seminary's perspective was that Bush *assumed what he was trying to prove*; citing as his clinching argument the dramatic language in Ezekiel – "spoken by Jehovah himself" – when declaring how the dry bones would live again. These words were so clear and powerful coming as they did directly from Jehovah, argued Bush, they sufficed with no further proof required.

Here is the passage in question (Ezekiel 37:1-14):

¹*The hand of the LORD was upon me, and carried me out in the spirit of the LORD, and set me down in the midst of the valley which was full of bones,*

²*And caused me to pass by them round about: and, behold, there were very many in the open valley; and, lo, they were very dry.*

³*And he said unto me, Son of man, can these bones live? And I answered, O Lord GOD, thou knowest.*

⁴*Again he said unto me, Prophesy upon these bones, and say unto them, O ye dry bones, hear the word of the LORD.*

⁵*Thus saith the Lord GOD unto these bones; Behold, I will cause breath to enter into you, and ye shall live:*

⁶*And I will lay sinews upon you, and will bring up flesh upon you, and cover you with skin, and put breath in you, and ye shall live; and ye shall know that I am the LORD.*

⁷*So I prophesied as I was commanded: and as I prophesied, there was a noise, and behold a shaking, and the bones came together, bone to his bone.*

⁸*And when I beheld, lo, the sinews and the flesh came up upon them, and the skin covered them above: but there was no breath in them.*

⁹Then said he unto me, Prophesy unto the wind, prophesy, son of man, and say to the wind, Thus saith the Lord GOD; Come from the four winds, O breath, and breathe upon these slain, that they may live.

¹⁰So I prophesied as he commanded me, and the breath came into them, and they lived, and stood up upon their feet, an exceeding great army.

¹¹Then he said unto me, Son of man, these bones are the whole house of Israel: behold, they say, Our bones are dried, and our hope is lost: we are cut off for our parts.

¹²Therefore prophesy and say unto them, Thus saith the Lord GOD; Behold, O my people, I will open your graves, and cause you to come up out of your graves, and bring you into the land of Israel.

¹³And ye shall know that I am the LORD, when I have opened your graves, O my people, and brought you up out of your graves,

¹⁴And shall put my spirit in you, and ye shall live, and I shall place you in your own land: then shall ye know that I the LORD have spoken it, and performed it, saith the LORD.

The passage clearly points out not only will God restore His people to their ancient land, but *he will put His Spirit within them,* something Christians believe is true of them (Christ, through His Holy Spirit comes to live *within* the individual believer permanently, thus we hear what can be a clichéd phrase, "receiving Christ"). *But this "person-to-person" (i.e., personal relationship) is uncharacteristic of how Jehovah relates historically to the Jews.* Therefore, this would be a *new state of being –* never before realized.

Furthermore, Jehovah's intent in bringing about this specific event is to prove to the Jews that it's He – *Jehovah –* and none other, who has caused this restoration and revival.[5]

FIGURE 64 - JOHN NELSON DARBY

At about the same time of Professor Bush's *apologetic* [an argument or defense] favoring the return of the Jew to his land, John Nelson Darby formed the *Plymouth Brethren* in England (circa 1840), a movement which begat a controversial perspective on biblical interpretation, known today as *Dispensationalism.* Although Darby's view was a hint in earlier scholars such as Jonathan Edwards (in 18th century America), this manner of interpreting the Bible was a major exodus from historic Christian orthodoxy. Today, we hardly realize this was such a drastic departure, since Dispensationalism is now the mainstream view held in conservative Christendom. Authors such as Hal Lindsey, Grant Jeffrey, Joel Rosenberg, Chuck Missler, Tim LaHaye, Gary Stearman, and J.R. Church (and this author), subscribe to this manner of interpretation. Because of these authors' significant influence, *the Rapture notion* (the sudden translation of believers into "their heavenly bodies") has become widely adopted throughout Evangelicalism.[6]

Drilling down, two characteristics help define the essence of Dispensationalism. The first attribute is *how the Bible is interpreted*, which is typically described succinctly *as literal interpretation* (although I chafe a bit with the adjective "literal" believing "plain meaning" to be a better catch phrase capturing the essence of the approach).[7] The second attribute relates to *the meaning of modern Israel*. The traditional Christian position rejects the notion that Israel remains "God's chosen people," believing instead that Christianity fulfills the promises God made to Israel. Dispensationalism strongly disagrees. God has two plans: One for the Church and one for Israel. His plan for Israel requires that a physical kingdom be realized upon the earth.

Hence, Dispensationalists have always believed that the political state of Israel must be recreated for God's ultimate program to be fulfilled.

**FIGURE 65 - MEMBERS OF FIRST ZIONIST CONFERENCE, 1898,
BASEL, SWITZERLAND**

When Israel became a nation in 1948, the Dispensationalists said, "See there. We told you it would happen. It proves we were right." However, the debate still rages today. The opponents to Dispensationalism, known today as *preterists* who espouse "replacement theology," are not convinced by Scripture or by the empirical facts themselves. They stick to their prophetic guns: Prophecy in the Bible has already been fulfilled. Christians are the recipients of the promises and covenants made to Abraham, Isaac, and Jacob. The Church *replaces* Israel. At issue is whether God's covenants are *conditional or unconditional*. My first book (*Are We Living in the Last Days?*) addresses this debate amongst Protestants in great detail, along with the issue of how the *Bible should be interpreted* from a prophetic standpoint to ensure a *consistent approach to interpretation* (aka *hermeneutics*).

Getting back to Professor Bush, he, along with the Dispensationalists, weren't the only persons in the 19th century puzzling over the meaning of Ezekiel's passage. The movement known as *Zionism* turned the focus of many Bible scholars to the Old Testament. There were an increasing number of politicians and theologians alike who were desirous that the Jewish people be restored to Palestine. The history of this movement is well outside the scope of our study; however, the key touch point is that it was through the prophecies of the Old Testament, especially Ezekiel's "Dry Bones" passage, that Zionism gained strength, leading to an alliance with many Anglo-Saxons (some who were English Dispensationalists), representing an *about face* amongst Christians regarding the importance of Judaism to God's grand plan.

To be sure, one could argue that this 19th century movement became the most important political idea of the era continuing to shape the political structure of our world today. *Zionism remains the fuel behind the fire in the Middle East.*

Undeniably, it's the view of Dispensationalists that the restoration of Israel is the single most important fulfilled prophecy demonstrating both the veracity of the Bible and clarifying God's intentions for the near future. But Ezekiel's prophecy hardly stands alone. Moses himself is recorded making the very same prediction in the Pentateuch (the first five books in the Bible). From Deuteronomy, Chapter 4:25-31:

25When thou shalt beget children, and children's children, and ye shall have remained long in the land, and shall corrupt yourselves, and make a graven image, or the likeness of any thing, and shall do evil in the sight of the LORD thy God, to provoke him to anger:

26I call heaven and earth to witness against you this day, that ye shall soon utterly perish from off the land whereunto ye go over Jordan to possess it; ye shall not prolong your days upon it, but shall utterly be destroyed.

*27**And the LORD shall scatter you among the nations**, and ye shall be left few in number among the heathen, whither the LORD shall lead you.*

28And there ye shall serve gods, the work of men's hands, wood and stone, which neither see, nor hear, nor eat, nor smell.

29But if from thence thou shalt seek the LORD thy God, thou shalt find him, if thou seek him with all thy heart and with all thy soul.

30When thou art in tribulation, and all these things are come upon thee, even in the latter days, if thou turn to the LORD thy God, and shalt be obedient unto his voice;

31(For the LORD thy God is a merciful God;) he will not forsake thee, neither destroy thee, nor forget the covenant of thy fathers which he sware unto them.

Because Israel has returned to the land, some orthodox Jews believe Messiah is at the door. This is *the later days*. Martin Buber, a famous Jewish author and philosopher wrote a book entitled *Gog and Magog* in which he voiced the traditional Jewish view that this war (Gog and Magog) is the final war of the nations against Israel and immediately precedes the coming of Messiah.

Likewise, Elie Wiesel, the Jewish Nobel laureate, also included the Ezekiel prophecy into his 1972 book, *Souls on Fire*. In an interview Wiesel commented, "Messianism is the gift of the Jew to the world, but in our tradition we believe that before redemption there will be a huge catastrophe. We call it the war of 'Gog and Magog.'"[8]

Christians and Jews differ on whether the "War of Gog and Magog" is the *one and only final battle* or whether it's merely one of a series. Indeed, the Christian view is that Ezekiel's war will commence the so-called *Time of Jacob's Trouble*, otherwise known as *Daniels' 70th Week* and/or the *Great Tribulation*. After the War of Gog and Magog, a false messiah will appear and will mislead many Jews. He will likely be a Jew himself (most scholars believe hailing from the so-called "lost tribe" of Dan). This false messiah is the aforementioned Antichrist. His appearance leads to turmoil of unequaled magnitude, culminating in another war at the end of the 70th Week known by the familiar name, *Armageddon*.

Because of these differing viewpoints, it's worthwhile to review what the Bible teaches about these distinct wars that collectively can be called, *World War III*. We will supply an overview of each of them in this chapter.

War I – The Battle of Those Who Know God by Another Name

The establishment of modern Israel in its native land is hardly the end of the matter of Jewish redemption. The Bible predicts that this event will set in motion a series of wars that will ultimately lead to the grandiose conflict between the *Antichrist* (dominated by Satan) and the *Messiah of Israel* who Christians profess is Jesus Christ. Many students of prophecy are aware of the so-called *Battle of Gog and Magog*. Most everyone is familiar with the notion of Armageddon. But few know that the Bible details yet another battle that appears to precede these other two wars; this war may be necessary to arrange the chess pieces before the "game" begins.[9]

The first war appears to be discussed in *Psalm 83*. We read of numerous tribes surrounding the Hebrews that equate to today's Lebanon, Syria, Jordan, and even the Palestinians. We see how *all* of these nations conspire together against their mortal enemy, Israel, to destroy them and *take away their land*:

¹Keep not thou silence, O God: hold not thy peace, and be not still, O God.

²For, lo, thine enemies make a tumult: and they that hate thee have lifted up the head.

³They have taken crafty counsel against thy people, and consulted against thy hidden ones.

⁴They have said, Come, and let us cut them off from being a nation; that the name of Israel may be no more in remembrance.

⁵For they have consulted together with one consent: they are confederate against thee:

*⁶The tabernacles of **Edom**, and the Ishmaelites; of **Moab**, and the Hagarenes;*

*⁷Gebal, and **Ammon**, and Amalek; the Philistines with the inhabitants of Tyre;*

⁸Assur also is joined with them: they have holpen the children of Lot. Selah.

⁹Do unto them as unto the Midianites; as to Sisera, as to Jabin, at the brook of Kison:

¹⁰Which perished at Endor: they became as dung for the earth.

11Make their nobles like Oreb, and like Zeeb: yea, all their princes as Zebah, and as Zalmunna:

12Who said, Let us take to ourselves the houses of God in possession.

13O my God, make them like a wheel; as the stubble before the wind.

14As the fire burneth a wood, and as the flame setteth the mountains on fire;

15So persecute them with thy tempest, and make them afraid with thy storm.

16Fill their faces with shame; that they may seek thy name, O LORD.

17Let them be confounded and troubled for ever; yea, let them be put to shame, and perish:

*18That men may know that thou, **whose name alone is JEHOVAH**, art the most high over all the earth.*

Chuck Missler, a leading authority on apocalyptic themes, recently began promoting this alternate view – which amounts to the next war between Israel and her neighbors. In his opinion, there will be a war between Israel and her Arab neighbors that's *round one* – it sets the stage for the subsequent Battle of

Gog and Magog. Missler points out that the nations listed in Psalm 83 are absent in the combatants list in the next two battles the Bible describes. Missler also identifies how the Psalmist underscores that the opponents to Israel mentioned in Psalm 83 don't realize they misunderstand God's proper name. In verse 18, the Psalmist asserts that God's name is YHWH or as usually translated, *"the LORD"* (YHWH has been translated by almost all versions of the Bible as LORD; but actually it could be translated and pronounced either as *Jehovah* or *Yahweh*). Is this clarification meant to underscore the fact that God's name *is not Allah?*

This seems precisely to be the

FIGURE 66 - NATIONS SURROUNDING JUDAH NEAR THE DEAD SEA

point. It's easy to forget that the God of the Bible doesn't "go by" the generic name *God*. Because we capitalize "God" when referring to the Judeo-Christian God, we may miss this point, assuming that this minor distinction is sufficient. But in contrast to our customs, *the name of the Hebrew God is a proper name*. And Allah isn't it.

Another relevant passage, which seems to reflect the same battle, is found in *Isaiah, Chapter 11:11-14 (emphasis mine)*.

> [11]*And it shall come to pass in that day, that **the Lord shall set his hand again the second time to recover the remnant of his people,** which shall be left, from Assyria, and from Egypt, and from Pathros, and from Cush, and from Elam, and from Shinar, and from Hamath, and from the islands of the sea.*

> [12]*And he shall set up an ensign for the nations, and shall assemble the outcasts of Israel, and **gather together the dispersed of Judah from the four corners of the earth.***

> [13]*The envy also of Ephraim shall depart, and the adversaries of Judah shall be cut off: **Ephraim** shall not envy Judah, and Judah shall not vex Ephraim.*

> [14]*But they shall fly upon the shoulders of the Philistines toward the west; they shall spoil them of the east together: they shall lay their hand upon **Edom** and **Moab**; and the children of **Ammon** shall obey them.*

Verses 11 and 12 clearly show that the re-gathering of Israel isn't just from the Middle East. It's from around the world. There is no historical precedent for a world-wide re-gathering. And this re-gathering is "for a second time."[10] From *whence* are they brought back to Israel? They return from *"the islands of the sea"* (this infers distant continents) and *"from the four corners of the earth."* Isaiah, like Ezekiel, predicts that Israel will be brought together again and will ultimately defeat those who seek to destroy Israel. *"Those who harass Judah will be cut off."* Israel will swoop down on the Philistines (typically to the south of Jerusalem, perhaps identified with Gaza – historically (and today) – a habitation of the Palestinians). Israel will plunder the sons of the east which would include Edom and Moab (to the east and southeast, the territory known today as Jordan), and the sons of Ammon (to the northeast, a reference to Syria). Interestingly, Ephraim, directly north of Israel, today's Lebanon, will not be jealous of Judah and Judah will not harass Lebanon. *This is eerily consistent with the political state of affairs during the past several decades.* While Hezbollah supported by the Syrians and Iranians, continues to threaten northern Israel from Lebanese territory, the government of Lebanon itself (until just recently) has been against the violence and has sought peace. So why is Lebanon not an enemy to Israel? History may have something to do with it. The land immediately north of Judah was the first "mission field" of the early Christians. It was at Antioch to the north that the followers of Jesus were first called, *Christians*. Perhaps the actions of the people of Ephraim remain a blessing to Lebanon to this day. And remember, this was prophesied almost 2,700 years ago.

The goal of the enemies to Israel in these passages is to "wipe it off the map" (or as Ahmadinejad proclaims, "A World without Zionism"). The battle is over *land*. This goal is different from the motives of the enemies of Israel in the Battle of Gog and Magog; the goal of that alliance is to "take spoil" as we will read shortly.

However, another startling passage that prophecy experts often cite as a future prediction yet to be fulfilled is the *destruction of Damascus*. This event has "stood out like a sore thumb" with scholars not knowing where to place it prophetically. But with the notion of a *third war* that is actually the first, preceding the Battle of Gog and Magog and Armageddon, it could easily be placed chronologically in the context of this first war, *the war of Psalm 83 and Isaiah 11*. We would see the destruction of *one of the world's longest inhabited cities* (meaning it has never been destroyed before) happening at this moment. Indeed, its desolation is prophesied in Isaiah:

¹ *The burden of Damascus. Behold, Damascus is taken away from being a city, and it shall be a ruinous heap.*

² *The cities of Aroer are forsaken: they shall be for flocks, which shall lie down, and none shall make them afraid...*

¹⁴ *And behold at eveningtide trouble; and before the morning he is not. This is the portion of them that spoil us, and the lot of them that rob us.*

Could Damascus be obliterated as part of a future war between Israel and its surrounding neighbors? Today's apocalyptic scholars agree this is Damascus' destiny and may not be far from happening. It's also possible that this first battle, the first war of World War III, has already been underway and we've been living through it for the past 62 years. The final event of this first battle is *the destruction of Damascus.* If so, the next battle looms on the horizon with an unmistakable climax.

War II – Gog and Magog

The Book of Ezekiel, chapters 38 and 39, describes the land of Gog and Magog, along with identifying other peoples (e.g., Rosh, Meshech, Tubal), that refer to tribes settling to the far north of Israel after the flood of Noah. Most conservative scholars believe that Gog and Magog are today's Russian people and the peoples geographically associated with them. These ancient names are the source for today's Russia and Moscow, while Tubal historically refers to the location of a tribe that settled in Eastern Europe. Furthermore, there is strong support that the people in ancient times knew Gog and Magog as the *Scythians*. Some Arab cultures referred to the Great Wall of China as *the Wall of Gog and Magog* (a wall built to keep Gog and Magog *out* of China!) Others suggest that Gog and Magog refer to tribes that settled in East Germany or Turkey. The Bible is clear that it's the peoples far to the north of Israel, which will come against the recently re-gathered Jews.

Here is how Ezekiel prophesies these events in Chapter 38:1-9:

¹And the word of the LORD came unto me, saying,

²Son of man, set thy face against Gog, the land of Magog, the chief prince of Meshech and Tubal, and prophesy against him,

³And say, Thus saith the Lord GOD; Behold, I am against thee, O Gog, the chief prince of Meshech and Tubal:

⁴And I will turn thee back, and put hooks into thy jaws, and I will bring thee forth, and all thine army, horses and horsemen, all of them clothed with all sorts of armour, even a great company with bucklers and shields, all of them handling swords:

⁵Persia, Ethiopia, and Libya with them; all of them with shield and helmet:

⁶Gomer, and all his bands; the house of Togarmah of the north quarters, and all his bands: and many people with thee.

⁷Be thou prepared, and prepare for thyself, thou, and all thy company that are assembled unto thee, and be thou a guard unto them.

⁸After many days thou shalt be visited: in the latter years thou shalt come into the land that is brought back from the sword, and is gathered out of many people, against the mountains of Israel, which have been always waste: but it is brought forth out of the nations, and they shall dwell safely all of them.

⁹Thou shalt ascend and come like a storm, thou shalt be like a cloud to cover the land, thou, and all thy bands, and many people with thee.

The prophet Ezekiel indicates that in the latter days there will be a coalition of nations led by Russia against Israel that includes Turkey (*Gomer and Beth-togarmah*), Persia (modern Iran), Libya (*Put*), and Ethiopia. Recall that these nations, especially Iran (*Persia*) are *not* mentioned in Psalm 83. This alliance is also unprecedented. Persia and Russia have not been allied in 2,500 years of recorded history. This predicted alliance was one of the primary reasons that doubting scholars in times past scoffed at the predictions in Ezekiel. But Ezekiel says this consortium will come together, *"in the latter years, after the inhabitants of Israel have been gathered from many nations to the mountains of Israel to the mountains of Israel which had been a continual waste."* Unlike the former battle with the immediate neighbors of Israel, this coalition will seek *"spoil."* And certain nations will sit back and do nothing. Continuing from Ezekiel 38:

10Thus saith the Lord GOD; It shall also come to pass, that at the same time shall things come into thy mind, and thou shalt think an evil thought:

*11And thou shalt say, **I will go up to the land of unwalled villages;** I will go to them that are at rest, that dwell safely, all of them **dwelling without walls,** and having neither bars nor gates,*

12To take a spoil, and to take a prey; to turn thine hand upon the desolate places that are now inhabited, and upon the people that are gathered out of the nations, which have gotten cattle and goods, that dwell in the midst of the land.

*13**Sheba, and Dedan, and the merchants of Tarshish**, with all the young lions thereof, shall say unto thee, Art thou come to take a spoil? hast thou gathered thy company to take a prey? to carry away silver and gold, to take away cattle and goods, to take a great spoil?*

Who are the nations that do nothing to come to the aid of Israel? Scholars insist that *Sheba and Dedan* refer to today's Saudi Arabia while the *merchants of Tarshish* likely refers to Spain or to ships that sailed the Mediterranean, likely a reference to the nations of Europe. We can readily hypothesize that should Russia attack Israel today, it's certainly probable that Saudi Arabia and Europe would protest, but take no military action just as verse 13 asserts.

At the time of this attack, Israel is *"living in a land of unwalled villages… villages… who are at rest, living securely"* (as translated by the New American Standard Version). Missler infers that the first war between Israel and her neighbors has placed Israel in a time of peace where it feels secure. But today there is a giant wall that separates East Jerusalem from the rest of the country. Israel isn't *unwalled*. From his perspective, something must happen that dramatically changes the current political situation in Jerusalem before the War of Gog and Magog could come to pass. That's why he presses the "alternative view" of the first war we've described. On the other hand, Joel Rosenberg, author of many books predicting the events leading up to and including the War of Gog and Magog, sees it differently. He believes that in many ways, peace is more real today in Israel that at any time since 1948. He quotes various authorities to cinch his argument. Rosenberg, also a Dispensationalist, interprets the "unwalled villages" as a metaphor of security gained not by "walls" but by diplomatic means. Since 1973, Israel has experienced progressively greater security despite occasional outbreaks of terrorism.

For the past two hundred years, even before Russia gained prominence as a world power, Bible scholars proposed that this battle would transpire just before or at the beginning of the Tribulation period (aka, *Daniel's 70th Week*). Evangelical scholars distinguish this battle from the final battle of Armageddon *as the participants and circumstances are quite distinct.* The description of the battle in Ezekiel indicates that the God of Israel comes to the aid of Israel. Against all odds, the LORD strikes down the armies of Gog and Magog. This demonstrates to the world that the God of Israel is alive and protecting His people. In Chapter 39, we read this amazingly detailed description:

7So will I make my holy name known in the midst of my people Israel; and I will not let them pollute my holy name any more: and the heathen shall know that I am the LORD, the Holy One in Israel.

8Behold, it is come, and it is done, saith the Lord GOD; this is the day whereof I have spoken.

*9And they that dwell in the cities of Israel shall go forth, and shall set on fire and burn the weapons, both the shields and the bucklers, the bows and the arrows, and the handstaves, and the spears, and they shall burn them with fire **seven years:***

10So that they shall take no wood out of the field, neither cut down any out of the forests; for they shall burn the weapons with fire: and they shall spoil those that spoiled them, and rob those that robbed them, saith the Lord GOD.

11And it shall come to pass in that day, that I will give unto Gog a place there of graves in Israel, the valley of the passengers on the east of the sea: and it shall stop the noses of the passengers: and there shall they bury Gog and all his multitude: and they shall call it The valley of Hamongog.

12And seven months shall the house of Israel be burying of them, that they may cleanse the land.

13Yea, all the people of the land shall bury them; and it shall be to them a renown the day that I shall be glorified, saith the Lord GOD.

14And they shall sever out men of continual employment, passing through the land to bury with the passengers those that remain upon the face of the earth, to cleanse it: after the end of seven months shall they search.

15And the passengers that pass through the land, when any seeth a man's bone, then shall he set up a sign by it, till the buriers have buried it in the valley of Hamongog.

16And also the name of the city shall be Hamonah. **Thus shall they cleanse the land.**

The explanation of what will happen seems like an *anachronism* – not only unlikely but chronologically out of sequence – unless one is thinking in terms of a war involving weapons whose substance could be used for fuel. However, such substances do exist today. And bows and arrows don't burn for seven years! Plus, the land itself appears contaminated and must be cleansed. Specialists will be commissioned to cleanse the land. The immensity of the problem of burying the dead is so great *it will take seven months to complete.* A careful search will be undertaken to make sure all of the dead have been buried. It takes little imagination to conclude that the nature of the battle involves some manner of nuclear or biological warfare. We can almost see these technicians walking around the desert in their hazmat suits. The detail of this passage is truly astounding as it depicts precisely what will happen to the battlefield after the War of Gog and Magog is finished.

When Does the War between Gog and Magog Occur?

Despite this peculiar information speaking to a future conflict uncharacteristic of Bible times, some prophecy scholars suggest that *this battle has already taken place.* Since the language used is of horses, crossbows and ancient types of warfare, it seems a literalist interpretation could not easily substitute these weapons for atom bombs or biological armaments. Of course, the counter argument from the other side contends that the events depicted are not easily associated with any former historical event when such an alignment of nations collectively made war on Israel. In this case, Ezekiel may have employed the names of archaic weapons metaphorically since he had no other words available for their depiction. That is one of the problems with taking things *too literally* since some literal statements aren't empirically accurate and aren't meant to be, especially when the category of fact is beyond the scope and capacity of the writers' language.

This section of scripture points out that the battle is in *the latter days*, which is an idiom slightly different from *the last days* and may suggest that the battle happens just *before the last days*. It does seem evident that the battle is not referring to any event that transpired prior to the first advent of the Messiah in 1 BC. In the New Testament book, *The Acts of the Apostles*, Peter quotes the prophet Joel to the masses shortly after the resurrection of Jesus. Here he uses the phrase "the last days." By doing so, Peter asserts that the epoch of *The Last Days* had therefore arrived. However, soon afterwards, Israel ceased to exist and remained dispersed for almost 1,900 years. Was the timing of *The Last Days* reset because of the Jewish nation's rejection of Messiah and His message? Was it reset to some point far into the future? Or was Peter simply mistaken about the day in which he lived? As I've argued elsewhere, this period could have been *the Last Days* – because there was an element of contingency. The outcome ultimately depended upon whether or not the Jews of that time chose to accept Jesus as their Messiah. Once it was decided Jesus didn't fit their framework and they rejected him, *The Last Days* were delayed. 2,000 years later, in our day it appears these battles could transpire in a few short years if not sooner.[11]

To clarify, it's logically necessary that the Battle of Gog and Magog happens *after* Israel comes together again and is restored. Since the description of the battle follows the passage we studied at the outset, the *Valley of Dry Bones* in Ezekiel 37, the latter days must refer to a time near the coming of the Jewish Messiah (which, for Christians, is the second coming of *Jesus Christ*) but may not be the same as a Battle within *The Last Days* also known as the *Day of the Lord*. Most commentators for the past 150 years have argued that the Battle of Gog and Magog is the next key event that must transpire leading the world into the Tribulation period, notwithstanding the War of Psalm 83 and Isaiah 11 that Missler has proposed (but which I believe may be depicting the ongoing conflict in the Middle East). Traditionally, Dispensationalists have predicted that if we witness a battle between Israel and the several nations led by Russia, through God's intervention Israel will miraculously prevail; secondly, *we should then begin the countdown to Armageddon.*

Because of this widespread perspective, students of prophecy seek to know what's happening behind the scenes with Russia and Iran. Are we now traveling down a path to war between Iran and Israel? Without a doubt, as we witness in the 2010 news, Iran continues to build extensive nuclear capability with Russian assistance. Those who study prophecy are very much on the edge of their seats since Russia has re-emerged as a power to *be reckoned with* in this new Millennium, and since it opposes the interests of the West once again. And as stated above, for the first time in recorded history, Russia and Iran are allies.

Rosenberg cites the words of former Iranian President Ali Akbar Hashemi-Rafsanjani shortly after the September 11, 2001 attacks on the World Trade Center and the Pentagon.

> On December 14, 2001, the Iran Press Service ran a story entitled **"Rafsanjani Says Muslims Should Use Nuclear Weapon against Israel."** According to the story, Rafsanjani asserted that a nuclear attack would "annihilate Israel," while costing Iran "damages only." He said, "If a day comes when the world of Islam is duly equipped with the arms Israel has in possession, the strategy of colonialism would face a stalemate because application of an atomic bomb would not leave anything in Israel but the same thing would just produce damages in the Muslim world." The article pointed out that… [it was] the first time that a prominent leader of the Islamic Republic openly suggest[ed] the use of a nuclear weapon against the Jewish State.

That was 10 years ago. And recall that Rafsanjani lost the election to an *even more radical personage*, Mahmud Ahmadinejad. Should Israel take military action against Iran, almost all prophecy experts will speculate the Battle of Gog and Magog is about to begin. As I write this chapter, *the possibility of hostility between Israel and Iran continues to increase.* The United States, under the current administration, steadily moves further away from military and political support for Israel, making the possibility of unilateral action by Israel more probable than ever.

It's also quite important to notice that the wording used in this passage suggests that this event is perhaps on the same level as the *Exodus, the most important salvation event in the history of Israel.* This event convinces the nation of Israel that God (aka *Yahweh*) does exist and that He, and He alone, has decreed their salvation. While today most Israelis are atheists or agnostics, that may be about to change. Furthermore, despite the fact that the names, "Gog and Magog" may be unfamiliar to most readers, *there is more detail about this battle than there is about the Battle of Armageddon.* Consequently, we should understand that the Battle of Gog and Magog is an enormously important event not only because it shakes up the political order of things, *but also because it's the single most significant episode that effectively reconciles Israel to Jehovah.*

War III: The Grand Finale – Armageddon

Armageddon is the English transliteration of the Hebrew, *Harmegiddo,* or the *Mountain of Megiddo.* Megiddo is in northern Israel. Megiddo is a valley with a wide and expansive plane that even Napoleon, upon seeing it declared could indeed contain all the armies of the world at one time. Most don't realize that Napoleon attempted, unsuccessfully, to conquer Palestine and create a homeland for the Jews in 1799. As mentioned earlier in this book, he went so far as to publish a letter on April 20, 1799, to Jews worldwide to encourage them to return to the Holy Land. After learning from his uncle, a Bishop in Paris, that the return of the Jews to their land was a precursor to "the end of the world," he immediately ceased his efforts.[12]

Armageddon is destined to be the final battle – the third of the three wars of World War III – it's the culmination of the *Apocalypse* and the *Day of the Lord* (or *Day of Jesus Christ* in the New Testament). According to Revelation, Chapter 16:

[12]*And the sixth angel poured out his vial upon the great river Euphrates; and the water thereof was dried up, that the way of the kings of the east might be prepared.*

[13]*And I saw three unclean spirits like frogs come out of the mouth of the dragon, and out of the mouth of the beast, and out of the mouth of the false prophet.*

[14]*For they are the spirits of devils, working miracles, which go forth unto the kings of the earth and of the whole world, to gather them to the battle of that great day of God Almighty.*

[15]*Behold, I come as a thief. Blessed is he that watcheth, and keepeth his garments, lest he walk naked, and they see his shame.*

[16]*And he gathered them together into a place called in the Hebrew tongue* **Armageddon.**

Clarifying the Battles of the Last Days

But how do we know that the battles of (1) Gog and Magog and (2) Armageddon are in fact *distinctive clashes?* As we noted above, Ezekiel tells us that after the Magog war, Israel will bury the dead for seven months and burn the weapons used by Gog and Magog for seven years (Chapter 39:9-11). John tells us that after the battle of Armageddon – the Messiah, Jesus Christ – immediately returns to set up his Kingdom on the earth. The Battle of Gog and Magog involves the hordes of peoples immediately north of Israel, along with Libya, Ethiopia, and Persia (Iran). The Battle of Armageddon is fought between the Antichrist and nations from all over the world (Isaiah 13:4, Zechariah 12:3), 'headlined' by the *Kings of the East* who bring an army of 200,000,000 through Asia (and across the *Euphrates River*, the ancient dividing line between *the east and the west*).

John indicates also about this final battle, that it's the battle of the *great day of our Lord.* The *Day of the Lord* or the *Day of Jesus Christ* is mentioned scores of times throughout the Scripture as the final event to which all of history is heading. Here are just a few examples:

Alas for the day! for the **day of the LORD** *is at hand, and as a destruction from the Almighty shall it come. (Joel 1:15)*

And the LORD shall utter his voice before his army: for his camp is very great: for he is strong that executeth his word: for the **day of the LORD** *is great and very terrible; and who can abide it? (Joel 2:11)*

Woe unto you that desire the **day of the LORD***! to what end is it for you? the* **day of the LORD** *is darkness, and not light. (Amos 5:18)*

The great **day of the LORD** *is near, it is near, and hasteth greatly, even the voice of the day of the LORD: the mighty man shall cry there bitterly. (Zephanish 1:14)*

For this is the **day of the Lord** *GOD of hosts, a day of vengeance, that he may avenge him of his adversaries: and the sword shall devour, and it shall be satiate and made drunk with their blood: for the Lord GOD of hosts hath a sacrifice in the north country by the river Euphrates. (Jeremiah 46:10)*

For several decades it's been debated whether any nation could field an army of 200 million. Back in the 1970's, China boasted that it could achieve this astronomical number. It was used as a data point by some writers such as Hal Lindsey to validate a *literal interpretation of this passage.*

It's remarkable that John selected this number given the population of the entire world in the first century was likely much less than this number. But John expressly states, *apparently to reinforce it was no mistake,* "I heard the number of them." It was as if he said, "Yep, that's right – 200 million troops – I heard it with my very own ears."

We read this in Revelation, Chapter 9:

13And the sixth angel sounded, and I heard a voice from the four horns of the golden altar which is before God,

14Saying to the sixth angel which had the trumpet, Loose the four angels which are bound in the great river Euphrates.

15And the four angels were loosed, which were prepared for an hour, and a day, and a month, and a year, for to slay the third part of men.

*16And the number of the army of the horsemen were two hundred thousand thousand: and **I heard the number of them.***

Armageddon and the Battle for Jerusalem

Oftentimes, we use Armageddon as a descriptive noun to include all the events associated with the Apocalypse. However, we should remember that Armageddon is a *place*. Specifically, it is a mountain (Megiddo) and a valley (also known by some as Jezreel) near the Sea of Galilee and Nazareth—Jesus' hometown (in fact, while growing up Jesus could look across the valley from his village every day). Secondly, as we stated above, Armageddon is a specific battle at the very end of the *Great Tribulation* period. At its conclusion, Jesus Christ returns.[13]

John the author of Revelation is not the only prophet to speak of this final battle. Paul the Apostle and most of the great prophets of the Hebrews, notably including Jeremiah, Joel and Zechariah all refer to *the Day of the Lord and offer further details*. There are passages elsewhere that talk of the battle for Jerusalem and seem to imply that *these are part of the same conflict*. We read the words of Zechariah (from Zechariah Chapter 12):

*3And in that day will I make Jerusalem a burdensome stone for all people: all that burden themselves with it shall be cut in pieces, though **all the people of the earth** be gathered together against it.*

⁴In that day, saith the LORD, I will smite every horse with astonishment, and his rider with madness: and I will open mine eyes upon the house of Judah, and will smite every horse of the people with blindness.

⁵And the governors of Judah shall say in their heart, The inhabitants of Jerusalem shall be my strength in the LORD of hosts their God.

⁶In that day will I make the governors of Judah like an hearth of fire among the wood, and like a torch of fire in a sheaf; and they shall devour all the people round about, on the right hand and on the left: and Jerusalem shall be inhabited again in her own place, even in Jerusalem.

⁷The LORD also shall save the tents of Judah first, that the glory of the house of David and the glory of the inhabitants of Jerusalem do not magnify themselves against Judah.

⁸In that day shall the LORD defend the inhabitants of Jerusalem; and he that is feeble among them at that day shall be as David; and the house of David shall be as God, as the angel of the LORD before them.

*⁹And it shall come to pass in that day, that I will seek to destroy **all the nations** that come against Jerusalem.*

The prophet indicates that *all the nations of the earth*, not just the list from Ezekiel 38, are gathered against Israel. He indicates that Jerusalem (i.e., Israel) will be seen as *the* enemy that all the nations agree *must be utterly destroyed.* However, Ezekiel indicates that the issue of Jerusalem will be like an immovable rock. Is this not a clear and unprecedented fulfillment of biblical prophecy in our day? Whoever tries to make the situation better seems to only make it worse for daring to do so. England's empire experienced it's twilight by fumbling the political process in the Middle East between World Wars I and II. America is hemorrhaging monies and lives in Iraq and Afghanistan primarily because it's trying to settle the question of Jerusalem (and the plight of the Palestinians). The Holy City is *the burdensome stone* – the immovable rock – that harms those who dare seek to move it.

Next, we read that God confuses the nations and blinds them. Furthermore, we learn that Messiah will first *secure* Jerusalem (verses 7 and 8), before going north to fight *His enemies at Armageddon.* This coincides with Zechariah's later prophecy that says that Christ will return first on the Mount of Olives and His touching-down will cause a great earthquake, the mount itself to split, and waters to gush forth forming new rivers, one to the Mediterranean Sea and the other running to the Dead Sea.

We read from Chapter 14 of Zechariah:

Zech 14 (handwritten annotation)

⁴*And his feet shall stand in that day upon the mount of Olives, which is before Jerusalem on the east, and the mount of Olives* **shall cleave in the midst** *thereof toward the east and toward the west, and there shall be a very great valley; and half of the mountain shall remove toward the north, and half of it toward the south.*

⁵*And ye shall flee to the valley of the mountains; for the valley of the mountains shall reach unto Azal: yea, ye shall flee, like as ye fled from before the earthquake in the days of Uzziah king of Judah: and* **the LORD my God shall come, and all the saints with thee.**

⁶*And it shall come to pass in that day, that the light shall not be clear, nor dark:*

⁷*But it shall be one day which shall be known to the LORD,* **not day, nor night:** *but it shall come to pass, that at evening time it shall be light.*

⁸*And it shall be in that day, that living waters shall go out from Jerusalem; half of them toward the former sea, and half of them toward the hinder sea: in summer and in winter shall it be.*

Zechariah proclaims that this day will be a day of darkness that will remain dark until evening and then light will return. Isaiah 13:10, confirms the same phenomena:

¹⁰*For the stars of heaven and the constellations thereof shall* **not give their light:** *the* **sun shall be darkened** *in his going forth, and* **the moon shall not cause her light to shine.**

When the Lord returns, whom Zechariah calls *"my God"* in 12:5 (Note: Zechariah identifies the Messiah as God, a non-orthodox Jewish view), *all of his holy ones will come with him.* This same idea is also contained in the book of Jude, in which Jude quotes from the book of Enoch (Jude 14 and 15):

See Rev 19:11 (handwritten annotation)

¹⁴*And Enoch also, the seventh from Adam, prophesied of these, saying, Behold,* **the Lord cometh with ten thousands of his saints,**

¹⁵*To execute judgment upon all, and to convince all that are ungodly among them of all their ungodly deeds which they have ungodly committed, and of all their hard speeches which ungodly sinners have spoken against him.*

These holy ones are not angels. Perhaps you may be surprised that most Bible pundits argue they're the previously *raptured* believers (the 'Saints'). These saints were raptured either immediately prior to the Messiah's return—the *traditional* Christian position, or *several years earlier*—the

Dispensational position).   In the book of Joel, Chapter 3, we read an extensive passage that refers to the *Valley of Jehoshaphat* (meaning "YHWH judges" according to the Jewish Encyclopedia).   There is no clear identification geographically of where this valley is.   It could be the Valley of Megiddo, or it could be the Kidron Valley outside of Jerusalem where tradition holds the last judgment will occur.   But the events described are clearly part of the *Day of the Lord*.   Note again, the timing of this event is when "the Lord brings down *His mighty ones*" placing it at His return, suggesting that the Valley of Jehoshaphat in this context is Armageddon.

Joel 3

¹*For, behold, in those days, and in that time, when I shall bring again the captivity of Judah and Jerusalem,*

²*I **will also gather all nations,** and will bring them down into the valley of Jehoshaphat, and will plead with them there for my people and for my heritage Israel, whom **they have scattered among the nations**, and parted my land...*

⁹*Proclaim ye this among the Gentiles; Prepare war, **wake up the mighty men**, let all the men of war draw near; let them come up:*

¹⁰*Beat your plowshares into swords and your pruning hooks into spears: let the weak say, I am strong.*

¹¹*Assemble yourselves, and come, all ye heathen, and gather yourselves together round about: thither cause **thy mighty ones to come down,** O LORD.*

¹²*Let the heathen be wakened, and come up to the valley of Jehoshaphat: for there will I sit to judge all the heathen round about.*

¹³*Put ye in the sickle, for the harvest is ripe: come, get you down; for the press is full, the fats overflow; for their wickedness is great.*

¹⁴*Multitudes, multitudes in the valley of decision: for the day of the LORD is near in the valley of decision.*

¹⁵*The sun and the moon shall be darkened, and the stars shall withdraw their shining.*

Importantly, Zechariah 12:10 adds that it's at this time that the residents of Israel no longer reject Jesus as Messiah.   We read:

¹⁰*And I will pour upon the house of David, and upon the inhabitants of Jerusalem, the spirit of grace and of supplications: and **they shall look upon me whom they have pierced, and they shall mourn for him, as one mourneth***

for his only son, and **shall be in bitterness for him, as one that is in bitterness for his firstborn.**

At this time, Christians believe that Israel will understand that their Messiah is in fact Jesus Christ, "the one they have pierced" (referring to the wounds He received at His crucifixion). After 2,000 years of denial, they will embrace the one they previously rejected. Christians and Jews will unite in worship of the Jehovah and His Son Jesus Christ. The *Dry Bones* won't just be raised from the dead, they are reanimated by the Spirit of the Lord, and *He will dwell within them.* As Paul says (in Romans Chapter 10):

11For the scripture saith, Whosoever believeth on him shall not be ashamed.

12For there is no difference between the Jew and the Greek: for the same Lord over all is rich unto all that call upon him.

13For whosoever shall call upon the name of the Lord shall be saved.

And also in Romans Chapter 11:

25For I would not, brethren that ye should be ignorant of this mystery, lest ye should be wise in your own conceits; that **blindness in part is happened to Israel, until the fulness of the Gentiles be come in.**

26And **so all Israel shall be saved:** *as it is written, There shall come out of Sion (Zion) the Deliverer, and shall turn away ungodliness from Jacob:*

27For this is my covenant unto them, when I shall take away their sins.

Evangelical Christians believe there are three battles in World War III while Orthodox Jews believe there are two. But both believe that at the culmination of these wars, Messiah comes. *It remains the culminating work of God* to awaken both Jews and Christians to the *identity* of His Messiah – *Messiah* being a biblical precept held in common; while today His identity continues to be a point of irreconcilable dispute. But that dispute amongst those who worship the God of the Bible is destined to be put to bed – and very soon as we move from "the latter days" to "the last days" and ultimately, to "the Day of the Lord."

Notes

[1]Although we should be note that Professor Bush's book on Mohammed was not particularly well received in Egypt during 2004 when it was pointed out that an ancestor to President Bush had commented on Islam. It created quite a stir. Bush's preference was to refer to Mohammed as "the Imposter." Not exactly a title that engenders Muslim support.

[2] The interpretation of the Rabbis was different from both of these of course. They believed the meaning is just the resurrection, *bodily*, of individual Jews at the beginning of the Messianic (Davidic) Kingdom.

[3] They also noted how Bush steered clear of the radical "millenarian speculation" espoused by those like Mr. Miller (the Millerites) who was notorious at the same time.

[4] Bush was the offspring of a brother, Timothy, an ancestor to the Bush family of 21st century fame, according to a short biography of an exhibition about him at the New York Public Library. In 1845, Bush became carried away with his apocalyptic fervor, leaving his Presbyterian commitment behind, joining Emanuel Swedenborg, founder of a far flung cult named after him, focusing on the 2nd Coming with occult overtones; therefore, he wound up adhering to a very **non**-orthodox approach. Professor Bush had earlier commented that the New Jerusalem and Temple later described in Ezekiel was a ridiculous concept; nevertheless, he believed *the prophecy regarding a revival of Israel as a political entity* was to be taken literally.

[5] The previous chapter, Ezekiel 36, is equally emphatic and clear about this unconditional promise (God will do this *in spite of* what Judah does by profaning God's name among the nations):

> [24]*For I will take you from among the heathen, and gather you out of all countries, and will bring you into your own land.*
>
> [25]*Then will I sprinkle clean water upon you, and ye shall be clean: from all your filthiness, and from all your idols, will I cleanse you.*
>
> [26]*A new heart also will I give you, and a new spirit will I put within you: and I will take away the stony heart out of your flesh, and I will give you an heart of flesh.*
>
> [27]*And I will put my spirit within you, and cause you to walk in my statutes, and ye shall keep my judgments, and do them.*
>
> [28]*And ye shall dwell in the land that I gave to your fathers; and ye shall be my people, and I will be your God.*

[6] Lindsey's book has sold over 35 million copies to date while Tim LaHaye and Jerry Jenkins have sold over 60 million copies of their series of books on the Second Coming, known as the *"Left Behind"* series.

[7] Plain meaning affords that symbols are symbols, figures are figures, and prose or poetic language that strongly infers a "space-time" fulfillment as what the author intended should be taken seriously ("space-time" fulfillment being what most interpreters mean by using the word "literal"). Said another way, don't put words in the prophet's mouth just because what the prophet describes requires a supernaturally-caused event to make it come about.

[8] Elie Wiesel, *Elie Wiesel: Conversations,* ed. Robert Franciosi, Jackson: University Press of Mississippi, 2002, pg. 138. Cited by Joel C. Rosenberg, *Epicenter 2.0,* pg. Wheaton, IL: Tyndale House Publishers, pg. 200.

[9] Perhaps a regrettable analogy since war is no game.

[10] When Isaiah wrote this prophecy, the first dispersion into Assyria (7th century BC) and Babylon (6th century BC) had not yet occurred. He looks past the first dispersion and speaks to the second which is world-wide in scope. He is speaking of the 20th century.

[11] Consequently, the timing of God's actions regarding the salvation of the Jewish people may be contingent, but the matter of whether or not it ultimately occurs, is not contingent.

[12] Cited by David Flynn in his book, *The Temple at the Center of Time,* pg. 173, citing John Holland Rose, *The Personality of Napoleon,* pg. 243.

[13] The *Day of Christ Jesus* is used in Acts 5:42, I Corinthians 5:13, Philippians 1:6, I Corinthians 1:8, and in many other places. The New Testament teaches that the *Day of the Lord* and the *Day of Christ Jesus* are synonyms. This is yet another example of orthodox Christian teaching that the Messiah is fully divine.

Chapter 14:
The Return of the King

And they asked him, saying, "Master, but when shall these things be?
And what sign will there be when these things shall come to pass?"
"And when these things begin to come to pass, then look up, and lift up your heads;
for your redemption draweth nigh.

And he spake to them a parable; Behold the fig tree, and all the trees; When they now shoot
forth, ye see and know of your own selves that summer is now nigh at hand. So likewise ye,
when ye see these things come to pass, know ye that the kingdom of God is nigh at hand.
Verily I say unto you, This generation shall not pass away, till all be fulfilled. Heaven and
earth shall pass away: but my words shall not pass away."

(Luke 21:7, 28-33)

"The board is set. The pieces are moving."

Gandalf, from J.R.R. Tolkien's *The Return of the King*

The Olivet Discourse

Matthew, Mark and Luke provide the details of a prophetic dialogue between Jesus and His disciples on the Mount of Olives
just outside the walls of Jerusalem. Prompted by seeing the
Temple perched on the Temple Mount just across the valley, they noted
the beautiful gleaming white stones and the fantastic construction; the
disciples commented to Jesus how amazing the building was.

Certainly some scholars list the first Temple of Solomon as one of the
Seven Ancient Wonders of the World (built circa 960 BC and destroyed in
586 BC). Estimates suggest that the cost to build that edifice today with the
same amount of gold and silver used would exceed $70 billion. But even
the second Temple, begun by Zerubbabel in 538 BC and still under construction by the Herodians as Jesus walked the earth, was a work of art and
a testimony to the fact that the Jews were survivors, overcoming a millennium of chaos and hardship.

Perhaps Jesus sensed from their questioning an assumption on the part
of the disciples which was likely consistent amongst all the Jews of His day.
Jehovah had brought the Jews back from exile and had allowed them over
500 years to build and enhance the glorious Temple they celebrated. Alex-

ander the Great bypassed them in 321 BC.[1] 160 years later they defeated Antiochus IV Epiphanes in the Maccabean revolt. More recently, in 63 BC, they withstood Pompey of Rome and achieved an uneasy peace. The Temple still stood as did their religion when Jesus walked the earth.

However, Jesus responded by warning them that very shortly, in less than 40 years from that moment, all its stones would be torn apart and thrown down. The destruction of the Temple would put an end to the center of Jewish religion. What seemed inviolable and stalwart was destined for utter destruction. *As invincible as Judaism seemed and as indestructible as its Temple appeared, both were to be destroyed with only their very foundations remaining.*

FIGURE 67 - THE MOUNT OF OLIVES - PANORAMA

In a word, the disciples were *dumbfounded*. This led to serious concern over what would happen to the nation of Israel and to the Kingdom of God, which they along with their Master had proclaimed over the past three years. They had invested their livelihood and had left everything to help commence this movement. What did the destruction of the Temple mean to their nation, their religion and to what would become of them as followers of their Christ? Their faith in Christ was in some ways tied to their belief in the "rock solid foundation" of Judaism based upon this amazing building of stone.

Jesus launched into a vast series of predictions, partially to reassure them that there was a plan and they were very much a part of it. He prophesied in broad brush strokes and sometimes in detail, the next 2,000 years of His followers' future.

The discussion assumed that (1) Jesus would come again to set up His Kingdom and His coming would be (2) at the end of the age.[2] We can read this dialogue in Matthew's gospel, Chapter 24:

3And as he sat upon the mount of Olives, the disciples came unto him privately, saying, Tell us, when shall these things be? and what shall be the sign of thy coming, and of the end of the world?

4And Jesus answered and said unto them, Take heed that no man deceive you.

5For many shall come in my name, saying, I am Christ; and shall deceive many.

6And ye shall hear of wars and rumors of wars: see that ye be not troubled: for all these things must come to pass, but the end is not yet.

7For nation shall rise against nation, and kingdom against kingdom: and there shall be famines, and pestilences, and earthquakes, in divers places.

8All these are the beginning of sorrows.

9Then shall they deliver you up to be afflicted, and shall kill you: and ye shall be hated of all nations for my name's sake.

10And then shall many be offended, and shall betray one another, and shall hate one another.

11And many false prophets shall rise, and shall deceive many.

12And because iniquity shall abound, the love of many shall wax cold.

The age before them, Jesus warns His disciples, portends eight distressing realities. But as horrible as these events will be, they are *not* the signs that testify to the final apocalypse and His coming. These eight signs will be characteristic of the time immediately *after* His departure and *before* His return "in the clouds." These are the signs of what has been called, *The Church Age.*

Citing these predictions specifically, we can summarize them as follows:

- *False Christs will appear and deceive many (verses 4, 5).*
- *Wars and people talking about wars — nation against nation, kingdom against kingdom will be commonplace (verses 6, 7).*
- *People will go hungry (verse 7).*
- *There will be earthquakes in many places (verse 7).*
- *Christians will be persecuted in every nation (verse 9).*
- *Many who professed faith will fall away, hating and betraying one another (verse 10).*
- *False prophets will appear and deceive many (verse 11).*
- *Evil will grow and people will lose the ability to love (verse 12).*

These occurrences are often cited as the signs of the end. Jesus expressly indicates that they are *not* symbols of the end... but events which must first take place before the signs of the end come to the forefront. Afterwards, Jesus then speaks of very specific prophecies that are the actual signs of the Apocalypse:

14And this gospel of the kingdom shall be preached in all the world for a witness unto all nations; and then shall the end come.

15When ye therefore shall see the abomination of desolation, spoken of by Daniel the prophet, stand in the holy place, (whoso readeth, let him understand:)

16Then let them which be in Judaea flee into the mountains:

17Let him which is on the housetop not come down to take anything out of his house:

18Neither let him which is in the field return back to take his clothes.

19And woe unto them that are with child, and to them that give suck in those days!

20But pray ye that your flight be not in the winter, neither on the sabbath day:

21For then shall be great tribulation, such as was not since the beginning of the world to this time, no, nor ever shall be.

22And except those days should be shortened, there should no flesh be saved: but for the elect's sake those days shall be shortened.

23Then if any man shall say unto you, Lo, here is Christ, or there; believe it not.

24For there shall arise false Christs, and false prophets, and shall shew great signs and wonders; insomuch that, if it were possible, they shall deceive the very elect.

25Behold, I have told you before.

26Wherefore if they shall say unto you, Behold, he is in the desert; go not forth: behold, he is in the secret chambers; believe it not.

27For as the lightning cometh out of the east, and shineth even unto the west; so shall also the coming of the Son of man be.

28For wheresoever the carcase is, there will the eagles be gathered together.

29Immediately after the tribulation of those days shall the sun be darkened, and the moon shall not give her light, and the stars shall fall from heaven, and the powers of the heavens shall be shaken:

30And then shall appear the sign of the Son of man in heaven: and then shall all the tribes of the earth mourn, and they shall see the Son of man coming in the clouds of heaven with power and great glory.

In this last passage, Jesus identifies six specific occurrences that plainly *signal His coming a second time:*

- The *gospel must be preached throughout the entire world* (verse 14). Many scholars believe that while this has been accomplished before, with the advent of modern technology it's being completed in our generation in a way surpassing all others.

- The *abomination of desolation* must take place (verse 15). This is the most decisive and unmistakable sign. We have described how this may be fulfilled figuratively through biogenetic transformation. However, this does not exclude a literal fulfillment by the Antichrist when he claims to the entire world to be the "god-man" in a newly constituted Temple in Jerusalem.

- False Christs and false prophets *will appear that do great signs and miracles* (verse 24). Since Jesus had previously mentioned both false Christs and false prophets (verse 4, 5, and 11), we could surmise that this third mention underscores something vastly more alarming about the frequent frauds that appear throughout the past 2,000 years. This may be a specific reference to the *Antichrist* and the *False Prophet*. Certainly the performance of *"great signs and miracles"* would be consistent with this conclusion. His metaphors *"far out into the desert"* and *"deep inside the house"* infer that all such 'christs' are easily detected when they are described as isolated and distant – it's therefore obvious that the true Christ won't come in secret! It will be a public display of power and authority over the Antichrist and his armies.[3]

- *Lightning that comes from the east can be seen in the west* (verse 27). Traditional commentators regard this metaphor as the mode of Christ's return: *Sudden, brilliant light, public, and seen by all.* In context with the previous contrast between the hidden false Christ and the real Christ, this would be the most likely meaning. This sign may be startling coming apparently after an extended period of time of darkness during the day and light during the night. Time will be difficult to detect with daytime darkness (refer to the "bright-night effect" discussed in Chapter 5 for what might be a possible explanation). Perhaps this fulfills *"no man will know the day or the hour."*

- *Signs in the heavens that are unmistakable*—the sun is darkened, the moon turns to blood, stars fall from the sky and *"the heavenly bodies are shaken"* (verse 29). Astronomical events like eclipses would seem to be far too commonplace to be the fulfillment of such signs. The fact that heavenly bodies "are shaken" suggests that something extraordinary will happen to the sun or moon beyond a mere change in appearance. The possibility of the sun storm as described in Chapter 5 could be a reasonable interpretation.

- The *"sign of the Son of Man will appear in the sky"* (verse 30). This could easily be interpreted as a spectral image of the cross appearing in the heaven. But how this will be accomplished or how it might actually appear if literally fulfilled we could only imagine. Chances are this sign appears only moments before Christ emerges along with *His mighty ones* – the Saints.

The Rapture

However, *the return of the King,* according to Dispensationalists, comes in two phases. *The first phase is very secret, the second very public.* We have just discussed the coming of Christ visibly to the earth. This appearance is for "all to see." Nonetheless, there are many verses in the Christian New Testament that speak of a secret coming of Christ just for His believers. This is the controversial secret coming of the King called *the Rapture.*

In the Apostles Creed, one of the creedal assertions is that "we believe in the resurrection of *the quick* and the dead." Immediately after Christ has resurrected the dead, then "the *quick" (which* refers to the *raptured* believers) meet Christ in the air. Believers alive at the time this event occurs do not die; God *transforms them* from one mode of *physical* life that is mortal to another form of *physical* life that is immortal. This concept was present very early in the life of the Church (and not as some might suppose *a later invention*). It was in Paul's *earliest letters* to Thessalonica and Corinth, letters that even liberal scholars consider *authentically Pauline.*

Indeed the Rapture doesn't just pertain to those that are alive. It covers two different circumstances. First, there are those that have already *'fallen asleep'* who Jesus Christ resurrects. Then, there are those that are alive at that moment and are *'caught up.'* To speak of the Rapture, one should be talking about both (1) the resurrection and *transformation* of the dead and (2) the *transformation* of living believers. *"Behold, I shew (show) you a mystery; we shall not all sleep, but we shall all be changed"* (I Corinthians 15:51).

Because of the immediate transformation of the *quick* as well as the dead, the Rapture is also known as *"the translation of believers"* — a metamorphous in the physical nature of our existence, from a corruptible (mortal) corporeal body to an incorruptible (immortal) one. The Apostle John also points out the unique change believers will experience. *"Beloved, now are we the sons of God, and it doth not yet appear what we shall be: but we know that, when he shall appear, we shall be like him; for we shall see him as he is"* (I John 3:2). The resurrected body of Christ, as depicted in the Gospel of John, provides many hints to the nature of this existence (see John 20 and 21). Jesus eats and drinks with his disciples yet can move through walls, jump from place-to-place, and assume an appearance that makes Him unrecognizable.

Indeed, unlike most other religions, Judaism and Christianity assert *the bodily resurrection*—not to a ghostlike spirit, but to a corporeal, spectacular existence—certainly *more like a flawless superhero than our typical depiction of an angel with wings, playing a harp, and sitting on a puffy cloud.* If the stereotypical idea of harps and clouds doesn't motivate you to seek the *hereafter,* you're not alone. After about three minutes of cloud sitting, I'd be looking for something else to do too. But that type of "pie in the sky, by and by" isn't what the Bible actually teaches. It will be as bright, beautiful and tangible as our experience of life is today – but even better. We will experience almost limitless possibilities where we can control and take command of the physical nature of the universe – never to another's harm, but only to promote what is good.

Paul goes on to say that our transformation will be "in a flash, in the twinkling of an eye, at the last trumpet. For the trumpet will sound, the dead will be raised imperishable, and we will be changed." Perhaps the most famous passage regarding the 'blessed hope' of the Church—the Rapture—is found in I Thessalonians 4:

13But I would not have you to be ignorant, brethren, concerning them which are asleep, that ye sorrow not, even as others which have no hope.

14For if we believe that Jesus died and rose again, even so them also which sleep in Jesus will God bring with him.

15For this we say unto you by the word of the Lord, that we which are alive and remain unto the coming of the Lord shall not prevent them which are asleep.

16For the Lord himself shall descend from heaven with a shout, with the voice of the archangel, and with the trump of God: and the dead in Christ shall rise first:

17Then we which are alive and remain shall be caught up together with them in the clouds, to meet the Lord in the air: and so shall we ever be with the Lord.

18Wherefore comfort one another with these words.

The Signal for the Rapture – The Trumpet (The Voice of God)

In this passage, Paul's words are most descriptive: Here he tells us the signal is like (1) a *loud command;* (2) with the *voice of the archangel* and (3) with the *trumpet call of God.* Having employed all of these descriptors, we sense that there is much more to "the trumpet" than merely the blowing of the Shofar.

The words in Revelation compare 'the Voice of God' to a trumpet. In Chapter 1, John relates the following:

> [9]*I John, who also am your brother, and companion in tribulation, and in the kingdom and patience of Jesus Christ, was in the isle that is called Patmos, for the word of God, and for the testimony of Jesus Christ.*
>
> [10]*I was in the Spirit on the Lord's day, and heard behind me a great voice, as of a trumpet,*
>
> [11]*Saying, I am Alpha and Omega, the first and the last: and, What thou seest, write in a book, and send it unto the seven churches which are in Asia; unto Ephesus, and unto Smyrna, and unto Pergamos, and unto Thyatira, and unto Sardis, and unto Philadelphia, and unto Laodicea.*

John indicates that hearing the voice of God is like hearing *the sound of a trumpet*. This simile appears again in Chapter 4:

> [1]*After this I looked, and, behold, a door was opened in heaven: and the first voice which I heard was as it were of a trumpet talking with me; which said, Come up hither, and I will shew thee things which must be hereafter.*
>
> [2]*And immediately I was in the spirit: and, behold, a throne was set in heaven, and one sat on the throne.*

And then in Revelation 11 we note regarding the resurrection of the amazing characters known as the *Two Witnesses*, that while the voice of God isn't compared to a trumpet it still utters the same words John heard in Chapter 4, this time as a *great voice* like a loud cry (in the New American Standard version): "*And they heard **a great voice from heaven** saying unto them, Come up hither. And they ascended up to heaven in a cloud; and their enemies beheld them.*" (Revelation 11:12).

One of the most interesting new notions I've come across in recent years is the possibility that *the last trumpet*, which sounds immediately before the Rapture (that signals the resurrection of the *quick and the dead*), is not a trumpet at all, but is the *Voice of God*.

In my first book, I called attention to some of the original insights of David W. Lowe in his work, *Then His Voice Shook the Earth*. Lowe's book examines the possibility that *the last trumpet* is in fact the *voice of God* and he offers this opinion as a compelling alternative view. This idea falls right in line with the concept of how God creates through the *Logos* – the Word. By merely speaking a command, His creation reacts and obeys. The shout of Jesus to Lazarus, "Come forth" immediately caused Lazarus to be resurrected. Likewise, in all the accounts of resurrection discussed in the New Testament, the voice of God commands the dead to rise and they do. *The last trumpet* may be the call of God for the resurrection and the rapture of the Saints to happen in the instant that it's spoken. It's like a trumpet because it's "loud and clear."

Rosh Hashanah, Pentecost, and the Jewish Holidays

NOTE

The traditional view links the *last trumpet* with the blowing of the Shofar, the ram's horn, *on Rosh Hashanah*. Rosh Hashanah is the Jewish New Year. Rosh Hashanah is also known as *the Feast of the Trumpets* – so there is a logical suggestion that the Rapture (which includes the resurrection of the dead), would take place on this day. The argument is that *the last trump* is the final blowing of the Shofar (one hundred times on each of the two days – unless it concludes on a Sabbath. Then the horn blows 100 times only on the first day). If so, this would tie the Rapture to *Rosh Hashanah* as the fulfillment of this key Jewish *high holy day*.

Indeed, the term officially used for all of the Jewish holidays is *convocation* – akin to a "dress rehearsal" (see Leviticus 23:2, 4, 37). Is Rosh Hashanah the day of the Rapture? Perhaps – but it's not the only candidate holiday that could be fulfilled by the rapture event as we will see.

There are *seven* Jewish feasts, commanded through Moses, given as part of the Law from the Mount Sinai experience. The feasts are divided into *fall* feasts and *spring* feasts – three in each. The seventh feast is Pentecost, transpiring 50 days after the 10 days of Omer. We will look at all of these briefly in this section. But since we have begun with the first of the *three fall feasts*, Rosh Hashanah, let's continue to describe the other two.

- *Yom Kippur*, the second fall *holiday* (literally holy day) Jews know as the *Day of Atonement*. It's most solemn of the Jewish holidays. On this day, according to priestly tradition, the High Priest enters the Holy of Holies and makes atonement for all the people by sprinkling blood on the Mercy Seat of the Ark of the Covenant. The Priests refer to this act as *propitiation*, in which God is satisfied with the offering and forgives the nation's sin. This day is also what many speculate will be the literal *day of the LORD*, the day Messiah rescues the nation from the Antichrist and the armies that surround it at Armageddon.

- *Sukkot (The Feast of the Tabernacles)* is the final fall holiday. It commemorates the dwelling of the people in tents during their wilderness wanderings for 40 years. It's also a reminder that God will dwell with the people in the Kingdom of God upon this earth, when David (and/or Christ) sits on the throne of God's Kingdom in Jerusalem. Dispensational Christians see the *Feast of the Tabernacles* symbolizing the Millennial Reign of Christ upon the Throne of David in Jerusalem. It's this feast, the Bible tells us, which all nations must observe during the Millennium – otherwise, their nation will see drought (Zechariah 14:18, 19).

Just as there are three festivals in the fall, there are three spring festivals: (1) Passover, (2) Feast of Unleavened Bread, and (3) Feast of First Fruits.

- *Pesach (Passover)* is of course the holiday reminding all Israel how the Angel of Death *passed over* the houses of the Hebrews in Egypt, sparing their first born but killing the first born of the Egyptians. This event caused the Pharaoh to "let the Hebrew people go" for the final time. Christians see Passover as a symbol of Jesus, as God's firstborn, sacrificed on the cross redeeming not only Israel's firstborn, but also all humankind.

- The *Feast of Unleavened Bread* is a period of seven days which reminds the people how fast they had to leave Egypt – they wouldn't have time to use leaven – there was no time for bread to 'rise.' Also, the Jews considered leaven a symbol of *sin*. To avoid leaven was a personal sacrifice, as unleavened bread is not as soft as leavened bread. Symbolically, avoiding leaven is avoiding sin. Christians see this period as speaking to the sinless nature of Christ and the sacrifice He made to save us.

- *Omer*, the Festival of First Fruits, is a time to celebrate harvest. The people gather the initial sheaves of the harvest during this 10-day period, bring them to the Priest, and then wave them before the Lord. Upon completing this event, harvest occurs for the next seven weeks. First Fruits is also seen by Christians as a symbol of the resurrection of Christ, in which Christ's rising is a symbol of being the "first among many brethren" to be resurrected. He is the first fruits of those rising from the dead.

Lastly, we come to the Festival of the Harvest, or *Pentecost*, occurring in springtime, but seen as the *middle* festival, lying between the fall and spring holidays. As stated above, Pentecost happens 50 days after the 10 Days of Omer. The possibility of Pentecost being the day of the Rapture would be symmetrical in that the church began on Pentecost and would conclude on that same day. It would be appropriate to interpret both dates figuratively as *days of harvest.* According to most scholars, God gave the Law to Moses on the day of *Pentecost.* Some traditions suggest that *David the King was also born on Pentecost.* I also speculate that this is the actual birthday of Jesus.[4]

As noted earlier, a few scholars suggest that the various *dispensations always commence on a Pentecost.* For Christians, Pentecost is indeed a major holiday! Orthodox Jews are to celebrate Pentecost by staying up all night, studying Scripture, and praying. Not many Christians, perhaps to our shame, follow this tradition.[5]

Additionally, the story of the Book of Ruth, associated with Pentecost, is a story that has probable *typology* involving the rapture of the Church. The book is about a gentile woman, Ruth, a Moabite, redeemed by a *kinsmen redeemer,* Boaz. In order to propose marriage between Ruth and Boaz, at the coaching of her mother-in-law from her prior marriage (Naomi), Ruth goes to the upper loft of the threshing floor and quietly lies down at the feet of Boaz where he is sleeping, uncovering his feet, and resting with him. Upon discovering Ruth, Boaz understands what amounts to a petition of Ruth to be cared for by Boaz; and therefore, he moves on to marry Ruth.

Tradition has it that this event occurs on *the day of Pentecost.* In fact, it's a story normally read on Pentecost by orthodox Jews. It symbolizes the marriage between God and Israel. Christians of course see in this story a symbol of the marriage between Jesus Christ and His Church—especially since Ruth, the bride, *is a gentile.* The date is also known as the only festival date *that cannot be established on a fixed date,* due to the fluctuation of Passover.

The sequence: Passover occurs on a the date of a full moon (which varies depending upon the blooming of the Almond Tree); (2) Omer is offered on the first day (Sunday) after the Sabbath (Saturday) after the Passover (which varies); (3) Pentecost or Shavuot was to be exactly seven weeks after the day following Sabbath (which would be Sunday), immediately after Passover (50 days after Omer).

In contrast, during Jesus' day the Pharisees fixed the date as the sixth day of Sivan (typically late May or early June). However, biblically, the date was always to be a Sunday and a *variable date* holiday. Christians of course supported Sunday as the holy day as it was a memorial to the day of Jesus' resurrection. [6]

Jewish Name	Common Name	Meaning of the Jewish Holy Day	Possible Christian Fulfillment
The Spring Festivals			
Pesach	Passover	• First full moon after the blooming of Almond trees. • Redemption of Israel through the Angel of Death 'Passing over' the Jews and striking the Egyptians' first born. • Individual salvation.	• The Crucifixion of Christ that Redeems All Humankind.
Pesach	Unleavened Bread	• Seven days eating unleavened bread—reminiscent of Exodus' quick departure. Leaven = sin.	• Pictures Sinless Life of Christ—His Death And Burial.
Omer	First fruits	• Celebration of initial harvest—First sheaves waved before the Lord.	• Resurrection of Christ—The 1st of Many Brethren.
Shavuot	Pentecost Festival of the Harvest Festival of Weeks	• Giving of Law at Sinai. • The Grain Harvest is complete. 50 days after 'Omer.' • The festival of the Bride and Bridegroom—Ruth.	• Coming of The Holy Spirit and The Birth of The Church (Acts 2). • The Rapture of The Church? *YES!*
The Fall Festivals			
Rosh Hashanah	Feast of the (Trumpets)	• Day of Creation. *YES!!* • *Seven* days afterwards are the *Days of Awe.* • Also, Jewish Civil New Year. • Time to Examine Oneself.	• The Rapture of The Church? • Return of Christ to Mount of Olives? • Days of Awe—The Tribulation Period?
Yom Kippur	The Day of Atonement	• 10 days after Rosh Hashanah. • High Priest enters the Holy of Holies in the Temple to make restitution for sin of the people. • National salvation.	• Judgment Day. • The Battle of Armageddon 10 Days after the Return of Christ to Mount of Olives?
Sukkot	Feast of Tabernacles	• 5 days after Yom Kippur. Lasts for 7 days. • The people are to dwell in 'booths' or tents to remind them of their dwellings in the wilderness. God will dwell with mankind in the Kingdom.	• The Millennial Reign of Christ. • The Holiday that All Nations Must Honor in the Millennium.

FIGURE 68 - TABLE OF JEWISH FESTIVALS & POSSIBLE CHRISTIAN FULFILLMENT

Additionally, the fact that the date of the festival couldn't be officially *known* until the blossoming of the Almond Tree, it infers that *"no man knows the day."* So it's for that reason many Christian scholars believe that the Rapture of the Church will happen on *Rosh Hashanah* (due to the correlation with the *Feast of Trumpets*) or on *Pentecost* (due to the typological factors implied in this festival).

No Man Knows the Day nor the Hour

However, we must also point out that scholars agree that Jesus taught that humankind won't know when He will return (Matthew 24:36) — specifically, we are told that we will not know *the day nor the hour* — therefore, we should always be *alert and ready.*

However, in a slightly non-traditional way, many argue this caution applies only to *the year* of His coming. The fulfillment of these festivals will indeed happen on the day of the festival (just as have all the others), but because we do not know the year, by inference *we won't know the day or the hour either.* Others would say that the statement, "we won't know when He's coming" is really directed at those who aren't earnestly watching. Those who are watching are not surprised when He comes *"like a thief in the night"* because we are *sons of the light.* We read in I Thessalonians 5:1-6:

¹But of the times and the seasons, brethren, ye have no need that I write unto you.

²For yourselves know perfectly that the day of the Lord so cometh as a thief in the night.

³For when they shall say, Peace and safety; then sudden destruction cometh upon them, as travail upon a woman with child; and they shall not escape.

⁴But ye, brethren, are not in darkness, that that day should overtake you as a thief.

⁵Ye are all the children of light, and the children of the day: we are not of the night, nor of darkness.

*⁶Therefore let us not sleep, as do others; but **let us watch and be sober.***

On the one hand, the Bible teaches that the *Day of the Lord* (which is usually understood as the *precise period of God's wrath* upon the earth) will come *"like a thief in the night"* (verse 2). On the other hand, Paul tells us that this shouldn't shock us because we're *"children of light and children of the day"* (verse 5). The Scripture charges us, nonetheless, to be alert and in control of ourselves (verse 6). Overall, *because we're alert* it suggests that *we may know the holy-day when the Lord is coming.*

So it's not necessarily the Rapture that the Lord suggests will come "like a thief." Instead, *it's God's judgment or the Day of the Lord* that will overtake those who do *not* understand the signs of the times – those that *are sons of the night.* We read that in Joel 3 earlier. The unbelieving assume peace and safety when destruction is lurking (verse 3).

What Comes After the Rapture?

The Dispensationalist (see reference to J.N. Darby earlier) believes there are many more events yet to come after the Rapture of the Church (from Revelation 19 and 20):

- The return of Christ will occur at the Battle of *Armageddon.*

- After defeating his enemies with the help of His Saints, Christ throws the *Antichrist* and *False Prophet* into the Lake of Fire.

- All believers will be united and attend the "marriage supper of the Lamb."[7]

- Satan is bound and thrown into a bottomless pit.

- Immediately thereafter, the Millennium commences and continues for 1,000 years.

- It's followed by yet another battle. In this battle, Satan is loosed from the bottomless pit for a little time and stirs up the nations of the world once more. He leads the armies of Gog and Magog to Jerusalem a second time for yet another battle against the Messiah.

- Satan fails once more and is thrown into the Lake of Fire, joining the Antichrist and the False Prophet.

- "The Great White Throne Judgment" takes place immediately after "the Second Resurrection." Only those unfavorably judged are resurrected here. These haven't been redeemed by the blood of the Lamb and are judged according to their works. Since their names aren't found in the Lamb's Book of Life, they're also tossed into the Lake of Fire.

- Coming forth like a new bride, New Jerusalem appears along with the new heavens and new earth.

- Eternity begins.

The Jewish Calendar Compared to the Mayan Calendar

Many prophecy experts consider *the Jewish calendar* to be God's time clock. By this they suggest that it's the holidays of the Jews as instituted by Moses (there are other holidays that Moses did not institute such as *Hanukkah*) that tell us specifically what is going to happen and when. Just as the "Spring Festivals" were fulfilled to the date by the Passion of Jesus Christ, the "Fall Festivals" will disclose exactly when Doomsday is and when Jesus Christ returns. The day that the Messiah publicly appears to save his people will be a *future Rosh Hashanah,* typically in September. A *future Day of Atonement*, usually in early October, is when Armageddon occurs. The Bible studied carefully and methodically, suggests clearly that Doomsday is in fact, a future Jewish date, *The Day of Atonement.*

To biblical scholars, this is no surprise. God has been setting dates and fulfilling his plan according to these dates throughout history. This is to demonstrate the Providence of God – His ability to bring His will to pass according to His Plan.

We infer from the Mayan calendar that December 21st, 2012, will be a "day of infamy" using the words of FDR. But Mayan timekeeping, as impressive as it was, is limited to tracking eclipses, planetary orbits, and approximately *when the sun eclipses the center of the Milky Way.* The Jewish calendar is far more comprehensive in its prophetic relevance, communicating much more about what will happen in the future. The only reason most of us don't know this is that culturally (in America) we decided a century or so ago to stop believing the Bible to be the *Word of God* – His verbal revelation to us – it became no better than a religious text supplying illustrations for Jungian psychology or existential philosophy.

Therefore, in our world, today, most pay no particular attention to what the Bible predicts about the future. However, perhaps with a few more startling fulfillments in the years to come regarding what the Bible's prophets foretold, this skeptical attitude will be reversed. Not that I'm personally predicting it will. It could only happen through massive shock treatments administered through fulfillment of biblically predicted events.

But then, Jesus said, "It is an evil and adulterous generation that demands a sign be given it." In other words, there are already enough reasons to believe. To demand yet more demonstrations just indicates one's unwillingness to come to grips with the truth.

The Last Generation

But how do we interpret Jesus' saying in Luke 21? "Behold the fig tree, and all the trees; when they now shoot forth, ye see and know of your own selves that summer is now nigh at hand. So likewise ye, when ye see these things come to pass, know ye that the kingdom of God is nigh at hand. **Verily I say unto you, this generation shall not pass away, till all be fulfilled. Heaven and earth shall pass away: but my words shall not pass away**." There used to be considerable debate about whether the fig tree had any meaning other than a very direct analogy of "once you see blooms you know leaves can't be far behind." But today, a consensus of scholars now seem satisfied that the fig tree indeed represents Israel.

There has been some research (I referenced Grant Jeffrey's work on this topic in my first book) that verifies the early Church believed *the fig tree* did represent Israel. The idea was simple: Once Israel returns to the land and officially becomes a nation again; the generation that witnesses this event will see all the predicted events come to pass. If true, the question is two-fold: Did the restoration of Israel in 1948 constitute *the budding of the fig tree*? Or did some other event before or after fulfill this prophecy? Secondly, what is the *length of a biblical generation*?

As to the first part of the question, Dispensationalists believe that either the 1948 Israeli Independence Day or the 1967 "Six Day War," in which Israel recaptured the Temple Mount, constitute the "start of the Doomsday Clock" (more precisely *the moment from which Jesus' predictions about the coming Apocalypse commence*).

Likewise, 1917 was once a date of great interest as it was the date of England's *Balfour Declaration*, declaring the intention to establish a Jewish homeland in Palestine, being the culmination of the Zionist efforts.[8] It was a date that the prophetically inclined (living in the first half of the 20th century) speculated to be *the budding of the fig tree*. But 1917 is a date long since past. Nonetheless, it's noteworthy that besides these three dates, no others have been popularly suggested as the "date of budding."

Regarding *the length of a generation*, the second part of the question, there are two *lengths* that scholars suggest. The first is a time period of 40 years. This seems corroborated by the fact that the generation of Jews who were responsible for the decision not to invade the land of Canaan was judged by God. As punishment, the Jews would wander for 40 years until everyone from *that generation* died. Secondly, Jesus predicted the length of one generation would span the time from His prediction regarding the destruction of the second temple until Jerusalem would be surrounded by armies and the Temple destroyed. Both time spans, according to Chuck Missler, lasted exactly 38 years. Others count 40 years. Either way, this tends to suggest that about 40 years is the length of a generation to which Jesus was referring. If so, neither 1948 nor 1967 would be the date that the "clock" started ticking. We are already past those dates.

Consequently, this is why many suppose it's a different length of time that Jesus had in mind. Some suggest 70 years is the proper length as the Bible in the Psalms prescribes the standard length of a human life to be 70 years (or 80 years if by God's grace – see Psalm 90:10). If 70 years is correct and 1948 is the year of the fig tree's budding, then *2018* would be the "last call" for this generation. If one subtracts Daniel's final seven years from 2018 to establish the date that the final "week of years" transpires, *we arrive at 2012*. (Seven years, counting them one-by-one: 1-2012, 2-2013, 3-2014, 4-2015, 5-2016, 6-2017, 7-2018). Am I setting a date? No indeed. Nevertheless I am always willing to consider the possibilities if the Bible is being interpreted properly.

I recently visited a web site that provides much more detail and justification for this date (*See www.feastsofthelord.net*). Bill Miller (who appears to have authored all its content), supplies us with extensive scriptural detail supporting this "doomsday date."

- September, 2011 will begin Daniel's 70th week, aka the 7-year Tribulation Period.

- *April, 2015* at Passover, will be the beginning of the final 3.5 years, aka the "Great Tribulation" or "Time of Jacob's Trouble." Some suggest (as does Miller) this period is also the same as "the Day of the Lord."

- October, 2018, at the *Day of Atonement*, will conclude the 70 Weeks [presumably, this is the *Battle of Armageddon*].

- The year that begins in 2018 is a "Year of Jubilee" and this is also when the millennial reign of Christ (aka the "Davidic Kingdom" for the Jews) begins.

- Miller points out that 70 years from 1948 concludes on 2018 and that 50 years (40 years from a generation plus 10 years corresponding to the 10 days of awe – for a time of repentance – concludes at this same time from the Six-Day War of 1967). He comments, "The 10 days 'Days of Awe' / 'Affliction' i.e., a time to repent between the Feast of Trumpets

> & the Feast of Atonement before Judgment, culminating at Jubilee; one day after Atonement, which starts at the 50th year, aka Jubilee / Millennial Kingdom."

This would all be fine and dandy *if* we knew for sure that 1948 is the start point and 70 years is the length of time in question. We do know from the teachings of Moses that a time of Jubilee is designated *every 50 years*. However, the reality is that we don't have enough evidence to be dogmatic that Daniel's 70th Week begins in 2011 or 2012. It's a fascinating date-setting attempt in and of itself that has allegorical scriptural support. Perhaps it even has empirical support too.

Consider certain lunar eclipses connect to key Jewish dates in 2015 and 2018, perhaps partially fulfilling the "signs in the moon and stars." It's curious too that these lunar eclipses all happen on Jewish feast days *all in one year*. This phenomenon hasn't happened since **1949** and **1967** respectively – ironically key years which might start the clock ticking as they're the key dates in the modern history of Israel). Nevertheless, *I can't condone such date setting without expressing reservations.*

On the other hand, lest we be guilty of being too hard to convince and failing to read the signs of the times, we best take this intelligent speculation with some seriousness. Moreover, it would be foolish to ignore how emphatic Jesus was in making this statement: "*Verily I say unto you, **this generation shall not pass away, till all be fulfilled.** Heaven and earth shall pass away: **but my words shall not pass away.**" His strong words suggest that he is deadly serious. We shouldn't fail to be "alert and sober," mindful that the culmination of history may be only a short time away.

For it's quite true that if we were able to firm up our confidence in the moment we should start the clock *and* the exact length of time it should run, *we would know the very day.* Jesus is emphatic that what He's predicted is going to happen exactly as He's stated. His credibility is on the line. And as the old scholars used to say quoting the Bible, "God is jealous regarding His word." He doesn't make promises that He fails to keep. "If He says it – that settles it."

That's another reason why the days given in the Book of Daniel – 2,520 days – are meant to be taken literally. It's the exact number of days from the time the future covenant between the 10-nation coalition of the Antichrist and the State of Israel is "inked" – *until the return of the Son of Man –* seven years later. Daniel's prophecy of days *can be counted on.* Why do I assert this so confidently? Because Daniel has an outstanding track record; that is, *there is historical precedent*. As presented earlier, Daniel predicted the time when the Messiah would present Himself to the nation. 173,880 days elapsed from the decree of Artaxerxes for the Jews to rebuild the walls of Jerusalem in 445 BC to Palm Sunday in 30 AD. This is no average prophecy to get right!

As to the admonition, "no one will know the day nor the hour," we have already suggested a number of reasons, biblically, that this warning was not intended for believers who are "children of the day" but for those who are "children of the night" who will be caught unawares. Jesus said, *"Behold, I come like a thief"* – but not to those who are *looking up and jubilant over His coming*. He said it instead to those who are *living in darkness* and *hiding from the light*. My question to you, "Are you living in the darkness or the light?"

NOTES

[1] Alexander left the Jews alone when he was confronted by the Priests who came outside of the walls in fine array to meet and honor him. Josephus the historian indicates that they shared with Alexander the prophecies of Daniel the Prophet which predicted how he would conquer many lands and be seen as one of the greatest empire builders of history. Astounded by the reception, Alexander did no harm to the Jews of that day.

[2] Proclaimed the "Great Commission" this passage places the Christian movement in this chronological context: *"Go ye therefore, and teach all nations, baptizing them in the name of the Father, and of the Son, and of the Holy Ghost: Teaching them to observe all things whatsoever I have commanded you: and, lo, I am with you always, even unto the end of the world."* (Matthew 28:19, 20).

[3] Many of the Masters talked about by the New Age leaders are characterized by these words. Supposedly, they are high in the Himalayas or in hidden deep in deserted places. Benjamin Crème describes *Lord Maitreya*, the Buddhist-cum-New-Age Christ, in this way.

[4] I also speculate that Jesus' birthday is on Pentecost. According to the star charts, if we take the statement in Revelation 12 about where the sun and moon are in relation to the "virgin" (Virgo — "at the feet of the virgin"), the annunciation to Mary by the Angel Gabriel, likely occurred in September 3 BC, possibly on Rosh Hashanah. Assuming that the conception of Jesus in the womb of Mary occurred at

this moment, nine months later would bring us to June 2 BC. The earliest that Pentecost can occur using our Gregorian calendar is May 10. The latest is June 13. My educated speculation is that Jesus' birth may have occurred then, June 2 BC.

[5] This tradition is reminiscent of Jesus' parable in which he mentions that the Master may return from the wedding feast in the 2nd or 3rd 'watch of the night.' So stay awake! (Luke 12:38) The Greek Orthodox Church actually celebrates this tradition too. Therefore, some Christians do stay vigilant on Pentecost.

[6] That the key day for the Jews is a Sunday not a Sabbath, is a remarkable typological detail – not incidental in my opinion – inferring identification of the Christians' by sanctifying their day of worship through this holiday.

[7] There is a strong argument that the Marriage Supper of the Lamb does not actually occur until after the Second Coming and immediately before the Millennial Reign begins. In this view, the 'Saints' of both Old and New Testament times will sit together at this event. In the former view, only New Testament Saints would be present.

[8] The *British Mandate* or *Balfour Declaration*: "His Majesty's government views with favour [English spelling]the establishment in Palestine of a national home for the Jewish people, and will use their best endeavors to facilitate the achievement of this object, it being clearly understood that nothing shall be done which may prejudice the civil and religious rights of existing non-Jewish communities in Palestine, or the rights and political status enjoyed by Jews in any other country."

Chapter 15:
Drawing Conclusions about Doomsday

He answered and said unto them,
"When it is evening, ye say, it will be fair weather: for the sky is red. And in the morning, it will be foul weather today: for the sky is red and lowering. O ye hypocrites, ye can discern the face of the sky; but can ye not discern the signs of the times?"

(Matthew 16:2, 3)

Doomsday – A Personal Experience

As we've seen, throughout history countless numbers of people have *misread the signs of the times* and miscalculated the moment when the final day dawns. While indisputable, it's a fact that supplies little comfort. Indeed, it is *extremely misleading*. History teaches us that cataclysms have happened many times before and will happen again. No matter whether we spell it with a big "D" or a little "d," *Doomsday* is a past, present, and future reality.

Furthermore, Doomsday is a *very personal experience*. If we die in a cataclysm, it will matter little whether it was "the Big One" or just a regional catastrophe that caused our death. We won't be around to assess the damage or evaluate the survivors' prognosis.

The fact is *doomsdays* happen in every century (indeed every decade). This makes it even more reasonable that we should face up to a potential *catastrophe* when planning our future.

For instance in the world of data processing, each facility that processes data for public companies must have a "disaster recovery plan." If the facility catches fire, experiences an earthquake, or is the victim of terrorism, management is responsible to put in motion a plan to recover the data and put the business back on-line within a reasonable timeframe. Failure to do this isn't just inept; it could be criminal.

It's reasonable that our personal planning horizon is rather short-term. We worry most about what might happen in our *immediate* future. Goodness knows we aren't as interested in what happens 70 years from now because we wager we won't be here. We want to know what might happen in the next ten years. Could our personal doomsday be soon? There's no doubt that if we

317

catch a glimpse *of the final scene in the play we call our lives,* we might choose to hold everything until we find out what our future holds.

I don't mean to suggest that Doomsday is *no more than a metaphor.* When we consider the magnitude of input from all the varied sources (in other words, *the fact that there's so much data on this topic*), it becomes exceedingly clear that *we may be living in a totally unique time with a distinct outcome.*

No generation has seen as much positive progress as ours on so many fronts. However, neither has any other generation experienced greater threats of self-imposed destruction. As such, it becomes all the more worrisome when pressures pile up and end times' prophecies happen right in front of our eyes. Scoffers abound always – but there comes a time when we see even the most steadfast skeptic silenced.

My point is this: *Decoding Doomsday* is not an optional or frivolous pastime. It deserves our upmost attention – especially now.

Prophesy vs. Predict

To evaluate the credibility of prophecy, first it's helpful to determine what we mean by the words we use. Specifically, I distinguish between the two words, *prophesying* and *predicting.* A dictionary may use the words interchangeably. However, in the context of history and the study of prophetic matters, there is a big difference. The processes are quite distinct. At the risk of being a bit tedious, let's consider these words for a moment.

To prophesy implies relying upon a source of knowledge outside the realm of the five senses. It infers a supernatural ability to acquire information that the five senses alone don't provide. Intuition, seeing spirits or ghosts, having a vision, hearing words spoken by an independent entity (e.g., the voice of god, or the channeling of a spirit), all are rightly considered a *sixth sense.* Likewise, dreams are vivid stories we encounter during our sleep. They are quite real, but we experience them outside our five senses.

Indeed, we see that prophecies in the Bible usually come from dreams or visions. These experiences might be normal for some people; however, we know they don't originate with our senses (i.e., seeing, hearing, touching, smelling, or tasting). Yet, dreams or visions are the most dramatic means by which we make contact with the divine or the spirit world. As we've seen, substances like DMT or LSD may enhance our ability to experience these phenomena. Nevertheless, the encounter is no less real to the individual whether or not chemical substances induce it.[1]

On the other hand, *predicting* is using our reason to make judgments. We say, "I predict the future," but defined this way, we are basing our prediction on prior history, patterns we've seen before, the weight of evaluated evidence, or the quality of information we've received from one or more witnesses. We may learn information (and usually do) through seeing *type* on the book page and assimilating what we read. We might learn through listening to a radio program. Alternatively, we can combine our senses and watch a documentary on television in which we gather new information through our ear sense and our eyesight. Predictions are built on the foundation of sense data (to gather empirical information – our perception) and our reason (our ability to process data and ultimately, draw conclusions).

Both prophecy and prediction can be wrong. A *prophecy* may not come true. We can miss a *prediction*. Both are subject to human frailty, to misinterpretation of the data, to drawing a conclusion based on too little or bad information (no matter what the source – natural or *supernatural*). Any source can mislead us and do so intentionally or unintentionally. That's why we shouldn't stake our whole-hearted commitment to any *prophecy* or *prediction* until we have done our best to *discern* whether we have *worthy* reasons to believe it.[2]

Probabilities vs. Certainties

In our world today, the weatherman predicts the weather making liberal use of the notion of *probabilities* (e.g., "we have an 80% chance of rain today") – by which the weatherman admits a 20% chance of being wrong. The weatherman doesn't prophesy – he (or she) *predicts*. The meteorologist identifies various factors, accumulates evidence, and provides explanation. The outcome is a *matter of probability*. And we pay attention to this type of advice. If we hear the weatherman predict an 80% chance of rain, we grab the umbrella as we head out the door.

It seems that the weatherman got smart some time ago. When you're in the business of making predictions every day, you best include a fudge factor because you endure no end of hostility if you get it wrong. In many respects, decoding Doomsday is like that – *it's a matter of calculating probabilities more than determining ironclad certainties*. It's a wonder that most Doomsday prophets are yet to catch on to the wisdom in this approach.

However, most seers do use particular language to provide wiggle room. Rarely is any prophecy 100% clear-cut from an interpreter's viewpoint. It's not because prophecy is subjective (that is, how we *interpret it*, what *it means to us*).

The reason why it's ambiguous is that it's usually encoded. Seldom do true prophets prophesy something specific which will happen *exactly in a certain way on a particular day*. For one reason or another, most prophets intentionally obscure their prophecies. Why is this so?

- We know that sometimes prophets had to be careful in what they said – therefore they used symbols, numerology, and images to cloak their message in order to protect themselves. John of Patmos who wrote the book of Revelation may have done this. Nostradamus certainly did.

- We can surmise that much is also encoded just because we don't understand the language or symbols of ancient times. Once we have the *Rosetta Stone*, we can *break the code*. The meaning becomes clear. Mayan hieroglyphics are like this. Egyptian monuments seem to possess this quality as well. And sometimes interpretation is merely a matter of good translation.

- It may also be the case that whoever is prophesying isn't eager to make his meaning clear – the source may elect to hide his message causing those who seek after truth to seek it earnestly. Jesus spoke in parables, some prophetic. He told his disciples he intended to conceal the truth. Only those meant to receive it would understand. "He who has hears to hear, let Him hear." Jesus claimed to be *the way, the truth* and *the life*. But he didn't force truth down anyone's throat. The hearer had to listen intently. The problem with many in his audience was simply that they didn't care enough to pay attention.

Can We Interpret Prophecy Accurately?

That being the case, is unlocking the exact meaning of prophecy impossible? In some sense, this might seem so. Even fulfilled prophecy is subject to debate. For example, did Jesus Christ fulfill the messianic prophecies of the Jews? To some, there appear to have been dozens of Old Testament prophecies that Jesus fulfilled. But there are more skeptics than you can count who doubt Jesus fulfilled any of these prophecies, either because they don't believe that the *messiah* would be a divine character who would die for our sins (the *Jewish* view) or because they don't believe in God and the supernatural (the *atheist's* or *naturalist's* view). Either way, scoffers insist Jesus failed to fulfill prophecy.

Therefore, we could conclude (wrongly I might add), that fulfillment of *prophecies past* is as uncertain as getting future ones right.

Another complication: Through the ages, knowledge is often subject to debate and skepticism. As Francis Bacon quipped (paraphrasing), "There is nothing ever been said that is so absurd that some philosopher somewhere hasn't said it." This includes a whole school of thought (following the lead of a skeptic like David Hume), which believes perception (such things as cause and effect) is *merely the way our minds work*, not necessarily the way things really are.[3] However, employing skepticism like this leads to a death spiral. We simply can't live our lives based on this perspective. As Anthony Flew, a long-time atheist now *believer* says, "When Hume left his office, he left his skepticism behind."

As with any author, I write with certain assumptions. However, I wish to expose mine plainly: *Truth exists, perception can be certain, information can be accurate, and prophecies can be subject to verification.* From a practical point of view, I might agree with the notion that "interpretation is in the eye of the beholder," but only to the extent that some interpretations of prophecy are obvious; others "not so much." The Bible says (the New American Standard Version's a bit clearer here): *"But know this first of all, that no prophecy of Scripture is a matter of **one's own interpretation**, for no prophecy was ever made by an act of human will, but men moved by the Holy Spirit spoke from God."* (II Peter 1:20, 21)

This scripture doesn't teach that truth is so obvious that everyone will agree on what any particular prophecy means. But it does emphasize that there is one and only one correct interpretation. The question of what the Bible means is much more a problem on the "hearing side" than it is on the "telling side." I may say something you don't understand; but that doesn't imply I don't know what I'm saying. Someone else may catch my drift perfectly without further explanation. That's the challenge of communication.

To get philosophical, knowing with *absolute certainty* is limited by our human condition and the reality that we are finite creatures with a finite capacity to know. Nonetheless, as the intellectual Francis Schaeffer clarified, "We can know truly, just not exhaustively." We live with this manner of truth in the court of law. Judgments are made and verdicts issued accordingly. Truth that is "beyond a reasonable doubt" is accepted as a normal course of human affairs. Indeed, we live this reality in our day-to-day lives.

Consequently, we return to the essential point: Prediction (and interpreting prophecy) unlike prophesying (the recounting of a form of knowledge outside ones' natural faculties), is *a matter of probability*. Probabilities we can deal with. Probabilities we can live with. We know that when we get on a plane, unfortunately, there is a chance we could crash. Nevertheless, the chance is well less than *one in 100,000* (0.00001%). From a practical standpoint, *that is certainty.* Therefore, we sit down in our chair, pull out our newspaper or magazine, read, relax, and try to enjoy the flight.

So how do we assess whether one interpretation of a prophecy is more probable than some other one? I argue it's *akin to being a weatherman.*

We identify the factors involved, we accumulate the facts (the evidence), and we try to explain everything with an interpretation based upon what seems to make the most sense – what takes into account all the facts. Through cross-reference and comparison of symbols, considering historical precedents, as well as examining the best scholarship available, we increase the odds our interpretation is correct. Then we arrive at a conclusion. We pronounce what a prophecy must mean based upon the analysis we've done. Sometimes we contend our interpretation is 90% likely – sometimes it may be less than a 10% chance. Establishing an exact percentage of certitude (or probability) isn't really as important as simply stating something is "highly likely" or "very unlikely." To summarize: *(1) We pay careful attention to what's highly likely; (2) we merely keep an eye out for a possibility; and (3) we mostly ignore what's unlikely or improbable.* By confidently adopting this approach, we can draw reasoned conclusions about the future and plan accordingly. We can conclude there are circumstances that rule out the possibility *we are living in the last days.* Conversely, we can evaluate the probability that Doomsday lurks only months or years ahead.

Furthermore, a methodology or process improves our evaluation.

I chose not to follow such a step-by-step process as the explicit structure for this book. After all, presenting doomsday data so methodically would make for a rather dry presentation. But, if you think back to how I approached my presentation, you will see the method in my madness. Stylistically, I attempted the following:

- *Clarify what was prophesized,* being as precise as possible, based upon the (a) language employed and the (b) typical meaning of symbols or numerology in the sources utilized.

- *Confirm its precedence.* Has such an event happened before? Could it happen again? What does history teach us? What does science say?

- *Consider the source.* Keep in mind that *more sources* are better than but a few; likewise, credible sources are better than sketchy ones. Numerous, reliable sources that agree lead to the conclusion the prediction is likely to come true.

- *Challenge the independence of the source.* Does it have an unspoken agenda that might color the perspective taken? Is there an "axe to grind?"

- *Calculate the odds.* Don't bother to get too mathematical. Is the predicted outcome: highly likely, merely probable, or dubious?

What is perhaps the most important of all these guidelines is "where the information is coming from." My mother taught me to shrug off meritless judgments on my character when she said, "Consider the source." As I've stated many times in the preceding pages, there are numerous reasons why most ancient sources (along with their current-day advocates), are less authoritative than the Bible. Why would I say this? Is it just my personal bias? To the contrary, there are some very strong and pertinent reasons why this is so:

- First, many commentators on "hot topics" today often fail to be authentic to the original source. Being unscientific, commentators may make bold assertions without much evidence to substantiate their point of view. Inspiration clouds insight. *"Proof texting"* isn't just a sin of many Bible enthusiasts. A simple quote usually doesn't do it.

- Secondly, as the reader has seen, most non-biblical doomsday sources are suspect because they're too open to interpretation or because very little is communicated – at best the information is vague. There just isn't that much said by ancient authorities when compared to the extensive material coming to us from the Bible. Only one opinion from one place and time isn't as convincing as ten statements from ten different places and times.

- Thirdly, unlike biblical prophetic erudition that has 2,000 years of work supporting it, when it comes to sources like the Maya or Egyptians (especially as seen by alternative history), there is a dearth of scholarship to compare one view against another. Well-regarded and well-researched studies are less than 50 years old.[4] Most studies of any caliber are less than 20 years old. Consequently, we have to take everything we read from such sources with a grain of salt. Discoveries and related analyses are very immature when compared to biblical scholarship that can be traced back for hundreds if not thousands of years.

With this methodology undergirding our endeavor, we can come to reasoned conclusions about what will transpire in the years ahead. In short, *we can decode Doomsday.*

Making use of these guidelines, allow me to draw the following conclusions about Doomsday. This will also serve as a summary of what we've learned in the previous 320 plus pages.

Evaluating the 2012 Prophecies

We've shown that a number of prophecies related to 2012 are suspect because of failures to pass the first test – merely conveying clearly and without ambiguity what the meaning of certain prophecies is. This appears to be the case with what we know as *the Bible Code*.

The idea that the Bible Code in fact exists is a reasonable conclusion given the many sources that support the assumption of divine inspiration. God may have chosen to provide additional validation that the Bible is uniquely His Word and merits our admiration and adherence. There are many prophecies in the Bible that millions consider proven true today and through the course of several thousand years have caused millions more to argue on behalf of the divine nature of the Bible and the accuracy of its prophets. Additionally, we should note that many believers in the Bible Code were initially highly suspect until they examined the evidence for themselves whereupon they became doggedly convinced. Furthermore, it's no small point that many of these supporters are intelligent scholars who are also specialists in code breaking and ciphers.

Nevertheless, declaring the Bible Code to be a genuine prophetic source is problematic. It's open to considerable speculation regarding what it predicts given there's so many possible interpretations to different ELS sequences. Plus, it's still a new aspect to Bible "science." Taking a stand claiming we should seek encoded prophecy in the Bible Code (looking for events yet to happen) appears out-of-bounds even among its staunchest advocates.

Other prophecies related to 2012 such as *Novelty Theory* and the prevalent interpretation of the *I Ching* remain ambiguous as far as defining both what is being asserted and why the assertions are worthy of consideration. Novelty Theory says that change will continue to increase at an exponential rate until change reaches a "zero point" (or perhaps an *infinity point*) where major change is constant. Today's interpretation of the *I Ching* proposes a similar end point when we reach this state (which is one-day later than the end of the Mayan Calendar). We're told that both discoveries point to either a radical transformation of life on earth or alternatively to its destruction – depending upon to whom you're listening.

However, this conclusion is not evident from the facts presented. The facts could be interpreted differently. Remember that the majority of those that put faith in the *I Ching* are not necessary advocates for the 2012 hypothesis. McKenna's is a relatively new theory of how the *I Ching* should be put to work. Indeed, neither contention has been verified by sources in a position of academic authority to authenticate his contentions.[5] Almost all enthusiasts for Novelty Theory are still part of the fringe element. From his findings, proponents leap to the conclusion that what McKenna has asserted reinforces the general theory around 2012 transformation – that it's another confirmation of an *omega point* around which all of creation is headed. But there is a hidden agenda here. Driving such enthusiasm is their inflated understanding of a self-directed divinity inherent within *Mother Nature* or what is mystically inferred by their notion of TIME.

It's not that the theories are without merit; they do provide some additional interesting data points. If 2012 brings a stunning change in our consciousness or Quetzalcoatl physically appears to guide us forward, we will look back and agree that there was something to it. Otherwise, we must suspect that proponents for these prophetic sources are reading *more into the prophecies than from them.* I conclude that McKenna's assertions, while bold and fascinating are unquestionably inconclusive. Even Daniel Pinchbeck, a 2012 author-cum-shaman, says McKenna was the first to admit that his proposal was highly subject to criticism because psychedelic drugs were a core element of his approach. "Most people would immediately dismiss the tangled complex of thoughts developed by the McKennas... as a projection of their own confused psyches, amplified by the uncontrolled ingestion of large amounts of psychedelics. McKenna freely admitted this." [6]

On the other hand, if we consider the calendars of all the North American indigenous populations from the ancient Maya to today's Hopi, it's significant that they all agree there's a major change coming to life on earth in 2012. It's true that one could simply dismiss this as a single voice arguing that the calendars and the prophecies originate from the same source historically (namely, the Olmecs and the Maya). But it's striking that over a course of 2,000 years the prophecies have expanded to include many more details about what will happen in 2012 – additional prophecies have been documented that support the same underlying contentions.

This does not mean that all sources agree on what will happen. The Aztecs believed that the return of Quetzalcoatl would cause "all hell to break loose" on earth. The Maya and their concept of Kukulkan which predates the Aztecs, appear to look forward to his return believing that with his coming, he will restore our true human nature and spirit centeredness, making us aware of the "invisible landscape" or the *Spiritus mundi* of Yeats. This revived attentiveness they deem to be an exciting rebirth of human life on earth.

The other side of the argument suggests that 2012 may be a great time of war and destruction. Today's Mayan shamans, taken from Lawrence Joseph's discussion with the Barrios brothers, are seriously worried about cataclysmic events in 2012. Based upon a cosmic sign from the stars (Venus eclipsing the Pleiades in the noon-day sun on December 21, 2012) and his interpretation of certain *pyramid prophecies*, Patrick Geryl is off looking for a safe place to ride out the storm of 2012. Likewise, hundreds of the rich and perhaps famous (and some governments) are convinced that a catastrophe of the first order of magnitude will occur, probably motivated by the fear of the predicted solar storms of 2012. They are busy retrofitting missile silos and constructing livable apartments to shield themselves from the coming disaster. It certainly appears that for every 2012 enthusiast you find anticipating a transformation of consciousness, you can hit upon a doomsday prophet who warns of the vast destruction set to transpire at exactly the same milestone. This fact alone shows the ambiguity of the predictions and should reduce our confidence in the precision of their fulfillment. *Be warned, take precautions, but don't sell everything and move to the hills.* The alert level is elevated, but there's no assurance a disaster *must* happen.

Science Weighs In

Science has given no quarter to the 2012 proposal that the eclipse of the dark rift by the sun in December 2012 portends horrific outcomes. First off, it points out that the eclipse already occurred in 1999 and 2000 and we didn't experience any detrimental effects. Next, it insists that there's no way to measure any manner of radiation from the galaxies center whose flow might be interrupted by such an eclipse. 2012 proponents believe it exists, but it's nothing more than an article of 2012 faith and dogma. This factor has such a low probability it's foolish to pay attention to it. Unlike biblical faith which is based on what its adherents believe are historical precedents (like the *Exodus event* or the *Resurrection of Christ*), there's no precedent or science to support the belief there's "radiation coming from the center of the galaxy" that is crucial to life on earth.

In contrast, Science offers the most tangible and frightening doomsday scenarios offered today. The possibility is very real that a devastating virus like Ebola could go global and decimate earth's population. As we described at the outset of this book, there's plenty of precedence for this occurrence (think of the *Plague* in the medieval times or the Spanish Flu of 1918). This probability is very high. We should perpetually be on guard against such a threat.

Likewise, a biogenetic creation gone wrong can devastate the human race just as the movie *Legend* portrayed. The prospect for a *Chimera* that harms rather than helps the evolution of humankind is a possibility that science itself discloses. As indicated in the latter portion of this book, this eventuality may have serious implications in fulfilling biblical prophecy. Plus, the ethical questions are enormous. It's an indictment to our culture that we aren't discussing what science is doing and asking questions whether we should allow such experimentation to take place. We seem stuck on embryonic harvesting of stem cells and the sensationalist issue of human cloning. However, Christians who believe we must stay awake and be aware of the coming of the Antichrist are asleep, failing to notice that through these happenings his advance guard is at the door. The probability is very high that major developments are coming down the pike, some good to be sure, but others to the detriment of humanity. My counsel: Be warned and be worried – very worried.[7]

Astronomers today are actively tracking possible near earth objects that could strike our planet causing a cataclysmic impact. The precedence for this hardly needs to be pointed out. We reviewed a number of events occurring in the past 3,000 years which indicate the probability of another such *deep impact* is very high. Many alternative history buffs and biblical "apocalyptics" predict this type of catastrophe is likely to occur in or around 2012. Science doesn't identify any particular object destined to actually strike the earth at this moment. Nevertheless, it's working on plausible scenarios and feasible ways to launch a defense against such comet assaults. We should be glad that so many scientists take this threat seriously. Unfortunately, it's unlikely that FEMA or anyone else has any plan to deal with a major calamity involving a million deaths from a meteor strike.

What may seem to be an "impossible prevention" we are pursuing; but the "essential response" we seem to be leaving unrehearsed.

When the subject moves to *volcanoes and earthquakes,* no one needs a scientific study to offer compelling evidence that such natural disasters will take place. In 2010, we saw a historic number of flights disrupted as a volcano erupted in Iceland. We witnessed a killer earthquake in Haiti killing over one million people. The prospect for some manner of natural disaster (many orders of magnitude greater) is an apprehension many live with every day. There's really no avoiding this one. Living in the Seattle area, I worry about the prediction that a "nine-plus" earthquake could strike our area with devastating results. The experts in plate tectonics predict that such a massive earthquake, virtually unprecedented in recorded history, could happen here at any time.[8] And that's if Mount Rainer doesn't blow its top first, just like its neighbor Mount St. Helens did in 1980.

In contrast, there are the pseudo-scientists that promote the possibility of Planet X, *aka Nibiru,* swinging by our planet in 2012 and being the trigger to the calamities typically depicted. But the most noted authority on this theory, Zecharia Sitchin, indicates that while he believes this has happened before and will happen again (as it repeats about every 3,600 years according to him), he asserts the next flyby is still 1,000 years away – *no relevance whatsoever to 2012.* Even if Nibiru exists, the evidence for feeling its presence in the short-term is nil. There are many advocates who predict it's another real element of the coming disasters in 2012 – but there's no empirical evidence to verify the claim.

Science certainly doesn't *prophesy* anything. But it *predicts* the likelihood of all sorts of catastrophic occurrences that could result in Doomsday (even weighting events with a mathematical probability). The highly likely near-term disaster is the predicted solar maximum of 2012. This one could be for real as *there is precedent and real science to support the concern.* As I indicated earlier, there are many persons and institutions committing serious resources to consider the issue and take precautions. We would likely be right to suppose the amount of effort falls below best efforts to be on guard against a real disaster. So continuing to sound the alarm on this possible cataclysm seems mandatory. Any readers who work with public utilities should encourage top management to do what's necessary to safeguard the power grid from this natural and frankly, highly predictable possibility. The crazy activity of the sun in 2005 likely precipitated the killer Hurricanes we experienced in the Gulf of Mexico. In that event alone, there's plenty of history suggesting we do whatever disaster recovery planning we can. There's also plenty of precedence for blaming those who fail to plan ahead. Just ask British Petroleum about off-shore drilling rigs. Do they feel they took sufficient steps to prevent blowouts or did the necessary planning for how to deal with wells spewing out vast volumes of oil at massive depths? It appears that the physics of a 5,000 foot depth were never factored in to their recovery plans. The *gulf oil spill of 2010* may yet be determined to be a result of criminal negligence.

Mysticism and the Search for Meaning

Mysticism and the occult heavily influenced many of the prophets and the prophecies we've discussed. We've seen a fantastic number of intellectuals and academics, convinced that the old-time religion is defunct who've discovered an alternative form of spirituality. Underlying the whole 2012 phenomenon is a search for some type of spiritual reality that can deliver a way out of our seemingly intractable dilemmas, be it global warming, nuclear self-destruction, or the individuals' angst about the meaning of life. By settling on the meaning of supposed prophecies believed coded into the many and infamous megalithic creations (such as the henges and the pyramids), the 2012 prophets hope a transcendent quality to life can be squeezed from these ancient works of stone.

Pyramidologists, of both the Egyptian and Mayan variety, are eager to find guidance in the artifacts of ancient civilizations. Their discoveries (if valid) warrant a belief that "something bigger than us" has been at work, directing us and moving us forward. The 2012 alternate historians have actually taken to ancestor worship – believing that our forebears were much smarter than what we've heretofore acknowledged. They look to the artifacts of ancient civilizations, hoping that once dusted off they will disclose our destiny. It's a bad pun, but this search gives new meaning to *fortune hunting.*

While the essential assumption is true – our forebears were a lot more intelligent than what we once thought – it's quite a leap to suppose that their artifacts hold the key to our future. Indeed, while the Mayan calendar stone (with its precision in dating) or Stonehenge (through its ability to measure the size of the earth) were both examples of sheer genius set in stone, neither justify placing hope in the hands of our pagan ancestors and their antediluvian star gazing ways.

The belief in ancient astronauts or divine-human hybrids (the demigod) as a substitute for the Judeo-Christian God is a frequent theme we've seen. Those who believe in such beings may contend that their primary point is that these (not-so-mythical) creatures are the origin of our concepts of God; but their real intent may be more *existential*. By relocating their "ground of being" to *super humans* or *extraterrestrials*, they seek relief from contemplating the lonely and unpredictable plight of humanity without God. They find comfort in the fact that our existential state isn't what they formerly feared it was. It's not just that they seek to know that we are not alone. Rather, it's their hope that we're *not on our own*. They fear what may happen to humanity left to its own devices. Indeed, expectations exist in a number of quarters that we might soon witness the unveiling of the existence of aliens by our governments. However, given their reluctance to come clean with the public before, there's really no telling what our leaders might choose to reveal. Should we really expect ET to have "come home?" This occurrence is a wild card that's almost impossible to predict. Whatever is motivating "extraterrestrials" to play hide and seek (should they even turn out to be ET) or our governments to cloak what they've discovered about them, it seems there's little reason to trust whatever we're finally allowed to learn. Given my personal belief that this whole phenomenon is a spiritual deception, I'll remain skeptical even if ET was to appear. Furthermore, given the history with our governments, how can we trust whatever meaning they ascribe to such beings in the upcoming *official disclosure* should it come to pass? Again I say, "Beware aliens bearing gifts" – or governments who fail to fully disclose them on a timely basis.

The contact with *spiritual agencies*[9] is a major sub-plot to the 2012 phenomenon and the prophecies for *a new world order*. Whether we're evaluating Madame Blavatsky, Alice Bailey, Heinrich Himmler, Adolf Hitler, Aleister Crowley, W. B. Yeats, Aldous Huxley, J.J. Hurtak, Benjamin Crème, or Terrence McKenna, we consistently discover the use of drugs as a door opener to channel spirit guides and encounter *the other side*. The conclusion we can draw from reviewing the statements and actions of this consortium of esoterics is that any spiritual encounter must be okay as long as it connects us to the spiritual realm and grants us an exhilarating experience.

But those who know better, like John Major Jenkins (who I quoted in the matter of *remote viewing*), understand that there are some spirit beings that aren't beneficent. Even Daniel Pinchbeck, who is all too eager to engage with spiritual entities or archetypes through imbibing drugs, has expressed the same warnings. Seeking trance states to communicate with *the other side* is a true walk on *the wild side*. As we often hear, "Kids don't try this at home."

Likewise, the chroniclers of the "Stargate Conspiracy" (Lynn Picknett and Clive Prince) throw up the yellow flag when it comes to handing over the controls of our government and our lives to the "Ennead 9" – the channeled masters who claim we live on "the only planet of choice." While they may be real disembodied entities, may exist outside of space/time, and we may be enthralled with the mere fact we can communicate back and forth, they haven't proven themselves worthy of our trust. In fact, just the opposite is true. It's instructive that Jesus warned his disciples as He did: *"Don't be impressed that demons are subject to your commands; be awed instead that your names are written in the book of life"* (Luke 10:20 paraphrased). Spiritual experiences may impress us and change our way of thinking, but they don't necessarily imply we'll be better off for the encounter. Our attitude toward the spirit world ought to be our attitude toward UFOs: There's no doubt the phenomenon exists, but what does it mean? And more importantly, what are we going to do about it? Are these phenomena pointing to a true "ground of being" or just the opposite – the potential for our beings being "ground up?"

Perhaps it's wonderful luck that all of these spiritual entities are eager to predict our future and interpret our past. It's staggering how many channeled sources there are to choose from; and yet, it's all-the-more sinister that these many voices say the same thing: *We are gods, we will achieve new levels of consciousness, and we can count on these spiritual sources to give us reliable predictions about the future.* Unfortunately, those that have gotten too close to these entities render a different verdict. Most of these forces prove to be menacing and self-seeking. They frequently voice not-so-subtle anti-Semitic statements. Historically they've proven to be behind some of humanity's worst moments and motivations. *Despite all protests to the contrary, there isn't much to be proud of in the history of mysticism and spiritism.* While occultists say they seek (in the new order) to overcome the divisions of the past and wish to help us achieve our ultimate destiny (i.e., realizing our divine nature), we're wise to ask whether their methods will again prove fascist and criminal exactly like the Nazi experience exemplified.[10] That history is the best evidence we have to go on. Historical precedent should cause grave doubt as to whether any good thing can come from this ages-old esotericism.

The World Religion to Come is Already Here

Friedrich Nietzsche provided an intellectual basis for seeking after a religion and science joined at the hip to create the *Übermensch*. Nietzsche believed that the only possible solution to the death of God is for man to buck up. Man must stand up, throw away any timidity, and become the measure of all things. *To overcome, humanity must become the "overman."*

At its core, the religion of the new age is fundamentally the same as ancient *Gnosticism* which likely influenced the Knights Templar to drift away from orthodoxy and likewise caused the Freemasons to posit a deistic god as the basis for their self-proclaimed "non-religious" religion. God exists – but to Masonry, he is a distant deity that only builds rules and rigor into the structure of the universe. He doesn't demand worship. He didn't send His Son for our redemption. God may be *the Great Geometrer* but He's neither our *savior nor* our *judge*. The dogma (and diagnosis) of this new-age religion (now widely adopted) is stated as follows, "The only thing wrong with human beings is our failure to realize we are 'gods.'" In other words, we don't need to be relieved of genuine moral guilt. We need to be unburdened of what the motivational speaker Zig Ziglar calls, *"Stinkin' thinkin.'"* Secret knowledge infused through initiation *(which is Gnosticism by definition)*, will bring us "home to ourselves." According to the world's oldest religion, this is the sort of salvation we need.

Indeed, who among the 2012 enthusiasts disagrees with the following article of faith? "At the center of the creation is humanity. We are the kings and queens of creation. In us, nature (and therefore God) becomes conscious." *New age* proponents, along with 2012 enthusiasts, encourage us to recognize our own godhood. Moreover, for our species to survive we must experience the transformation of consciousness that will engender absolute self-knowledge – surely, "we are 'gods' and knew it not." Or as the Snake said tempting Eve, "Eat the apple and you will be like God, knowing both good and evil."

To the biogeneticist, this article of faith is a license to go forth and reconfigure the building block of humankind and the animal kingdom – our very DNA. To be sure, what could be a better way to lay claim to our own godhood than to get busy and build better human attributes in the physical world? The era of the transhuman isn't coming soon – it's already here – and we've been asleep at the wheel for ten years or more while it's gained momentum. Now we must worry if it's already too late to stop the train.

In my analysis, America has been positioned to be the caretaker bringing forth this new reality. Now, don't get me wrong: I like to wave the flag and even play John Phillip Souza marches. I'm very proud of America. We remain the greatest nation on earth. But we've fallen from the pedestal we once occupied. Additionally, I don't think it's such a good idea for our patriotism to be melded to our religious aspirations. Call it separation of Church and State. That's why I don't think it's unpatriotic to raise the question of what our Nation's Founders really had in mind when they erected the pagan structures in Washington DC. No doubt we may be achieving the destiny that our forefathers planned for us. Perhaps Francis Bacon would be proud. Like the evil Emperor in *Star Wars* when referring to the ominous *Death Star*, Bacon might gush "The New Atlantis is now FULLY operational." But as we've discussed, if our biblical worldview continues to wane, what this really portends is opening a doorway for hell to come on earth.

Yet, when all is said and done, the final question we must ask is, "Can we really trust ourselves to bring forth this secular utopia? Will humanity alone with no God to ground our morals and ethics be able to birth this brave new world?" History suggests that we should question whether *humanity* operating on its own moral sense remains *humanitarian*. The American Revolution went the right way, but the French Revolution led to *Madame Guillotine*. This is because the American Revolution mixed Freemasonry with Presbyterianism. In contrast, the French Revolution was a straight shot of classical paganism operating without reference to the God of the Bible. Liberty suffered. And so did many innocents.

Connecting Biblical and 2012 Prophecies

Christian *apologists*, among whom I include myself, are always looking for stronger defenses for the faith. For instance, if we believe that science has made a discovery to help prove intelligent design we are quick to make the most of it. We rejoice if archeology unearths something proving a challenged detail in the Bible to be true. Often feeling attacked by modernism from every angle, this is our predictable recourse. However, when it comes to whether prophecy in the Bible supports the *2012 prophecies*, a word of caution is in order.

There are many predictions coming from many different sources from around the world, from different periods of history, and from different peoples. There are the prophecies of Nostradamus and the predictions of Newton. There is the Zohar's testimony that the Messiah will come to the Jews in 2012, the prophecy of St. Malachy that there's only one more Pope before Rome is destroyed; and although we've chosen not to discuss it, there is *Webbot* which a few believe has a good track record in predicting cataclysms. It too warns of 2012. All of these voices harmonize that something big will happen in 2012. It's compelling that so many sources sound the same alarm. It's almost incomprehensible that nothing will come of 2012, given the warnings of so many voices from many continents and many different times. Indeed, the probability seems impossibly low that *nothing will happen in 2012 that smacks of the apocalypse.*

But since these voices are from pagan sources or outside the auspices of Judeo-Christian orthodoxy, we must exercise *discernment*. The possibility for a massive deception is real, particularly if you believe as do I that there are spiritual forces at play that mean us harm. For fellow Christians who may be reading, please take my caution into advisement. For casual readers and the undecided, please be clear on my position: *2012 isn't disclosed in the Bible as a date of particular import.*

As we saw at the close of the last chapter, there are interpretations of selected passages, particularly the Book of Daniel, which may lead some to conclude that the "final seven years of human history *as we know it*" may be kicked off in 2012. The probability is clearly higher than at any other moment in the past 2,000 years, given the many predictions that something big seems sure to happen and that doing the math shows select dates to be particularly portentous.

Nevertheless, a yellow light of caution should be flashing brightly. If we've learned anything, we should surely recognize that predicting Doomsday is a tricky business; there's no reward for being accurate and there's penalty aplenty for being wrong.

Having made that point clear, I nonetheless believe that the likelihood for something significant to happen in 2012, as it relates to the apocalyptic future, is more than possible – it's *probable*. 2012 may be a year like no other. I, for one, will sleep with one eye open.

334

Notes

[1] Alternatively, as Ebenezer Scrooge suggested to the apparition he witnessed (the ghost of Jacob Marley), Scrooge wasn't willing to believe in him because he might merely be an *undigested morsel of meat*, or an *undercooked potato.*

[2] Discernment also involves *wisdom*. Experience teaches us a great deal; we often correlate the education of life experience with what we label wisdom. However, I will stop with the anatomy of "predicting" at this point less the discussion get too philosophical.

[3] The philosopher, Immanuel Kant, based his philosophy upon this *admission*. In effect, he accepted that human beings couldn't absolutely know that what we sense is the way things really are. However, once we understand *how* we sense and think, we can nevertheless build a foundation for knowledge based upon "how our minds work." He called the former type of knowledge "*transcendent* knowledge" which only God could have. Humans can have only "*transcendental* knowledge." The core issue is whether there really is any meaningful difference once we acknowledge that all knowledge humans have, by definition, is only *human* knowledge.

[4] Lest I be guilty of a circular argument, allow me to clarify. Regarding the Pyramids, there are scholarly studies from the 19th century, but generally, today's academicians don't acclaim them. More recent findings challenge many of the old conclusions. If we are dealing with information that is open to scientific investigation, "newer" is probably better. However, with information that is not open to such poking around, "newness" is not necessarily helpful. Scholarship surrounding the Bible is useful even if it is very old. Indeed, the opposite value seems to be true when studying ancient manuscripts. Commentaries that are closest to the time of the source material may be the most valuable. In the case of the Maya, if we had manuscripts describing the Mayan religion, their calendars, etc., dated from the 1st century, these would likely be much more valuable than most research done today.

[5] Not that academic confirmation is totally necessary. Much of academia has been shown to reinforce the status quo out of self-interest. Recently, the whole issue of global warming was cast in doubt when it became clear that many academicians were fudging the facts to reassure a continued flow of financial research monies from the government to analyze the phenomenon.

[6] Daniel Pinchbeck, *2012: The Return of Quetzalcoatl*, pg. 102.

[7] Notwithstanding, Christians who believe God is "in charge" should continue to believe that God's providence is real and "the whole world is in His hands." But preparation is still mandatory.

[8] The Alaska "Good Friday" earthquake in 1964 near Anchorage measured 9.2 in strength and is perhaps the strongest on record. The Pacific Northwest should be wary.

[9] Or *Jungian archetypes* could be the selected phrase depending upon how clinical your language need be to derive a personal sense of credibility.

[10] It's also curious that the sources for this out-of-this-world information are so critical of Judaism and Christianity – especially given that the adherents of these new age dogmas like to use Christian words and biblical names, but their meaning is clearly heterodox. It takes no time at all to sniff out how variant to traditional and respected views their interpretations are. It's easy to draw the conclusion that these mystical agents of "the other side" are very much at war with the forces most of us consider good. It's all too easy to draw the conclusion that these agents really mean us harm, not help, when we examine their fruit.

Chapter 16:
The Denial of Doom

And as it was in the days of Noe (Noah), so shall it be also in the days of the Son of man. They did eat, they drank, they married wives, they were given in marriage, until the day that Noah entered into the ark, and the flood came, and destroyed them all.
Likewise also as it was in the days of Lot; they did eat, they drank, they bought, they sold, they planted, they builded (built); but the same day that Lot went out of Sodom it rained fire and brimstone from heaven, and destroyed them all.
Even thus shall it be in the day when the Son of man is revealed.

(Luke 17:26-30)

*Knowing this first, that there shall come **in the last days scoffers**, walking after their own lusts, and saying, "Where is the promise of his coming? For since the fathers fell asleep, all things continue as they were from the beginning of the creation." For this they willingly are ignorant of, that by the word of God the heavens were of old, and the earth standing out of the water and in the water: Whereby the world that then was, being overflowed with water, perished.*

(II Peter 3:3-6)

Ernst Becker and the Denial of Death

In 1973, an important book was published that crossed the lines of philosophy, anthropology, and psychology. Written by Ernst Becker, it was entitled, *The Denial of Death*. It won the Pulitzer Prize for non-fiction in 1974.

Becker relied on the prior work of Søren Kierkegaard, Sigmund Freud, Erich Fromm, and especially Otto Rank. A good writer, Becker made the obscure wisdom of *existentialism* and *psychoanalysis* accessible to many people. "As Becker clearly states himself, *The Denial of Death* was to 'fix' Sigmund Freud with the help of the lesser known, once disciple of Freud, Otto Rank. Whereas Freud explained the motivations and neuroses of human nature to unconscious instinctual drives [mostly sexual], Becker and Rank see man's problems based on his basic split between his limited body and his limitless mind. This basic dualism is a universal form that can be seen throughout history in all works."[1]

Becker asserts that, when it comes to the subject of our mortality, *human beings are double minded*. On the one hand, we know we will die. On the other, we seem called to do something with our lives that is heroic, which proves our meaning. We seek a positive legacy. In short, *we strive to amount to something.* Becker says, "The hope and belief is that the things that man creates in society are of lasting worth and meaning, that they outlive or outshine death and decay, that man and his products count."

Our nightmare is that *death* is certain and permanent while *significance* is not only fleeting, it's ultimately fictional. Our lives are full of attempts to deny death. We build our character and our identity upon our claim to fame. We try to attach our worth to something we do or something we believe we are. This endeavor consumes us.

Becker believes that this effort is a necessary exercise for human beings to live in the world. However, this "immortality project" (as he calls it) prevents self-knowledge. We live in denial, hiding in dark shadows throughout our days, avoiding any light of awareness that might uncover the truth that we are nothing more than limited beings with an unpredictable destiny. As Shakespeare laments in Macbeth's soliloquy:

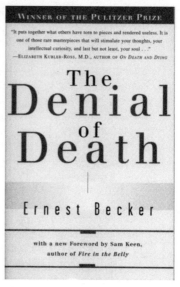

FIGURE 69 - *THE DENIAL OF DEATH*

> *Tomorrow and tomorrow and tomorrow,*
> *Creeps in this petty pace from day to day*
> *To the last syllable of recorded time,*
> *And all our yesterdays have lighted fools*
> *The way to dusty death. Out, out, brief candle!*
> *Life's but a walking shadow, a poor player*
> *That struts and frets his hour upon the stage*
> *And then is heard no more: it is a tale*
> *Told by an idiot, full of sound and fury,*
> *Signifying nothing.*

In short, whether it's conscious or not, we persist in our self-deception. We ignore the Socratic admonition, "The unexamined life is not worth living." We disregard the hard truth about what makes us tick. We may fool others – but we surely fool ourselves.

Becker presses the point that *evil* is what happens when we *deny our mortality and seek to destroy all threats to what we deem our source for meaning.* Religious wars would certainly fall into this category, but so would the efforts to overturn religion in the name of science. Becker states:

> For all organisms, then, opposing and obliterating power is evil – it threatens to stop experience... men are truly sorry creatures because they have made death conscious. They can see evil in anything that wounds them, causes ill health, or even deprives them of pleasure. Consciousness means too that they have to be preoccupied with evil even in the absence of any immediate danger; their lives become a meditation on evil and a planned venture for controlling it and forestalling it.

While Becker may be guilty of dramatizing *the evil that men do* being so heavily influenced as he was by the holocaust, it's inadequate to offer a summary characterization of his views with no more than a clichéd phrase like *human behavior is selfish and self-seeking*.

Indeed, his insight into our underlying motivation is a genuine breakthrough: We do evil primarily to protect our *immortality project*, our claim to fame. If someone dares to upset what we perceive substantiates our self-worth, we are quick to strike out against any and all such perpetrators. We are compelled to eliminate such threats because we preserve the foundation for our life's meaning – it's sacred – there's nothing more important to us whether we are conscious of it or not.

While Becker didn't use these exact words, nonetheless they concisely state his position: Our *quest to protect life's meaning becomes the root of our evil.* Let's administer a self-test: Ask yourself these three questions:

- What is your most "cherished" belief that gives meaning to your life?

- *What happens when someone challenges this belief?* Are you angry or threatened? Are you quick to strike back?

- *What is the reason for your belief?* Is the foundation of your faith immune to any sort of *proof to the contrary?*

If you're honest, any contradiction posed to your most treasured belief, if you haven't examined why you believe it, is a *flash point.* You won't be able to let the matter go, to walk away. You will strike back, no holds barred, to reassure yourself that you still have it right. My point being: It's dangerous to ask yourself why you believe what you do; but it's even more dangerous *not* to face the possibility that your beliefs could be dead wrong.

How Doomsday Exposes Meaning – or Meaninglessness

In light of the insights that mirror so much wisdom from many other religions and philosophers through the ages, how should we understand what we popularly label, *Doomsday*?

If we're like most people, we avoid thinking about it. At some point, however, we may conclude, it's a topic we can't evade. After all, as I have demonstrated, there is now so much discussion about the threats of war, disease, planetary catastrophe, and wild weather – the apprehension grows daily. *Doomsday is impossible to ignore.*

Confronted as we are with the realistic possibility of *Doomsday*, how do we react? Certainly, we must feel endangered. However, isn't this fear easily dismissed? Isn't Doomsday just like *the denial of death*, but on a "whole-species" basis? After all, is there anything more shattering to our notion of meaning, if something – no matter how straightforward or sinister – was to wipe our entire species off the face of the planet?

It quickly becomes apparent that our notion of God (is He or isn't He real?) has a lot to do with how we handle our predicament. For those who believe in an infinite creator God, a personal being who broods over his creation, that (as Evangelical Christians preach) wants to have a "personal relationship with us," how could we possibly believe that God would allow such a thing to happen? Certainly, we base our *shared sense of meaning* upon an overt notion that our existence on this planet is no accident. Something or someone greater created us – there is no way that God would allow all of life to expire. Surely, he would even overturn our free will if we were hell-bent on destroying the planet (and ourselves). For those of us who believe in the reality of a divine presence in the universe (however we understand *the divine being*), there is little doubt about our conclusion: *Evil won't prevail.* The good guys will come out on top.

On the other hand, if we believe there is no God, perhaps we might sooner come to grips with at least the theoretical possibility that a future cataclysm will end civilization and the entire human species. With the absence of *God as a protector*, there is no longer any insurance against annihilation – there is no guardian upon which we can rely – there is no higher-power that can watch out for what happens to us. We are *left to our own devices.*

Some would state stoically that the sooner we accept this bleak truth, the better off we are. Indeed, many would counsel that this is a much more honest way to approach the matter of Doomsday. After all, isn't counting on God to intervene on our behalf – to stop us from destroying ourselves – dishonest, negligent, and even reprehensible? Doesn't atheism, in this context, demand we take responsibility for our actions far more than relying upon God?

For the moment, let's say this is so. The question then arises, "When it comes to whether we should dismiss all meaning to our existence, is the atheist capable of being consistent with his or her own presuppositions?" Can he or she actually get comfortable with the starkness of a universe without God? We ask this question because we know that, despite what we say we believe, at the end of the day, we are all very much alike. The quest for meaning is part of our DNA just as much as our denial of death; in fact, it's one and the same.

Just consider how the *unbeliever* acts when tragedy occurs. He might cry out, "Why me?" like anyone else; when he should remember that such a question implies a belief in life's purpose – which his stated belief system expressly denies. How can there be *misfortune* if we begin with no guarantees and no destiny? If there is no God to offer an explanation, how can we obtain an answer? If there are no fates to cause the occurrence, how can we look for a reason?

When bad things happen to good people, the last person that should be shocked is the atheist. The atheist can't label any catastrophe *a tragedy*. It is what it is. The cry goes out to the stars and the sky, but the universe answers with silence.

That's why atheism is so inconsistent with humanity's wiring. When calamity strikes, *even the most pessimistic atheist is stunned*. The unbeliever, just like the believer, expects better. The atheist too feels the same initial *sense that there must still be hope*. Accordingly, we shouldn't wonder why the atheist, just like a person of faith, gets upset if something bad happens. The reality is that *even the atheist loses his or her equanimity* when an outcome seems brutal or unjust. In our better moments, we all anticipate social justice and positive outcomes. It may be only instinctual, but we believe somewhere there is *a guarantor for the good*.

That's why, even for the atheistic materialist, there is an indisputable aspect of human expectation insisting *there is something beyond ourselves*. The reality of this underlying conviction defies even the hard-core atheist to mutter "so what" at our demise. Our optimism, our *assurance* (that often needs to be *re-assured* by our loved ones, a good book, or an uplifting sermon!) is simply a fact of humanity's essence. Therefore, we build our love and aspirations upon a rock called *meaning*. What happens *does matter*, not just to us, but also to *the grand scheme of things*. We want to believe every person deserves a happy ending. It's my belief that we all share this confidence in life's meaning because God planted it in our being. It's *an innate testimony to God's existence* since it inspires our best moments and causes us to seek justice, love, and ultimately Him.

Perhaps paradoxically, and very much on the other hand, I would insist that we meditate on the impossibility *of a universe without a God*. Even the faithful should thoughtfully consider this possibility despite its appearing to be a moment of infidelity.

Speaking purely theoretically, the search for *meaning* could indeed be nothing more than a primal delusion to which we all succumb – a survival mechanism we should outgrow. We may all share in a happy but false fantasy about what life means. Perhaps it's nothing more than *a diabolical curse* because every day we uncritically quest after fairness and significance. If it's indeed no more than a diabolical trick, our best and most noble ambitions are destined to fail.

While our optimism may be nothing more than a deception that makes life bearable, Becker (and others who consider themselves existentialists), would nevertheless insist that we squarely face this possibility, however theoretical. The absurd could be our lot. Before we search for a way out of this dungeon, we should recognize that we might not find a doorway. We must consider the distinct possibility we can't rid ourselves of our chains of meaninglessness.

As a teenager, I remember a popular expression cast about by many to help keep things in perspective: *Today is the first day of the rest of your life.* This notion was a refreshing way of recognizing that we can put our past behind us and start anew. Yet, the abrupt converse of this statement may be better medicine awakening us to our "existential situation:" *Today could be the last day of our life.*

For believers and unbelievers alike, we don't awaken in the mornings with this thought keeping it firmly in mind as we live out each day. If we did, we probably wouldn't get out of bed. However, it doesn't make the possibility any less stark. The fact is, a bus could run over us today or tonight an asteroid could decimate our planet. Either way, our mortal life ends. Our consciousness comes to a halt. Perhaps we can avoid the former by staying at home. However, the latter possibility is one we can literally do nothing to circumvent.

So how should we deal with such fear? How do we *put Doomsday into perspective?*

Avoiding the Consequences of What Could Happen

When they are young, we read fairy tales to our children. But the tales we read today are highly sanitized versions of the old *Grimm's Fairy Tales* (first published in 1810). What we may not realize is just how grim these fairy tales used to be. The monsters and witches were much darker then, heroes were much more vulnerable, and the deaths of the villains much more gruesome.

Why did our forebears tell such frightful stories to their children? We know now it was how parents prepared their children for the reality of the dark world in which they lived. Evil was commonplace. Better to scare them to death early exposing them to the horrors of life, for such things were to be their firsthand experience sooner rather than later. It was in the parent's best judgment this sort of *tough love* conditioning was necessary as part of growing up.

This perspective contrasts so much with our protective methods of child rearing today, perhaps we should ask ourselves, "Which generation was right?" Should we teach our children that evil is easy to overcome, that death is easy to cheat? On the other hand, do we help our children understand that death is a part of life? Should they learn that evil sometimes wins and disasters occur? What type of reassurance is the proper balance between hoping for the best and not being surprised if bad things happen?

We sometimes talk about how we go *whistling in the dark* if we're afraid to face the dire circumstances in our way. What do we mean by this? What is the underlying motive for such behavior?

FIGURE 70 - HANSEL AND GRETEL FROM 1909 EDITION OF *GRIMM'S FAIRY TALES*

In essence, our whistling is our method to *normalize* the situation, to make it seem less imposing. Sometimes psychiatrists will describe this phenomenon as *minimizing* whatever threat disrupts our normal course of life. You know the familiar phrase, "The bigger they are the harder they fall." We may not believe it. Nonetheless, by saying this we muster the courage to face our enemies.

My family did this so very well it took me many years to learn how to deal with death and suffering. Our approach was to laugh it off or get things back to normal as quickly as we could. We might typically say something like "It's no big deal." We wouldn't face the possibility that the worse could happen and that we might not be able to cope. Instead of learning to square up to bad times and face the music, it was our habit to escape the pain. This failure to come to terms with tragedy and suffering almost ended my marriage 26 years ago when my father-in-law died from Lou Gehrig's disease (ALS) and I couldn't relate to my wife's feelings as she watched her father's health disintegrate before her eyes.

My supposition is that we have two essential methods of dealing with death from Doomsday – one healthy, the other, not so much. These are deep-seated human techniques to cope with drastic situations. The two phenomena outlined above give us a glimpse of what these methods are.

Method One: *Recognize that the cataclysm not only can happen, but also is eventually inevitable.* Furthermore, our encounter may be immediately ahead. We can embrace it and figure out how we should live our lives in light of it. We can make our meaning no longer contingent upon the denial of mortality and our particular and cherished plan for self-worth. We can recognize that we are finite trusting that our value is secured only after we link it to something that is much bigger than we are. In the case of those in the Judeo-Christian tradition, we can connect who we are and what our life means *to God*, who is infinite and assures our meaning. He is our point of reference. In other words, *we have meaning because God tells us we mean something to Him.* Moreover, the proof is in His promise that our lives are so valuable He will transform them – making them fit for eternity. As the Francis Schaeffer pointed out, *finite beings have meaning only if they have an infinite point of reference.* Otherwise, as the existentialist bemoans, we remain trapped in an absurd existence with "no exit" (Sartre).

Method Two: *Find ways to downplay Doomsday's potential occurrence.* As we read early on, our culture now more than ever is obsessed with the theme of *the end of days.* Doomsday captivates us. Our popular culture is replete with examples. So then, do we *really* deny Doomsday? At least on the surface, it seems that nothing could be further from the truth. However, sometimes things aren't quite what they seem.

In our defense, we might insist that we are taking action. We seek to dispel the worry and the gloom of doom. We read books. We go to movies. However, it's my contention that our captivation is much more akin to *whistling in the dark* than a medicinal assimilation of the frightening images of the fairy tale. We encounter the darkness to reassure ourselves that it isn't a menacing presence after all. We vaccinate ourselves with just enough of what could happen to comfort ourselves that it won't. It simply is too fantastic – so out of the question – that we would be foolish to lose any sleep over it. We venture out to a movie to watch the world end in the best special effects ever. After all, it's *only a movie*. The sun will rise again tomorrow. Life will go on.

So, in the final analysis, what does the doctor prescribe? Simply this: It's best to acknowledge that the end can happen *at any moment*. We may realize our worst fear. We shouldn't deny it. We should embrace it. Even if we cling, I believe rightly, to faith as our means to overcome anxiety and to resolve what may only appear to be absurd, it's wise to recognize the dilemma in which humankind finds itself. Once we appreciate our *existential* condition, we live a life that is far more authentic. That's the message we hear from true spirituality and philosophy.

Even from the perspective of the most pious and stalwart Christian, before any one of us can fully appreciate *the salvation message*, we should fully understand *our predicament without it*.

Who hasn't experienced a narrow escape, when someone you loved nearly "bought the farm?" Perhaps it was a spouse. Perhaps it was a child. When the reality your loved one is fine finally quiets your worst fears, you still never quite forget the feeling of *dread*. Being grateful, you may be forever changed. Living in light of that experience reminds you to keep your eyes wide open, be a bit more cautious, and take extra pains to protect those you love. If you fail to forearm yourself in this way, you've wasted what the calamity sought to teach.

A wise person once said, "Pagans waste their pains" – which is a statement of concise conviction that something greater than ourselves is teaching us a lesson we must learn. Even Nietzsche scolded his readers for not recognizing that all progress comes through pain. Seeking only pleasure as a cherished goal in life is a death knell for personal growth and meaning.

The Meaning Behind Our Attempt to Decode Doomsday

This being so, why do we seek to decode Doomsday? That is, as they used to say, the $64,000 question. History discloses time-after-time how humankind covets *the truth about the end of the world*. Many criticize this endeavor for a whole variety of reasons not the least of which is that no one has succeeded so far, although as we have seen, countless have tried. However, there are two other obvious explanations why we might want the world to end (which we rightly criticize):

- The first and most apparent negative reason is palpable: We seek to escape. Life has gotten too tough. We just can't handle the truth. We no longer have hope. We hate our lives. It's better if the whole shebang just blows up into a million bits.[2]

- The second is equally irresponsible. We throw in the towel and lament, "the world is going to hell in a hand basket. Why fight the battle any longer? I am such a small cog in the wheel, what difference can I really make?" In short, despair paralyzes us.[3]

On the other hand, could there be worthy motives? Is there justification to decode Doomsday? *Shouldn't we seek to decipher the date?*

It's my contention that we should – at least to the point of quantifying probabilities as I discussed in the previous chapter. To do otherwise is to avoid the reality of our species' finitude, failing to accept our limitations.

We can distinguish a number of solid and sound reasons to do so. In fact, there are no less than five valuable reasons why we should press on in our efforts to decode Doomsday.

The first reason is this: We attempt to break the doomsday code because we believe someone smart is (or was) out there, who knows (or knew) about Doomsday and is trying to help us to prepare ourselves for it – or to find a means to avoid it altogether. This someone could be the God of the Bible speaking through the Scripture, it could be our human ancestors from many millennia ago who left advice embedded in ancient documents or artifacts, or it could be extraterrestrials who may have had a hand in our evolution and are passing messages to us in unconventional channels.[4] The help is from the past or it's from above whether it's spiritual beings from another dimension or spacemen from some nearby region in outer space. Either way, we believe that we have access to truth that is out of this world (or at least out of the ordinary), and therefore it can make a big difference in how we live our lives. We quickly reckon (because it is far from obvious) that if this knowledge exists, it is encoded, and we must seek it earnestly in order to decipher it.

Secondly, if we discover this information does exist, *it throws a completely new light on the issue of meaning.* What would happen if we uncovered detailed information about the Mayan prophecies that really was beyond doubt? What if the biblical passages regarding the end time's scenario in fact mirror what happens in the months ahead? What if a spaceship lands on the White House lawn and proclaims that life exists throughout the universe – with radiant alien beings being *the living proof*? Furthermore, what if alien life forms inform us (as many science fiction and new age authors have ventured), that they have been *caretakers of life here on earth*? We should note that these outcomes are not necessarily mutually exclusive (that is, two or more of these discoveries could be true at the same time). However, the important point is that once transcendence has been proven (that something bigger than us does exist outside of our empirical everyday world); you can bet that life will never be the same. Our meaning may now have a stamp of legitimacy. *Decoding Doomsday may be the means to validate this transcendence.* It's a strong motivation to put our hands to the plow and unearth such evidence.[5]

Thirdly, for believers in the Judeo-Christian concept of afterlife or the kingdom of God (however it's interpreted), the supposition is that life to be will simply be much better than life today. Certainly, *we want our problems and pain eliminated by the coming of Messiah.* It may be Doomsday for the world, but because we experienced salvation, we look forward to the Kingdom of God, we see it as *our solution,* and it's our way out. Decoding Doomsday could tell us just how quickly we can get the heck out of Dodge. The sooner the better!

While we earlier correctly labeled this motive *irresponsible,* it does have a good side. From a biblical perspective, avoiding hardship is ultimately judged based upon whether such pain and suffering is self-induced or whether it's from genuine persecution or peril which resulted from a commendable stance we've chosen. As we've stated, the event that Christians call the *Rapture of the Church,* they also label "the Blessed Hope." There is no question that the Bible commends those believers who look forward to the return of the Christ and for those who seek the Kingdom of God. For instance, the *Book of Revelation* is the only book of the Bible *to promise a blessing to those who read it.* True Christianity, as I argued in my first book, *advocates the Apocalypse as an ever-present possibility that must guide the manner in which we live.* There should be no surprise at all that Christians (and Jews too) have tried to determine when Messiah comes (or comes back). It's the essence of the Bible's message from the time of the Bible's prophets forward.

Fourthly, for believers who take the Bible as a sacred book (that is to say – *literally* – as this is the most common shorthand expression for this approach), *seeking to know the time and seasons is simply a means to remind ourselves to be ready.* "Watch for you know not when the Son of Man comes." Being a good Christian means keeping an eye out for the Master. We do this not because we're afraid to get caught in a regrettable action, but because Jesus' disciples were admonished to be watchful. Like the wise and foolish virgins, we're to keep our "lamps trimmed" and buy extra oil in case the groom of the wedding feast tarries and doesn't show until the wee hours of the morning. To do otherwise (as stated in another of Jesus' parables dealing with the same subject), is to be "disobedient and foolish servants."

From the perspective of sharing the gospel message, what happens if we find evidence of the soon return of Christ? Wouldn't that cause unbelievers to rethink what they believe? Wouldn't it be smart to point out this truth since the consequences might be eternal for everyone alive today? *Compelling evidence derived from decoding Doomsday might just cause many to change their ways.* Salvation might be highly prized after all – before it's too late! Additionally, despite today's contrarian naysayers, it might even make the world be a better place in the meantime. *It's not just about fire insurance.* It's about standing up straight and doing the rights things.

Finally, there is another practical and wise reason to decode Doomsday. What if we find out that the world is ending due to a natural cataclysm that we can avoid with adequate preparation? What if we find out that the Mayans correctly prophesied the world's end? *Doomsday will happen in 2012 just as some Mayan authorities contend* – we learn the Maya did know a natural cyclical cataclysm happens every 5126 years! Is it best to stay in the dark?

No doubt, some disasters can't be avoided. However, there are some examples where taking action ahead of time can forestall or reduce the destruction that otherwise might be inescapable.

This is where most believers in *the end of days* agree. Whether it's because we advocate, "an ounce of prevention is worth a pound of cure," because we want to achieve some manner of spiritual transformation, because we can settle the question of life's meaning, or it's for the reason "our faith constrains us," *breaking the doomsday code is a worthy task.* Knowing what's ahead may allow us to take steps to prevent the worst from happening. Maybe there will be time to *build an ark* and protect a remnant of humanity. Perhaps we can create the right type of missile defense system to fend off a killer asteroid. It's even possible that Jesus Christ is set to return and establish his Kingdom.

It's not wrong to cry wolf when we hear the wolf growling. With one moment's notice, at least some of the sheep can be spared.

Tom Horn mentions the connection between *Apollo and the wolf.*[6] He indicates that Herodotus discussed a great people to the north of Greece known as the Hyperboreans, who worshipped Apollo and made an annual pilgrimage to the land of Delos, where they participated in the famous Apollo festivals there. Lycia, a small country in southwest Turkey, also had an early connection with Apollo, where he was known as *Lykeios, which ties* to the Greek word *Lycos* and means "wolf." "Wolfmen" are called *Lycans or lycanthropes* for this reason.[7]

Apparently since *Apollo and the wolf* are connected, perhaps the wolf is a good image we should associate with the coming Antichrist.

Consequently, two questions come to mind that you might wish to consider: First, *"Do you hear the growling of the wolf?"* And then secondly, *"What will you do about it?"* If you think the wolf is lurking just outside the light of the campfire, it might be time to get prepared. On the other hand, if you doubt the wolf is roving just outside of camp, perhaps you're content to remain as you are, asleep and warm in your sleeping bag.

Yet I wonder, given all that we've covered about what might be happening in the months and years just ahead, are you willing to bet your life and your eternal destiny that everything you've read is only me "crying wolf?"

My hope and sincere prayer for you is that you will conclude the very opposite. May you find your way to a relationship with "the Great Shepherd" whose name is Jesus Christ.

In the Gospel of John, Chapter 10, we read:

[7] *The said Jesus unto them again, Verily, verily, I say unto you, I am the door of the sheep.*

[8] *All that ever came before me are thieves and robbers; but the sheep did not hear them.*

[9] *I am the door; by me if any man enter in, he shall be saved, and shall go in and out, and find pasture.*

[10] *The thief cometh not, but for to steal, and to kill, and to destroy; I AM COME THAT THEY MIGHT HAVE LIFE AND THAT THEY MIGHT HAVE IT MORE ABUNDANTLY.*

[11] *I am the good shepherd; the good shepherd giveth his life for the sheep.*

[12] *But he that is an hireling, and not the shepherd, whose own the sheep are not, seeth the wolf coming, and leaveth the sheep, and fleeth; and the wolf catcheth them, and scattereth the sheep.*

[14] *"I am the good shepherd, and know my sheep, and am known of mine.*

[15] *As the Father knoweth me, even so know I the Father; and I lay down my life for the sheep.*

The Apostle John opened his gospel with the simple explanation of what we must do to become one of His sheep:

But as many as received him, to them gave he power to become the sons of God, [even] to them that believe on his name. (John 1:12)

May God lead you down the path to His safekeeping soon. Receive Him now. For our time, I'm afraid, grows shorter day-by-day.

Notes

[1] From the summary article on the unofficial Ernest Becker web site. See *http://www.ernest-becker.com/thedenialofdeath.*

[2] Even Freud once said that "death must be sweet" in a moment of despair.

[3] This is one extreme of neurosis, the other extreme involves being so ebullient about the possibilities, we live in unreality.

[4] I am of course only mentioning this "God as an alien astronaut" as a possibility, not that I give it equal credence to the other possibilities.

[5] In this regard, I endorse Kierkegaard's solution to dread. We must risk the meaning of our existence on the leap of faith that God is there. But unlike SK, the leap doesn't have to be an irrational one in the sense that there are "no good reasons" for believing. The predictions the Bible makes about what is going to happen "in the last days" provide compelling reasons to trust that the Bible is true and God is there.

[6] Horn, op. cit., pg.163.

[7] The original search engines included not only Yahoo! but also *Lycos*, whose symbol was a dog.

Bibliography

Andrews, Synthia and Colin, *2012: An Ancient Look at a Critical Time,* Penguin Books, New York, 2008, 318 pages.

Baigent, Michael and Leigh, Richard, *The Temple and the Lodge,* Arcade Publishing, New York, 1989, 306 pages.

Becker, Ernet, *The Denial of Death,* Free Press Paperbacks, New York, 1973, 314 pages.

Bauval, Robert & Gilbert, Adrian, *The Orion Mystery: Unlocking the Secrets of the Pyramids,* New York, Three Rivers Press, 1994, 325 pages.

Braden, Gregg, *Fractal Time: The Secret of 2012 and a New World Age,* Hay House, Inc., Carlsad, CA., 2009, 253 pages.

Braden, Russell, Pinchbeck, Jenkins, et al., *The Mystery of 2012,* Sounds True, Boulder CO., 2009, 465 pages.

Bradley, Michael, *The Secrets of the Freemasons,* Barnes & Noble, New York, 2006, 208 pages.

Busch, David Winston, *Appointed,* ACW Press, Eugene, OR., 2003, 318 pages.

----------, The Assyrian: Satan, His Christ, and the Return of the Shadow of Degrees, Xulon Press, United States, 2007, 339 pages.

Butler, Alan and Dafoe, Stephen, *The Knights Templar Revealed,* Barnes & Noble, New York 1999, 233 pages.

Byrne, Rhonda, *The Secret,* Atria Books, New York, 198 pages.

Church, J.R., *Hidden Prophecies in the Song of Moses,* Prophecy Publications, Oklahoma City, OK., 1991, 363 pages.

Collins, Andrew, *Beneath the Pyramids: Egypt's Greatest Secret Uncovered,* Virginia Beach, VA, A.R.E. Press, 2009, 262 Pages.

Cornuke, Robert, *Relic Quest,* Tyndale House Publishers, Wheaton, IL, 2005.

Dawkins, Richard, *The God Delusion,* First Mariner Books, New York, 2008, 463 pages.

DeStefano, Tony, Publisher, *Unlocking Mysteries with Solomon's Key,* TD Media, 2009, 143 pages.

Drosnin, Michael, *The Bible Code,* Simon & Schuster, New York, 1997, 249 pages.

----------, *The Bible Code II: The Countdown,* Penguin Books, New York, 2002, 283 pages.

Ehrman, Bart D., *Truth and Fiction in The Da Vinci Code,* New York, Oxford University Press, 2004, 207 pages.

Ferguson, Marilyn, The Aquarian Conspiracy: Personal and Social Transformation in the 1980s, J.P. Tarcher, Los Angeles, 1980, 448 pages.

Flew, Anthony, *There Is A God,* Harper One, New York, 2007, 222 pages.

Flynn, David, *Temple at the Center of Time: Newton's Bible Codex Deciphered and the Year 2012,* Official Disclosure, A Division of Anomalos Publishing House, (Crane, Mo.), 2008, 296 pages.

Geryl, Patrick, *The World Cataclysm in 2012: The Maya Countdown to the End of Our World,* Adventures Unlimited Press, Kepton, Illinois, 2005, 273 pages.

Hagee, John, *Jerusalem Countdown: A Prelude to War,* Front Line Publishing, Lake Mary, FL., 2007, 265 pages.

Hale, Christopher, *Himmler's Crusade,* Edison, NJ, Castle Books, 2006, 422 pages.

Heron, Patrick, *The Nephilim and the Pyramid of the Apocalypse,* Citadel Press, Kensington Publishing Corp., New York, 2004, 241 pages.

Hitchcock, Mark, 2012: The Bible and the End of the World, Harvest House Publishers, Eugene, OR., 2009, 184 pages.

----------, *The Apocalypse of Ahmadinejad,* Multnomah Books, Colorado Springs, CO., 2007, 208 pages.

Hildebrand, Lloyd B., *2012: Is This the End?* Bridge-Logos, Alachua, FL., 2009, 258 pages.

Hogue, John, The Essential Nostradamus for the 21st Century & Beyond, Vega Press, London, England, 272 pages.

Horn, Thomas R., *Nephilim Stargates: The Year 2012 and the Return of the Watchers,* Anomalos Publishing House, (Crane, MO.), 2007, 232 pages.

----------, *Apollyon Rising: 2012,* Anomalos Publishing, Crane, MO., 2009, 352 pages.

Horowitz, Mitch, *Occult America,* New York, Bantan Books, 2009, 290 pages.

Howarth, Stephen, *The Knights Templar,* Barnes & Noble, New York, 1982, 321 pages.

Jeffrey, Grant R., *Countdown to the Apocalypse,* WaterBrook Press (Colorado Springs, Co.), 2008, 227 pages.

----------, *The New Temple and the Second Coming*, WaterBrook Press, Colorado Springs, 2007, 204 pages.

Jenkins, John Major, *Maya Cosmogenesis 2012*, Bear & Company Publishing, Rochester, Vermont, 1998, 425 pages.

Jenner, Greg, *Planet X and the Kolbrin Bible Connection*, Silver Springs, NV, Your Own World Books, 2008, 78 pages.

Jones, Marie D., *2013: The End of Days or a New Beginning?* New Page Books, Franklin Lakes, NJ., 2008, 286 pages.

Joseph, Frank, *Atlantis and 2012*, Rochester, Vermont, Bear & Company Books, 2010, 246 pages.

Jung, C.G., Flying Saucers: A Modern Myth of Things Seen in the Skies, MJF Books, New York, 1978, 138 pages.

Knight, Christopher, and Butler, Alan, *Before the Pyramids: Cracking Archeology's Greatest Mystery*, Watkins Publishing, London, 2009, 271 pages.

LaHaye, Tim, *The Rapture: Who Will Face the Tribulation?* Harvest House Publishers, (Eugene, OR), 2002, 255 pages.

Lawrence, Joseph E., *Apocalypse 2012: An Investigation into Civilization's End*, Broadway Books (New York), 2007, 2008, 262 pages.

Livio, Mario, The Golden Ratio: The Story of Phi, the World's Most Astonishing Number, Broadway Books, New York, 2002, 294 pages.

Lowe, David W., Then His Voice Shook the Earth: Mount Sinai, the Trumpet of God, and the Resurrection of the Dead in Christ, Seimos Publishing, 2006, 167 pages.

Marrs, Jim, *Rule by Secrecy*, Harper Collins, New York, 2000, 467 pages.

Marzulli, L.A., Politics, Prophecy, and the Supernatural: The Coming Great Deception and the Luciferian Endgame, Anomalous Publishing ,Crane, Mo., 2007, 248 pages.

Missler, Chuck, *The Magog Invasion*, Western Front Publishing, Coeur d'Alene, Idaho, (date not disclosed), 311 pages.

----------, *Prophecy 20/20: Profiling the Future through the Lens of Scripture*, Thomas Nelson Publishers, Nashville, Tn.), 2006, 280 pages.

Nietzsche, Friedrich, *The Antichrist: A Criticism of Christianity*, New York, Barnes and Noble Publishing, 2006, Originally Published in 1896, 77 pages.

Nostradamus, *The Complete Prophecies of Nostradamus*, A & D Publishing, Radford, VA, 2007, 151 pages.

Newton, Sir Isaac, *A Dissertation upon the Sacred Cubit of the Jews,* from Miscellaneous Works of Mr. John Greaves, Professor Astronomy in the University of Oxford, Vol. 2, PP. 405-433, London, 1737.

Newton, Sir Isaac, *Revised History of Ancient Kingdoms: A Complete Chronology,* Larry and Marion Pierce, Editors, Master Books, Green Forest, AR., Revised Edition, 2009. 205 pages.

Ramotti, Ottavio Cesare, *Nostradamus: The Lost Manuscript,* Destiny Books, Rochester, NY, 1998, 167 pages.

Ravenscroft, Trevor, *The Spear of Destiny,* Samuel Weiser Inc., York Beach, Maine, 1st American Edition, 1973, 362 pages.

Redden, Wayne, 2012 in Bible Prophecy, with Shadow Mayan Tradition Clearly Cast Behind It, Winepress Publishing, Enumclaw, WA., 2008, 422 pages.

Rosenberg, Joel C., *Epicenter 2.0 Version: Updated and Expanded,* Tyndale House Publishers, Carol Stream, IL., 401 pages.

Ross, Scarlett, *Nostradamus for Dummies,* Wiley Publishing, Hoboken, N.J., 2005, 362 pages.

Ryrie, Charles C., *Dispensationalism, Revised and Expanded,* Moody Bible Institute, 2007, 265 pages.

Picknett, Lynn and Prince, Clive, The Stargate Conspiracy: Revealing the Truth Behind Extraterrestial Contact, Military Intelligence and the Mysteries Of Ancient Egypt, Berkley Books, New York, 1999, 425 pages.

Pinchbeck, *Daniel, 2012: The Return of Quetzalcoatl,* New York, Penguin Group, 2007, 411 pages.

Price, Randall, Searching for the Ark of the Covenant: Latest Discoveries and Research, Harvest House Publishers, Eugene, Oregon, 227 pages.

------------, *Searching for the Original Bible,* Harvest House Publishers, Eugene, Oregon, 2007, 293 pages.

Sanger, Mel, *2012: The Year of Project Enoch?* Rema Marketing, London, 2009, 253 pages.

Sherman, R. Edwin, Bible Code Bombshell: Compelling Scientific Evidence that God Authored the Bible, New Leaf Press, Green Forest, AR., 2005, 301 pages.

Stenger, Victor J., God: The Failed Hypothesis, How Science Shows That God Does Not Exist, Prometheus Books, Amherst, NY., 2007, 294 pages.

Szwast, Bruce, *The Life and Times of Archbishop James Ussher*, Master Books (New Leaf Publishing), Green Forest, AR., 2005, 311 pages.

Thomas, I.D.E., *The Omega Conspiracy: Satan's Last Assault on God's Kingdom*, Anamolous Publishing, Crane, MO., 2008, 195 pages.

Vision Revisited, *The Antichrist Identity*, Prime Republic Ltd., London, 2008, 179 pages.

von Daniken, Erich, *Chariots of the Gods*, Berkeley Books (Penguin Putnam), New York, 1999, 200 pages.

Winchester, Simon, *Karkatoa: The Day the World Exploded, August 27, 1883*, Harper Collins, New York, NY, 2003, 403 pages.

Woodward, S. Douglas, *Are We Living in the Last Days*? Woodinville, WA., 2009, 312 pages.

Index

About the Author

S. Douglas Woodward ("Doug") is currently an independent consultant serving emerging companies. Over the past twelve years, Doug has served as CEO, COO, and CFO of numerous software and Internet companies. Prior to his tenure in entrepreneurial efforts, he worked as an executive for Honeywell, Oracle, Microsoft, and as a Partner at Ernst & Young LLP. His technical background is in enterprise business strategy, software development and most recently in venture financing and business strategy.

Doug grew up in Oklahoma City, going to high school and college nearby (Norman). At 15, Doug was struck with a serious form of adolescent cancer, *Rhabdomyosarcoma*, which forced him to lose his left leg as a means to treat the disease. At the time of his illness (1969), recovery was likely in only 10% of the cases diagnosed. The experience had a dramatic impact upon Doug's spiritual life, linking him with dozens of family members, friends, ministers, nurses and doctors who showed great compassion and provided him with remarkable support. Doug cheated death however, through the great efforts of many doctors and the prayers of parents, brothers, family and friends.

Doug attended the University of Oklahoma where he received an Honors Degree in *Letters* (Bachelor of Arts), graduating Cum Laude. His studies focused principally on religious philosophy and theology as well as European history and Latin. In particular, Doug studied under Dr. Tom W. Boyd, a renowned professor, teacher, and speaker there. Doug actively participated in *Young Life* and *Campus Crusade for Christ* throughout his college experience. Upon graduation, Doug served as a Youth Minister and Associate Pastor in the Methodist and Reformed Churches for three years before experimenting with the computer industry as another possible career choice. He grew to love it and has spent thirty-five years in various capacities there. He has written various articles and spoken at many conferences and seminars throughout his career. During his experience at Oracle and Microsoft, much of his efforts were devoted to education and introducing new approaches for better efficiency, making use of distanced learning technologies. Through the years, Doug has served in various capacities in Methodist, Presbyterian, and Reformed Churches. Most recently, Doug served as Elder in the Presbyterian Church.

Doug is married to Donna Wilson Woodward and together they are celebrating thirty-five years of marriage. The Woodward's lived in Oklahoma City until 1987 then moved east. For six years they lived in New England and then have spent the last eighteen years in Woodinville, Washington, a suburb of Seattle. They have two children, Corinne, 31, and Nicholas, 26, and four dogs that are treated far too well.